The Napoleonic Wars 1803–1815

The Napoleonic Wars
1803–1815

David Gates
Deputy Director of the Centre for Defence and International Security Studies, Lancaster University

A member of the Hodder Headline Group
LONDON • NEW YORK • SYDNEY • AUCKLAND

First published in Great Britain in 1997 by
Arnold, a member of the Hodder Headline Group,
338 Euston Road, London NW1 3BH
175 Fifth Avenue, New York, NY 10010

Distributed exclusively in the USA by
St. Martin's Press, Inc.,
175 Fifth Avenue, New York, NY 10010

British Library Cataloguing in Publication Data
A catalogue entry for this book is available from the British Library

Library of Congress Cataloging-in-Publication Data
Gates, David.
    The Napoleonic wars, 1803–1815 / David Gates.
        p. cm. — (Modern wars)
    Includes bibliographical references and index.
    ISBN 0–340–69184–0 (hardbound). — ISBN 0–340–61447–1 (pbk.)
    1. Napoleonic Wars, 1914–1918—Campaigns.   2. Napoleonic Wars.
1800–1815—Naval operations.   3. Napoleon I. Emperor of the French,
1769–1821—Military leadership.   4. Military art and science—
History—19th century.   I. Title.
DC226.3.G38   1997
940.2'7—dc21   96–14188
                                                                    CIP

ISBN 0 340 69184 0 (hb)
ISBN 0 340 61447 1 (pb)

Typeset by Phoenix Photosetting, Chatham, Kent
Printed in Great Britain by JW Arrowsmith Ltd, Bristol

Contents

List of Maps

General Editor's Preface

One of the most famous images of Napoleon is Jacques Louis David's fanciful evocation of the young general crossing the Great St Bernard pass in 1800. At one level, this is a canvas which confirms David's categorization as a neo-classicist: although there are no elephants, the comparison with one of the greatest commanders of the ancient world, Hannibal, is more than implicit. But at another level neo-classicism is usurped by romanticism. The Alps had proved a powerful lure for the brooding imaginations of late-eighteenth-century artists. This is Napoleon the hero, his hair still long, his face swarthy, and his waist girt with a general's sash – the tricolour of revolutionary France. In case the latter point should be lost, the red of his swirling cloak contrasts with the blue of his coat, and both are set off against the white of the snow. Beneath the rearing charger, chiselled in block capitals on a conveniently sited rock, is the simple legend 'BONAPARTE'.

Dr David Gates's absorbing study takes up the story at the point where youthful ambition gave way to self-assured maturity. The conventional portrayal of Napoleon as emperor was radically different from that of Bonaparte as revolutionary general. The colours were primary – the black of his cocked hat, the grey of his riding coat, and the white of his breeches. Even his horse, 'Marengo', was a grey. His thinning hair was now cut short, his physique podgy. The paintings of the period up to 1802 tell a story of vertiginous ascent; those after 1803 of gradual decline.

The theme of the years from Austerlitz to Waterloo is the loss of control. The state of Napoleon's health – his piles, his sexual potency, and even his possible poisoning – continues to be adduced as a cause of his eventual defeat. But fanciful speculations concerning the former are not necessary for an understanding of the latter. Dr Gates provides economic and military explanations of much greater substance. It was, of course, the later Napoleon who provided the basis for the argument of Tolstoy's *War and Peace*, that great men do not shape the events of which they are a part.

However, Dr Gates is not a historian who would suppress the role of the individual when he is set against the background of wider forces. Napoleonic scholars have never had much truck with Tolstoy. The very presence of the French army in Russia in 1812 is inexplicable without reference to the emperor's driving ambition. Recently Charles Esdaile, in a book whose broad sweep comes close to eschewing campaign history entirely, still opted for a title that emphasized the personal over the collective, *The Wars of Napoleon* rather than *The Napoleonic Wars*. If the interpretation of the past is ever to be contingent on the impact of great men, then Napoleon must be one of them.

The massive paintings of David and his pupil, Gros, are part of this cult of the personality. Like many previous rulers, Napoleon recognized the role of the visual arts in propagating and mythologizing his regime. The plans for rebuilding Paris dwarfed even the Bourbons' creation of Versailles. The empire of Napoleon was in this respect an extension of the absolutism of Louis XIV. Dr Gates, like one of Napoleon's most distinguished French biographers, Georges Lefebvre, links Napoleon to the notions of eighteenth-century enlightened despotism. The fact that this was so helps explain the comparative painlessness, in a domestic context, of the Bourbon restoration in 1815. The great powers had no need to undo the revolution of 1789. Napoleon has already put the lid on Jacobinism and through the medium of his empire even recreated elements of the old order.

A similar point must be made in a European and international context. True, both national boundaries and systems of government were irrevocably altered by the impact of France's armies as they cut across the continent. But Dr Gates is at pains to stress the paucity of political radicalism. In Prussia, popular patriotism was the preserve of a few intellectuals. Guerrilla warfare as practised in Spain was little more than licensed brigandage, and elsewhere no self-respecting king and few generals were willing to entrust their futures to such methods. Napoleon's defeat was not the achievement of a movement for national liberation.

Where the French revolution enjoyed its greatest vitality was in the French army. The revolution reshaped the army, bestowing on it many of the characteristics that gave it victory: conscription, mass, manpower, ideology, and – above all – a youthful, ambitious and professional officer corps. That army gave Napoleon his opportunity, as David's painting made clear. But it also meant that Bonaparte's political standing was as secure as his last victory. To ask why Napoleon could not settle for international compromise between 1803 and 1807 is in part to misunderstand the roots of his domestic authority. The revolution had fused the nation with the army, and made war its business. If he stopped fighting, the state's principal activity would no longer be the one on which Napoleon's power was based. Napoleon's dilemma was that the casualties sustained in fighting, and especially those of the punishing battles of 1807 and 1809, eroded the very instrument on which he relied. It may be worse than trite to talk of inevitability in history, but the interlocking nature of Napoleon's reliance on continued war and on the French army implied that defeat would follow when the latter's powers of regeneration were exhausted.

The story told by this book begins with the honing and perfection of *La Grande Armée*, assembled in 1803 for the invasion of Britain. So well trained and so well organized was this force of 200 000 men that in 1805 it was able to march 200 miles in four weeks, envelop an Austrian army at Ulm in October, and go on to smash a Russian one at Austerlitz at the beginning of December. The latter was a victory achieved despite inferior forces. Through the *levée en masse* the French revolution may have inaugurated the idea of the mass army, but it was not the mass army *per se* that gave Napoleon his most impressive victories. The mobility and flexibility of the French armies had the effect of multiplying their effectiveness. In operational terms they enabled envelopment, the *manœuvre sur les derrières*. In tactical terms, they permitted the same unit to fight successive actions at different points in the same battle.

Robert M. Epstein has called this 'distributed manœuvre', and categorized it as a key feature of modern war. After 1809, and in particular after the 'drawn' battle of Aspern–Essling, Napoleon no longer had the monopoly on 'distributed manœuvre': other armies adopted the divisional and corps structures that gave articulation to mass. In 1813–14, as Dr Gates makes clear, the armies of Napoleon's opponents now had the means to bring strength to bear against weakness, and Napoleon's brilliance in manœuvre could no longer compensate for his growing weakness in manpower.

Moreover, as Dr Gates underlines, prolonged warfare had done more than drain France of men; it had also, and arguably wth even more dire consequences, exhausted the supply of horses. Napoleon's increasing reliance on artillery made draught for guns a first priority. But this left too few animals for the movement of supplies. The starvation of Napoleon's army in Russia was caused not so much by inadequate food stocks as by the inability to distribute those stocks. Furthermore, the ratio of cavalry to the whole army declined. The consequent curtailment of scouting and reconnaissance undermined Napoleon's intelligence services. When he managed to bring his opponent to battle, he could not pursue, and so could not convert tactical success into operational or strategic victory.

In the face of these explanations, other reasons for Napoleon's eventual defeat become less important. Dr Gates's rebuttal of the idea of national liberation leaves little room for ideology or even nationalism as potent factors in the mobilization against Napoleon. Those who have argued that Napoleon's campaigns rested on improvisation and good luck, and that eventually the latter ran out, have always had to contend with the fact that they were stretching a point. Dr Gates has little truck with them, arguing that Napoleon habitually aimed to minimize the role of chance by careful planning. Indeed, it may be safer to argue the reverse, that Napoleon's successes encouraged him to become formulaic in his responses: the operational methods that had served him well before 1809 were those to which he returned in 1813–14. By the same token, the explanations for defeat which transfer blame from Napoleon to the inadequacies of his subordinates, and especially of Ney, have to confront two difficulties. First, these same corps commanders had brought victories up until 1809. Second, there was no obvious change in Napoleon's operational principles nor in his willingness to convey them to his subordinates.

Napoleon's operational methods helped define modern war. Tactically, his techniques were less distinctive, not least because the technology of warfare was little different from that of earlier wars. Industrialization had not yet proceeded far enough to inaugurate major changes in weapons production. But we should not therefore conclude that in economic terms the Napoleonic Wars were 'pre-modern'. At a strategic level, nothing could be further from the truth. Dr Gates makes comparisons with the effort and impact of the First World War. In round figures, five million died in the former and 10 million in the latter, but in the interim the population of Europe had doubled. The French wars cost Britain about £830 million, most of which was met by borrowing, and the burden of which was diminished by inflation. Income tax, introduced by Pitt to fund the fight with the French, was – in the Napoleonic Wars as in the First World War – more a means to curb monetary inflation and to confirm the government's creditworthiness than it was an effective engine for the generation of revenue. The massive change in the power of the state enabled a mobilization of material and financial resources to a level that was not to be repeated until 1914–18, and in some respects was not to be surpassed even then.

This long-term perspective, which sets the Napoleonic Wars in the context of the succeeding century as a whole, masks important short-term discontinuities. In 1815 the warring powers reduced their armies. Through the reimposition of long service, they broke the links between armies and societies which the French Revolution had fostered. The soldiers were put back into their boxes. Fifty years would elapse before short service would return, and with it a higher level of military participation. In the years before 1914 the ideas of the 'citizen army' would again constitute a focus for contemporary debate.

The continuity given to the practice of modern war by Napoleon was due less to the ideas of 'the nation in arms' and more to the work of two theorists, both of whom saw extensive service in the campaigns Dr Gates describes. Antoine-Henri Jomini shaped and systematized what Napoleon had done. His concern was with 'grand tactics', or what today would be called operations. Jominian principles provided the underpinning by which the armies' professional independence was consolidated. The merging of manœuvre with decisive battlefield success, as mediated by Jomini, his heirs and successors, became the object lesson of the Napoleonic Wars for the general staffs of 1914.

The second theorist was Carl von Clausewitz. It can be argued that Jomini's thinking was shaped by the early Napoleon, Clausewitz's by the later. Certainly the emphasis in *On War* is on big battles, on killing rather than manœuvring. Clausewitz's influence waxed during the Cold War. It did so not because of what he had to say about the nature of late Napoleonic warfare, which is after all the bulk of *On War*, but because of his reflections on the nature of war and politics. These, concentrated in the opening and closing books of his study, are the bread of the sandwich, albeit a bread which does not become stale. Indeed, they were Clausewitz's attempt to give a universal relevance to observations derived very largely from one war and one style of fighting.

Clausewitz's preoccupation with the relationship between war and politics seemed less remarkable to his contemporaries than it does to us. After all, eighteenth-century monarchs, pre-eminently Frederick the Great, had fused supreme political and military authority in their persons. Napoleon thus represented continuity in this as in some other aspects of kingship. But Napoleon also embodied change: he was a general who intervened in politics and claimed a popular mandate as the basis of his success on the battlefield. He was evidence that professional soldiers could not be politically neutral. And what he had done others could also do. As Dr Gates points out, Napoleon abdicated in 1814 because his marshals were no longer willing to support him. When he returned from Elba in 1815, his bid for power became credible because the French army embraced him once more. In immediate terms, the army confirmed that it was the sole foundation of Napoleon's authority in France; more widely, it reminded emerging constitutional governments of their vulnerability to a more generalized and persistent form of Bonapartism. The fear of an over-mighty army dominated the political life of the Third Republic, and poisoned the relationships between soldiers and politicians. It would take another general turned politician, Charles de Gaulle, to lay the bogey.

Napoleon helped shape modern French politics, as much as he determined the nature of modern warfare. When the war was over, the peace settlement concluded at Vienna could not revert to the state boundaries of 1792. Thus he also redrew the map of Europe more effectively than his eventual defeat suggested was likely. Dr Gates's book is a sure guide to the wars whose effects were felt well into the twentieth century.

Hew Strachan

Acknowledgements

I am indebted to several institutions and people who helped me in the production of this book. The Master and Fellows of Gonville and Caius College, Cambridge, did me the great honour of electing me a Visiting Fellow, providing me with an environment which was as enjoyable as it was intellectually stimulating. I am also grateful to Dr Philip Towle and Dr Ian Clark of the Centre of International Studies, Cambridge University, for their kindness and support. Dr Norma Potter of the Codrington Library, All Souls College, Oxford, provided me with immense help in tracing copies of several rare pieces of literature, as did the staff of the University Libraries in Cambridge, Lancaster and Freiburg im Breisgau, Germany. I am also particularly indebted to the staff of the Manchester Central Library, the British Library, the Public Record Office, the *Militärgeschichtliches Forschungsamt*, formerly of Freiburg and now in Potsdam, Germany, and to the *Chef du Service Historique* at the Château de Vincennes, France. Last but by no means least, my colleagues at the University of Lancaster, notably Professor R.D. McKinlay, Professor Martin Edmonds, Dr Audrey Darell and Pauline Elliott, are to be thanked for their encouragement and assistance. Any mistakes are, of course, mine.

David Gates
Lancaster, 1996

Abbreviations

The following abbreviations are used in the Notes that appear at the end of each chapter.

ASH   Archives of the *Service Historique de l'Armée de Terre*, Château de Vincennes, France.

CREP   *Consortium on Revolutionary Europe Proceedings*.

NC   *Correspondance de Napoléon Ier* (32 volumes, Paris, 1858–69).

WD   *The Dispatches of Field Marshal the Duke of Wellington during his various Campaigns . . . from 1799 to 1818* (edited by R. Gurwood, 13 volumes, London, 1837–39).

WSD   *Supplementary Dispatches and Memoranda of Field Marshal Arthur, Duke of Wellington* (edited by his son, 15 volumes, London, 1857–72).

Introduction

With the possible exception of the life of Jesus of Nazareth, Napoleon and
his times have formed the theme of more literature than any other historical subject. All of 10 years ago, it was calculated that there were at least
220 000 works on them, and many new ones have appeared since.
Biographies of prominent figures, notably military commanders, have
proved a particular favourite with writers, as have studies of campaigns
and individual battles. Many of these latter works, however, date from the
nineteenth century or are based almost exclusively on studies that do.
Indeed, many of our basic perceptions of the Napoleonic Wars need refin-
ing in the light of more recent scholarship. In particular, there has been
little attempt in the past to present a 'total' approach to the history of the
conflict, partly because methodologies have altered over time but also
because there is so much material which one might legitimately include.
War encompasses all of human experience; the parameters of its history
are practically impossible to draw.

   In endeavouring to produce a work of digestible proportions which, as
far as is possible, provides an up-to-date account of the principal military
operations and sets them in their political, social, economic and cultural
framework, I have inevitably had to exercise a good deal of selection. My
aim has been to give the reader an insight into what factors shaped the
way these wars were conducted, who fought them, and why and how they
influenced the development of warfare. In so doing, I have had to grapple
not only with my own eclecticism and that of previous historians, but also
with a number of other historiographical problems. For of all the areas of
historical studies, none presents as many challenges to the scholar as the
history of war. Not even the parameters of the subject can be easily
defined, since the range of considerations which can be of relevance is
immense: psychology, technology, economics and history itself are just
some of the factors which have influenced the conduct of war. There is
also the conundrum of what actually constitutes 'history'. Whereas
almost all history has a didactic purpose – it is merely a question of degree

– so emotive a subject is warfare, so central to national honour and identity can the perception of past struggles be, that it is not a theme which lends itself to dispassionate treatment.

The Napoleonic Wars are unexceptional in this regard. Two of the most celebrated battles in history occurred in the conflict: Trafalgar and Waterloo. Their memory is perpetuated by, among other things, monumental pieces of architecture and, in the case of Waterloo, two dioramas, which were assembled by Captain William Siborne during the 1840s in the light of information given to him by British officers who participated in the battle.[1]

Siborne's account became the basis of subsequent views of Waterloo. Yet he has been taken to task by one recent writer, for example, who observes that:

> For reasons of sycophancy, veniality, and national prejudice, Siborne, in the model and history resulting from his researches, wilfully suppressed and distorted facts. He omitted whatever was unflattering about any of the officers who financed him during his work, or which did not accord with a hagiographic portrayal of the Duke [of Wellington], or was less than Homeric in its account of the actions of the British army.[2]

The same critic then proceeds to attack other writers on the subject of Waterloo for their failure to relay 'the true picture'; in the course of his explorations, 'it became evident that Siborne had not been alone in his selective approach to history. The eminent French *fin de siècle* Napoleonic historian, M. Henri Houssaye, had chosen his sources carefully to shed only a warm light on his hero.'

That there is a degree of veracity in these remarks cannot be denied. However, in making them, the author puts his faith in the notion that, somewhere beneath all this bias, deception and misunderstanding, there is a 'true picture', an objective version of history by which all others are to be judged. This is nonsense. 'History' is not ultimate truth, but rather an ineluctably incomplete portrayal of past experience which has been passed on by written or spoken word – media which are themselves capable of giving rise to ambiguity. Whereas the amount of evidence relating to recent events can be so enormous that we have to be highly selective if we are to come to any conclusions about it whatsoever, the dim and distant past is so often just that. Indeed, the history we do *not* know is of at least as much significance as that of which we are aware. In short, what we are presented with as 'history' is the unavoidably eclectic opinions of past historians, broadly defined. Furthermore, not only were their interpretations shaped by a host of subjective and objective influences, but also such variables continue to colour the perceptions of subsequent

analysts, leading to 'revisionist' versions of this or that historical phenomenon.

Revisionism, moreover, is not always just a matter of seeking to put
some fresh interpretation on the known 'facts'; sometimes it involves
changing them. Examples of this process abound, but, for illustrative purposes, the problems encountered by the author of a recent chronicle of
Napoleon's Russian campaign will serve our purposes. He discovered, as
is often the case, that eyewitness accounts of the same incident do not
always tally with one another. 'It was often difficult to ascertain what was
fact and what was the author's bias,' he complains. His method for over-
coming this complication was, he goes on to say, that:

> When several sources were reviewed, the most commonly reported and
> plausible account was more heavily weighted. . . . If none of the accounts
> agreed very closely in their detail, a composite account was developed and
> the most obvious nationalistic biases were removed.[3]

This demonstrates how historians are as much a part of the problem as
they are of the solution. Some alter 'history' with, no doubt, the best of
intentions, yet often attribute inconsistencies in the accounts of others to
bias of one description or another. As far as eyewitness descriptions of
Napoleonic battles are concerned, however, influences other than deliberate prejudice should be allowed for. Wellington himself, in an oft-quoted
remark, observed that:

> The history of a battle is not unlike the history of a ball. Some individuals
> may recollect all the little events of which the great result is the battle won
> or lost; but no individual can recollect the order in which, or the exact
> moment at which, they occurred, which makes all the difference as to their
> value or importance.[4]

Of course, matters are actually more complicated still. People's reminiscences might not be all that accurate to begin with and become less so
with the passage of time. Most memoirs of the Napoleonic Wars were
written long after the event, and it would be astonishing if men, particularly those who participated in year after year of marches, skirmishes and
battles, were able to retain so much as an accurate sense of their chronol-
ogy, let alone the details of everything they saw. In any case, they can at
best furnish us with a glimpse of events. Even if they were in a position to
enjoy a bird's-eye view of a particular engagement – and very few of them
ever were, if only because of the sheer size of Napoleonic battles – most
ordinary soldiers were far too busy trying to keep themselves and their
comrades alive to worry about the grander affairs going on around them.
As an acquaintance of Captain Kincaid, the celebrated diarist, stated
about Waterloo (or, at least, so Kincaid assures us):

I'll be hanged ... if I know anything at all about the matter, for I was all day trodden in the mud and galloped over by every scoundrel who had a horse; and, in short ... I only owe my existence to my insignificance.[5]

Indeed, of the 200 000 men or more who fought in the battle, only a few dozen have left us any record at all of what they did, saw and felt. The others' experiences are the history we do not know. For instance, men in the leading ranks of the French Imperial Guard's assault could doubtless have furnished us with a fascinating insight into this phase of the contest. They never did, however; those who lived to tell the tale either could not or would not pass on their reminiscences in a form that survived. Similarly, if only because of the illiteracy which prevailed among the lower ranks of all armies of the period,[6] most British, Dutch and German eyewitness chronicles of Waterloo were written by officers, whose perceptions inevitably contrasted with those of the men under their command. The handful that were not were either produced, like most accounts, long after the events they describe, or by means of an amanuensis, or both. Thus, the 'autobiography' of Sergeant William Lawrence, for instance, was actually composed by somebody else to whom this veteran soldier recounted his tales some 35 years after the occurrences in question. Among detectable inaccuracies is Lawrence's failure to get his own year of birth correct: he states he was born in 1791; the relevant parish register records that he was baptized in November 1790.[7] There are bound to be other distortions, too, be they deliberate or unintentional, but we have no way of knowing how many or what they are. We can only trust that Lawrence's memory prevailed over his imagination and that he resisted the temptation to exaggerate his and his colleagues' triumphs and play down the inauspicious parts of their performance.

This is a leap of faith, however. It is revealing that Wellington himself, whose written English is strikingly prosaic, was strongly opposed to the production of 'what is called a history of the battle of Waterloo', precisely because:

> If it is to be a history, it must be the truth, and the whole truth, or it will do more harm than good and will give as many false notions of what a battle is, as other romances of the same description have.[8]

Although we sense here the tendency for an individual to regard his or her perspective as being synonymous with 'the truth', with what really happened, Wellington's failure to contribute any evidence to Siborne's study of Waterloo is conspicuous.

Notes

1. Many of their submissions can be found in H.T. Siborne (ed.), *The Waterloo Letters* (London, 1891 and 1983). The larger of the two dioramas can be seen in The National Army Museum in Chelsea, London. The smaller model is in the Royal Armouries, The Waterfront, Leeds, England.
2. D. Hamilton-Williams, *Waterloo: New Perspectives: The Great Battle Reappraised* (London, 1995), p. 12.
3. G.F. Nafziger, *Napoleon's Invasion of Russia* (Novato, CA, 1988), pp. xiii–xiv.
4. WD, VIII, pp. 231–2.
5. Captain Sir John Kincaid, *Adventures in the Rifle Brigade and Random Shots from a Rifleman* (Glasgow, 1981 edition), p. 173.
6. According to C. Trebilcock, *The Industrialization of the Continental Powers, 1780–1914* (London and New York, 1981), p. 446, as late as 1835 no more than 50 per cent of recruits to the French Army, for instance, could write. Even this seems to be a very liberal estimate.
7. See E. Hathaway (ed.), *A Dorset Soldier: The Autobiography of Sgt. William Lawrence, 1790–1869* (Stapleton, Kent, 1993), p. 13.
8. WSD, XIV, p. 619.

1

The Belligerents

Of all the belligerents of the Napoleonic Wars, none arouses stronger passions than the eponymous emperor himself. This has long been the case. As long ago as 1837, Captain Elzéar Blaze, who had served in *La Grande Armée* and had few illusions as to what life in its ranks entailed, highlighted the polarization of opinions with regard to Napoleon. He recalled that, shortly after the Battle of Eylau, he beheld 'for the first time, that surprising man, of whom some would fain make a god, while certain idiots insist that he was but a fool. He has proved that he was neither the one nor the other.'[1] Blaze expressed the expectation that, one day in the distant future, when enthusiasm and animosities should have died away, 'a man free from passions, consulting the thousands of volumes written, and that are yet to be written, will be able to find truth in the well'.[2] But, as Pieter Geyl so rightly observed in his work *Napoleon: For and Against*:

> To expect from history . . . [such] final conclusions, which may perhaps be obtained in other disciplines, is . . . to misunderstand its nature. . . . It is impossible that [any] two historians, especially two historians living in different periods, should see any historical personality in the same light. The greater the political importance of an historical character the more impossible this is. Is there anyone whose decisions have been more affected by the ever-widening network of international relations than Napoleon? Is there anyone whose decisions have had greater consequences for the whole of Europe? . . . No human intelligence could hope to bring together the overwhelming multiplicity of data and of factors, of forces and of movements, and from them establish the true, one might almost say, the divine, balance. That is literally a superhuman task. . . . Truth . . . assumes many shapes to men. . . . The study even of contradictory concepts can be fruitful. Any one thesis or presentation may in itself be unacceptable, and yet, when it has been jettisoned, there remains something of value. Its very critics are that much richer. History is indeed an argument without end.[3]

This book is not concerned with trying to prove whether Napoleon was good or evil, however one might define such terms. But with power

comes responsibility; and Napoleon, as ruler of France, cannot evade all
blame for the horrendous wars which tore Europe apart between 1803 and
1815. That said, it is difficult to accept the thrust of Charles Esdaile's
recent history, for example, which depicts the 'responsibility for the endless conflict' as being Napoleon's 'and his alone'. 'The Wars of Napoleon'
is thus seen as a subtly apt title for Dr Esdaile's wide-ranging study, which
he even dedicates to his family in the hope that 'they will never know
another Bonaparte'.[4] Emotionally appealing though this might be, it is not
very satisfying from an intellectual standpoint. War is, in the final
analysis, always about power – its acquisition, its retention or consolidation – and is a reciprocal activity. Napoleon might have played a role,
arguably the major role, in provoking the wars in question, but he
assuredly did not start them all; there was a conscious decision on the part
of others to, as Clausewitz was to term it, continue 'political intercourse
with the addition of other means'.[5] Austria's conduct at various stages,
particularly after armed conflict had failed to fulfil its purpose in 1809,
shows that there was an alternative: peaceful coexistence. To end the
fighting, all that Napoleon's opponents had to do was simply give him
what he wanted. That they chose not to and instead resisted French hegemony is legitimate enough, but this does not justify the conclusion that the
fault for the continuation of the wars lies with none but Napoleon. Surely,
it lies at least as much with the British, Austrians, Prussians, Russians,
Swedes and other belligerents, who not only fought against the French but
intermittently against one another, too.

Moreover, the Napoleon of 1803 seems to have been a very different
person from the Napoleon of 1808 or 1812, with contrasting aspirations.
Among other things, his capacity for work, his cerebral powers, including
his phenomenal memory, and his not inconsiderable courage make him
stand out as an extraordinarily gifted man. However, he was mortal just
like the rest of us and was well aware of the implications of the physical
deterioration to which we are all subject, commenting in 1805 that: 'One
has only a certain time for war. I will be good for six years more; after that
even I must cry halt.'[6] He did not; and we must wonder why. At times, he
seems to have been surprised by the sheer extent of his success during the
period 1805–7. Opportunities were created which he could not have
envisaged, but so too were difficulties. The refusal of Britain especially to
grant him a period of genuine peace in which to consolidate his gains
ensured that the war dragged on, leaving him with few policy options
which were not likely to prove counterproductive in the longer term. Nor
was he infallible. Having gradually lost his political acumen, he finished
up trying to solve all of his problems through military means. This was
simply not sustainable, however reluctant he became to accept that fact.

Nevertheless, his final defeat was both costly to achieve and a long time in coming. It required no fewer than seven coalitions and 12 years of incessant warfare. At least a partial explanation for this lies in Napoleon's martial prowess. This, like every other facet of his personality, has come under attack, most recently from Owen Connelly, who, echoing a work by Correlli Barnett,[7] tries to depict the emperor as a commander who 'scrambled' his way to victory through luck rather than by carrying out a preconceived plan.[8] Frankly, this appears fatuous. Not only is Connelly's analysis of Napoleon's campaigns often impossible to reconcile with much of the available documentary evidence, but his conclusion is also founded on a misconception. For Napoleon *did* have a preconceived plan in all of his wars: the destruction, in battle, of the enemy's armed forces and, thereby, his means to resist. This approach contrasted with the military doctrine of the eighteenth century, which emphasized attritional, manœuvre warfare. 'He who has an understanding of these things can initiate military operations with geometric strictness', wrote General Henry Lloyd in a piece which is representative of much of that period's military thought, 'and can constantly wage war without ever finding it necessary to be forced to fight'.[9] While Frederick the Great argued that 'Battles determine the destiny of states. When you go to war you must seek to bring on a rapid decision,' during the Seven Years War especially '*Alter Fritz*' found this ideal unattainable and was obliged to depend upon a strategy of interior lines. Although the fighting of pitched battles featured in this, their objective was not so much the annihilation of the enemy as the gaining of time and liberty to redress a deteriorating position elsewhere in the theatre of war.[10] Similarly, when he attempted to pursue offensive warfare in the conflict over the Bavarian succession in 1778–9, Frederick discovered that a combination of his own physical frailty, the prudency of the enemy's dispositions and the growing shortcomings in his own forces thwarted his bids to bring on a decisive encounter. The Prussian army was gradually worn down not so much by fighting as by strategic consumption in a campaign which was as lengthy as it was essentially uneventful.

The evasion of major engagements as an instrument of policy was feasible largely owing to the unitary structure of armies in the eighteenth century; unless the commanders of hostile forces effectively agreed to fight, it was very difficult to embroil them in a battle because of their strategic cumbrousness. However, Napoleon's forces were designed with very different operations in mind. Influenced by the Enlightenment's military thinkers, notably Pierre de Bourcet, Joseph du Teil and Jacques de Guibert, by the 1790s the French Army had adopted the use of semi-autonomous, self-contained brigades and divisions. In 1800, Napoleon furthered this principle by splitting it into *corps d'armée*, each comprising several infantry and cavalry divisions with organic artillery and engineer units. This remains the basis for the organization of armies to this day and offers far more flexibility than unitary forces at both the strategic and tactical level. So far as Napoleonic warfare is concerned, it enabled the French to impose battle as the culmination of strategic manœuvres which were often executed by means of more than one axis of advance. Only in Spain was this engagement-oriented strategy to prove inapplicable, necessitating a reversion to eighteenth-century practice with its siege and other attritional warfare operations. As Wellington, the architect of the French defeat in the Iberian Peninsula, commented: 'It was always [their] ... object to fight a great battle; my object, on the contrary, was in general to avoid to fight a great battle.'[11] Since the whole purpose of any such clash was to secure a rapid end to hostilities, the failure of French doctrine in Spain was to have grave consequences. Similarly, in Russia in 1812, Napoleon was to discover that his Pyrrhic victory at Borodino was not sufficient to destroy the Russians' capacity to go on resisting him; the conflict dragged on with momentous repercussions.

Connelly's critique also shows a lack of understanding of war's sheer intractability. Clausewitz judged that 'No other human activity is so continuously or universally bound up with chance.' He depicted it as a

> remarkable trinity – composed of primordial violence, hatred, and enmity, which are to be regarded as blind natural force; of the play of chance and probability within which the creative spirit is free to roam; and of its element of subordination, as an instrument of policy, which makes it subject to reason alone.

He also stressed the role of 'friction ... the force that makes the apparently easy so difficult'.[12] Given all of this, it is unsurprising that few wars have followed the pattern envisaged in theory. Napoleon, however, excelled at seizing the initiative and imposing his will on his opponents. While, as one of his aides confirms, he 'never devised any other than a vague plan, preferring to take counsel of opportunity, a system more conformable to the promptitude of his genius',[13] like a chess grandmaster, having chosen a particular gambit to open a game, he was almost unerringly good at predicting his adversary's responses, allowing for any contingency, misfortune or opportunity which might arise, and calculating the risks and benefits of every possible course of action. Occasionally, to assist him in this, he would commit his thoughts to paper. A few specimens have survived, leaving us with a fascinating insight into the mind of one of history's greatest captains.[14] Nevertheless, no general can guarantee success, and Napoleon suffered defeats at Aspern–Essling, Leipzig and Waterloo. On other occasions, notably Eylau and Borodino, he was held to a draw. Yet he fought all of 60 battles in his career, emerging victorious from nearly all of them, even if he did not always win the war. Moreover, he triumphed against a variety of adversaries, earning the respect of generations of soldiers; as Wellington, who finally sealed his downfall at Waterloo, 'the nearest run thing that you ever saw', freely acknowledged: 'I have had experience enough to know how very exact a man must be in his calculations and how very skilful in his manœuvres to be able to do that.'[15]

A detailed analysis of all of the military undertakings of the Napoleonic era cannot be accommodated in a work of this size; Sir Charles Oman required seven huge volumes to chronicle the occurrences of the Peninsular War alone. However, a fairly detailed analysis of Napoleon's greatest and most controversial campaigns has been included to provide the reader with both the sequence of events and an insight into how operations were conducted and how warfare evolved during this period. While the minutiae of battlefield tactics occasionally feature in all of this, an exhaustive examination of the doctrines and drills of the various armies is, again, something which lies beyond the purview of this book.[16] However, to help illustrate the part that tactical innovation played in the development of Napoleonic warfare, some discussion of its salient points is essential.

For many years before and after Napoleon appeared on the scene, European military technology scarcely altered at all. Likewise, the various branches within armies – the cavalry, infantry, artillery, engineers and other support units – remained the same. In their employment, although at Wagram and elsewhere he retrieved one dangerous situation after another with his tactical finesse, Napoleon primarily concerned himself with strategy, sensibly leaving tactical matters to his field commanders' judgement in the light of the circumstances prevailing at the time. Moreover, the fundamental principles of his forces' tactics had been fashioned in the furnace of Enlightenment thinking and the Revolutionary Wars, the latter also providing a substantial pool of officers and men who had combat experience.[17] Just as Napoleon was able to draw on these trained manpower reserves when creating the first Imperial armies, he merely adapted ideas which were already there, applying them with consummate skill and on an unprecedented scale.

The pyramid-like structure he devised for the French Army of 1800 was to become the model for all of Europe's larger armies in the course of the Napoleonic Wars. Until battlefield defeat served as a catalyst for change, however, the forces of Austria, Prussia and Russia continued to be organized along Frederician lines: the basic building block was the cavalry or infantry regiment, typically 800–1000 men strong, larger units being cobbled together on an *ad hoc* basis. While there were a few rifled weapons in service, these, though more accurate, were slower to load and, being difficult to mass-produce, were prohibitively expensive; they had to be the preserve of a handful of specialist units. Consequently, the basic infantry firearm remained the smoothbore flintlock musket which had hardly changed since Marlborough's day and was still to be in widespread use in the 1850s. It fired a lead ball weighing roughly 25 grams and was highly inaccurate, necessitating a reliance on volley, rather than individual or aimed, fire at worthwhile targets and at ranges of no more than 100 metres. The nature of European feudal society also influenced tactics in this sense. Soldiers were traditionally recruited from its dregs and were kept under control with Draconian discipline. The rank and file were flogged and drilled into being more afraid of their officers than they were of the enemy, and any hint of initiative was suppressed. This made them ill suited for duties where the onus was on the individual. Russian serfs were probably the most inflexible of soldiers in this regard. Tenacious in the extreme, they 'let themselves be killed like automatons; they are not taken alive', as one French general noted at Borodino.[18] Similarly, a British observer remarked that: 'Taken from a state of slavery, they have no idea of acting for themselves when any of their superiors are by.'[19] The French, by contrast, were naturally adept as skirmishers, owing, it would seem, to what Clive Trebilcock has termed the 'atomistic individualism' brought about by the impact of Revolutionary thought. Certainly, Rousseau's concept of the 'natural man' manifested itself in the form of soldiers for whom firing and moving at will were second nature. Austrian, British and Russian troops, on the other hand, seemed to lack this instinctive adroitness and had to be drilled in the arts of *la petite guerre*, which rather defeated the object and was only partially successful.[20]

Indeed, at the start of the Napoleonic Wars, in the light of changes in the European countryside brought about by afforestation, enclosure and urbanization, creating an environment in which such forces were as useful as they were essential, the French Army had invested heavily in light troops, both on foot and on horseback. In addition to the single company of *voltigeurs* or *tirailleurs* found, along with several 'centre' companies and one of grenadiers, in each battalion of the Line, there were numerous regiments designated as *infanterie légère*. But, as we shall see, such was the sophistication of Napoleon's footsoldiers that, as frequently occurred during the 1809 campaign, for example, whole Line regiments could be deployed in skirmish order when appropriate. Normally, however, the heavy infantry of all armies would be arrayed shoulder-to-shoulder. Frederician drills emphasized the use of linear formations – usually three ranks deep – which maximized firepower. To this, the French, drawing on the thinking pioneered by Guibert in his *Essai Général de Tactique* and embodied in the *Ordinance* of 1791,[21] added the use of handy battalion and regimental columns, which permitted an optimal blend of *l'ordre profond* and *l'ordre mince*, thus fusing firepower with mobility and French *élan*.

Under Napoleon, the cavalry, which was also divided into heavy and light regiments, acquired a greater role both on and off the battlefield. Used for bold shock action against enemy formations weakened by infantry attacks and artillery fire, it was often employed *en masse* – something which the Austrian horse, for instance, was neither trained for nor accomplished at.[22] The superior commitment found among Napoleon's soldiery also allowed the emperor to entrust his cavalry particularly with missions of a type which most Frederician-school generals would have been loath to risk, notably extensive screening operations to mask his strategic manœuvres and sustained pursuits, such as occurred in the Jena campaign. Napoleon's troopers were also provided with close support by numerous horse-artillery batteries, whose crews rode on horseback rather than marched alongside their pieces as in the foot companies. Indeed, equipped with mass-produced Gribeauval guns, which had interchangeable parts and standardized ammunition, easing supply problems, the artillery was allotted a more independent and prominent role. Ordnance worked on the same principle as a musket but was on a grander scale. Cannon fired solid metal shot weighing up to 10 kilograms over distances of up to 1000 metres. Short-range, anti-personnel projectiles included bagged grape and canister. Howitzers, capable of both direct and indirect fire, could also deliver fused shells. These weapons had no recoil mechanisms and had to be manhandled back into position after each shot. A gunner by training, Napoleon was keenly aware of the material and psychological damage which artillery fire could inflict. He increased the numbers, range and power of his forces' ordnance and used it *en masse* for maximum effect.

The key to tactical success in Napoleonic battles lay in the dexterous coordination of infantry, cavalry and artillery, a process evidently assisted by the employment of mixed-arm units. Covered by concentrated artillery barrages and a fusillade of aimed fire from swarms of skirmishers making use of any available cover, French heavy infantry, deployed in a flexible mixture of lines and columns, would move to within striking range of an opponent's forces. Every effort would be made to reduce his firepower. With their morale and numbers weakened by the bombardment and sniping, his infantry would be forced from line into defensive squares by actual or threatened cavalry attacks. Meanwhile, his guns would be silenced by counter-battery fire. When sufficient damage appeared to have been done, the heavy infantry columns would advance, deploying into line for a fire-fight if necessary. Once the opposition began to falter, the cavalry, supported by horse artillery, would press home its attacks, eventually leading the pursuit of the beaten foe, which might continue for days on end.

The increased capacity for manœuvrability and flexibility on the tactical plane enhanced it at the strategic level, too. In the eighteenth century, logistical and command problems made it as counterproductive as it was difficult to concentrate a force in excess of 70 000 men. But, by rejecting unitary structures, Napoleon was able to field the vast numbers of soldiers which conscription put at his disposal. Divided into semi-autonomous *corps* – each a miniature army capable of maintaining itself until help could arrive – his forces could safely scatter when on the move and, yet, be swiftly concentrated for battle. Dispersed across the countryside, his troops were able to live, to a large extent, off the land rather than having to rely on cumbersome supply convoys – an expedient which the proliferation of readily usable root crops, such as potatoes and turnips, also helped make feasible. By dint of these measures and hard marching, his armies, the infantry and cavalry moving cross-country, leaving the roads for their artillery and vehicles, achieved unprecedented mobility and size.

That the Napoleonic era was a paradigm of manœuvre warfare is, one suspects, at least a partial explanation for the fascination it holds for so many people. Because of the limitations of the technology at their disposal, commanders had perforce to bring their troops to within a few metres of their adversaries to engage them. The ingenuity of Napoleon's moves especially was often as astounding as their scope was huge. Immense areas of Europe would become war zones as the scattered components of his armies would outmanœuvre and converge on their prey. Whereas Marlborough had marched some 40 000 men from the Netherlands to the Danube in order to secure his triumph at Blenheim in 1704, Napoleon's 1805 offensive involved five times as many troops and penetrated not just to the Danube but ultimately to Austerlitz, a total distance of 1000 kilometres. In 1812, he was to lead his army as far as Moscow in search of victory.

More will be said about the armed forces which opposed Napoleon elsewhere. However, as they were ineluctably reflections of the societies which produced them, a thumbnail sketch of the latter is appropriate at this point.

On the eve of the Napoleonic Wars, Britain's population was just under 16 000 000 but was expanding so rapidly that, by 1811, it had exceeded 18 000 000. A large proportion of her people was concentrated in urban areas. London, with 1 100 000 inhabitants, was the biggest city in Europe, while Birmingham, Edinburgh, Manchester, Liverpool and Glasgow all had between 71 000 and 83 000 residents. Comprising around 132 000 personnel in May 1803, her army was predominantly officered by nobles and gentry, wealth, even on a modest scale, being a cardinal route to a commission. Britain's fleet was the most powerful in the world and, together with her comparatively advanced level of industrialization, which generated considerable prosperity, was to afford her tremendous advantages in the impending struggle. Although her insular nature made it difficult for her to influence continental affairs directly, on the other hand she was shielded from invasion and thus spared the ravages of war suffered by most of her neighbours. Indeed, day-to-day life continued largely uninterrupted, with the economy proving robust enough to survive Napoleon's attempts at strangulation and with the population, some industrial unrest – notably the Luddite riots – aside, evincing remarkable cohesion.

The Austrian Empire's population at the start of the Napoleonic War was around 27 000 000, of whom 5 000 000 lived in Hungary. Vienna was the largest city, with 250 000 residents, while Prague and Budapest had 75 000 and 54 000 respectively. Like all of the continental states, Austria was at the proto-industrialization stage of development. Roughly a third of her people worked in farming, forestry or fisheries, with the only sizeable concentration of industry being in Bohemia, where textiles furnished most of the nonagricultural employment. The productivity of the agrarian sector ranged from high in Bohemia and the Habsburgs' hereditary lands, where farming methods were quite advanced, to low in the backward areas of eastern Galicia. Second only to Britain in her persistent resistance to French hegemony, Austria suffered severely in the wars. Her economy was ravaged by debt and rampant inflation, and the empire's cohesion was strained at times. Nevertheless, primarily through eighteenth-century methods, she maintained an army, officered for the most part by gentry and nobles, of between 250 000 and 425 000 troops.

Prussia, too, was overwhelmingly rural and, in the course of the war, saw her population fall from around 9 000 000 to 5 000 000 as Napoleon's annexations took their toll. Prussian society was strongly feudalistic; some 75 per cent of it comprised peasants and, until the reforms in the wake of Jena, the army's officer corps was drawn almost exclusively from the *Junker*. By 1813, she had, on paper at least, the largest army in proportion to her population of all the Allied powers, roughly 300 000 men.

Russia's population amounted to 38 000 000 at the start of the conflict with Napoleon. Virtually everybody lived and worked on the land. Indeed, there was only a handful of large towns and cities, notably St

Petersburg and Moscow, which had 220 000 and 250 000 residents respectively. Although Russia had led the world in iron production in 1780, she had long since been overtaken by Britain and, in general, was barely at the proto-industrialization level of development. Poor communications and her sheer size inhibited the exploitation of her huge natural resources and the transportation of goods. Like Austria, she suffered heavily from inflation during the war, the value of the paper rouble falling dramatically. Russian society was rigidly feudalistic, with most of the population comprising serfs who toiled on private estates. The army's officer corps was made up of boyars and gentry, while the rank and file were recruited for 25 years by an annual levy. As in 1812, emergency measures could be used to conscript more men if required. In fact, that year Russia had approximately 600 000 under arms, although most of them were committed to internal and broader security duties rather than to fighting the French. She also maintained small fleets based on the Black and Baltic Seas.[23]

In the armed forces of all these countries discipline was maintained with capital and severe corporal punishment; offenders were shot, hanged, flogged, made to run the gauntlet and, in the navies, keel-hauled. Brutal though this seems, it should be pictured against the harsh everyday life which the lower orders especially had to endure in civilian society, including that in Britain. If the Russian serfs have been aptly described by one historian as 'baptised chattels', it should not be forgotten that the slave trade was not outlawed in Britain until 1807 and that, despite the endeavours of William Wilberforce and Thomas Clarkson, it was 1833 before slavery was abolished throughout the British Empire. Enslavement could also take the guise of transportation, with thousands of (white) British subjects being sentenced to what usually amounted to exile for life in one of His Majesty's very remote, penal colonies. Whereas the first Factory Act – which put a 12-hour limit on the daily labour of pauper apprentices in textile mills – was only passed in 1802, some 230 crimes – including impersonating a Chelsea Pensioner – were punishable by death, the full rigour of the law being applied not only to adults but also to children as young as 9. Indeed, for the curious, a visit to the criminal court in Lancaster's ancient castle brings home some of the grim reality of our forbears' concepts of justice. Built in 1800, the dock's panelling houses a small vice which was used to restrain a convicted person's hand while it was branded with an 'M' – for malefactor. Court records confirm that such stigmatization was still being carried out there until at least 1811.

We should also briefly mention the role of the Established Churches, particularly the Catholic Church, in the societies which the Napoleonic Wars affected. After the Concordat of 1801, Napoleon's relations with the

Pontiff were to deteriorate steadily, culminating in the annexation of Rome in 1810. By this time, Pius VII had moved to excommunicate the French emperor, but had been arrested and exiled. Yet what really concerned the faithful was not so much the Pope's treatment or events in Rome as French religious policy and its impact on local life. Besides their work in poor relief and education, the Established Churches not only gave existence spiritual meaning but also, through their rituals, festivals and customs, endowed it with a temporal framework. French anticlericalism thus threatened a rhythmic, familiar lifestyle as well as people's religious beliefs. Equally, Napoleon's attempts to emancipate and integrate Europe's Jews offended many gentiles, while proving a rather mixed blessing for Judaism.

The disruption of local life by French taxation, conscription and religious policies was one of the factors which contributed to the few outbreaks of popular resistance which occurred within the Napoleonic Wars. In the eighteenth century, most rulers balked at the mere thought of encouraging the civilian population to rise against an invader. Even Frederick the Great only resorted to such tactics once, and then in extreme circumstances;[24] war was regarded as the prerogative of the Crown and the people had no right to determine their own future or strive for political liberties. Reforming monarchs had, however, occasionally provoked rebellion among some of their own subjects by undermining their traditional way of life. Indeed, during the Revolutionary epoch peasant risings erupted in Calabria, France and the Tyrol, among other places.

The last of these cases perhaps best illustrates the common motives behind the phenomenon of popular resistance. Austria's Joseph II alienated the Tyroleans during the 1780s with his reforming fervour. These devout Catholics resented the emancipation of Protestants and Jews and the dissolution of local monasteries. They also objected to the loss of regional government through the centralization of power and to attempts to impose conscription and taxation measures which took no account of local practice and sensitivities. By 1789, the Tyrol was in uproar. Its diet, which had one Andreas Hofer among its members, protested to Joseph, who eventually rescinded most of the offending reforms. The area thus returned to its customary ways until 1806, when, annexed by Bavaria, it found itself threatened again with change, this time as a result of the Napoleonic revolution. At the instigation of Count Montgelas and the Bavarian functionaries he put in charge of the region, the Tyrolean assembly was done away with and the former (Austrian) currency debased. Taxation, conscription and administrative innovations very similar to those which Joseph had vainly sought to introduce were effected, as was reform of the Church. In 1809, the Tyrol exploded into armed revolt.

In *On War*, Clausewitz identified five conditions for the successful prosecution of guerrilla warfare: the conflict had to be waged in the country's interior; it must not be decided by a single stroke; the theatre of operations needed to be fairly large; the countryside had to be mountainous, forested, or otherwise rough and inaccessible; and the population's character had to be suited to armed resistance.[25] In all of the regions where popular participation in warfare occurred during the Napoleonic Wars – in Calabria, Spain and Portugal, and in the Tyrol – these prerequisites were fulfilled. In the case of the Tyrol, there was a long-established military tradition; the inhabitants took responsibility for their own security by raising *Schützenbünde*, just as in Portugal and Spain one found local militia units – the *ordenança* and *somatenes*, respectively – which combated the brigands and smugglers who abounded in inhospitable areas especially.[26] Predictably, in the turmoil caused by invasion and war, the scope for such lawlessness increased, with the result that the distinction between armed resistance to an occupying power and simple banditry was not always evident. Whereas many of the Spanish guerrilla *partidas* were composed of patriots, some had less noble aspirations, as did most of the partisans in Calabria.[27] As Captain Blaze observed about the Spanish rising:

> The love of country was not the sole motive of the insurrection; it had furnished the pretext for it – that was all. Most of the guerillas, when they found nothing to do against the French, plundered their own countrymen: all were alike to them. They thought only of enriching themselves, leaving the country to settle its business as it best might. . . . In many villages the peasants called the French and the guerillas brigands. When I one day asked an alcalde: 'Is it long since you had the brigands in this part of the country?' he inquired: 'Which do you mean? The French or the Spaniards?'[28]

Certainly, none of the mass risings seems to have been inspired by any developed sense of political consciousness, and they were largely supplanted by the actions of distinct guerrilla bands once the French intruders receded from the neighbourhood. In any event, the mobs of armed civilians which intermittently strove to combat Napoleon's legions were mostly ineffective, while, given enough resources, French commanders could invariably suppress if not destroy even the best partisan bands, as was to occur in the Tyrol and Calabria. In the Peninsula, on the other hand, the presence of hostile regular armies prevented them focusing their efforts on either this threat or the one posed by the partisans. Within the framework of a conventional war, the irregulars could not only evade annihilation but also be more efficacious, leaving the French forces with insufficient strength to contain both them and the Allied field armies. Often, they could do no more than cling to major towns.

However, the majority of Napoleon's empire was wholly unaffected by insurrection. Sporadic attempts to stir up revolts in Germany proved fruitless, while the small risings which occurred in Holland and northern Italy in late 1813 followed rather than preceded the French withdrawal. Nevertheless, in so far that they blurred the distinctions between combatants and noncombatants and pointed to a time when the people would assert the right to determine their own future, the isolated cases of popular resistance which did take place constituted a significant step towards 'total' war. Nor were the French the only nation caught up in this trend. One British officer, who, following service in the Iberian Peninsula, participated in the 1812 war against the USA, took the view that:

> In absolute monarchies, where war is more properly the pastime of kings than the desire of subjects, non-combatants ought to be dealt with as humanely as possible. Not so, however, in States governed by popular assemblies. By compelling the constituents to experience the real handicaps and miseries of warfare, you will soon compel the representatives to vote for peace; and surely that ... conduct is, upon the whole, most humane, which puts the speediest period to the cruelties of war. There are few men who would not rather endure a raging fever for three days, than a slow lingering disease for three months. So it is with democracy at war. Burn their houses, plunder their property, block up their harbours, and destroy their shipping in a few places; and before you have time to proceed to the rest, you will be stopped by entreaties for peace.[29]

Notes

1. E. Blaze, *Life in Napoleon's Army: The Memoirs of Captain Elzéar Blaze* (London, 1995 edition), p. 12.
2. Blaze, *Memoirs*, p. 13.
3. P. Geyl, *Napoleon: For and Against* (London, 1964), pp. 15–16.
4. C.J. Esdaile, *The Wars of Napoleon* (London, 1995), pp. 36, 29, xiii and *passim*.
5. Carl von Clausewitz, *On War*, ed. M. Howard and P. Paret (Princeton, 1976), p. 605.
6. Quoted in D.G. Chandler, *The Campaigns of Napoleon* (London, 1966), p. 733.
7. C. Barnett, *Bonaparte* (New York, 1973).
8. O. Connelly, *Blundering to Glory: Napoleon's Military Campaigns* (Wilmington, DE, 1987).
9. Quoted in H. Delbrück, *History of the Art of War [Within the Framework of Political History]: The Dawn of Modern Warfare*, trans. W.J. Renfroe (Westport, CT, 1985), p. 388.
10. See C. Duffy, *Frederick the Great: A Military Life* (London, 1985), especially pp. 78, 301–6 and 263–78.
11. Philip Henry (5th Earl) Stanhope, *Notes on Conversations with the Duke of Wellington, 1831–51* (Oxford, 1938 edition), p. 113.
12. Clausewitz, *On War*, pp. 85, 89, 121.
13. P. de Ségur, *History of the Expedition to Russia undertaken by the Emperor Napoleon in 1812* (2 vols, London, 1825), I, p. 188.
14. See, for example, his *Notes* in NC, XXVII, pp. 26–31, and XXVI, pp. 153–7.

15. Stanhope, *Conversations*, p. 12.
16. A detailed study can be found in B. Nosworthy, *Battle Tactics of Napoleon and his Enemies* (London, 1995).
17. See J.A. Lynn, *The Bayonets of the Republic: Motivation and Tactics in the Army of Revolutionary France, 1791–1794* (Chicago, 1984).
18. J. Hanoteau (ed.), *Memoirs of General de Caulaincourt, Duke of Vicenza* (2 vols, London, 1935), I, p. 201.
19. Cited in A. Palmer, *Russia in War and Peace* (London, 1972), p. 106.
20. See D. Gates, *The British Light Infantry Arm, c. 1790–1815* (London, 1987), *passim*.
21. See J. Colin, *La Tactique et la Discipline dans les Armées de la Révolution* (Paris, 1902); A. Gat, *The Origins of Military Thought* (Oxford, 1989), pp. 43–53.
22. See G.E. Rothenberg, *Napoleon's Great Adversaries: The Archduke Charles and the Austrian Army, 1792–1814* (London, 1982), p. 152.
23. For more details of European society just before and during the Napoleonic era, see, for example: F.L. Ford, *Europe, 1780–1830* (London, 1970 and 1989); G. Rudé, *Revolutionary Europe, 1783–1815* (London, 1964 and 1985); C. Emsley, *The Longman Companion to Napoleonic Europe* (London, 1993).
24. Duffy, *Frederick the Great*, p. 296.
25. Clausewitz, *On War*, p. 480.
26. See Blaze, *Memoirs*, pp. 101–2.
27. See D. Koening, 'Banditry in Napoleonic Italy', CREP (1975); A. Grab, 'Popular Risings in Napoleonic Italy', CREP (Bicentennial Consortium, 1989); M. Finley, 'Patriots or Brigands: The Calabrian Partisans, 1806–12', CREP (1991).
28. Blaze, *Memoirs*, p. 57.
29. G.R. Gleig, *An Officer: A Narrative of the Campaigns of the British Army at Washington and New Orleans, 1814–15* (London, 1821), p. 386.

2

The Austerlitz Campaign

The Treaties of Lunéville and Amiens that concluded the War of the Second Coalition could have formed the basis of a more enduring peace had the signatories honoured them in both their spirit and letter. These agreements sought to conserve the balance of power which had emerged in the course of the Revolutionary Wars and which, if not wholly satisfactory for all concerned, was not unbearable either: France, enlarged and revitalized, regained her former influence in Western Europe; Austria, though eager to reassert herself in both Italy and Germany, was exhausted and prepared to compromise in return for peace with security; Britain, too, showed signs of coming to terms with French power and a willingness to barter with Napoleon; while Russia, now under Alexander I, who had connived in the assassination of his own father, not only had an invulnerable sphere of influence in Eastern Europe but also saw herself as a key guarantor of the Lunéville settlement, thus aspiring to a leading role in the affairs of the West.

This, however, together with the perennial Romanov interest in expansion towards the Baltic, Turkey and Mediterranean, was less a potential source of friction between Russia and France than between Russia, Austria and Britain. Indeed, the last of these three countries in particular faced several pressing concerns as events unfolded. Forsaken by their allies, more interested in colonial than European issues, war-weary and hard-pressed financially, the British had agreed at Amiens to make substantial concessions. They were to return nearly all of the overseas conquests made in recent years – only Trinidad and Ceylon were to be retained – and acquiesce in France's virtual control of Holland and northern Italy, not to mention Spain, her ally. Two strategically sensitive areas – Egypt, the key to the Levant and Orient, and Malta, Britain's only naval base in the eastern Mediterranean – were to be returned to Turkey and the Knights of St John respectively. The knights' grand master, however, just happened to be the Tsar, whose designs on the Baltic, the principal source of supplies and materials for the Royal Navy, were already causing

London some disquiet. After all, Tsar Paul had, only months after fighting alongside the British in 1799, joined the revived League of Armed Neutrality against them in pursuit of a new balance of power, and had even seemed willing formally to align himself with Paris in order to achieve it.

In the event, though, it was not Russia but France that was to prove the greater threat to Britain. Embarking on a series of economic, administrative, financial, legal and educational reforms that transformed the country, Napoleon consolidated his own position while giving France a period of stability and prosperity which stood in marked contrast to the tumultuous Revolutionary era. As early as 1792, Robespierre had prophesied that war would jeopardize the Revolution by benefiting its enemies within France, among them elements of the army.[1] Although Napoleon preserved the principles of fraternity and equality of opportunity, political liberty soon fell victim to the needs of his regime. The object of various conspiracies, he turned these to his advantage by portraying his own survival as being vital for the preservation of order. An accommodation with the Catholic Church and the continuation of the Revolutionary land settlement helped, among other judicious measures, to win over still more elements of French society until the majority of the population were, in the early years at least, his tacit if not enthusiastic supporters. Life Consul from 1802, he saw benefits for both himself and France in the re-establishment of hereditary rule, yet did not want to be king. He felt that title had been debased by the Bourbons and was anxious to avoid any association with the *ancien régime*, insisting that he was 'not the successor of the French Kings but of Charlemagne'.[2] Accordingly, he sought and secured popular endorsement for the creation of the French Empire through a plebiscite held on 6 November 1804. The necessary legislation had already been passed by the Senate and enfeebled Tribunate as early as May; and, on 2 December, in the splendid surroundings of Notre Dame, he was formally crowned emperor of the French.

By this time, open hostilities had resumed between France and Britain. The latter's hopes for a commercial treaty with the former had come to naught, and France's *de facto* control over the Scheldt and Antwerp threatened both Britain's trade and security. More worrying still were Napoleon's signals of intent. Between 1801 and 1802, he virtually annexed Piedmont, Parma, Elba and Holland, while, in the following year, another French attempt to seize Egypt seemed on the cards. Since the Treaty of Lunéville and the *Reichsdeputationshauptschluss* of April 1803, France, rather than Austria or Prussia, had been the dominant power in the Rhineland and had gradually tightened her grasp on adjacent areas of Germany and Switzerland. As in the War of the Second Coalition,

French aspirations now evidently extended far beyond the old objectives of the Brissotins. This was a danger that London could not ignore and, by May 1803, renewed conflict was looming on the horizon. Refusing to evacuate Malta, Addington – shortly to be superseded by Pitt as prime minister – issued France with a virtual ultimatum: she was to withdraw from Holland and Switzerland, and Britain was to be conceded control of Malta. Napoleon responded by suggesting Russian mediation, which, predictably, London rejected. In the meantime, the Royal Navy commenced a blockade of the French coast, and Napoleon began forming an 'Army of England' along the Channel.

On 16 May, Britain finally declared war and France wasted little time in occupying Naples and Hannover. The latter was the electorate of George III and constituted almost the only territory where Napoleon could exert direct pressure on British interests. For, at this juncture, the war was essentially economic and maritime; Napoleon would have to overcome the Royal Navy's dominance of the Channel at least if his awesome army was to be of any use, and there was no immediate prospect of that occurring. Equally, however, apart from strangling French commerce with their maritime cordon, there was little that the British could do to incommode Napoleon; only continental allies could furnish the land forces necessary for any conclusive struggle with the 'Corsican Ogre'.

They were not long in coming. Napoleon's unilateral meddling in Germany was already irritating the Tsar when, in March 1804, French troops kidnapped the Bourbon Duc d'Enghien from his residence in neutral Baden. Tried by a military court for conspiracy against France, he was condemned and shot. Even Fouché, the unscrupulous head of Napoleon's secret police, disapproved: 'It was more than a crime; it was a mistake.'[3] Certainly, while the prince's execution effectively ended the danger of Bourbon conspiracies against Napoleon, it sent a wave of revulsion through Europe's royal households. Although he had murdered his own father, Alexander was particularly outraged by the incident, broke off diplomatic relations with Paris, and began making overtures to London and Vienna for a new anti-French alliance.

The Austrians, however, were initially reluctant to participate. They feared that the British and Russians were, for very selfish reasons, seeking to pitch them into the forefront of another calamitous war against France. Austria's leading general, Archduke Karl, cautioned against her involvement in another conflict. She should, he argued, stay on the defensive: her army was relatively weak and unprepared for war, and her economy would be ruined by hostilities. Peace, on the other hand, offered the chance to 'improve relations with France and thus to regain a decisive role in European affairs'.[4] But, thanks to devious intrigues at the Austrian court, Karl was, at this time, being eclipsed by *Feldmarschall-Leutnant* Mack, the *Generalquartiermeister,* who presented a much more optimistic assessment of Austria's capabilities and prospects to the *Kaiser,* Francis. Although Karl and others viewed the Russians with suspicion and feared that, as allies, they would require substantial material support, Mack and the rest of the faction favouring war secured Francis's tacit consent to open negotiations with the Tsar. The outcome was a nebulous, preliminary pact. Signed in November 1804, this pledged the parties to field 350 000 troops in order to enact a campaign plan which would be elaborated later. Neither party was to conclude peace separately, and the Tsar was to seek British financial subsidies for his Austrian partners. London eventually agreed to provide £400 000 each year, as well as a substantial advance in gold to defray the costs of mobilization. However, hostilities actually commenced before much of this money arrived, and the Austrian war-effort suffered commensurably.

By April 1805, Francis had stopped vacillating and had concluded an alliance with the Tsar. The Convention of St Petersburg detailed the objectives of the impending war: France's frontiers were to be rolled back to those of 1791.[5] Britain, meanwhile, had already forged agreements with Sweden and Russia, and was labouring to secure the latter's and Austria's entry into the war against France. A fresh piece of provocation on Napoleon's part furnished the pretext for this. With a sequence of events, ranging from the Basle Treaty and the Congress of Ratstatt in the 1790s to the Lunéville accord and the *Reichsdeputationshauptschluss* in the early 1800s, France had already displaced the Austro-Prussian condominium within Germany, craftily exploiting the antipathy between the two great powers of the *Reich* to remould the geopolitical structure of the region to her own advantage. So great were these changes that almost 60 per cent of the German population found themselves under new rulers.[6] For Vienna especially, this was quite humiliating and worrying enough, but there was also a simultaneous threat to her interests south of the Alps. In May 1805, Napoleon was crowned king of Italy and quickly assimilated Genoa and Savoy into his new realm. These were the last nominally independent parts of the peninsula west of the Adige. France's actions were not just an affront to the Habsburg emperor but also sullied Austria's standing in a region which, despite the setbacks of recent years, she regarded as her preserve. She believed herself to have stopped the rot with the Lunéville accord, but even that now seemed in jeopardy. An official protest was lodged in Paris and, during August, London's formal proposal for an alliance was accepted.

The Third Coalition disposed of strong forces by both land and sea. However, it was not quite as powerful as its architects had hoped.

Although Napoleon might have goaded Austria, Russia and Britain into fighting, Europe's other major power, Prussia, maintained the aloof posture she had adopted with the Treaty of Basle in 1795. A rival to Austria for hegemony in Germany, she was also dissuaded from joining the war by an adroit blend of coercion and bribes; the propinquity of French troops in Hannover appeared as menacing as Napoleon's offer to give Prussia the electorate was tempting. Lesser German rulers than Frederick William III were won over with similar means. Austria's conduct in recent years had already alienated several of them, pushing them into France's arms – a trend which was about to continue with the brusque handling of Bavaria. In any case, collaboration was both a more pragmatic and fruitful policy than resistance. The Elector of Württemberg, for instance, when confronted with 30 000 French troops demanding passage through his territory, hinted to Napoleon's envoy that various neighbouring possessions were 'in his way, and that if he had them and his electorate were made a kingdom, matters might still be arranged'. On being informed of this, Napoleon laughed, saying: 'Well, that suits me very nicely; let him be a king, if that is all that he wants.'[7]

Nevertheless, the overall balance was tilted heavily against the French emperor. Around 400 000 front-line Allied troops were being set in motion against him along an arc that extended from the Adriatic to the Baltic. Archduke Karl regarded Italy as the 'first and most preferable theatre of war'.[8] French and Austrian units were already glowering at one another over the Adige, and an enemy offensive here might penetrate the unfortified Alpine provinces and endanger Vienna. Accordingly, Karl argued that the bulk of Austria's disposable troops – some 94 000 men – should be deployed here under his immediate command, with a further 22 000 under the Archduke John covering his right in the Tyrol. Eventually swinging north, these forces would initiate a two-pronged offensive, linking up with an Austro-Russian army which would thrust down the Danube Valley, through the Black Forest and on into France.[9]

This second force would comprise 72 000 Austrians, nominally led by Archduke Ferdinand, an Italian Habsburg aged 24, but primarily under Mack's direction, and 35 000 Russians commanded by General Kutusov. He was to arrive at Braunau on the Inn by 20 October, and would be followed by a further 40 000 Russians under General Buxhöwden. Further north, a third Russian column, led by Marshal Bennigsen, would skirt Prussian territory and enter Bohemia. Meanwhile, 32 000 Russian and Swedish troops would debouch from Stralsund in Swedish Pomerania, while 25 000 Russians and 9000 British would assemble in Corfu for a landing in Naples, where they would unite with the Neapolitan army and march northwards. Britain's main contribution, however, was to consist of an enormous effort to clear the French from Holland and, in conjunction with the Stralsund corps, liberate Hannover. Anxious to provide tangible evidence of their commitment to their continental allies, the British cabinet planned to allocate every available soldier – perhaps 65 000 in all – to this undertaking, which on paper had much to recommend it. Besides reversing the humiliation of losing George III's electorate, the geostrategic importance of Hannover and the Dutch littoral was immense; control of them would greatly strengthen London's hand both during the war and in any subsequent peace negotiations.[10]

To these vast armies, Mack was eager to add the resources of Bavaria. He also wanted to bring his forces alongside those in the Tyrol by taking up positions along the Lech, where his own right flank would also be afforded some protection by the Prussian enclave of Ansbach to the north. Though far from fully prepared, his army marched into Bavaria on 8 September. They encountered neither friends nor foes; the elector's 22 000 troops had already withdrawn northwards into the Main Valley, while Maximilian himself, having made a secret pact with Napoleon, had left Munich that very day.[11] Rumours that enemy troops were already crossing the Rhine at Strasbourg both reinforced Mack's conviction that any French thrust into Germany would come through the southern Schwarzwald and persuaded him to hurry westwards to meet it head on. Accordingly, he advanced his main force to the Iller, concentrating some 50 000 men between Ulm and Memmingen. While 12 000 troops under General Kienmayer were left in the vicinity of Ingolstadt to liaise with the approaching Russians and keep an eye on the Bavarians, General Jellacic's 11 000 bayonets and sabres were summoned from the Tyrol and ordered to fan out towards the Bodensee and beyond. Archduke Ferdinand objected to these dispositions, which conflicted with the plan of campaign originally envisaged by Archduke Karl, but his demand that Mack pull back to await the Russians fell on deaf ears. Mack was hopeful that, if and when the enemy attempted to debouch from the aptly named Höllental and other Schwarzwald defiles, Jellacic would destroy them piecemeal. At worst, the line on the Iller, which was being fortified at key points, would stop them in their tracks.

In fact, Napoleon's blow was to come from the east, not the west. Following the collapse of the Peace of Amiens, his principal forces were stretched along the Channel, through Holland and into Hannover. He planned to invade England with an army of 150 000 men, but, unable to do so in the face of British naval power, settled his troops into a network of camps centred on Boulogne. They spent their time perfecting their drills and manœuvres, while barges and other shipping were assembled for the projected invasion. It never came. Although Napoleon took great pains in preparing his army, the crossing could not be attempted until Britain's 'wooden walls' had been overcome. As late as the summer of 1805 this had still to be accomplished; and Napoleon, aware of the incipient rise of a new coalition against him, was anxiously looking over his shoulder. Finally, in the early hours of 13 August, he learned that Admiral Villeneuve had, instead of confronting the British Channel fleet, retired to Ferrol. The emperor was furious. 'Do you know where that bloody fool Villeneuve has gone?' he bellowed at Count Daru, the *Intendant-Général*. 'He's at Ferrol! . . . That is the end of it; he will be blocked up there. What a navy! What an admiral! What useless sacrifices!'[12]

Even if Villeneuve had evinced some sign of outwitting Nelson and his colleagues, Napoleon now dismissed an invasion of England as being as imprudent as it was impractical: 'Austria, at the instigation of Russia or England, might renew the war the moment I set foot on the British Isles,' he reasoned, 'and we might, by this doubtful expedition, lose the fruits of ten years of victory.'[13] As early as March he had warned his corps commanders to prepare for a dramatic change of plan,[14] and he now issued orders accordingly. 'By September 17th, I shall be in Germany with 200 000 men,' he told Talleyrand, his foreign minister.[15] Prevented from striking directly at Britain, he would do so indirectly by turning on her hard-won coalition partners.

So as not to betray their departure to prowling British warships, the French Army withdrew from the coast under a smokescreen of ingenious deception techniques and strict secrecy. Only an observation corps of 30 000 men under General Brune was left to secure the littoral. Napoleon himself dallied at Boulogne until 3 September, and even then he headed for Paris rather than immediately rejoin his forces. There, in the midst of resolving a financial crisis and summoning 80 000 conscripts to the colours through emergency measures, he learned that Mack had ventured as far as the Iller, but that the Russians were still way to the east.[16] This is precisely what he had hoped for. 'If I have the good fortune to catch the Austrian army asleep on the Iller and in the Black Forest for three or four more days,' he told Marshal Bernadotte, 'I will have outflanked it, and I hope only the debris will escape.'[17]

Napoleon's own field force – now dubbed '*La Grande Armée*' – comprised some 194 000 personnel with 396 guns, divided among seven corps, the Imperial Guard and a Cavalry Reserve containing around 23 000 of the army's 29 000 horsemen. While much of the Cavalry Reserve, under Marshal Murat, kept Mack's attention fixed on the southern Schwarzwald with brief but elaborate feints, the II, III, IV, V and VI Corps, commanded by General Marmont and Marshals Davout, Soult, Lannes and Ney respectively, would assemble between Mainz and

Strasbourg. They would then pass over the Rhine and, following separate routes to avoid congestion and ease supply problems, sweep, on an ever-diminishing front, towards the Danube before curling southwest to strad-dle Mack's communications with the Russians and Vienna. Bernadotte's I Corps would slip away from Hannover to join the outer flank of this colossal turning movement and to establish contact with the Bavarian army beyond the Main, while Augereau's VII Corps, having marched all the way from Brest, would, together with the Guard, bring up the rear. Murat, meanwhile, after having pinned Mack to his forward position, would also join *la manœuvre sur les derrières* by withdrawing into Schwabia to form the fulcrum and vanguard of Napoleon's army.

The offensive commenced on the night of 24–5 September. Thanks to the meticulous preparatory work done by Napoleon's staff, and the mobil-ity and flexibility conferred by the corps and foraging systems, there were few hitches; the various columns averaged about 30 kilometres a day and soon reached their initial objectives. While Guardsman Coignet joked that the emperor made war not with his soldiers' arms but with their legs, this hardened veteran also admitted that:

> Never was there such a terrible march. We had not a moment for sleep, marching . . . all day and all night, and at last holding on to each other to pre-vent falling. Those who fell could not be wakened. . . . Blows with the flat of the sabre had no effect on them. The bands played and the drums beat; nothing got the better of sleep.[18]

Whirlwind advances and living off the land also had dire implications for those unfortunate enough to live in the army's path, as a member of Davout's corps observed. Although 'We were only billeted on the local population twice,' he recalled:

> the speed of our march made it impossible for supplies to keep up with us, and so we were often short of bread despite all the efforts of our comman-der. . . . Fortunately, it was the height of the potato season, and they were plentiful. . . . How many times did we ruin the hopes of the villagers! We pillaged from them the fruits of an entire year's work.[19]

The Allies' cause was about to sustain grievous setbacks, too. Transfixed by the feints in the Schwarzwald, Mack had no inkling of the storm that was gathering beyond the Schwabische Alb. The British, mean-while, encouraged by reports that Bernadotte had all but evacuated Hannover, resolved to land their expeditionary force in the electorate itself rather than proceed via Stralsund. London severely underestimated the logistical difficulties involved in transporting a force of the size envis-aged to the continent and then sustaining it, but it was anticipated that the mustering of up to 100 000 Allied troops in northern Germany would prod or entice Prussia into tacitly or actively aiding the coalition. British hopes rose further when Bernadotte's soldiers, linking up with the Bavarians, violated Prussian neutrality by cutting across the Ansbach enclave as they descended on Ingolstadt. Bernadotte, however, took pains to minimize any resentment this caused: 'I am bivouacking only on lands where the harvest has been taken in,' he advised Napoleon's headquarters, 'and am paying for everything at full price with ready cash.'[20] In any case, Prussia's neutrality was more the product of irresolution than deliberate policy. Like that of Franciscan Austria, her ruling hierarchy was almost paralysed by factionalism. In the event of a serious French reverse, it is conceivable that she might have joined the Allies. As it was, Frederick William III protested about Bernadotte's behaviour and compensated the Allies by permitting Bennigsen's column to cross Silesia, but refrained from declaring war. Although on 25 October London's representative at Charlottenburg opined that such a declaration was 'almost inevitable',[21] this optimism was to prove as misplaced as it was ephemeral. By early December, with disturbing rumours emanating from the Italian and Danube theatres, Allied attempts to enlist Prussian support were becoming desperate. The Tsar visited Berlin and Britain offered £250 000 in subsidies, but Frederick William found the prospect of gaining Hannover more tempting. Simultaneously, strained relations between Sweden and Prussia jeopardized the Stralsund project, while Denmark, Saxony and Hesse-Cassel, which had been expected to join the coalition against France, all followed Prussia's example and remained neutral. The only good news was that of Nelson's triumph at Trafalgar on 21 October.

Even this, however, was more than offset by the succession of bad tidings that reached the Allies' capitals over the next few weeks. Despite deteriorating weather conditions, *La Grande Armée* maintained the tempo of its advance and, by 6 October, having covered over 300 kilometres in just 13 days, was irrupting into the Danube Valley both to the west and east of the confluence with the Lech. On the night of 6–7 October, its spearheads began seizing the Danube bridges and, over the next few days, almost all of Napoleon's forces passed to the south bank, swinging west to envelop Mack's army on the Iller.[22]

According to Napoleon's calculations, Mack now had three options open to him: he could abandon the approaching Russians and flee into the Tyrol; or fight a holding action on the Lech; or try to re-establish his communications by attacking up one, or both, of the Danube's banks. The last of these possible courses of action seemed the most probable, but, while Mack was making up his mind, Napoleon disposed of his own troops in a fashion that was equally suitable for defence or attack. One by one, the few avenues remaining to the enemy were closed, as the French both consolidated and extended their grip on the area, quashing isolated pockets of resistance as they did so, notably a force at Wertingen and a smaller one which had ventured across the Danube at Gunzburg. A French assessment of the enemy's movements at this juncture concluded that the Austrian generals were 'already beginning to lose their heads'.[23]

In fact, Mack, alerted by Kienmayer to Napoleon's approach from the northeast only on 5 October, had interpreted his adversary's movements in a way which was as bizarre as it was misguided. Utterly fallacious rumours of a British landing at Boulogne had persuaded him that Napoleon's incipient dash for the Iller was the start of a retreat into France via the Schwarzwald.[24] Initially, he responded by ordering his outlying units to concentrate around Gunzburg, with the intention of probing up the highway to Augsburg, from where he could hamper the supposed withdrawal. So dispirited was he by the defeat at Wertingen, however, that he pulled his entire force back to Ulm and then sought a way eastwards along the Danube's northern bank. This led to a bitter engagement in which just 4000 French, under General Dupont, held off around six times that many Austrians in the vicinity of Albeck and Haslach. Expecting a major battle on the Iller as the Austrians tried to re-establish contact with Vienna and the Russians, Murat had summoned most of Ney's VI Corps to the Danube's southern side. This premature move left Dupont's division exposed and briefly jeopardized Napoleon's plans; the Austrians, pushing back Dupont's few troops, threatened to break out of Ulm and evade encirclement. The emperor, however, swiftly realized what was afoot and, reprimanding his brother-in-law, issued instructions that, over the next few days, were to seal Mack's fate: Ney's Corps, followed by Lannes's, hurried back to succour Dupont; II Corps and the Guard cordoned off Ulm on the south side; Soult's IV Corps moved round to block its western egress; while Davout, Bernadotte and the Bavarians liberated Munich and prepared a suitable reception for any Russians that materialized.[25]

Early on the 14th, Ney, exhibiting his usual gallantry, led his men in an attack on the partially demolished bridge at Elchingen and, overthrowing its 9000 defenders, pushed on to save Dupont's hard-pressed units, who were locked in renewed fighting along the Brenz road.[26] Within 36 hours, Ulm was ringed with French troops and batteries. Some Austrians had eluded the trap; Jellacic had dodged Soult and headed for the Vorarlberg with 5000 bayonets and sabres, while Kienmayer managed to extricate part of his force and join the Russians. Werneck, who had helped brush Dupont aside, tried to escape with 8000 men towards Heidenheim; and Archduke Ferdinand, determined to deprive the French of 'the glory of capturing a Habsburg', followed him at the head of a clutch of other senior officers and 6000 cavalry. But Murat was not far behind. Indeed, so unrelenting and skilful was the French pursuit that few of these men ever reached Werneck and most of those who did were compelled to surrender with him on the 19th. Although Ferdinand eventually gained Bohemia with a handful of squadrons, Murat captured an immense amount of *matériel* and thousands of prisoners.

Meanwhile, Mack, cooped up in Ulm, frittered away precious time in recriminatory squabbles with what remained of his staff. 'He screamed and shouted, behaving in a way which was truly insane,' one general recalled, while the packed city, now under bombardment from the surrounding hills, 'was a latrine, permeated with a pestilential stench'.[27] Summoned to capitulate, Mack haggled over the terms; believing the Russians to be close at hand, and Jellacic and Werneck still to be at large, he sought to play for time.[28] In fact, Kutusov's column was still 160 kilometres distant, and Werneck's had been exterminated. On hearing of this, Mack finally abandoned all hope. On 20 October, some 24 000 Austrian troops trudged out of Ulm into captivity. Napoleon watched the spectacle amid a group of dignitaries from both sides. A Frenchman asked one of the Austrians to point out their commander to him. 'You see before you the miserable Mack,' came the reply.[29]

The calamity at Ulm, however, was but a part of the ongoing discomfiture of the Allied armies. In Italy, Archduke Karl found himself opposed by 50 000 troops under Marshal Massena, who had been enjoined to pin his adversary down.[30] Of the Russo-British corps that was supposed to land in Naples there was no sign; and, even if it were to appear, a further 18 600 French troops under General St Cyr, not to mention the formidable fortresses of Central Italy, threatened to block any move northwards. Deterred from opening his planned advance, Karl was soon thrown onto the defensive by Massena's aggressive probing of the Adige basin. News of Mack's deteriorating position placed him in a dilemma, but he resolved to move east rather than north, particularly as enemy troops were already threatening the detachments in the Vorarlberg: Augereau's VII Corps had come up through the Schwarzwald and, although footsore, eventually cornered and captured Jellacic's force; while Ney, once released from the investment of Ulm, joined Bavarian troops in a pincer movement which ultimately engulfed Innsbruck and imperilled the Brenner Pass. After checking Massena, first at Caldiero on 29 October and then in a series of smaller actions along the Rivers Brenta, Piave, Tagliemento and Isonzo, Karl eventually united with John's army by way of Lienz. Indeed, by late November, he had amassed some 80 000 men in Carinthia.

In the Danube basin, events had, meantime, proceeded apace. Napoleon, having eliminated Mack, set out to try conclusions with Kutusov's Russians, whose vanguard had reached Braunau only on 12

October. Exhausted by their long march, 27 000 men were slowly accumulated here, to which were added some of Kienmayer's remaining troops and miscellaneous reinforcements, giving a total of 50 000 bayonets and sabres. On 23 October, Mack, having been released on parole, arrived at Kutusov's headquarters 'bearing news of the complete annihilation of the army under his command'.[31] Kutusov, anxious to preserve his, immediately ordered a retreat towards Vienna. The French were already snapping at his heels,[32] and the first clashes between them and the rearguard, under Prince Bagration, occurred within days. Battling through the sleet and snow to force a way over the Enns at Steyr,[33] Murat's pursuing units penetrated between the Russians and the Austrians. The latter, in accordance with obsolete orders from Vienna, had largely diverged from Kutusov's columns and were endeavouring to escape into Hungary. But Napoleon, determined to keep the Allied forces along the Danube isolated from those in the Tyrol and Carinthia, had pushed forward the II and III Corps along the edge of the Alps. Davout overtook the hapless Austrians at Maria Zell and routed them.[34] Murat, however, after a stiff fight with Bagration at Amstetten, was burning to seize Vienna and, dashing off towards the Austrian capital, left Kutusov almost unmolested and unobserved. The wily old Russian intended getting his army out of Napoleon's reach at the earliest opportunity, and he now hurried it across the Danube at Mautern and Krems, demolishing the bridges behind him.

The only French force of any size on the far bank was Marshal Mortier's VIII Corps, a makeshift unit that Napoleon had constructed when reorganizing his army after the fighting around Ulm. One of its three divisions, Gazan's, was pounced on by Kutusov at Dürrenstein on 11 November. With their backs to the Danube, Gazan's 6000 men fought all day against 15 000 opponents who came at them from three sides. Even Mortier himself, conspicuous by his height, was 'forced to kick aside or sabre some of the most determined assailants'.[35] Although rescued in the nick of time by Dupont's battered regiments, Gazan lost half his strength and was unable to impede Kutusov, who, having gathered in various detachments and reinforcements, now disposed of over 40 000 troops.[36]

However, Napoleon was already adjusting his army's dispositions to renew the pressure on the Russians. Besides receiving a scolding for his impulsiveness, Murat was enjoined to seize one of the Vienna bridges and pass his cavalry, the III and IV Corps, onto the north bank. Soult would support this movement with the bulk of the V Corps, while the balance would hold Mautern. Bernadotte, too, would cross simultaneously at Melk. Mortier, meanwhile, was to maintain contact with the enemy unless seriously molested. The various columns were to converge on Hollabrunn in order to envelop Kutusov's army as, continuing eastwards, it crossed their front.

Capturing the Tabor Bridge in Vienna's suburbs by means of a ruse which was as daring as it was outrageous,[37] Murat initiated this manœuvre on 12 November. But Bernadotte's crossing in particular was badly delayed.[38] Moreover, the Russians, mindful of Murat's deceitful conduct at the Tabor Bridge, repaid the prince in his own coin: he was fooled into concluding a provisional armistice with the skimpy units covering Kutusov's retreat eastwards.[39] On discovering this, Napoleon was furious,[40] but, by the time Murat had been spurred into renewing the chase, Kutusov had slithered away again, losing no more than 2400 casualties.[41] Racing after him, the French were too late to prevent him assimilating reinforcements led by Buxhöwden and the Tsar. Prince Liechtenstein also appeared with a ragbag corps of Austrians, swelling Kutusov's army to all of 80 000 bayonets and sabres.

By this time, the Austrian court, mandarinate and military had long since fled Vienna, leaving it in the hands of the triumphant French. However, *La Grande Armée* was at the end of its tether. Its spearheads occupied the fortress city of Brünn on 20 November, where, as in Vienna and Braunau, the Allies had, in their haste to escape, abandoned substantial stocks of provisions and *matériel*. While these alleviated the deprivations of some of Napoleon's '*Grognards*', many more were left in a lamentable state. After eight weeks of ceaseless operations which had taken them nearly 1000 kilometres from their homeland, the once resplendent divisions were as tattered as they were weary and cold. The cavalry, who had been almost constantly to the fore, were in a particularly bad way. 'Our regiment was a walking infirmary,' recalled a trumpeter of the 8th *Chasseurs*.[42] Napoleon himself complained about, and cracked down on, the 'dirty train of cripples and camp-followers and plunderers' that followed in the army's wake, an 'inevitable evil, a . . . result of forced and sudden marches, by means of which . . . heads were saved by legs'.[43] On the whole, however, the locals viewed the French as well behaved and even saw them as their liberators from the Russians, whose conduct tended to be abominable.[44] Napoleon's troops frequently encountered genuinely warm receptions. This was just as well, as it was clear that his forces needed to rest and recuperate; and, on 23 November, he duly called a halt.

If the scene immediately before Napoleon was worrying, the broader, strategic situation was scarcely better. Not only had the initiative passed to the Allies, but also fresh threats were emerging all around the becalmed and over-extended *Grande Armée*. Following the Tsar's visit, Prussia was slowly mobilizing an 'army of observation'[45] and had undertaken to engage in 'armed mediation' between the coalition and France should the war drag on into December. It seemed that 200 000 Prussians might descend on Napoleon from the north before too long. Nor was his southern flank entirely secure. Although the French now controlled Vienna and the Danube Valley, Archduke Karl might march northwards from Carinthia through Hungary. Marmont, who had taken up a position between Leoben and Graz, could retard any such development, but was insufficiently strong to prevent it. Much depended on Massena pressing Karl 'without relaxation', which he was again urged to do. However, news arrived that Naples had repudiated the neutrality pact it had concluded with France and had permitted the Anglo-Russian expeditionary corps of General Lacy, some 30 000 men, to start disembarking.[46] Elsewhere, the Archduke Ferdinand was known to be mustering fresh forces in Bohemia, while a steady stream of Russian reinforcements continued to flow into Kutusov's camp, among them the formidable Imperial Guard. Napoleon realized that, unless he was to retreat and thus effectively throw away the fruits of the campaign so far, he would have to secure a decisive encounter by luring Kutusov into a premature attack on *La Grande Armée*. This he proceeded to do with consummate skill.

With so many of his forces detached to protect the theatre's strategic flanks, the emperor was left with comparatively few men to hand: Bernadotte's I Corps and some Bavarians were at Iglau, keeping a watchful eye on Ferdinand's column, which was creeping forward from Prague; Davout and Mortier's corps were on the Danube between Vienna and Pressburg; the Guard and Lannes' V Corps were at Brünn itself; while Murat's Cavalry Reserve and Soult's IV Corps were out in front, scrutinizing Kutusov's army in its positions around Olmütz. During the closing days of November, this last group of French forces – some 53 000 men – were deliberately dispersed and dangled under the Allies' noses in order to tempt them onto the offensive. In fact, the French units were carefully kept within supporting distance of one another and were in little immediate danger. The Allies, with roughly twice as many troops available, were gradually lulled into believing otherwise. They now disposed of close to 90 000 men, giving them a considerable numerical advantage over Napoleon. On the other hand, their extemporized logistical support was insufficient to satisfy the demands these hordes made upon it, and there was little shelter available for them either. If the army was not to be ruined by cold and hunger, a channel had to be reopened to an adequate source of supplies. This pointed to a move back to Brünn if not Vienna.

Besides the Tsar, the *Kaiser*, a fugitive in his own country, was present at Allied headquarters, trying to reassert himself after the disasters of recent weeks. He stood to lose more in the event of defeat and pardonably favoured postponing any advance until Karl and Ferdinand could unite their respective forces with those of Kutusov. At Olmütz there were barely 16 000 Austrian soldiers. Outnumbered not only by his enemy's forces but also by the Tsar's, Francis was anxious that his few men should be neither destroyed by the former nor squandered by the latter. But he was in an invidious position. Whereas Kutusov sympathized with him and counselled temporization, the Tsar tended to dismiss the Austrians as a broken reed and had little respect for any of them except Weyrother, the chief-of-staff, who, like him, was all for assuming the offensive. Alexander, it was noted, 'seemed to be confident of a victory that would place him at one stroke above the man who as yet had no equal, let alone a rival on the battlefield'.[47] Little wonder that, when Francis proposed an armistice to Napoleon in order to buy time for Karl to arrive, the French emperor seemed inclined to accept, sending General Savary to meet the Allies. Besides taking a surreptitious look at the enemy's dispositions, Savary skilfully manipulated the conversation. Hinting that Napoleon was keen to avoid a battle at this juncture, he soon discerned the factions within the Allied leadership and was able to give his master a sound insight as to their mood.

Sure enough, the Austro-Russian army stirred on 27 November, sending several columns back towards Brünn. Straddling the highway on the Pratzen Heights near the village of Austerlitz (Slavkov), Soult's troops awaited the onslaught. On the 29th, however, Napoleon, prior to requesting a meeting with the Tsar, directed the IV Corps to abandon this position completely. Likewise, Murat's cavalry offered just token resistance before pulling back in feigned panic. All of this helped persuade Alexander, and the young hotheads he liked to surround himself with, that Napoleon was terrified and desperate. Not deigning to meet the 'chief of the French government' himself, the Tsar eventually sent one of his favourites, Prince Dolgorouky. He 'laid down the law with an impertinence hard to imagine'; Napoleon could have peace in return for evacuating the Rhine's west bank, Belgium and Italy. 'The Emperor controlled his indignation with difficulty, and this young man . . . returned full of the notion that the French army was on the eve of its doom.'[48]

The Allies spent the next couple of days shuffling onto the undulating terrain between Austerlitz and the course of the Goldbach. On 1 December, Napoleon and his entourage joined Murat's cavalry pickets on the Pratzen Plateau. 'I could certainly stop the Russians here, if I held on to this fine position,' he commented; 'but that would be just an ordinary battle. I prefer to abandon it to them and draw back my right. If they then dare to descend from the heights to envelop my flank, they will surely be beaten without hope of recovery.'[49] In keeping with this, the French relinquished the heights to their opponents in the course of the day. However, marshalling the 89 000-strong Austro-Russian army and its 287 guns proved no easy task and, by nightfall, was still incomplete. Napoleon, meanwhile, having familiarized himself and his staff with every metre of the anticipated battlefield, was putting the final touches to his own plans and dispositions. Not wanting to frighten his adversaries off, he had been incrementally and stealthily concentrating his troops in the vicinity of Brünn for some time. More importantly, he had also summoned more men from further afield. With yet more astonishing forced marches, Bernadotte's I Corps covered the 90 kilometres from Iglau in just 36 hours, joining the French left-rear on 1 December, while Davout's III Corps came up from Vienna at a still faster pace. Although Davout himself had joined Napoleon by dusk on the 1st, most of his men remained strung out along the highway; only Friant's infantry division and Boucier's dragoons were nearing the battlefront.

Actually, this was to suit Napoleon quite well, for he wanted his right, in the vicinity of Tellnitz, to appear weak in order to encourage the 'hirelings of England' to assail it. Indeed, an exchange of fire occurred here well into the night, and Napoleon galloped down to investigate in person. The shooting, however, rapidly petered out, and Napoleon strolled back to his headquarters at the northern end of the line. Exactly a year had passed since his coronation and, quickly recognized, the emperor and his entourage found themselves thronged by cheering soldiers holding improvised torches and shouting '*C'est l'anniversaire! Vive l'empereur!*'. Napoleon was deeply touched by this spontaneous exhibition of enthusiasm and affection. 'It has been the finest evening of my life,' he murmured as he drifted into sleep on his straw bed.[50] He did not get much rest. Reports arrived confirming the continued massing of enemy troops beyond Tellnitz and, in any case, he had arranged to meet his senior commanders at dawn. At 7am on 2 December, the skirmishing around Tellnitz began again and steadily intensified as the Allies, just as Napoleon had hoped, fed one unit after another into the assault. 'It is a shameful movement,' he muttered. 'They must think me a greenhorn.'[51]

Indubitably, the Allies might have treated the greatest captain of their age with more circumspection. That they did not is a measure of both their own complacency and the success of his stratagems. Their plan, punctiliously prepared by Weyrother, called for four columns, totalling 56 000 men, to sweep round to the south, driving the French out of Tellnitz and rolling up their line along the Goldbach. Meanwhile, the bulk of the Allied cavalry, under Liechtenstein, together with Bagration's 13 700 men, were to pin down Napoleon's troops astride the Olmütz road. The Russian Guard, around 10 500 bayonets and sabres under Grand Duke

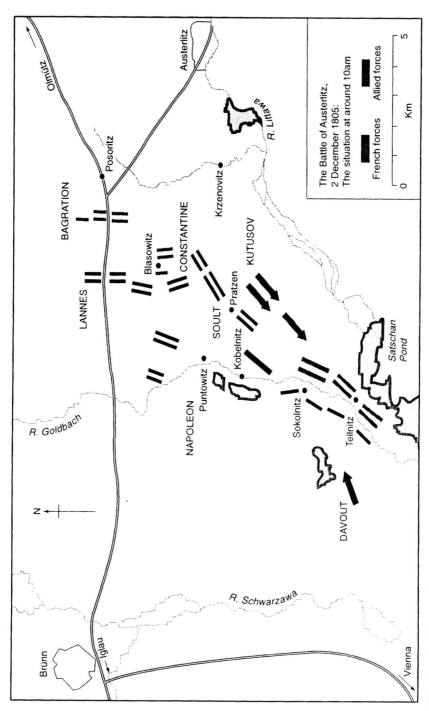

The Battle of Austerlitz.

Map labels:

Brünn

Olmütz

Posoritz

Austerlitz

R. Litawa

BAGRATION

LANNES

Blasowitz

CONSTANTINE

Krzenovitz

KUTUSOV

SOULT

Pratzen

Kobelnitz

Satschan Pond

NAPOLEON

Puntowitz

Sokolnitz

Tellnitz

R. Goldbach

DAVOUT

Iglau

R. Schwarzawa

Vienna

N

The Battle of Austerlitz,
2 December 1805:
The situation at around 10am

French forces   Allied forces

0   Km   5

Constantine, was to remain in reserve to their left, along the summit and eastern slopes of the Pratzen Heights. As the turning manœuvre alone involved nearly as many men as Napoleon was estimated to have altogether, the Allies rightly believed that they possessed a considerable numerical superiority, even after allowing for sick and stragglers. Moreover, as the Austrians had performed manœuvres in the selfsame area in 1804, they had an intimate knowledge of the ground. This, it was assumed, would offset the Allies' uncertainty as to the precise whereabouts and strength of the French units, most of which were still cloaked in mist or screened by terrain features when the battle began. Napoleon's army, tired, homesick and demoralized, would doubtless disintegrate as it was hustled northwards.

It was not to be. The emperor watched with growing satisfaction as the Allies continued to denude their centre of troops in order to overpower the defenders of Tellnitz and the other settlements on the right of his line. For Tsar Alexander, who was viewing the spectacle from the Pratzen, however, matters were proceeding much too leisurely. In one of the most celebrated episodes in military history, which was later to be embroidered so vividly by Tolstoy in *War and Peace*, he demanded to know why Kutusov had not yet committed the fourth and last column to the turning movement. When told that the general was waiting for the others to get into position, the Tsar retorted that 'We are not on the Empress's Meadow, where we do not begin a parade until all the regiments are formed up!' 'Your Highness,' Kutusov protested, 'if I have not begun, it is because we are not on parade, and not on the Empress's Meadow. However, if such be Your Highness's order.'[52]

As a consequence of this, by 9am the entire left and left-centre of the Austro-Russian army was crowding into the irregular triangle between the lower Goldbach, the frozen Satschan Pond and the southwestern reaches of the Pratzen. At about 8.30, however, Napoleon, with nigh perfect timing, ordered Soult's corps – the French centre – to ascend the plateau and fall on the flank and rear of the unsuspecting Allied columns. Emerging from the smoke and fog into the brilliant sunshine on the upper slopes, his troops clashed fiercely with the tail of the Allied forces pressing southwest, elements of which about-faced to confront this unforeseen threat. They were soon bowled over; and, as the victorious French columns swept onwards, the Tsar, Kutusov, now injured, and the rest of the Austro-Russian high command were scattered, leaving their army virtually decapitated. Napoleon, by contrast, maintained almost total control over both his forces and events. At about 9.15, given Soult's progress, he directed Lannes and Murat to lock horns with Bagration and Leichtenstein, thus tying up the Allied right and protecting IV Corps' inner flank. As more ground was won in the centre, Bernadotte's corps, the Guard and the rest of the reserves advanced to occupy it in a fashion which was as orderly as it was awe-inspiring: the martial music, the drumming and the lavish uniforms of the Guard especially conjured up an atmosphere that 'was enough to make a paralytic move forward'.[53]

The Guards' Russian counterparts were also astir. At around 11am, as Napoleon shifted his headquarters to the Pratzen, it was dawning on Constantine that his 10 500 men were the only Allied force left on the right-centre of the line. Unsure of developments so far, he had been feeling his way from the Raussnitz Brook up to the hamlet of Blasowitz, when an urgent appeal arrived from his brother, the Tsar, on the Pratzen. He detached a battalion of the Izmailovsky Regiment – which was subsequently embroiled in the ruin of the Allies' fourth column – and infiltrated some skirmishers into Blasovitz. But this last position soon proved untenable in the face of Lannes' advance against Bagration. Indeed, by now the latter's defence was crumbling before skilfully coordinated cavalry and infantry assaults, backed by powerful artillery batteries. Constantine retrieved his *Jäger* and then sought to extricate his whole force by shifting south, intending to combine with the Allies' main body. Some Austrian cavalry, fugitives from the fighting further north, joined him *en route*. He had not got far, however, when he blundered into the path of the advancing French centre, which was regrouping, having just dispersed the Allied fourth column. Left with little alternative, he wheeled to engage it.

A desperate struggle ensued, as the gigantic Russian Foot Guards flung themselves against the infantry of General Vandamme's division. Their mounted colleagues charged forward, too, riding down two French battalions. Napoleon had just arrived on a nearby hilltop and, as the survivors streamed past him and his retinue, they mechanically panted out '*Vive l'empereur!*'. Not even he could stifle a smile.[54] The light horsemen of his own Guard now surged forward to plug the gap, followed by some horse artillery, a squadron of *grenadiers à cheval* and, eventually, the leading division of Bernadotte's corps. Soon, the Pratzen was littered with the wreckage of the Russian Household regiments, among them *Le Chevalier Garde*, the cream of Alexander's nobility. By 2.15, the hill was irretrievably in French hands.

Napoleon was now ready for the battle's concluding phase. While Bernadotte pushed the dregs of the enemy's centre towards Austerlitz, and Lannes hustled Bagration back along the Olmütz road, Soult's divisions pivoted southwards, followed by the Guard and the remaining reserves. Throughout the morning, the balance of the Allied turning force – the other three columns, comprising about 35 000 men in all – had been endeavouring to hack its way through the settlements, vineyards and orchards along the lower Goldbach. The defenders – initially around 11 000 bayonets and sabres, but gradually bolstered by the arrival of elements of Davout's corps – made up with spirit what they lacked in numbers. Despite heavy casualties and periodic reverses, they not only clung to their positions but also mounted several ripostes, the last of which coincided with the descent of Napoleon's *masse de décision* against the enemy's exposed flank and rear. Striving to elude this pincer movement, the bewildered Austro-Russian wing steadily disintegrated, with several clumps of infantry, horsemen and artillery, some in disorder, others still in ranks, trying either to retrace their steps or to flee over the icy ponds and marshes which hemmed them in to the southeast. Several French batteries were now brought to bear against the ice so as to break it up, further impeding the Allies' flight. Although scores of guns were lost or abandoned in the retreat, contrary to some claims,[55] few men perished in the freezing but shallow waters; most scampered to safety over the thicker floes, various causeways and the odd rickety bridge. Nevertheless, as the sun set and fresh sleet began to fall, the banks of the Satschan Pond and its tributaries witnessed the harrowing climax of the battle. Thousands of shivering Allied soldiers were slain, wounded or captured by their pursuers, while those that escaped the slaughter were hopelessly scattered amid the gathering darkness and deteriorating weather. Only Bagration's troops, far to the north, quit the field in any semblance of order.

By 4.30pm, it was all over. While the defeated and dishevelled Tsar slumped beneath a distant tree, weeping into a cloth, Napoleon picked his way across the field to the Olmütz highway, he and his staff listening intently in order to hears the moans of the wounded, who were then given what help was available.[56] The casualties of *La Grande Armée* were astonishingly few: 1305 dead, 6940 injured and 573 captured. The Allies, by contrast, had lost no less than one third of their army in killed, wounded and prisoners.[57] It was a crushing defeat which, following close on the heels of Mack's annihilation at Ulm, dismembered the Third Coalition. The Tsar insisted on withdrawing what remained of his forces, while Francis, forsaken by the Russians, was obliged to accept whatever terms Napoleon stipulated. Although Archduke Karl's army was still intact, the Austrian monarchy did not dare run the risk of yet more defeats and the concomitant loss of territory and prestige. Accordingly, in late December, the humiliating Treaty of Pressburg was signed, by which Austria ceded Venice, Dalmatia, Istria and Friuli to the Kingdom of Italy. Napoleon's German allies were also rewarded for their loyalty: the Vorarlberg and Tyrol were given to Bavaria, while Baden and Württemberg received assorted German enclaves. Moreover, the duke of Baden became a grand duke, while the electors of Bavaria and

Württemberg were, in keeping with Napoleon's promise, proclaimed kings.

The failure of the Allies' principal military effort also had fatal ramifications for the diversionary operations in Italy and northern Germany. By mid-December, Lacy had tardily assembled around 30 000 men in Naples, only to re-embark them in the aftermath of Austerlitz: the Russians made for Corfu; the British for Sicily. None of these troops had fired a shot in anger and, although they had caused some alarm and preoccupied part of the French Army in Italy, they had utterly failed to distract Napoleon from his decisive confrontation with the Austro-Russian army in Central Europe. Nor did the expedition to Hannover come to much. Reeling at the tidings of Austerlitz, Pitt's government initially tried to draw nearer to the vacillating Prussians, but, by the time of his death in January 1806, the prime minister himself was having second thoughts. Compelled to extricate her forces from Hannover and go back onto the defensive, Britain's disillusionment with her continental partners was already intense when Prussia's annexation of the electorate completed her alienation. Indeed, the new 'Ministry of All The Talents', under Grenville, went so far as to declare war over the issue, reasoning that Berlin had acted more like a French confederate than a neutral party. Anglo-Russian relations were also affected, for the Tsar had abetted Prussia's coveting of Hannover.

Thus, old enmities and rivalries returned to divide the great powers at a time when unity might have served them better. Just as Prussia's prevarication had helped ensure the defeat of the Third Coalition, her duplicity was now to deepen her isolation and to embroil her in a catastrophic confrontation with France.

Notes

1. See, for example, G. Michon, *Robespierre et la Guerre Révolutionnaire* (Paris, 1937), pp. 51–5.
2. Quoted in A. Fournier, *Napoleon I: A Biography* (2 vols, London, 1911), II, p. 145.
3. L. Madelin (ed.), *Mémoires de Joseph Fouché, Duc d'Otrante* (2 vols, Paris, 1945), I, p. 217.
4. See O. Criste, *Erzherzog Karl von Österreich* (Vienna, 1912), II, pp. 252–7.
5. Details of the aims of Britain and Russia at this juncture can be found in C.K. Webster (ed.), *British Diplomacy 1813–15: Select Documents Dealing with the Reconstruction of Europe* (London, 1921), appendix I, pp. 389–94.
6. J.J. Sheehan, *German History, 1770–1866* (Oxford, 1989), p. 251.
7. P. de Ségur, *Histoire et Mémoires* (7 vols, Paris, 1887), II, pp. 355–6.
8. M. Angeli, 'Ulm und Austerlitz,' *Mitteilungen des K. und K. Kriegsarchivs*, 3 (Vienna, 1878), pp. 378.
9. See Criste, *Erzherzog Karl*, II, pp. 319–26.
10. C.D. Hall, *British Strategy in the Napoleonic War, 1803–15* (Manchester, 1992), pp. 118–19.

11. See E. Klessmann (ed.), *Deutschland unter Napoleon in Augenzeugenberichten* (Munich, 1982 edition), pp. 42–3 (hereafter cited as *Augenzeugenberichten*); J.L.A. Colin and P-C. Alombert, *Campagne de 1805 en Allemagne* (5 vols, Paris, 1902–4), II, pp. 336–8: 'Bulletin' and Napoleon to Bernadotte.
12. Ségur, *Mémoires*, II, p. 339.
13. A.H. Jomini, *Life of Napoleon* (4 vols, Kansas, 1897 edition), I, p. 312. It is difficult to accept the opinion of Connelly and some other writers that the whole invasion project was an elaborate bluff. See O. Connelly, *Blundering to Glory: Napoleon's Military Campaigns* (Wilmington, DE, 1987), pp. 78–9; and ASH, C2 200–1 'Expédition d'Angleterre'.
14. Sir Peter Hayman, *Soult: Napoleon's Maligned Marshal* (London, 1990), p. 58.
15. NC, XI, p. 133.
16. See Murat's report to Napoleon, 21 September, in Colin and Alombert, *Campagne*, II, pp. 305–6. Also see the reports on pp. 325–9.
17. NC, XI, pp. 251–2.
18. J. Coignet, *The Note-Books of Captain Coignet, Soldier of the Empire 1799–1816* (London, 1985 edition), pp. 117 and 120.
19. E. Fairon and H. Heusse, *Lettres des Grognards* (Paris, 1936), p. 98.
20. A. Palmer, *Bernadotte: Napoleon's Marshal, Sweden's King* (London, 1990), p. 125. Also see Bernadotte's letters of 3 and 4 October in Colin and Alombert, *Campagne*, II, pp. 703–4, 707, 761; and *Augenzeugenberichten*, pp. 44–6.
21. Hall, *British Strategy*, p. 120; *Augenzeugenberichten*, pp. 45–6, 52–3.
22. Copies of documents detailing the progress of *La Grande Armée* up to this point can be found in Colin and Alombert, *Campagne*, II, pp. 391–888.
23. Colin and Alombert, *Campagne*, p. 871.
24. See Chandler, *Campaigns*, p. 396; C. Duffy, *Austerlitz 1805* (London, 1977), p. 48.
25. See *Augenzeugenberichten*, pp. 42–4.
26. See E. von Loeffler, *Das Treffen bei Elchingen und die Katastrophe von Ulm im Jahre 1805* (Ulm, 1904).
27. Quoted in Duffy, *Austerlitz*, p. 49.
28. See Ségur, *Mémoires*, II, pp. 395–408.
29. Ségur, *Mémoires*, II, p. 409. For further details of Ulm consult: A. Krauss, *Der Feldzug von Ulm* (Vienna, 1912); F.N. Maude, *The Ulm Campaign, 1805* (London, 1912); ASH, C2–14 'Prisonniers'.
30. See Colin and Alombert, *Campagne*, II, pp. 367–8.
31. Duffy, *Austerlitz*, p. 54. By 1 November, French estimates of Austrian losses totalled 64 300 men. See Colin and Alombert, *Campagne*, IV, pp. 399–401.
32. For dispositions of *La Grande Armée* at this juncture consult Colin and Alombert, *Campagne*, IV, pp. 711–70, 'Situations'.
33. See Colin and Alombert, *Campagne*, IV, pp. 482–6.
34. Colin and Alombert, *Campagne*, IV, pp. 621–9.
35. Ségur, *Mémoires*, II, p. 433.
36. See R. Egger, 'Das Gefecht bei Dürnstein-Loiben, 1805', *Militärhistorischeschriftenreihe*, 3 (Vienna, 1965); Colin and Alombert, *Campagne*, IV, pp. 683–5.
37. See J.L.A. Colin, *La Surprise des Ponts de Vienne en 1805* (Paris, 1905).
38. See Palmer, *Bernadotte*, pp. 126–7.
39. See Chandler, *Campaigns*, p. 408; Duffy, *Austerlitz*, pp. 66–7.
40. See NC, XI, p. 415.
41. R. Egger, 'Das Gefecht bei Hollabrunn und Schoengraben, 1805', *Militärhistorischeschriftenreihe*, 27 (Vienna, 1974).
42. T.J. Aubry, *Souvenirs du 12ème Chasseurs 1799–1815* (Paris, 1889), p. 42.
43. Ségur, *Mémoires*, II, p. 427.
44. See, for example, Murat's comments about Russian excesses in Colin and Alombert, *Campagne*, IV, p. 383.

45. See Colin and Alombert, *Campagne*, IV, pp. 404–5.
46. Hall, *British Strategy*, p. 117; M. Finley, *The Most Monstrous of Wars* (Columbia, SC, 1994), p. 12.
47. Quoted in Duffy, *Austerlitz*, p. 74.
48. NC, XI, p. 447; Ségur, *Mémoires*, II, p. 448.
49. Ségur, *Mémoires*, II, pp. 451–2.
50. C. Manceron, *Austerlitz: 2 December, 1805* (Paris, 1960), p. 215.
51. Ségur, *Mémoires*, II, p. 464.
52. Contrast Duffy, *Austerlitz*, p. 103, and L. Tolstoy, *War and Peace* (2 vols, Harmondsworth, 1957 edition), I, pp. 321–2.
53. Coignet, *Note-Books*, p. 124.
54. Ségur, *Mémoires*, II, pp. 469–70.
55. See, for instance, Baron M. de Marbot, *The Memoirs of Baron Marbot* (2 vols, London, 1988 edition), I, p. 200.
56. A.J.M.R. Savary, Duc de Rovigo, *Mémoire sur l'Empire* (8 vols, Paris, 1828), II, p. 209.
57. For more details of Austerlitz, consult: P. de Clermont, *Le Soleil d'Austerlitz* (Paris, 1934); Manceron, *Austerlitz*; Chandler, *Campaigns*; F.W. Rüstow, *Der Krieg von 1805 in Deutschland und Italien* (Fraunfeld, 1853); A. Slovak, *La Bataille d'Austerlitz: Documents Inédits* (Paris, 1908); K. Stitterheim, *Die Schlacht bei Austerlitz* (Hamburg, 1860); Colin and Alombert, *Campagne*, V. In addition to the material reproduced in Colin and Alombert, the following French archival sources relate to the 1805 campaign; ASH, C2 1–10 and C2 201 *'Correspondance'*; C2 16 *'États des tués, blessés et prisonniers'*; C2 17 *'Austerlitz: Renseignements divers'*; C2 253 *'Correspondance du chef de l'État-Major'*; C2 15 *'Prisonniers faits à Austerlitz'*.

3

The War at Sea

The overall political and geostrategic situation in 1803 dictated that the Napoleonic Wars would begin as a maritime struggle between Britain and France. As the fragile Peace of Amiens finally crumbled, London placed an embargo on French shipping and, on 10 May, issued a virtual ultimatum. Within a week this had been followed by a declaration of war, the first shots being fired in a clash between a Royal Navy frigate and a French convoy in the English Channel.

For Britain, naval power and the capacity to intervene abroad through amphibious operations were clearly vital. Her insular nature made her hard to invade but, conversely, also rendered the task of attacking an enemy that much more difficult, particularly at a time when, as during the Napoleonic Wars, sufficient forces had to be kept back for the protection of the homeland base, the colonies and sea-lanes. Thus, although the Royal Navy was an instrument of power-projection, its mission so far as the conflict with Napoleon was concerned was essentially defensive. Realizing that, if the French were left at liberty to concentrate their available strength at a crucial point in time or space, they would be well placed to exploit the vulnerability of Britain's coastline, overseas possessions and trade-routes to maximum effect, within days of hostilities being declared the Royal Navy penned the enemy's warships into their harbours by means of an unrelenting blockade. But the fear that this cordon might be breached by audacious sorties or that an armada might otherwise be assembled was to haunt Britain for most of the war's duration. That Napoleon might, by alliance, conquest or construction, secure even a temporary maritime advantage was a sufficiently worrying prospect to push London into taking precautions against such an eventuality which were often as drastic as they were inflammatory. As Henry Dundas, later Viscount Melville and First Lord of the Admiralty, observed:

> From our insular position, from our limited population not admitting of
> extensive continental operations, and from the importance . . . of our com-
> merce and navigation, it is obvious that, be the causes of the war what they

may, the primary object of our attention ought to be by what means we can most effectually increase those resources on which depends our naval superiority, and at the same time diminish or appropriate to ourselves those which might enable the enemy to contend with us in this respect.[1]

Thus, in October 1804, the Royal Navy mounted a surprise attack on a Spanish bullion convoy off Cadiz. Spain, at this juncture, was neutral but on cordial terms with France, and Britain's action was allegedly designed to make her show her hand. She declared war on 'Perfidious Albion' and subsequently allied herself with Napoleon, placing her substantial fleet at his disposal, whereupon the Royal Navy added Spain's principal naval bases – Ferrol, Port Mahon and Cadiz – to the French ones already under blockade. As we shall see, this process was to continue as Napoleon's influence expanded across Europe, with Britain taking passive or active measures to prevent Danish, Russian, Portuguese and Dutch vessels being employed against her. Not only were ports such as Bolougne, Calais, Dieppe and Antwerp bombarded or subjected to amphibious assault in a bid to destroy their shipping and dockyards, but also the need to foster and defend trade outlets, help preserve the Royal Navy's freedom of movement, and deny hostile – or potentially hostile – maritime forces control of key sea areas obliged Britain to occupy permanently various strategic islands, littorals and choke-points around the globe, irrespective of whether there was a discernible threat to their security.

Besides consuming a huge proportion of the army's manpower in the form of garrisons, this commitment put an immense strain on the Royal Navy. At the outbreak of hostilities it had 32 men-of-war immediately available and, within a year, with reserve ships being brought into service, this number had risen to 82.[2] Indeed, during the course of the Napoleonic Wars British seapower attained its zenith so far as the age of sail is concerned. By 1809, for instance, there were 108 ships of the line, 150 frigates and 424 sloops in commission.[3] Even so, this huge fleet was insufficiently large given its numerous and widespread obligations. If, in 1796, Britannia's grip on the Mediterranean had been loosened by the ramifications of the First Coalition's collapse,[4] the sheer tempo and extent of Napoleon's conquests in the period 1805–9 led to the Royal Navy being seriously overstretched. Not only had its capital ships and frigates to maintain a constant vigil off the various enemy naval bases, but they were also needed to patrol the Baltic, Mediterranean and Atlantic, to mount colonial expeditions, to escort convoys, and to support coastal operations involving British or friendly troops.

Besides scattering them around the globe, this also meant that the Royal Navy's vessels spent a very high proportion of their time at sea, where they were battered by the winds and waves if not the enemy. In fact, out of the total of 317 ships lost during the Napoleonic Wars, no fewer than 223 of them were wrecked or foundered.[5] French and Spanish losses, by contrast, were mostly incurred in engagements. Indeed, although Napoleon's squadrons, bottled up in their havens, might slowly rot at anchor, the wear and tear on the Royal Navy was a more pressing problem. Whereas in 1793 the British fleet had been comparatively new and in good condition, by the start of the Napoleonic conflict its state of repair had declined appreciably. In 1807, the Portland government sought to rectify this by refitting older vessels and building new ones. Besides helping to push up the cost of the service from £15 million in 1806 to a peak of over £20 million in 1813,[6] this added to what was already a huge demand for building materials and naval stores, as well as the need for dockyards with the facilities and skilled labour necessary to keep ships seaworthy. Plymouth, Portsmouth, Sheerness and Chatham were capable of constructing and maintaining the larger vessels, but Woolwich and Deptford could only accommodate smaller ones. Repairs were, moreover, complex and time-consuming affairs, often requiring months for their completion. Indeed, it has been estimated that, typically, around 20 per cent of all the men-of-war and 16 per cent of all the navy's lesser vessels would be out of commission awaiting repairs.[7]

The quest for naval supplies was complicated by developments at home and abroad. The Continental System instituted by Napoleon jeopardized the flow of timber, flax, hemp, tallow, pitch, tar, linseed, iron ore and other necessities. In the main, Russia and Sweden satisfied British demand for these commodities, many of them being exported via Danzig and Memel (Klaipeda). Consequently, the Baltic became of vital strategic importance to Britain, and she was to maintain a substantial flotilla there throughout the ice-free months.[8] Nevertheless, in 1810, after Napoleon had consolidated his grip on the region, British shipping losses reached their peak – 619 merchant vessels – and the trade in nautical supplies was badly disrupted.[9] There were alternative sources, but the products were of inferior quality and the Royal Navy was reluctant to endorse their use. At the start of the war, Earl St Vincent, the First Lord of the Admiralty, was labouring to streamline and improve the dockyards and to control naval expenditure. Besides discharging many workers, he alienated the lumber merchants who fulfilled the fleet's requirements by disposing of surplus stocks and insisting on supplies of high-quality timber at peacetime rates. The result was a shortfall in the provision of English oak especially, necessitating the use of inferior foreign lumber and even unseasoned wood. As the latter rotted much more quickly, this had obvious implications for the fleet's seaworthiness. Several ships were nearly lost because of decay in their hulls, while others, though newly built, very rapidly became unserviceable.[10]

This particular problem was to persist throughout the war as the demand for matured timber repeatedly outstripped supply. However, as first Viscount Melville and then Lord Barham superseded St Vincent at the Admiralty, relations within the dockyards improved,[11] the lumber merchants' cartel being left at liberty to control supplies and increase their prices. Although this pushed up costs, it did allow more vessels to be repaired and refitted, with numerous older ships being able to put to sea as a consequence.[12] While often only capable of performing limited duties, these patched-up vessels were none the less a timely accession of strength.

But ships were of little use without crews, and the Royal Navy was to experience chronic manpower shortages as the fleet was enlarged and the rigours of war took their toll. Although Parliament voted for progressive increases in the number of marines and mariners – the theoretical strength of the Royal Navy expanding from 100 000 men in 1804 to 145 000 by 1810 – sufficient recruits were not forthcoming and the service invariably suffered from a shortfall of between 3000 and 16 000 personnel. Life aboard Britain's 'wooden walls' was scarcely appealing. Protracted periods at sea on tedious, unglamorous blockade or convoy duties added boredom to the omnipresent ills of Draconian disciplinary codes, cramped and insanitary living conditions, low pay and poor rations.[13] Such tribulations had spawned mutinies within the fleet in 1797. However, during the Napoleonic conflict manpower shortages were as much a product of competition as they were of unenticing employment conditions. Many sailors elected to serve with the privateers in the profitable *guerre de course*, while others worked aboard coasters and merchantmen where their remuneration was up to five times that enjoyed by Royal Navy seamen and life was generally much more agreeable.[14]

It is little wonder in view of all of this that, despite the inhumane practice of impressment[15] and the extensive recruitment of foreigners, many British warships were left with either insufficient crewmen or none at all. Thus, in October 1805, Barham was to grumble about numerous vessels 'lying inactive in Port' for want of sailors,[16] while HMS *Victory* fought at Trafalgar with 134 men missing from her official complement of 837 officers and ratings.[17] Nor, once found, were sailors easy to retain. Although great progress was made in improving the health of ships' crews, the old curses of smallpox and scurvy being gradually eradicated by means of inoculation and lemon juice respectively,[18] desertion remained a serious problem, with many seamen seeing service in the New World especially as an ideal chance to start afresh. Not only did life there seem to offer all manner of exciting opportunities for material enrichment, but also the USA's contrasting political order inevitably appealed to the many disaffected and discontented Britons who had been pushed or dragged into His Majesty's service. Indeed, the Royal Navy's attempts to counter this menace by combing American vessels for alleged deserters was one of the issues which was to lead to the Anglo-American War of 1812.

Aspects of that conflict will be dealt with in more detail elsewhere. It should be noted here, however, that it formed one of the few opportunities Britain had after Trafalgar to use her maritime might in an offensive mode. That encounter, though perhaps the most celebrated naval clash in history, was the only major sea battle of the lengthy war against Napoleon and, thereafter, the British had to rely primarily on more indirect means of dissipating his nautical strength. Apart from a handful of comparatively minor engagements between small flotillas and individual squadrons, there were to be no more occasions on which the opposing fleets locked horns with one another.

This situation must have proved rather frustrating for the many enterprising commanders within the Royal Navy during our period. As Napoleon adopted a minatory posture by keeping his flotillas in their ports and adding to their size through various shipbuilding programmes, the British navy was largely reduced to mounting an interminable blockade of the enemy's bases. The equally unexciting work of enforcing the Orders-in-Council – London's response to the Continental System – was the other major task that fell to the fleet. Such duties, though essential, afforded little scope for the Royal Navy to perform the mission at which it excelled and instinctively preferred: the destruction of an adversary's warships in open battle. Although British vessels were, on the whole, slower and often inferior in design, better signalling systems and superior discipline and seamanship made them formidable opponents once they engaged the enemy. In the hands of astute commanders such as Cornwallis, Collingwood, Keith and, of course, Nelson, British squadrons exploited their capacity for precise, rapid and bold manœuvre to the full, penetrating the enemy's formations to rake his ships from close range with rapid and accurate broadsides. The carronade, a highly manœuvrable gun which fired large projectiles from close quarters, was an important innovation in this regard, since it encouraged Royal Navy captains to thrust into the hostile fleet, suppressing the guns on opposing vessels with superior firepower. Once they had edged alongside the enemy ships, the British would complete their victory by boarding them.

Indeed, by the late 1790s the British naval dominance that was to be confirmed during the Napoleonic Wars was already emerging. At the Battle of the Nile on 1 August 1798, Nelson, relying on the polished seamanship of his crews, sailed into shallow, unchartered waters, actually enveloping the French fleet by passing some of his ships along the leeward edge of the enemy's anchorage. The Royal Navy's superior manœuvrability, gunnery, training and morale did the rest: of the 16 French ships of the line and four frigates, 11 of the former and two of the latter were lost, together with some 4000 personnel who were killed, wounded or captured.[19]

Whereas Nelson and his colleagues were to implement a similarly daring and aggressive plan at Copenhagen in April 1801,[20] the French naval commanders of the period never exhibited such tactical flair. Throughout the eighteenth century French maritime doctrine had suppressed initiative and emphasized the husbanding of resources rather than the pressing home of attacks to achieve the annihilation of an opponent's fleet. More generally, too, the navy that Napoleon was to inherit was no match for its British counterpart, and the latter's overall strategy was to help ensure it stayed that way.

When hostilities resumed between Britain and France after the abortive Peace of Amiens, the French Navy was dispersed among its principal bases – Rochefort, Brest, Lorient and Toulon – and was scarcely ready for action. Its dockyards were on the verge of being improved, as was its fleet: to facilitate communications between the naval bases and Paris, the erection of aerial telegraph systems devised by Claude Chappe had already commenced,[21] while new warships, often superior in their design and construction to those of the British, were being commissioned.

The cardinal defects of the French Navy, however, lay in its personnel rather than in its vessels and supporting infrastructure. Demoralized by repeated defeats and weakened by purges during the Revolutionary period, its officer corps was in the midst of regenerating itself and had yet to adjust fully to the style of maritime warfare pioneered by the British in recent years.[22] Besides a shortage of competent commanders, the training of the ratings in basic skills like gunnery was also markedly inferior to that found in the Royal Navy, while, given the constraints imposed by the latter's blockade, there were few opportunities for the French to improve their seamanship or to practise the manœuvring of substantial numbers of ships. The exception to this general rule appears to have been the Toulon flotilla, which, after being severely mauled at Trafalgar, was refitted and enlarged with newly constructed vessels until it amounted to 24 men-of-war. Unable to maintain a tight blockade of Toulon because of its comparative remoteness from their bases and the prevailing wind's direction, the British were haunted by the fear that the squadrons here might slip past them and strike a blow somewhere in the spacious Mediterranean. This had already occurred in 1798, when Admiral Brueys's fleet had not only escorted the convoy taking the French expeditionary force to Egypt but had also captured Malta into the bargain.[23] Similarly, in 1808, a sortie from Toulon came close to jeopardizing Britain's hold on Sicily, her nodal base in the Mediterranean. Admiral Ganteaume's ships were to have embarked 9000 soldiers at Naples and land them near Messina, while other Imperial troops crossed the straits from Calabria. In the event, however, Ganteaume was diverted into resupplying Corfu's garrison, and the invasion of Sicily was set aside.[24] It was to be September 1810 before the French Army in Calabria felt strong enough to be able to contemplate the venture again. Napoleon himself doubted whether, without naval support and adequate transport vessels, such an amphibious operation was likely to succeed.[25] In fact, the 3000 Neapolitan troops who did manage to land on the island proved quite insufficient for its conquest and had to beat a hasty retreat.[26] But this abortive attempt again underscored the potential danger posed to Britain's position in the Mediterranean by the Toulon fleet.[27] In the face of this, the retention of Sicily alone imposed an appreciable drain on London's resources. The island's governing regime, the fugitive Neapolitan Bourbons, was neither the most dependable of allies nor the most popular of rulers. The British, fearing that internal strife or secret negotiations between the Bourbons and Napoleon constituted as much of a threat to their grip on the island as did the prospect of a French invasion, sought to safeguard Sicily with a large garrison, a naval presence and generous subsidies. Nevertheless, it remained vulnerable to a French *coup de main*.[28]

While it was largely counterbalanced through Napoleon's dramatic conquests by land, the Royal Navy's dominance of the waves contained, if it did not eliminate, the threat posed by his battlefleets and amphibious forces. The danger of a French landing in Ireland, England or the Mediterranean receded, while the overseas possessions of Napoleon and his vassals were, once cut off from their motherlands, progressively subdued. This latter process was significant not only because of the virtual monopoly it conferred on Britain in the production and distribution of colonial goods, but also because it deprived her enemies of distant havens. Acknowledging their inability to challenge the Royal Navy in fleet-to-fleet confrontations, its opponents steadily resorted to commerce-raiding as a maritime strategy. Although Alfred Thayer Mahan, the nineteenth century's 'evangelist of sea power',[29] was to be rather scornful of the impact that this *guerre de course* had on the course of the Napoleonic conflict,[30] it was, as Paul Kennedy has observed, more successful in terms of its effect on British seaborne trade than any since the War of the Spanish Succession.[31] With thousands of continental mariners rendered idle by the decline of their own countries' battle and merchant fleets, the privateers were not short of willing crewmen. Nor were they lacking talented leaders who knew how to prey efficaciously on Britain's global trade web.[32] Although, among other countermeasures, the Royal Navy organized escorted convoys and patrolled its home waters with 'Q-ships', armed vessels disguised as innocuous merchantmen, protecting the multitude of potential targets which, at any one time, were plying between Great Britain and her trading partners, especially the more distant ones, was palpably impossible. Ineluctably, substantial numbers of ships were lost to the privateers, marine insurance rates rose commensurately[33] and, in conjunction with the Continental System, Napoleon's *guerre de course* had a significant effect on international trade, the bedrock of Britain's prosperity.[34] Nevertheless, the Royal Navy managed to limit the damage sufficiently and, by means of blows against commerce-raiders based in such diverse places as San Domingo (1806), Cape Town (1806), Mauritius (1810) and Java (1811), went a long way towards eradicating the threat posed by these licensed pirates.[35]

We should not forget that, in addition to the dangers arising from enemy action, all mariners faced a formidable common foe, the sea itself. Although he knew from bitter experience how much weather conditions could affect the prosecution of war by land, Napoleon never seems to have fully appreciated the extent to which maritime operations in the days of sail were governed by the elements. (In one notorious incident in 1804, for example, he insisted that a flotilla based at Boulogne put to sea for a review, despite an imminent gale. A number of gunboats were capsized and several hundred men drowned.[36]) Indeed, the winds and tides could plunge even the best-planned operations into turmoil. An adverse, little or no wind could delay movements, while a tempest might scatter or even destroy a fleet. As ship-to-ship communications were effectively limited to, at most, the range of the human eye, once dispatched, vessels were difficult to recall or redirect if circumstances altered. Thus, protracted voyages were eschewed as far as possible, with the emphasis being placed instead on sudden *coups* against vulnerable targets not too remote from friendly waters. Similarly, logistical problems tended to circumscribe naval campaigns. Replenishment at sea was as hazardous as it was difficult to arrange, and so ships had to be as self-sufficient as possible and remain within comfortable range of friendly ports. The need for adequate supplies of fresh water was but one constraint among many. Moreover, when, as often happened, warships doubled as transport vessels, logistical difficulties increased correspondingly. Not only might men-of-war be expected to accommodate dozens of infantrymen alongside their crews, but uncomprehending draught and cavalry horses were occasionally squeezed aboard, too. Clearly, given their needs, these poor creatures were far less able to adapt to such an environment than their human masters. To curtail mortality rates, the duration of voyages had to be kept to a minimum. This, as we shall see elsewhere, helped to curb the scope and size of amphibious operations.

Whereas Spain's navy was never to recover fully after Nelson's victory at Trafalgar on 21 October 1805,[37] France made a determined effort to rebuild hers. In fact, Napoleon was quite sanguine about the eventual course of the war at sea. In 1811, at the height of his power, with most of Europe's shipyards at his disposal, he was to predict that:

> In four years I shall have a fleet. When my squadrons have been three or four years at sea we shall measure swords with England. I know I may lose three or four naval engagements . . . but we are brave . . . we shall succeed. Before ten years are passed, I shall have conquered England.[38]

While this might appear to be wishful thinking on Napoleon's part, it was a possibility which the British Admiralty took very seriously. In a memorandum of February 1813, Lord Melville was to point to the French Empire's capacity for shipbuilding and the implications this would have for the maritime balance of power, warning that, by January 1816, Napoleon would be able to muster 'a fleet of 108 Sail of the Line'.[39] But, overtaken by events elsewhere, nothing ever came of the emperor's grand plan; as a result of the *débâcle* in Russia, for instance, he was compelled to transfer 20 000 men from the navy to the army in 1813. In the meantime, his maritime ambitions were effectively frustrated by the repercussions of Britain's blockade. However much the quality of their vessels and dockyards improved, French commanders could not endow their ships' crews with the degree of professionalism, discipline and proficiency which was found in the Royal Navy. Deprived of essential experience at sea, Napoleon's fleet would never acquire the dexterity necessary to confront that of the British *en masse*. Indeed, after Trafalgar, Britannia's maritime supremacy was to go unchallenged not only for the rest of the conflict with Napoleon but also for 100 years thereafter.

Notes

1. Quoted in P. M. Kennedy, *The Rise and Fall of British Naval Mastery* (London, 1983 edition), p. 128.
2. C.D. Hall, *British Strategy in the Napoleonic War 1803–15* (Manchester, 1992), p. 29.
3. Hall, *British Strategy*, p. 1.
4. See O. von Pivka, *Navies of the Napoleonic Era* (London, 1980), pp. 49–51.
5. Hall, *British Strategy*, p. 47; Pivka, *Navies*, pp. 239–45.
6. See B.R. Mitchell and P. Deane, *Abstract of British Historical Statistics* (Cambridge, 1967 edition), pp. 288–96; P.K. Crimmin, 'Admiralty Relations with the Treasury', *Mariner's Mirror*, 53 (1967).

7. See R. Morriss, *The Royal Dockyards during the Revolutionary and Napoleonic Wars* (Leicester, 1983), pp. 18–25, 44.

8. See A.N. Ryan, 'The Defence of British Trade with the Baltic, 1808–13', *English Historical Review*, 74 (1959).

9. Kennedy, *Rise and Fall*, p. 131.

10. See P.L.C. Webb, 'Construction, Repair and Maintenance in the Battlefleet of the Royal Navy, 1793–1815', in J. Black and P. Woodfine (eds), *The British Navy and the Use of Naval Power in the Eighteenth Century* (Leicester, 1988); R.G. Albion, *Forests and Sea Power* (Cambridge, MA., 1926).

11. R.A. Morriss, 'Labour Relations in the Royal Dockyards, 1801–5', *Mariner's Mirror*, 62/4 (1976).

12. Hall, *British Strategy*, pp. 30–1.

13. See P. Kemp, *The British Sailor: A Social History of the Lower Deck* (London, 1970); M. Lewis, *A Social History of the Navy, 1793–1815* (London, 1960); C. Lloyd, *The British Seaman 1200–1860: A Social Survey* (London, 1968).

14. Hall, *British Strategy*, p. 11.

15. See, for instance, J.F. Zimmerman, *The Impressment of American Seamen* (New York, 1925).

16. Quoted in Hall, *British Strategy*, pp. 11–12.

17. Hall, *British Strategy* pp. 11–12.

18. See C. Lloyd and J.L.S. Coulter, *Medicine and the Navy (1714–1815)*, vol. III (Edinburgh and London, 1961); C. Lloyd (ed.), *The Health of Seamen* (London, 1965); E.H. Turner, 'The Naval Medical Service, 1793–1815', *Mariner's Mirror*, 46 (1960); P.D.G. Pugh, *Nelson and his Surgeons* (Edinburgh and London, 1968).

19. C. Lloyd, *The Nile Campaign: Nelson and Napoleon in Egypt* (New York, 1973).

20. See D. Pope, *The Great Gamble: Nelson at Copenhagen* (London and New York, 1972).

21. See F.L. Petre, *Napoleon and the Archduke Charles* (London, 1976 edition), p. 65. For details of the British equivalent, see T. Holmes, *The Semaphore: The Story of the Admiralty to Portsmouth Shutter Telegraph and Semaphore Lines, 1797–1847* (Ilfracombe, 1983).

22. See R.V.P. Castex, *Les Idées Militaires de la Marine du XVIIIᵉ Siècle* (Paris, 1911).

23. See G. Lacour-Gayet, 'La Traversée de la Mediterranée en 1798', *Revue des Études Napoléoniennes*, 12 (1923).

24. See P. Mackesy, 'Collingwood and Ganteaume: The French Offensive in the Mediterranean, January to April 1808', *Mariner's Mirror*, 41 (1955).

25. See NC, XX, p. 373.

26. See Pivka, *Navies*, pp. 125–7.

27. See P. Mackesy, *The War in the Mediterranean, 1803–10* (Cambridge, MA, 1957).

28. See D. Gregory, *Sicily: The Insecure Base: A History of the British Occupation of Sicily, 1806–15* (Rutherford, NJ, 1988); R. Muir, *Britain and the Defeat of Napoleon, 1807–15* (New Haven, CT, 1996), pp. 165–70.

29. See A.T. Mahan, *The Influence of Sea Power upon the French Revolution and Empire* (2 vols, London, 1892).

30. See A. Gat, *The Development of Military Thought: The 19th Century* (Oxford, 1992), pp. 197–8.

31. See Kennedy, *Rise and Fall*, pp. 130–1.

32. See P. Crowhurst, *The French War on Trade: Privateering 1793–1815* (London, 1989).

33. See C. Wright and E. Fayle, *A History of Lloyds* (London, 1928), p. 191.

34. Kennedy, *Rise and Fall*, pp. 130–2. Also see C.N. Parkinson, *The Trade Winds: A Study of British Overseas Trade during the French Wars, 1793–1815* (London, 1948).

35. See Pivka, *Navies*, pp. 107–9, 114–15; C.N. Parkinson, *War in the Eastern Seas, 1793–1815* (London, 1954).

36. D.G. Chandler, *The Campaigns of Napoleon* (London, 1966), p. 323.
37. For some details of the Spanish Navy in 1806, for instance, consult: G.H. Lovett, *Napoleon and the Birth of Modern Spain* (2 vols, New York, 1965), I, p. 38. Also see J. Harbron, *Trafalgar and the Spanish Navy* (London, 1988) and J. Harbron, 'Spain's Forgotten Naval Renaissance', *History Today*, 40/8 (1990).
38. Quoted in A. Fournier, *Napoleon I: A Biography*, II, p. 145. Also see pp. 147–8.
39. National Library of Scotland, Melville Papers: MS 1045/94: Memorandum by Lord Melville, 25 February 1813.

4

From Jena to Tilsit

As the Austrians discharged their obligations under the Treaty of Pressburg, Napoleon gradually withdrew his forces westwards. His principal concerns at this juncture were to stabilize his fledgling empire and to allow France and *La Grande Armée* to recuperate after the strains of the recent war. Indeed, between March and September 1806, he remained in Paris, preoccupied with his country's financial difficulties and other internal matters. However, although he seemed uninterested in fresh conquests, consolidation at home ineluctably involved the resolving of several issues further afield, notably in Germany and Italy.

Following Austria's defeat, large chunks of territory and scores of thousands of inhabitants had been transferred to new rulers. In Germany, this, together with the secularization that resulted from the dismemberment of ecclesiastical territories, had further enfeebled the tottering *Reich* and rendered its time-honoured institutions anachronistic. Throughout the eighteenth century, the growth in the power of individual states – notably Prussia and Austria – and their pursuit of their own interests had worked to the detriment of the Holy Roman Empire. As early as 1804, Francis, while still keeping the Roman–German crown, had attempted to develop a national role with imperial trappings by adopting the title 'Hereditary Emperor of Austria'. By May 1806, however, following a report by Count von Stadion, his foreign minister, he had concluded that the *Reich* was more of a burden than an asset; its crown had been useful in the past in defending Habsburg interests, but it appeared inadvisable to retain it 'under current conditions'.[1] France had now secured preponderance in German affairs, but, when offered the crown, Napoleon declined it. Instead, in July 1806 he established the Rhenish Confederation. This was to vary in size over the next few years as new territory was assimilated or existing lands were transferred from one polity to another, but, in substituting around 30 substantial, independently minded states for the hundreds of entities that had existed under the *Reich*, it transformed the geopolitics of the region and provided the framework within which modern Germany was to evolve.[2]

As a result of all this, in August 1806 Francis abdicated as emperor of the *Reich* and released its members from their constitutional obligations.[3] To the east, France now had a network of friendly, robust states which would serve as a buffer zone for her frontier or, if necessary, as a bridgehead for fresh military operations against the Central European powers. Napoleon also consolidated his position in Italy: Naples, having abrogated the neutrality pact it had concluded with him, and having allowed Allied forces onto its territory, was invaded. Dismissed by Napoleon as 'threefold liars', the ruling Bourbon family fled to Sicily and the emperor's brother, Joseph, was proclaimed king.[4] Soon after, another sibling, Louis, ascended to Holland's throne. The French hold on the first of these countries was, however, endangered by an insurrection, while their grip on both of them continued to be menaced by British maritime power. Napoleon, particularly eager to eliminate this last threat and the ongoing economic blockade, tried to woo the 'Nation of Shopkeepers' into ending the war. Charles Fox, the ailing foreign secretary in the 'All the Talents' ministry, strongly favoured peace, but suspicions over Napoleon's intentions concerning the Mediterranean rendered negotiations difficult; the emperor insisted that Sicily be given up, which was something 'Perfidious Albion' would not consent to. Indeed, the island's garrison was gradually strengthened to all of 17 500 men.[5]

Yet, without allies, there was little that Britain could do militarily to lift the danger Napoleonic France posed to her security. Indeed, a noxious blend of disenchantment with continental partnerships and a dearth of viable strategic alternatives pushed London into trying to exert pressure on Paris by means of colonial expansionism. This approach was an old weapon in Britain's armoury, but, in 1806, was to culminate in rash adventures that did nothing to alleviate her difficulties. Throughout that and for much of the following year, her insularity was as political as it was geographic. Even when hostilities finally erupted between France and Prussia, London remained aloof, observing the latter's eventual demise with perverse satisfaction. Nor was Russia's re-entry to the fray to elicit any practical assistance; both Frederick William III and the Tsar were seen as waging war in defence of their own interests, whereas Britain wanted operations that would achieve the objectives of the defunct Third Coalition.[6]

But when Grenville's administration first took office, and for some considerable time thereafter, it seemed improbable that Prussia would fight at all. Only days before Austerlitz, Napoleon had received Berlin's foreign minister, Count Haugwitz. He was supposed to have given the emperor a virtual ultimatum, but proved no match for the guileful Corsican; outmanœuvred, he was packed off to Vienna to await the imperial pleasure.[7]

When, contrary to expectations, tidings arrived of Napoleon's victory, Haugwitz endeavoured to extricate himself and his country from what now seemed a potentially suicidal course of action by extending his king's congratulations on the emperor's success. Napoleon was unimpressed; he was well aware of Prussia's machinations in recent months. He deliberately made Haugwitz wait a further two weeks before granting him another audience, during which he turned the tables on him by issuing his own ultimatum: Frederick William was to sign an immediate and exclusive pact aligning himself against Britain; and many of Prussia's possessions in southern and western Germany were to be surrendered to France or Bavaria. By way of compensation, Berlin would receive Hannover and additional territory around Bayreuth.[8]

With the Austrians defeated, the Russians in retreat and Britain increasingly suspicious, Prussia suddenly found herself isolated and exposed to the full might of the French Empire and its satellites. Only nominal allies remained to help her: Saxony, which was susceptible to browbeating by her powerful neighbour, and Sweden, which shared Britain's mistrust of the scheming Hohenzollern. Nor was the mobilization of her own army sufficiently advanced for war to be a viable, let alone desirable, option. Hoping that time might rectify some of these shortcomings, Haugwitz endeavoured to gain some. But, again, Napoleon outwitted him. Suspecting that Prussia, given her circumstances, could and would not fight, however provocatively he behaved, he coerced Haugwitz into signing a preliminary convention before he left Vienna.[9] When, in a further bid to win a stay of execution, Berlin subsequently tried to reopen the negotiations, Napoleon insisted that the treaty be formalized, ratified and implemented at once. He also incorporated clauses stipulating that the north German ports were to be closed to British shipping and merchandise. Although humiliated, the Prussians were indeed reluctant to fight, just as he had surmised; by the end of February, they had acceded to his terms.

As one historian commented, it seems as least doubtful that Napoleon 'was ever more dishonest than Prussia was in 1805–6'.[10] Britain declared war in response to Berlin's actions, while Napoleon, having discredited Frederick William and deepened both his and Britain's isolation at one fell swoop, now tried to entice the Russians into ending hostilities. However, what Alexander's envoy, Count d'Oubril, agreed to, the Tsar subsequently disavowed. Nor did Napoleon's attempts to placate Britain lead to anything, even when he offered to barter Hannover for Sicily. But, whereas this suggestion failed to conciliate London, its impact on Franco-Prussian relations was predictably harmful; and when, shortly after, Francis of Austria laid aside the Roman crown, and Napoleon proclaimed the establishment of the *Rheinbund*, Berlin began to fear for its own traditional sphere of influence within the moribund *Reich*.[11] Although Paris now proposed that a counterbalancing north German confederation might be created under Frederick William's auspices, his expectations exceeded what Napoleon was prepared to concede. The emperor would not, for instance, permit the inclusion of the *Hansestädte,* while his championing of the causes of Saxony and Hesse-Kassel, which had understandable misgivings about Prussia's intentions, appeared to be a calculated impediment to the fulfilment of Berlin's aspirations.

All of this provoked indignation within Prussian society in general and within the army and ruling elite in particular.[12] The Francophobic Karl von Hardenberg had superseded the neutralist Haugwitz in the handling of foreign affairs. He, together with a group of proud, patriotic generals and courtiers, began advocating war with France. Queen Louise was no less bellicose. Napoleon once described her as 'the only real man in Prussia'. Certainly, her tender beauty belied her strong personality, which contrasted starkly with that of her pusillanimous husband. By early August, however, even he had been persuaded of the need to make a stand. Although still assuring Napoleon that he could depend on their continuing cooperation, the Prussians began to prepare for hostilities in earnest.

Ever since its triumphs in the Seven Years War, the Prussian Army had enjoyed a formidable reputation which its lacklustre performance in the First Coalition against Revolutionary France had done little to diminish. Just as Wellington was to dominate the thinking and practice of the British Army for decades after Waterloo, so was that of Prussia to be inspired and haunted by Frederick the Great's successes. The inherent conservatism that this led to manifested itself at every level: the soldiers were, for the most part, equipped, clothed and trained just as they had been in the days of '*Alter Fritz*', while their doctrine and the mechanics of their logistical support were as geared to the ways of the mid-eighteenth century as were their generals' minds. In fact, most of the senior officers had first seen action alongside Frederick and, consequently, were in their 70s at least.[13] As products of a feudal society, largely untouched by the social and political turmoil of recent years, they were all of noble birth and imbued with a sense of natural as well as professional superiority. They were confident that they would put paid to the Corsican upstart.[14] But, as Clausewitz remarked, 'behind the fine façade, all was mildewed'. When the Prussian Army took the field in summer 1806, it embarked on its first major operation for 11 years, and the atrophy which had occurred over the previous 20 quickly revealed itself.[15] Once the very symbol of Prussia's strength, her army had become the most dangerous manifestation of her political vulnerability.[16]

Until early September, Napoleon remained persuaded that hostilities with Prussia might be avoided. However, the death of Fox on the 13th extinguished any lingering hopes of a reconciliation with Britain, and the Tsar's rejection of the draft treaty agreed with Count d'Oubril also boded ill. It seemed to Napoleon that another coalition was in the offing, and he began mobilizing his army. But the Prussians had no intention of waiting for Russia to come to their assistance. The cocksure war party was bent on taking the offensive without further ado; the country's honour and security demanded nothing less. Hoping to catch the French forces while they were still dispersed, the Prussians proposed to move via Erfurt and Wurzburg towards Schwabia. Accordingly, while an army of 50 000 men under Prince Hohenlohe lumbered towards Dresden to pressgang Saxony into supporting Frederick William, the Prussian main force, some 70 000 troops under the septuagenarian duke of Brunswick, plodded through Leipzig towards the Thuringerwald. A 16 000-strong reserve, led by Eugen of Württemberg, followed in its wake, and a further 30 000 troops, commanded by General Ruchel, moved up on its right from Hannover. Although Frederick William's forces totalled around 250 000 personnel, many units had still to be activated, while others were left garrisoning distant fortresses. Indeed, even at this late stage, the rusty bureaucracy had only succeeded in mobilizing about two thirds of the available manpower to confront Napoleon: 35 000 sabres, 115 000 bayonets and 15 000 gunners with 300 heavy cannon and 250 lighter pieces intended to furnish close support for the infantry. Brunswick, who, as the Allied *generalissimo*, had fought the Revolutionary armies at Valmy and in the Rhineland, was aware of, and concerned about, the numerical strength at France's disposal. He favoured peace and had strong reservations about actions which might precipitate hostilities.[17] Nevertheless, on 25 September, Berlin issued an ultimatum demanding the immediate withdrawal of all French forces to beyond the Rhine; negotiations for the settlement of all outstanding points of dispute; and the return of key enclaves. Moreover, France was to refrain from interfering in Prussia's establishment of a confederation encompassing all the north German polities not yet included in Napoleon's *Rheinbund*.

Since the Prussians had resolved to go to war weeks beforehand, it is doubtful whether they really wanted or expected a response to these demands, but any answer was to be at Brunswick's headquarters by 8 October. Napoleon, however, sensing that hostilities were imminent, had already left Paris to join his troops and only received the missive on the 7th. His reaction was to unleash *La Grande Armée*. In the aftermath of the Austerlitz campaign, most of it lay spread across southern and western Germany, with the III, IV and VI Corps cantoned in a crooked triangle with its base on the Rhine and its apex at Munich, while the VII, V and I

Corps lay along an arc from around Siegen in the northwest to Nuremberg in the southeast. These units totalled 160 000 personnel, including 32 000 horsemen, with in excess of 300 guns. A few recruits who had replaced the last campaign's casualties aside, the infantry consisted entirely of seasoned, enthusiastic soldiers, as did the cavalry, which had also had an infusion of good-quality mounts captured from the Austrians. True, there was a shortage of limbers and caissons, and many of the troops' uniforms were rather threadbare, but, however rough, these six corps, together with the elite Imperial Guard at Paris, comprised the diamond of the Napoleonic armies. Besides them, General Brune's men maintained their vigil on the Channel, while King Louis's 20 000-strong Franco-Dutch corps safeguarded the Dutch littoral and, simultaneously, menaced Hannover.[18] A further 90 000 troops secured the French possessions in Italy and ensured that Austria remained dormant.

The Prussian leadership had little information as to the precise whereabouts of Napoleon's army. Nor could they agree on a plan with which to confront it. In a series of protracted and often acrimonious councils of war, they repeatedly adopted new schemes, only to jettison them shortly afterwards. Unlike their adversary's, their army's basic building block remained the regiment; there was no permanent structure of corps or divisions, and foot, horse and artillery units were cobbled together as and when required. Neither was there a general staff to coordinate the activities of the army's myriad elements, nor a clear chain of command to implement any decisions that were taken. Compendious orders had to be drafted for each unit, yet, such was the scope for misunderstanding, senior officers were routinely summoned to headquarters for clarifying briefings. The whole cumbersome and time-consuming system was a relic from a bygone age when armies, moving slowly and methodically among networks of depots, had sought to gain marginal advantages over their enemies in a prolonged, essentially attritional war. Against opponents operating within the same ethos, it had worked effectively enough. Against Napoleon, who regarded ensnaring his adversaries in a decisive battle on terms favourable to him as the sole object of strategy, it was to prove as fatal as it was inflexible.

Indeed, barely had the Prussian leadership issued their ultimatum than the limitations of their command and control procedures began to show. Because of constant changes of plan, several units wearied themselves in pointless marches and countermarches, while others were paralysed by uncertainty. Napoleon, meanwhile, having considered his own and, as far as he could discern them, his adversaries' options, had concluded that, ideally, the enemy should not be tackled head-on as this would risk pushing them back towards Berlin, their depots and, worse still, the Russians.

With simple frontal offensives ruled out, a turning movement as far east as possible had most to recommend it. Although this would entail traversing the difficult country which formed the watershed of the Saale and Main, and would leave the heads of the French columns vulnerable to a counterstroke as they debouched onto the rolling plains south of Leipzig, it promised to isolate the advancing Prussian army from both Saxony and Berlin. Accordingly, with its customary speed, *La Grande Armée* began assembling east of a line running through Bamberg and Nuremberg,[19] leaving the territory between the former and Mainz wholly unoccupied. Its own lines of communication were rerouted southwards to place them out of harm's way, while, just in case the Prussians should veer through the Fulda Gap towards the middle Rhine, Mainz especially was put in a state of defence.[20] Until the concentration was completed, however, *matériel* and troops continued to pass through here *en route* to the army. Among them was the Guard, which, by means of hard marching and rides on requisitioned carts, covered the 550 kilometres from Paris in just over a week.

By 7 October, Napoleon had amassed approximately 200 000 troops and 300 guns in an area 60 kilometres wide by 60 deep. Comprising three principal columns, each within supporting distance of its neighbour and with their constituent parts likewise separated by no more than a day's march, this '*bataillon carré*', as he described it,[21] was, terrain features permitting, capable of movement in any direction. Should a section of its frontage encounter the enemy, the rest would converge to support it, wrapping itself around the victim like some enormous bolas.

At dawn on the 8th, this huge formation, masked by Murat's light horse, rolled over the Prussian–Saxon frontier between Coburg and Bayreuth. The centre column consisted of the I and III Corps, the Guard and the balance of the Cavalry Reserve. It headed through Kronach for Schleiz. The left-hand prong was formed by the VII and V Corps, and made for Saalfeld via Coburg. The right-hand column, meanwhile, squeezed into the defiles between the eastern end of the Thuringerwald and the Fichtelgebirge, debouching at Hof. The mountains, soaring to 800 metres, contained but a few Prussian picquets; and, apart from some clashes between them and Murat's screens, there was no fighting on the 8th.

During 4–7 October, owing to their interminable councils of war, the Prussians almost ceased active operations. By the French offensive's start, their forces were still spread along a 140-kilometre front: Ruchel was at Eisenach, with a detachment commanded by the duke of Saxe-Weimar at Vacha on the Werra; Hohenlohe was at Jena, with his vanguards dotted along the upper Saale between Rudolstadt and Hof; while Brunswick was in the vicinity of Erfurt with, like Ruchel, outposts as far forward as the Werra. Frederick William himself was at the duke's headquarters. Prone to wavering at the best of times, the young monarch felt overawed by the elderly, distinguished and experienced warriors around him and, although titular commander-in-chief, meekly acquiesced in most of their decisions. This made his presence as much of a liability as an asset; it further warped the twisted pyramid of command. Occasionally, the king did overrule or openly question his subordinates' prescriptions, leaving the lower ranks uncertain as to who was actually at the helm. As things stood, they had grounds enough to doubt their leaders' judgement. Until a reconnaissance patrol discovered that the French had evacuated the Main Valley west of Bamberg and were thrusting northeast, the Prussian high command barely had an inkling of Napoleon's dispositions and intentions. Once the situation became clearer, however, all thought of mounting an offensive was abandoned; the army would have to sidle eastwards to bar the enemy's path. Brunswick ordered a preliminary concentration in the area bounded by Jena, Weimar and Rudolstadt, while Saxe-Weimar, with all of 11 000 troops, was dispatched to harry the French communications which, it was assumed, were now dangerously exposed. Württemberg's corps was also brought forward to Halle.

Once again, the inadequacies of the Prussian staff work led to debility and confusion. After a clash between the spearheads of the French central column and a detachment under General Tauenzien near Schleiz on the 9th, Hohenlohe sought to gather his forces together and move to his subordinate's support. Regrettably, his orders to Prince Louis, who was at Saalfeld with 8000 Saxons and Prussians, nervously monitoring the approach of Napoleon's left-hand column, were woefully nebulous and gave the prince the impression that he was to gain time while Hohenlohe slipped away to succour Tauenzien and Brunswick shifted east to fill the void.[22] In the event, Brunswick did not budge; he recalled Hohenlohe and directed Louis to fall back on Rudolstadt, shunning combat. However, by the time these orders arrived, at 11 am on the 10th, the latter was irretrievably engaged with Lannes's corps just south of the Saale. The battle ended in the prince being slain in hand-to-hand fighting and the dregs of his command streaming north over the river in utter disorder.[23]

Studying reports of the actions at Saalfeld and Schleiz, Napoleon now concluded that the Prussians' main body was still further north or west than he had expected. Thirty-six hours after the Saalfeld encounter, the bulk of his own forces – the Foot Guards, and the I, IV, V and VII Corps – were between the Elster and the Saale in an arc which extended from Gera through Weida and Neustadt to Saalfeld. Ney was at Schleiz, with Davout's III Corps and most of Murat's heavy cavalry to his front astride the Gera road. As the Prussians were evidently west of the Saale, the French army started pivoting towards it during the 12th, Lannes's and Davout's spearheads eventually probing across it at Kahla and Naumburg respectively. The sheer pliability of the '*bataillon carré*' greatly facilitated this vast manœuvre: in wheeling westwards, the troops of Soult and Ney, who had originally formed the army's right-hand column, became its spine, effectively changing places with Davout's and Bernadotte's corps. None of these units encountered any opposition. Indeed, the day's only engagement was a skirmish involving Lannes's vanguard and some Prussian outposts as the V Corps, still on the French left, neared Jena on its march up the Saale's west bank. The marshal repelled the enemy easily enough, but his 19 000 men were now becoming dangerously detached from the rest of *La Grande Armée*. Augereau's VII Corps should have been close by, but had fallen behind owing to a combination of belated instructions and a needlessly circuitous route; by evening on the 12th, it was at Kahla.

As Napoleon initially intended giving his footsore troops a rest on the 13th, few new movements were ordered; the hindmost units were directed to close up to those already along the Saale. However, fresh intelligence reports persuaded the emperor that the Prussians were retreating towards Magdeburg, although there was a risk that they might turn on Lannes. Accordingly, just after 9am, new directives roused *La Grande Armée* again. Most significantly, in order to close the gap between Lannes and Davout, who was at Naumburg, Murat's and Bernadotte's forces were to move 'as quickly as possible' to Dornburg, from where they could assist either the V or III Corps according to circumstances. Meanwhile, Napoleon left Gera for Jena to ascertain for himself what the enemy was doing.[24]

By 3pm he was nearing his destination. Already alarmed by the distant rattle of musketry, he now received a letter from Lannes, the marshal's first report that day, stating that he was confronted by a powerful Prussian contingent on the plateau between Weimar and Jena. Apparently, having penetrated the latter town at dawn, Lannes's leading division, Suchet's, had continued harassing the picquets they had encountered the previous evening. These, however, had steadily withdrawn, relinquishing the wooded Landgrafenberg to their pursuers, where, as the morning mist dispersed, Suchet's 4000 infantry had found themselves looking at three imposing lines of troops, totalling as many as 40 000 bayonets and sabres.

Napoleon himself ascended the Landgrafenberg around 4pm. The Prussians seemed disposed to attack. With most of his corps still to arrive, Lannes had but a handful of infantry battalions with which to meet any immediate onslaught. Nevertheless, Napoleon was determined to retain the Jena bridgehead and he promptly summoned reinforcements: the Foot Guard and the remainder of V Corps were to occupy the Landgrafenberg; Augereau was to hasten his advance from Kahla; while the IV and VI Corps, together with the heavy cavalry of Murat's Reserve, would proceed to Jena with all speed. If Davout and Bernadotte heard heavy firing around that place during the evening, they too were to advance from Naumburg and Dornburg respectively, seeking to envelop the enemy's left.[25]

In the event, however, the night passed without incident. Personally supervising the work, lantern in hand, Napoleon had his troops widen and level the steep, narrow track up the Landgrafenberg from Jena so as to ease the flow of men and, more importantly, artillery.[26] By dawn on the 14th, 46 000 soldiers had crowded into position, while, from the south and east, thousands more were converging on Jena, the inhabitants of which, 'half-clothed carrying ... their children', were fleeing blazing buildings and the impending fighting.[27] Assuming that Brunswick's main force now stood before him, Napoleon envisaged a major battle, perhaps over two days, in which the French would, first, consolidate their foothold on the plateau and gain space for manœuvre before, second, enveloping and destroying their adversaries. In fact, the troops that were deployed between the settlements on the fogbound plateau were only a portion of Brunswick's army. Commanded by Hohenlohe, they had been left to cover an all-out retreat on Halle via Kösen and Freyburg. How had this come about?

The mauling of Prince Louis's contingent at Saalfeld on the 10th had come as a dreadful shock to the Prussians and their reluctant Saxon allies. Louis, the king's nephew, had been regarded as one of their most promising leaders, and the 33-year-old's needless if heroic death even moved Napoleon to convey his condolences. But, if the fact that the demise of Louis's force had been caused, at least partly, by the seemingly ceaseless blunders in the army's staff work was unsettling, the realization that the French tactics at Saalfeld had proved more than a match for the vaunted Frederician line was demoralizing in the extreme. Indeed, the reverse had a psychological effect that was far worse than the material damage inflicted. Many Saxon units in particular lost all faith in their commanders and, as Hohenlohe extricated Tauenzien's troops and his other detachments from beyond the Saale and passed through Jena the following day, they were gripped by mindless panic.[28] Order was not easily restored and continued to be fragile as the troops' deprivations mounted.[29] For one thing, the complex network of depots and convoys that sustained the army in the field was not functioning properly. '*Alter Fritz*' had waged most of his campaigns on his own territory and, reluctant to impoverish and alienate the population by letting his soldiers live off the land, had discouraged the practice more than most eighteenth-century commanders. In the living museum that was the Prussian Army, little had altered since his day and, lacking both permission and the techniques for orchestrated foraging, the troops were almost exclusively dependent on the commissariat. As hunger compounded the fatigue caused by pointless marches and countermarches, the army was steadily enfeebled, both psychologically and physically.

Finally convinced of the need to concentrate every available man, the Prussians regrouped their forces. Dusk on the 12th saw Württemberg at Halle, while Hohenlohe was between Jena and Weimar, with Brunswick behind him and Ruchel still further west beyond the Ilm. Saxe-Weimar, who had searched widely but vainly for Napoleon's putative supply lines, was only expected to reach Ilmenau the following evening. By that time, however, Napoleon was guiding Lannes's corps and the Guard into position on the Landgrafenberg, while Brunswick, fearing for his links with Magdeburg, had left Ruchel to await Saxe-Weimar and had headed north along the Ilm's left bank for Freyburg, where he hoped to assimilate Württemberg's force.

Expected to screen the other Prussian contingents, Hohenlohe had considered falling on the French debouching from Jena, but was enjoined to stay on the defensive, both strategically and tactically.[30] In any case, he dismissed the enemy's activity here as insignificant, being more concerned by reports of French troops at Dornburg and Camburg.[31] The chance to deliver a spoiling attack against the incipient French concentration was thus allowed to slip, and the assembly of Napoleon's forces continued unimpeded. Such were the advantages conferred by the structure of his *'bataillon carré'* that, in under 24 hours of initiating the move, all of 96 000 men had been massed around Jena.[32] Moreover, Napoleon believed, a further 55 000, under Bernadotte and Davout, would also be close at hand, threatening the enemy's left-rear from beyond Apolda.

This assumption was to prove as unfounded as Napoleon's conviction that he was facing the bulk of Brunswick's army. In fact, this was now well to the north, while the French I and III Corps were not quite where the emperor believed them to be either. As we have seen, Davout and Bernadotte had been enjoined to advance immediately on Jena in the event of them hearing heavy firing. This had not occurred and, around 4am on the 14th, Davout, still at Naumburg, received fresh directions. Believing that a decisive engagement was imminent, Napoleon now instructed him to advance on Apolda via the Ilm's western bank, adding that, if Bernadotte was still with him, the two were to march together: 'The Emperor hopes, however, that he will be in the position assigned to

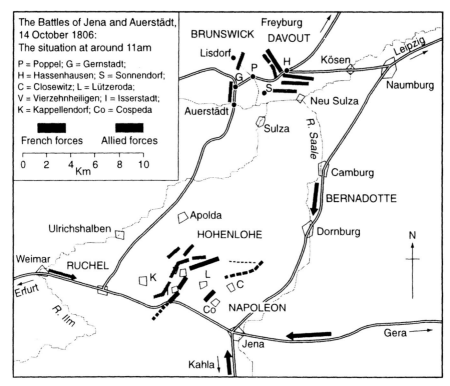

The Battles of Jena and Auerstädt,
14 October 1806:
The situation at around 11am

P = Poppel; G = Gernstadt;
H = Hassenhausen; S = Sonnendorf;
C = Closewitz; L = Lützeroda;
V = Vierzehnheiligen; I = Isserstadt;
K = Kappellendorf; Co = Cospeda

French forces   Allied forces

0   2   4   6   8   10
         Km

The Battles of Jena and Auerstädt

him at Dornburg.'[33] In fact, the I Corps was still near Naumburg, and Bernadotte was promptly given a copy of the new orders by Davout. But the I Corps' jealous commander chose to disregard it, later citing a number of essentially fatuous and puerile reasons for refusing to cooperate with his colleague. This nearly had disastrous consequences, and it was purely because of Napoleon's clemency that Bernadotte was spared a court-martial and firing-squad.[34]

Yet, if Napoleon's view of matters was obscured somewhat by the fog of war, Hohenlohe and Brunswick were still worse informed as to the strategic situation. Until he came under heavy attack on the 14th, the latter remained convinced that the developments at Jena were inconsequential and that he faced only a flank guard of *La Grande Armée* as it continued towards Leipzig and Dresden. Reports of French troops in Naumburg were interpreted in the same light, but Hohenlohe did take the precaution of deploying 5000 men on the plateau above Dornburg on the 13th. As a result of this extension to his line, his 38 000 bayonets and sabres were scattered along a 14-kilometre front: Tauenzien confronted the French on the Landgrafenberg with just 8000 troops, while General Holtzendorf supervised the outposts towards Dornburg. The balance of Hohenlohe's force was spread for some distance along the northern edge of the Jena–Weimar road, to the right-rear of Tauenzien's formations.[35]

Just as Hohenlohe failed to anticipate a major engagement on the 14th, so too did Brunswick. Accompanied by the king, his 50 000 men, with 230 guns, set out from Weimar for Freyburg at 10am on the 13th. So great was the pandemonium within the ranks, however, that, slow in comparison with the French at the best of times, the Prussians proceeded at a snail's pace. The foremost units, under General Schmettau, got no further than Gernstadt, just beyond Auerstädt, by dusk, while the rearmost, despite marching well into the night, were several kilometres behind them. Indeed, the French were closer; Davout's reconnaissance parties had probed over the Saale at Kösen late on the 13th, clashing with Prussian hussars. At around 5am, however, the marshal, in accordance with his latest orders, set the whole III Corps – 26 000 men with 44 guns – in motion for Apolda. Groping through dense fog, Gudin's division followed a small vanguard towards Gernstadt, while Colonel Burke, Davout's aide, trotted ahead to ascertain the position and strength of the opposition.

Blundering into the Prussian vanguard – 600 cavalry commanded by the fiery if elderly Blücher – Burke and his escort scurried back to alert their compatriots, who now began deploying along the rough crescent of hills which embraced the settlement of Hassenhausen and overlooked the Liesbach. With the enemy barring his path to the Kösen Pass and Freyburg, Brunswick frantically started disentangling combat units from the army's baggage trains and feeding them into an action that spiralled in scale and intensity.[36] Blücher, heavily reinforced, led a series of cavalry charges which, though determined, utterly failed to break the French infantry squares; they coolly mowed down their assailants with musketry and canister. By 8.30am, Blücher's troopers had been routed, whereas Davout's second division, Friant's, had begun to reinforce the French line. The next Prussian attack did not occur until after 9am and was executed by Schmettau's infantry and several regiments of General Wartensleben's command that had trickled across the solitary, choked bridge at Auerstädt. As at Saalfeld, the tactical superiority of the French quickly showed. Ensconced in buildings, sunken lanes, orchards and other enclosures, skirmishers inflicted heavy casualties on the ponderous Prussian lines long before their own close-order formations were engaged, while the French cannon made up with accuracy and rapidity of fire what they lacked in numbers. Both Schmettau and Brunswick were mortally wounded as, once again, the Prussian efforts to dislodge their opponents from Hassenhausen ended in gory failure.

South of the road which bisected the battlefield, however, sheer weight of numbers began to tell. The faltering French line was curling back on Hassenhausen when Davout's third division, Morand's, arrived and spearheaded a counterattack which restored his fortunes. Virtually all of the remaining Prussian cavalry was now utilized in a bid to stem Morand's advance, but their commander, Prince William of Prussia, failed to commit his units *en masse* or to coordinate their attacks; regiments came up piecemeal and were, like Blücher's before them, received by the French in squares. Unsupported by infantry, the Prussian squadrons eddied and swirled around these resilient formations, suffering heavy losses to little effect. Exhausted and demoralized, their remnants soon reeled back, allowing Morand to resume his progress along the horn of hills between Hassenhausen and the Ilm.

With their right flank being enfiladed at a time when Friant was also making gains against their left, the Prussians responded by throwing yet more of their reserves against Morand. This attempt to stop the rot was also unsuccessful, and the wreckage of the attack recoiled over the Liesbach with Morand in hot pursuit. Simultaneously, Gudin's powder-stained regiments struck at the forces stalled before Hassenhausen itself, while, further north, Friant's men splashed through the Liesbach and ousted the Prussians from the settlement of Poppel. Around noon, General Kalreuth, at the head of the last reserves, tried to establish a new line along the heights between Gernstadt and Auerstädt, but Brunswick's army was by now on the verge of dissolution. Turned out of this position, too, it made off in disorder, leaving Davout's exhausted but jubilant men in possession of the field, 115 guns and 3000 prisoners. No less than 15 000 Prussians had also been killed or wounded, compared with French losses totalling 7000 – a quarter of Davout's force.[37]

While all of this had been happening, Napoleon had assailed what he took to be the main Prussian army at Jena. At around 6am, both sides' artillery commenced firing, and Lannes initiated the breakout from the Landgrafenberg bridgehead: picking their way through the dense, morning mist across the saddles and hollows of the plateau, his troops advanced in a mixture of lines and columns, preceded by skirmisher swarms. Progress was slow in such an environment, and it was 7.30am before they got to grips with Tauenzien's front line between the villages of Closewitz and Lützeroda. The fighting was heavy and confused – some Saxons in the latter place were bombarded by their own gunners, who could barely distinguish friend from foe in the fog[38] – but Tauenzien's troops were eventually ejected from the settlements and surrounding woods. While they regrouped between Vierzehnheiligen and Isserstadt, Soult's and Augereau's corps squeezed in on Lannes's right and left respectively, occupying the space cleared by V Corps' advance.

Despite the approaching thunder of battle and several frantic messages from Tauenzien, Hohenlohe remained reluctant to believe that anything serious was afoot and became quite irritated when one subordinate started moving his cavalry towards the sound of the gunfire.[39] At last persuaded that his left was in genuine jeopardy, he summoned Ruchel from Weimar and directed Tauenzien to fall back on the reserves between Apolda and the Weimar–Jena road. Tauenzien, who, with some success, had just commenced a counterattack, promptly complied. The V Corps continued to edge forward in his wake, but was insufficiently strong to tackle the new Prussian line. While Lannes's troops marked time, however, a new threat emerged on their right-rear in the form of Holtzendorf's contingent, which, alerted by firing to the south, had spent the previous three hours concentrating and marching to join Tauenzien. Finding the V Corps across his path, Holtzendorf was tempted into assailing the exposed French flank, but had still to complete his preparations when his own troops came under fire from the woods on their left. This was the work of Soult's corps, as it sought to come abreast of Lannes's formations. Holtzendorf instantly aborted his attack. He was too close to disengage easily, though, and was soon beset by a swarm of hussars and *chasseurs*. Several units were overthrown, and the rest had to flee towards Apolda, from where, menaced by Bernadotte's corps as it approached from Dornburg, they headed for the Ilm at Ulrichshalben.

In crossing the plateau Lannes's two divisions had inclined somewhat to the north, opening up a gap in the French left-centre. This was plugged initially by a 25-gun battery. As the advanced guard of Ney's corps arrived on the field, however, its 4000 men not only crammed in between this artillery and Lannes's left but also surged towards the Prussian positions around Vierzehnheiligen. This move, unsanctioned by Napoleon, provoked an immediate response from the Prussian cavalry, which had been massing for an attack on the stalled V Corps. Forty-five squadrons swept down on Ney's panting men, forcing them into squares and cutting them off from the rest of the French line. To extricate them, Napoleon had to commit the few cavalry reserves he had to hand – Murat's troopers were only just reaching the battlefield – and to implore Lannes to renew his advance. Augereau was also enjoined to intensify the pressure on Isserstadt. Although these emergency measures saved '*le Rougeaud*', the cost was considerable. Lannes's weary men clawed their way through Vierzehnheiligen and tried to debouch into the fields beyond, but recoiled at the approach of virtually all of Hohenlohe's remaining infantry, some

20 000 men. Similarly, VII Corps' leading elements doggedly moved tree by tree through the Isserstadt woods and into the village, but ground to a stop just beyond it.

Indeed, by noon, the entire battlefront was essentially static. For the moment, Ney's, Augereau's and Lannes's regiments could make no headway, whereas Hohenlohe, unwilling to attack until Ruchel had arrived, rejected his subordinates' pleas for an immediate advance. The pause was to work to Napoleon's advantage, however. In accordance with his plans, thousands of reinforcements were pouring onto the field every few minutes and were forming up in support of the front line. Once these actively joined the fray, the Prussians, hopelessly outnumbered, would be unable to prevent their positions being overlapped. In any case, the ongoing exchange of fire was proving far more destructive for Hohenlohe's troops than for their adversaries. Ordered to deploy within musket range of the latter, the former dutifully went through the intricate manœuvres of the Frederician drill while being riddled with sniper fire. Once in line, they sought to reply with orchestrated salvoes, which had a negligible impact on the French skirmisher screens; dispersed, and firing at their discretion from behind any available cover, they were far more elusive targets than the close-order formations pitted against them. Of course, as they afforded optimum firepower on a given frontage, easier control and the mental comfort men derived from being part of a mass, shoulder-to-shoulder formations had much to recommend them and, more than a century later, were still regarded by many as possessing a sufficiently potent blend of psychological and physical strength to overcome even machine guns and quick-firing artillery which could engage targets at unprecedented ranges.[40] Nor should one be surprised that the Prussian army relied on the tactical formations and procedures of its own antiquated doctrine; it was trained with nothing else in mind. But, like more than a few commentators since, many a French officer must have been astounded to see his Prussian counterparts pointlessly expose their soldiers to this destructive skirmisher fire for so long. Seeking neither to retire nor to advance, they stood stoically before the French positions for perhaps 90 minutes, until in places 'the fronts of companies were only marked by individual files still loading and firing, while all their comrades lay dead and dying around them'.[41]

In so doing, the Prussian infantry displayed courage which was surpassed only by their tactical inflexibility and, in this instance, the ineptitude of their senior commanders. As Clausewitz was to observe: 'It was not just a case of a style which had outlived its usefulness but the most extreme poverty of the imagination to which routine has ever led.'[42] So demoralized and physically enfeebled was the Prussian line as a consequence of this ordeal that it was already crumbling when the French renewed their assault at about 1.15pm. Although a few cavalry units withdrew in some order and, on the far right around Isserstadt, the Saxon brigades were still trying to hold their ground, all but one regiment of the entire centre and left of Hohenlohe's army buckled before the onslaught. Retreat swiftly degenerated into rout as Murat, contemptuously wielding a riding-crop instead of a sabre, led 11 cavalry regiments into the voids between Vierzehnheiligen and Isserstadt.

The pursuit continued pitilessly for 3 kilometres towards the Weimar road. Here, however, the French cavalry, having left their own infantry far behind, slithered to a halt as, battling their way through the crowds of fugitives, came Ruchel's battalions, deployed *en échelon* to form a vast spearhead. His approach had been leaden-footed to say the least: he had taken four hours to cover the 8 kilometres between the Ilm and Hohenlohe's right-rear. Nor had he been able to gather in Saxe-Weimar's contingent, which, despite hard marching, was still beyond Erfurt. This gave him just 15 000 men with which to rescue Hohenlohe, though he was also deeply perturbed by the roar of battle far to the north around Auerstädt; indeed, he had no sooner deployed his troops for action at Jena than a belated plea for help arrived from Brunswick. Hohenlohe, assuming command of Ruchel's men, committed the whole force not to a covering action but to a riposte. Marching eastwards, supported by the remaining horsemen, the wedge of battalions crested the hills before them only to encounter overwhelming numbers of French infantry backed by numerous artillery batteries. Within 30 minutes, Ruchel was critically wounded and what remained of his corps had dissolved into the torrent of fugitives around it.[43]

This calamity also sealed the fate of the Saxons who were still grappling with Augereau's corps around Isserstadt. Although ousted from the village at around noon, they had continued to dispute every metre of ground for approximately three hours, becoming increasingly cut off as the Prussians to their left were displaced by Frenchmen. Once Ruchel was discomfited, however, their isolation was complete. Faced with annihilation, no less than 6000 surrendered to Murat's circling squadrons. Of the 20 000 Saxons who had fought under Prussian leadership at Saalfeld and Jena, nearly half were now prisoners and hundreds more were dead or wounded. This military defeat was soon to be mirrored in a broader capitulation: while Napoleon treated his Saxon captives very generously after the battle,[44] he secured their elector's renunciation of his alliance with Prussia and imposed a hefty indemnity. As a compliant member of the Napoleonic order, Saxony was also obliged to participate in the boycott of British goods and to provide resources for *La Grande Armée*. Although enlarged, at Prussia's expense, and, like Bavaria and Württemberg before her, elevated to a kingdom, she came to realize that Napoleon had only allies or victims, and that the distinction between the two was often a subtle one.[45]

Napoleon had utilized just 54 000 of the 96 000 troops at his disposal utterly to rout the 53 000 men commanded by Hohenlohe, Ruchel and Holtzendorf. Fewer than 7000 casualties had been sustained, whereas around 11 000 Prussians and Saxons were slain or injured, and 15 000, together with 200 guns, were captured. The whole Allied army was scattered and dispirited and, by the time the exhausted French halted their pursuit for the day, had been chased over the Ilm at Weimar and Ulrichshalben.[46] It was a tremendous victory, but it was apparent to Napoleon that only half of Brunswick's total force had been involved in the *débâcle*. Where was the rest? And where were the III and I Corps?

Though weary, the emperor pondered these questions well into the night, until reports, among them one from Davout, furnished the answers. That Brunswick's main body had been at Auerstädt and had been defeated by a solitary *corps d'armée*, was astonishing; the III Corps had, Napoleon acknowledged, performed wonders.[47] Above all, Brunswick's defeat dispelled his principal fear: the enemy no longer possessed a substantial body of troops which had not been beaten. Although Bernadotte's failure to participate actively in either of the battles at Jena and Auerstädt had helped the Prussians evade complete annihilation in one or both, the shattered armies of Brunswick and Hohenlohe were now converging in indescribable confusion beyond the Ilm. The French could exploit and consolidate their victory with impunity.

Accordingly, at 7am on the 15th, *La Grande Armée* embarked on what was to become one of the most thorough and rapid pursuits in military annals. While Murat, Soult and Ney maintained the pressure on the Prussians, who were retreating towards Erfurt and Sommerda, Bernadotte raced north to Halle to bar the routes to Magdeburg and the Elbe. The corps of Augereau, Lannes and Davout, after recuperating, followed in his wake. Murat's *l'épée dans les reins* chase soon reaped a rich harvest. Prussian discipline and morale were at their nadir, and thousands of starving, mutinous men were rounded up as they rampaged through houses, barns and crop-fields in search of food. Abandoned guns, tonnes of *matériel* and hundreds of wagons also fell into Murat's hands. Erfurt, he discovered, was packed with 10 000–12 000 fugitives. Saxe-Weimar, who was lurking nearby, hoped to extricate these troops and unite them with his own force, which was still intact. Erfurt capitulated without firing a shot, however, and the duke made for Heiligenstadt with no more than 12 000 bayonets and sabres, while Murat and Ney swung northwards towards the Harz Mountains, herding the main body of Frederick William's stricken army before them. Meanwhile, Bernadotte's spearheads had reached Halle, where Württemberg's 16 000-strong reserve corps was still lingering, uncertain what to do. Attacking on the 17th, Bernadotte crushed the Prussians' half-hearted attempt to retain the town, inflicting all of 5000 casualties; his amounted to 800 at most.[48]

Over the next few days, all the country between the Saale and the Elbe was relinquished to the advancing French as they thrust towards Berlin, which was abandoned to its fate. Meanwhile, the bulk of the beaten Prussian armies, including Saxe-Weimar's contingent, which had come up from Heiligenstadt by a circuitous route, converged on Magdeburg prior to moving northeast to the Oder, where the Russians were expected. On the 21st, as Hohenlohe left Magdeburg for Stettin with a hotchpotch of 40 000 troops, Davout's and Lannes' corps began debouching onto the Elbe's right bank through Wittenberg and Dessau respectively. Berlin was entered in triumph by the III Corps on the 25th,[49] while the I Corps, nearing Brandenburg, and the IV Corps, together with much of Murat's cavalry, at Potsdam, were just to the south of Hohenlohe's fleeing columns. These, separated so as to ease their supply problems amid the region's countless lakes and watercourses, were gradually overtaken and either forced or tricked into surrendering by Murat's horsemen.[50] Hohenlohe himself capitulated at Prenzlau with 12 000 exhausted, famished and utterly demoralized men. He could probably have cut a path to the Oder, but his courage had finally failed him. More shameful perhaps was the surrender of the powerful fortresses of Stettin and Magdeburg, both of which were sumptuously garrisoned and supplied. At the former, 5000 men meekly capitulated to General Lasalle's few hundred horsemen; at the latter, over 24 000 troops surrendered to Ney's 17 000 after a blockade lasting just two weeks.

On the same day that this occurred, the remnants of the last significant Prussian field force also laid down their weapons. Saxe-Weimar's column had been assimilated into one commanded by Blücher, who, cut off from Hohenlohe's main force and likewise faced with encirclement, had fled westwards in the hope of gaining a port and sailing for Allied territory. Pursued by Bernadotte and Soult, he fought a series of desperate rearguard actions but, on 5 November, was cornered when he forcibly occupied the neutral, opulent *Hansestadt* of Lübeck by the Danish frontier. The French stormed the perimeter and, with converging assaults, massacred their opponents in bitter street fighting: 3000 Prussians were killed or wounded, 6000 captured and the rest ejected from the town. When, the next day, he finally agreed to surrender since he had 'neither bread nor ammunition',[51] Blücher could muster barely a third of the 21 000 soldiers he had had just seven days earlier. A small force of Swedish troops also fell into Bernadotte's hands.[52] As we shall see, this was to have important ramifications.

The military and political collapse experienced by Prussia was as complete as that which France herself was to undergo in 1940. The whole campaign had lasted precisely four weeks, during which forces totalling 145 000 personnel had been annihilated and every single engagement lost. In contrast to Vienna the previous year, Berlin had to host a humiliating victory parade by its conquerors, in which prisoners from Frederick William's Noble Guard were a prominent feature. These arrogant young aristocrats, who, only weeks before, had provocatively sharpened their swords on the French Embassy's steps,[53] were now compelled to trudge past it to the jeers of the watching citizens, who accused them of having involved the king in a ruinous war.[54] But Napoleon's *Blitzkrieg* had not only destroyed Prussia's martial reputation; it threatened to cost her her status as a great power, too. Whereas the rickety Habsburg Empire had survived years of war and defeat at France's hands, the hard-won gains of generations of the Hohenzollern dynasty were jeopardized after just a few weeks. Frederick William himself, a fugitive in Königsberg (Kaliningrad), hoped to salvage what he could through diplomacy, but his wife and advisers like Hardenberg grasped at the straw of salvation proffered by Russia.

Realizing that further fighting was likely, Napoleon endeavoured to reduce the odds against him. Turkey, encouraged to take advantage of Russia's distractions in Central Europe, obligingly prepared for hostilities on the lower Danube and, in January 1807, also declared war on Britain. Austria was too enfeebled by her recent defeat to consider renewing hostilities against France, but she was now well placed to mimic Prussia's conduct in the events of 1805. An astute blend of intimidation and conciliation was used to obtain a pledge of her neutrality. Britain, by contrast, was as implacable as ever. As the paymaster of the various coalitions that had arisen against France, cowing her was a necessary if not sufficient measure for securing a wider peace. But as she remained beyond the reach of Napoleon's military might, the only leverage available to him was an intensification of the economic blockade. Accordingly, on 21 November 1806, the Berlin Decrees were issued, closing all ports and coastlines under French control to British trade.[55] London was to retaliate the following January with Orders-in-Council which regulated neutral trade with the French Empire. However, Napoleon's Continental System could only have much prospect of success if it, first, genuinely involved all the continent and, second, was applied long and consistently enough. With much of the Baltic littoral still admitting British merchandise, such economic sanctions were bound to fail. Moreover, intelligence reports suggested that around 60 000 Russian troops under Bennigsen were already nearing the Vistula, with thousands more following on their heels. The Prussians, too, had a 15 000-strong corps here under General Lestocq, as well as several substantial garrisons dotted along the Baltic and throughout Silesia. Once united, these forces might pose a serious challenge to the French grip on the territory west of the Oder.

Given these considerations, Napoleon decided to move his army further east before going into winter quarters. If he could occupy Thorn and Warsaw, his forces would, he reasoned, be perfectly poised to cover operations against the various Prussian bastions or to launch a springtime offensive against the Russians, should that prove necessary. Furthermore, he was keen to exploit the Poles' latent nationalism; their country had recently been partitioned out of existence by Prussia, Russia and Austria. While anxious not to antagonize the last two, Napoleon was quite prepared to continue Prussia's dismemberment by forming her Polish provinces into a semi-autonomous polity.[56] As always, this 'liberation' occurred within the framework of French hegemony, but the emperor's opportunism was to win him considerable support among the Polish people. As late as 1814, appreciable numbers of Polish volunteers could be found among his soldiery, while Countess Marie Walewska, Napoleon's lovely Polish mistress, showed the emperor a lasting devotion which was as patriotic as it was romantic.[57]

The campaign in Poland

In mid-November, the vanguards of *La Grande Armée* crossed the Oder and headed east in search of the Russians. The abominable Polish roads and saturated fields proved the main obstacles. As Coignet recalled: 'The weather was terrible: snow, rain and thaw. . . . We sunk down up to our knees . . . and our shoes would stick in the wet mud.'[58] Both he and Aubry of the 12th *Chasseurs* recollect numerous men committing suicide in the face of the deprivations they encountered on the barren steppes.[59] Warsaw was finally reached on the 28th, but Bennigsen had already decided to fall back to Pultusk on the Narew and coordinate his operations with those of Marshal Buxhöwden's approaching army. Simultaneously, Lestocq forsook Thorn and, shadowed by the I and VI Corps, retired northeastwards. Little changed over the next few days but, by mid-December, Napoleon, concerned that the Russians were retreating beyond his reach and seeking to join up with Lestocq, initiated a pincer movement that was intended to keep the Allied armies separated, sever their communications and provoke a decisive battle. In fact, his adversaries were edging forwards, not back. A number of encounters ensued, notably at Pultusk and Golymin.[60] None proved conclusive, but the Russians were sufficiently chastened to start a general withdrawal. Although the French attempted to pursue them, the barren countryside, soaked by torrential rain, followed by hard frosts and abrupt thaws, alternated between being a mudbath and an ice-rink. Progress was painfully slow; the various corps became overextended and drifted out of touch with one another; the supply system all but collapsed; and '*les Grognards*' were left exhausted, hungry and homesick.

Such developments were only to be anticipated after weeks of forced marches punctuated solely by battles. Certainly, discipline in *La Grande Armée* had been fraying at the edges since mid-October, when Soult especially had been compelled to take Draconian measures to curb the 'devastation and crimes atrocious almost beyond belief' that were occurring in the wake of some units.[61] If Napoleon was successfully to tackle the tenacious hordes of Holy Russia,[62] his forces would first need to rest, re-equip, regroup and assimilate reinforcements. Accordingly, the next few weeks were spent in frenzied endeavours to restore the army's vitality. Pay bonuses were dispensed, new footwear and clothing issued, stocks accumulated and rations improved.[63] To garrison his lines of communication and new conquests, Napoleon called up fresh conscripts prematurely and ordered a recruiting drive among his allies. Around 23 000 foot and 10 000 horse were also added to the existing establishment of the army's regiments, increasing each infantry company to a theoretical strength of 140 men and augmenting every cavalry regiment by a fifth squadron. Seasoned horsemen were brought from as far afield as Italy to help meet these targets, and scores of millions of francs were exacted from Prussia, Saxony and Napoleon's German vassals especially in order to finance them. Nevertheless, the demands imposed by the ongoing war threatened to outrun the means to support it. It was vital that *La Grande Armée* avoided disturbing the Russian Bear's hibernation before Napoleon's preparations were complete and a decisive encounter could be contrived.

But the enemy was already astir. Bennigsen, at the head of the combined Russo-Prussian forces, was bent on surprising the French in their winter cantonments, although he was unsure as to their precise whereabouts. A sudden lunge against elements of the I and VI Corps – the French left – south of Königsberg in late January heralded the coming storm. Napoleon raced to join his mobilizing forces from Warsaw and, rightly concluding that Bennigsen was making for the lower Vistula, swung them onto a west–east axis in search of his opponent's exposed left and rear. This manœuvre was executed amid great secrecy and, for a time, it seemed that Bennigsen would be ensnared. However, a young, inexperienced staff officer bearing an unencoded dispatch for Bernadotte was captured by prowling Cossacks. The information on him revealed to the Russians that their apparent progress against the I Corps was illusory; Bernadotte was deliberately luring them southwest, while Napoleon pivoted against their communications.[64] Bennigsen promptly countermarched towards the Alle, where, on 3 February 1807, the converging armies brushed against one another. Again, however, the Russians managed to slip away before the French, toiling along atrocious roads, could arrive in sufficient strength to impede them. Dawn on the 4th revealed that Bennigsen had continued his retrograde movement throughout the night, extricating all of his columns. The shivering French hurried after them, dislodging their rearguard from positions near Hof and Preussisch-Eylau, and threatening to penetrate between the Russians and Lestocq's Prussians to the north.

The battle that ensued around Eylau (Bagrationovsk) on the 8th was one of the most gory and confused engagements in military history. Buried beneath up to a metre of snow, the rolling field, broken up by frozen brooks and marshes, was swept by an Arctic wind which, intermittently, brought blinding blizzards with it. It seems improbable that Napoleon ever intended mounting a major attack early that day. Although determined to pin the Russians down, he was still awaiting the arrival of much of his army and apparently wanted to do little more than consolidate his grip on Eylau itself and the low ridge to either side; besides being a fairly good defensive position, it offered at least some protection from the elements.[65] Bennigsen, his forces arrayed along a parallel ridge, enjoyed a considerable numerical superiority; he disposed of nearly 70 000 men, whereas Napoleon had but 45 000 close at hand, mostly in a block to the south of Eylau. Both sides were expecting reinforcements in the course of the day: Lestocq was endeavouring to unite his 9000 troops with the Russians, while Napoleon was awaiting Ney's and Davout's appearance on his left and right respectively. Bernadotte was also thought to be coordinating his movements with those of the VI Corps. In fact, Ney's instructions arrived late,[66] and Bernadotte, whose advance had been delayed by the capture of his orders as mentioned above, was trailing badly. Once the I, VI and III Corps materialized as anticipated, however, Napoleon hoped to sever the Russians from both the Alle and Königsberg with a double envelopment that would culminate in their encirclement.

After a night during which the temperature fell to $-10°$ C,[67] the two sides began exchanging artillery fire at about 8am. The Russians had assembled colossal batteries, but their fire found relatively few victims among the sparse French formations, many of which were masked by buildings and hillocks.[68] At 8.40, encouraged by the approach of Davout's vanguard, Friant's division, the emperor had Soult stage a diversionary attack against the enemy's right so as to fix Bennigsen in position and distract his attention from the southern tip of his line, where the real danger would eventually loom. However, although they advanced with tremendous *élan*, Soult's frostbitten men were soon being pushed back by superior numbers, while, detaching a powerful cavalry force from his ample reserves, Bennigsen managed to check Friant's advance, too. By 10am, the French left had recoiled to its starting positions. Napoleon, anxious to ease the mounting pressure on Soult, reluctantly decided to utilize Augereau's VII Corps, originally designated part of *la masse de décision*, ahead of schedule. St Hilaire's division of the IV Corps, which constituted the right of Napoleon's line, would also move forward in support. Augereau's 9000 troops, deployed in lines and squares, dutifully stumbled through a dense if cursory blizzard towards what they took to be the Russian left. In fact, they were inadvertently veering towards Bennigsen's centre and its 70-gun battery. Caught in a crossfire between this and their own artillery, which continued to shoot blindly into the snow squalls, thousands of men were killed or wounded in a few minutes.[69] Beset by cavalry and infantry, the survivors streamed towards Eylau, with odd regiments, notably the 14th *Ligne*, attempting to cover their retreat.[70] Brushing these aside, Russian cavalry swung against St Hilaire's exposed flank, while a column of 4000–6000 infantry penetrated into Eylau itself, jeopardizing both Napoleon's headquarters and the improvised hospitals in some nearby barns. Seeing this, the solitary squadron of Guard *chasseurs* forming the emperor's escort selflessly charged the intruders head-on. Simultaneously, a Foot Guard battalion hastened to intercept the Russians' advance, while General Bruyere's light horsemen wheeled against their rear.

Driven from the village in a ferocious *mêlée*, the surviving Russians were hacked down by Bruyere's troopers as they made off towards their own lines; hundreds were slain or wounded. Nevertheless, Napoleon's position remained precarious. His left and left-centre had suffered a severe mauling, and his entire right had come to a standstill. Moreover, the VI Corps, which had marched from Landsberg early that morning, had encountered detachments left by Lestocq to cover his flank as he strove to link up with Bennigsen;[71] embroiled in a series of minor actions, Ney could neither prevent the balance of the Prussians – about 7000 men – joining the Russians, nor intervene on the field of Eylau before evening. Denied all hope of reinforcements for the present, Napoleon had to look to his dwindling reserves to save the situation. Accordingly, at about 11.30, Murat deployed his cavalry – three dragoon divisions and one of *cuirassiers,* some 9000 men in 70 squadrons – and led them in a tremendous charge against Bennigsen's left. After routing the cavalry menacing St Hilaire's division, General Grouchy's dragoons fell on the horsemen of the Russian centre, driving them back on their own infantry and guns. Successive waves of *cuirassiers* now joined the fray. Stabbing and trampling infantry and gunners, they penetrated Bennigsen's first and second lines, carrying death, confusion and terror into the midst of his army. After charging approximately 2500 metres, however, the *cuirassiers,* as breathless as their mounts, found themselves cut off; with typical tenacity, the battered Russian foot regiments were reforming in their wake. Fortunately, help was at hand. Yelling 'Heads up, by God! Those are bullets, not turds!',[72] General Lepic of the *Grenadiers à Cheval* led the Guard cavalry through a hail of fire to rescue Murat's blown squadrons. Once again, the Russian lines were shattered; and the French troopers, a trail of dead and injured men and horses marking their route, retraced their steps.

The respite they thus gained saved their army and gave it fresh heart. By 1pm all of Davout's 15 000 men were enveloping Bennigsen's southern flank, and the French centre had regained its composure. Gradually, the Russians were prised from their positions east of Eylau. With his left wing bent back at right angles to his line, Bennigsen was compelled to divert every available soldier to trying to stem Davout's advance, and the battle elsewhere degenerated into an artillery duel as the focus of the fighting shifted northeastwards. Still the Russian position continued to deteriorate. As, at 5pm, Friant's battalions overran the village of Kutschitten, however, Lestocq reached Schmoditten at the far side of the field with around 5600 men.[73] In response to Bennigsen's urgent entreaties, he immediately deployed these and, rallying the broken Russians, spearheaded a riposte which regained Kutschitten and checked Davout's progress. Ney, meanwhile, still grappling with Lestocq's rearguards, forced his way onto the field at around 8pm, uniting with Lasalle's light cavalry on Napoleon's left near Althof. Continuing his advance, he stormed Schloditten, all but completing the encirclement of the Russo-Prussian army. Indeed, Bennigsen made an abortive attempt to retake it at around 10pm. Ney, however, had no plans to retain the settlement and abandoned it shortly afterwards.[74]

Darkness had long since fallen, and the battle now petered out. Bennigsen, having sustained at least 25 000 casualties, and having no food and little ammunition left, drew his army off towards Königsberg during the night. The French, too exhausted to mount a pursuit, followed as best they could. Their dead and wounded amounted to perhaps 28 000, and Napoleon's plan had again been foiled. As Ney observed when dawn revealed the scale of the carnage to him: '*Quel massacre! Et sans*

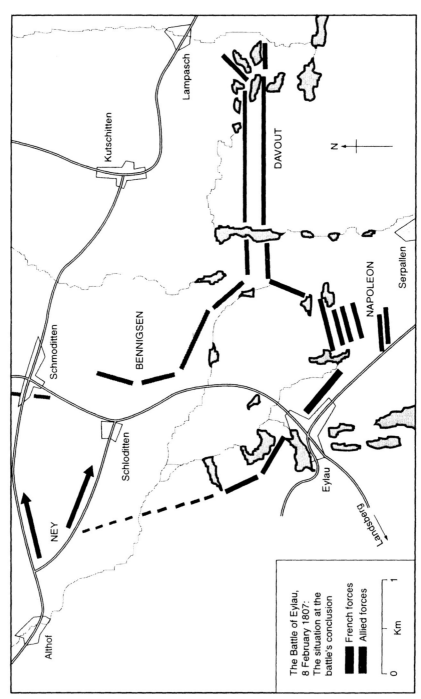

Lampasch

Kutschitten

DAVOUT

N

Schmoditten

BENNIGSEN

NAPOLEON

Serpallen

Schloditten

NEY

Althof

Eylau

Landsberg

The Battle of Eylau,
8 February 1807:
The situation at the
battle's conclusion

French forces
Allied forces

0   Km   1

The Battle of Eylau

résultat!'[75] Certainly, the loss of experienced troops suffered at Eylau was one which Napoleon could not make good, and the inconsequential engagements of the campaign so far had marred his martial reputation; it was imperative that Austria especially be kept in awe lest she be tempted to renew hostilities against France. Accordingly, the emperor deliberately delayed a return to winter quarters for a few days, during which he began implementing another bout of measures to repair the moral and physical strength of *La Grande Armée*: the wounded were evacuated, reinforcements summoned from throughout the Empire, and fresh cantonments prepared nearer the Vistula. Further, the shattered VII Corps was disbanded and a new one, still under Lefebvre, created to besiege Colberg, Graudenz and Danzig.

Securing the last of these was accorded particular importance. The garrison of the prosperous port comprised all of 16 000 troops; and Napoleon, fearful that his adversaries might ship in still more, took the precaution of creating a special reserve, under Lannes, to support Lefebvre's X Corps in the event of an amphibious operation to relieve the fortress. This proved wise, for, in mid-May, 57 transport vessels laden with Russian soldiers were to try just that. Although repulsed, the landing highlighted the danger Danzig posed to Napoleon's position. Moreover, Britain's new government, under Portland, was being pressed by the Russians and Swedes to send soldiers to the Baltic and, in April, was to earmark 10 000 for the reinforcement of Stralsund, which was being menaced by Mortier's VIII Corps.[76] In the event, though, matters proceeded too quickly for the Allies: Mortier concluded a local ceasefire with the Swedes in Pomerania on 29 April and, joining Lefebvre before Danzig with most of his troops, had helped obtain its surrender within a month.[77] By the time the British expeditionary force had sailed for Stralsund, not only was Danzig lost but, as we shall see, Bennigsen's army had been crushed and, in the ensuing diplomatic realignment, most of the Baltic states had turned hostile.

Indeed, 1807's opening weeks witnessed the start of what was to prove a particularly gloomy period for the British. In June 1806, a bold raid by Commodore Sir Home Popham had led to Buenos Aires being seized as part of London's dubious, new quest for overseas markets and possessions. However, the tiny garrison's position was quite untenable and, confronted by a popular uprising, it had surrendered shortly after. News of this reverse reached Britain only on 25 January 1807,[78] by which time a second military setback was in the offing. Vice-Admiral Duckworth's squadron, dispatched over two months earlier to persuade the Porte, by force if necessary, to surrender its fleet, finally reached the Dardanelles, but, arriving too late to cow or conciliate the Turks, was driven from the

Straits by massive shore batteries on 3 March.[79] Just days after this occurred, a force under Major-General Fraser, which had been sent from Sicily to occupy Alexandria – a prospective naval base and the key to Egypt, a region of great strategic importance to Britain – was also defeated while trying to secure the hinterland. Although Fraser retained Alexandria itself, he sustained 1400 casualties and had to be reinforced.[80]

This placed a further strain on the overextended forces in the Mediterranean. Despite a successful action against French troops at Maida in Calabria in August 1806, the British had been unable and unwilling to keep more than a toehold on the Italian mainland and had withdrawn to Sicily.[81] Now, merely clinging to this and other outposts seemed demanding enough. The fugitive Neapolitan Bourbons were intensely unpopular with their Sicilian subjects. Ever since the 1780s they had been trying to curtail the feudal privileges of the Sicilian nobility, who resented being exploited, as they saw it, and dominated by the Neapolitans. The British were increasingly fearful that this internal unrest would eventually benefit France. If the rival political order just beyond the Messina Straits did not prove sufficiently alluring to disaffected Sicilians for them to depose the Bourbons themselves, the danger that the French would suddenly invade and topple the regime was ever present. Queen Maria Carolina was perfidious at the best of times and was sus- pected of secretly negotiating with Napoleon – a suspicion which was subsequently discovered to be well founded. She was reluctant to cooperate fully with London and, over the next few years, was to alienate a succession of British commanders as they struggled to safeguard the island against French attack. Nor were the troublesome Bourbons Britain's only problem in the region. Fraser's mission, which, like Duckworth's, was intended to aid the Russians by distracting Turkey while simultaneously safeguarding British interests, scarcely achieved either: Russia was intensely suspicious of British aspirations concerning the Mediterranean; the Turks were antagonized but hardly incommoded; and, as with the Latin American ventures, which were continuing with General Whitelocke's Rio de la Plata campaign, the resources devoted to these operations might have been more productively employed else- where.

For, while all of this was occurring, 115 000 Russians and Prussians were squaring up to 220 000 French and Imperial troops in Poland.[82] Despairing of any assistance from Britain and Sweden, let alone Austria, on 2 June Bennigsen ventured west again, seeking to catch Napoleon's forces in their billets. However, his plan for doing so was unduly compli- cated and, poorly executed, only succeeded in alerting his adversary to what was afoot.[83] With Danzig under his control, and the former siege corps now available for other assignments, Napoleon surmised that, this time, the enemy's main thrust would be directed against Ney's and Soult's units between Spanden on the Passarge and Guttstadt on the Alle; another offensive towards the lower Vistula would have little to recommend it, as would one down the Narew towards Warsaw, where Marshal Massena had been posted with a powerful corps of observation. Sure enough, on 5 June, Ney was hustled back across the Passarge by overwhelming numbers, and Napoleon began concentrating 148 000 men along that river's western bank. By early on the 8th, though, Bennigsen, having lost his nerve, was in retreat for Heilsberg, where he had prepared an entrenched camp. Napoleon immediately assumed the offensive, his spearheads clashing with the enemy's rearguards in the vicinity of Guttstadt, before assailing Bennigsen's main body in its redoubts along the Alle on the 10th.

The impetuous, piecemeal and uncoordinated assaults were, however, repelled with heavy casualties: the French lost 10 000 men; the Russians 8000.[84] Under the circumstances, no other outcome was likely. But their stout defence of the fortified heights overlooking Heilsberg left the Russians vulnerable to encirclement as the rest of Napoleon's army neared the Alle. Bennigsen contemplated prolonging the struggle, but, on learning that Davout was hurrying up the Landsberg–Eylau road, began to fear for his communications with Russia and Königsberg.[85] He therefore decided to withdraw along the Alle's eastern bank to its confluence with the Pregel at Wehlau, while a detachment of 9000 men, under General Kamenskoi, crossed the Alle at Bartenstein to unite with Lestocq's Prussians, who, in the aftermath of the abortive offensive on the Passarge, had rebounded towards the Frisching. Shadowed by French cavalry, Bennigsen's main force duly hastened northwards, the vanguard reaching Friedland (Pravdinsk) at 6pm on the 13th. Beyond the Alle, *La Grande Armée* was dividing into two bodies so as to threaten both Königsberg and Domnau: 60 000 troops under Soult, Davout and Murat marched for the former place, while the rest cautiously advanced on the latter.[86]

On reaching Friedland, Bennigsen's vanguard had overwhelmed some cavalry picquets belonging to Lannes's Reserve Corps. Later that night, Lannes received a warning from Napoleon that the Russians seemed bent on crossing the Alle here. However, the emperor was as yet unsure whether this was their main body or merely a detachment: since it appeared to be part of a general and direct move on Königsberg, Kamenskoi's march northwards had clouded matters.[87] Indeed, he and Lestocq had assembled 25 000 troops just south of the city and, on the evening of the 25th, were already skirmishing with Murat's pursuing horsemen. Hence Napoleon's decision to allocate no fewer than 60 000 men to this part of the front. He anticipated that Bennigsen would commit every available unit to protecting Königsberg – an expectation shared, incidentally, by Lestocq and Kamenskoi.

Bennigsen, however, had other ideas. Persuaded that, at Friedland, he was confronted by a solitary division, he was tempted to destroy it before continuing his retreat to Wehlau or, if circumstances seemed propitious, marching directly on Königsberg. Accordingly, during the early hours of 14 June, he began diverting his army onto the Alle's western bank via the Friedland bridge, which was supplemented by three constructed from pontoons. The town stood at the end of a virtual peninsula formed, on the south side, by the broad, meandering Alle and, on the north, by the smaller Mühlen River. The latter dissected the plateau to the west of the town; and, to facilitate his army's deployment here, Bennigsen had four further bridges erected to span the rivulet. The plain itself was fan-shaped, being bounded by an arc of heights running from Heinrichsdorf, on the Königsberg highway, to Grunhof. Although open to the north, south of the Mühlen River the plateau was broken up by the Sortlack Forest.

Lannes, realizing that Bennigsen was entering a bottleneck, corked it up by deploying his troops to either side of Posthenen on the hills enclosing Friedland. The first clashes occurred at 3am, when he had just 9000 bayonets and 3000 sabres to hand. By 9am, another 5000 cavalry – the first of many reinforcements sent by Napoleon – had arrived, whereas Bennigsen had gathered no less than 46 000 troops and scores of guns, many of which were placed in batteries on the ridge overlooking the Alle from the east. The French managed to maintain their position largely through superior tactics, but Bennigsen does seem to have been taken aback by the robust resistance he encountered. After determined attempts to oust the enemy from Posthenen and Heinrichsdorf had failed, he remained quite passive, contenting himself with a desultory cannonade and some skirmishing, notably in Sortlack Forest. He was already thinking of breaking off the action and withdrawing.

Lannes, however, strengthened by a steady trickle of reinforcements, kept him occupied until Napoleon could appear. Arriving at noon at the head of yet more troops, the emperor took control and began preparing a counterstroke. By 5pm, he had amassed close to 80 000 men and, deploying them so as to exploit the palpable flaws in Bennigsen's dispositions, set them in motion: masked by the woods, Ney's VI Corps, backed by Latour–Maubourg's cavalry, suddenly fell on the Russian left around Sortlack, while his guns suppressed the batteries on the far side of the Alle; General Victor's I Corps began debouching from Posthenen; and, all along their line, the French artillery commenced a devastating bombardment of the exposed Russian formations.

Bennigsen, summoning his few remaining reserves from beyond the

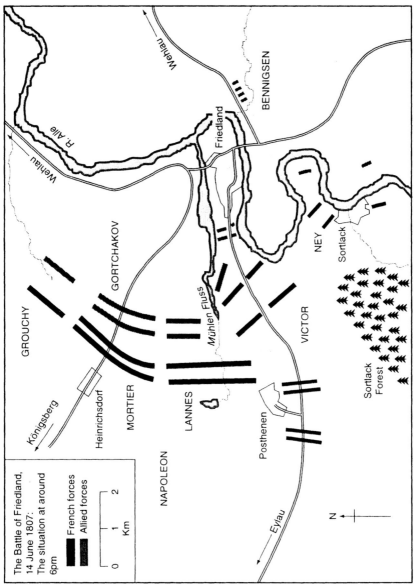

GROUCHY

GORTCHAKOV

Königsberg

Heinrichsdorf

MORTIER

NAPOLEON

LANNES

Mühlen Fluss

Wehlau

R. Alle

Wehlau

Friedland

BENNIGSEN

NEY

Sortlack

VICTOR

Posthenen

Sortlack Forest

Eylau

N

The Battle of Friedland

Alle, unleashed a swarm of cavalry to try to stem Ney's advance. Supported by Bagration's infantry and guns, they succeeded for a time. As Latour–Maubourg's troopers drove them off, however, VI Corps renewed its assault along the river, while Victor's troops crowded in between its left and the Mühlen River. Soon, thousands of Russians, some fleeing, some endeavouring to advance, were corralled on the Friedland peninsula. Victor's artillery, directed by General Alexandre Senarmont, former commandant of the gunnery school at Metz, seized its chance. Accompanied by a few squadrons and an infantry battalion, 30 guns bounded forward, raking the squirming masses from ever-diminishing ranges until they were just 50 metres distant; entire battalions were scythed down by blasts of grapeshot. Nor could the remnants of the Russian cavalry quell the impudent gunners; the withering fire instantly reduced the charging squadrons to bloody, tangled heaps of men and horses.

Clogging the streets of Friedland, the dregs of the Russian left made for the Alle bridges. Ney's infantry followed, quashing pockets of resistance, while the French artillery maintained its murderous fire. This, besides causing immense slaughter among the densely packed fugitives, set several buildings ablaze. By 7.30pm, the flames had engulfed the bridges, forcing the fleeing Russians to take to the river. Dragged down by their heavy clothing and accoutrements, hundreds perished in its depths.

By 8pm, Ney had gained undisputed control of Friedland, closing the trap on the enemy's centre and right wing beyond the Mühlen River. Commanded by General Gortchakov, these troops had remained steadfast under intense fire for hours. Enfiladed by Ney and Victor, and threatened by Lannes's units and Mortier's VIII Corps to their front, they now realized that retreat was imperative. But to where? Covered by their cavalry, the two southernmost divisions fought to regain access to one of Friedland's bridges, only to find it ablaze. Thereafter, they, and the rest of Gortchakov's forces, ravaged by gunfire and harried by infantry – the tired French horse mostly stayed quiescent – either fled north or crossed the Alle by means of a ford which, luckily, had just been discovered. Although this enabled Bennigsen to extricate more of his stricken army than Napoleon would have wished, he lost roughly half its strength in dead and wounded alone. Thousands more men were scattered, though, as usual, few had preferred surrender to death. French casualties totalled 7000.[xx]

In the wake of this *débâcle*, the Allies all but acknowledged defeat. Königsberg, packed with stores and 7000 sick and wounded, was relinquished to Soult, who also blockaded Pillau. Meanwhile, the main French forces chivvied the dispirited Russo-Prussian army across the Pregel towards Tilsit (Sovetsk), harassing its retreat at every opportunity. Here, Bennigsen received all of 30 000 men in reinforcements, but even these were insufficient to fill his army's depleted ranks. The only other Russian force of any size in the region comprised 16 000 troops under General Tolstoi on the Narew. Despite the threat posed by the Turks, most of these had been summoned from the 'Army of Moldavia' and were themselves in retreat following a defeat at Massena's hands in an engagement on 12 June.

With the strategic situation looking increasingly unfavourable, the Allied sovereigns proposed an armistice to Napoleon.[89] On 25 June, in a somewhat theatrical meeting on a raft moored in the Niemen's midst, he and Tsar Alexander negotiated an agreement that was to transform the map of Europe. Contemptuously excluded from the proceedings, Frederick William could only look on as his realm was dismembered by Napoleon and his erstwhile ally. Prussia's eastern boundaries returned to those of 1771: most of her Polish provinces became Napoleon's Grand Duchy of Warsaw, under the traditional tutelage of Saxony's monarch, and the rest were ceded to Russia. All of Prussia's lands west of the Elbe were also forfeited, becoming, together with Hesse-Kassel, the Kingdom of Westphalia. Bestowed upon Jerome Bonaparte, this new polity was as large as the remaining rump of Prussia, which, compelled to join the Continental System, saddled with reparations and occupied by French troops, ceased to be a great power. In fact, Westphalia provides the classic paradigm of how Napoleon's quest for political compatibility between France and her vassal states necessitated the mixing of foreign and domestic policy in a way which led to an enduring influence. Not only was the kingdom given the first constitution in German history – one which, moreover, embodied the emancipatory ideals of the French Revolution[90] – but also model institutions. Patched together from disparate bits of territory lacking common religious or cultural traditions and dynastic loyalties, Westphalia was largely endowed with a sense of cohesion by a legalistic and administrative framework. This process was under way throughout the *Rheinbund*. Indeed, the formation of the foundations of modern Germany owes much to a generation of bureaucrats, such as Montgelas in Bavaria and Reitzenstein in Baden, who recognized the challenges and opportunities presented by the Napoleonic era. As Von Hardenberg observed, any state that did not embrace the Revolutionary principles faced 'either their forcible imposition or its own extinction'.[91] Many of the changes these men implemented were irreversible and outlived their instigator, Napoleon.

Of all its more immediate ramifications, the Tilsit treaty's impact on the European balance of power was the most important. Russia's accession to the Continental System was followed by her formation, with France, of an anti-British maritime league. She also ceded the Dalmatian coast and the Ionian Isles. Napoleon, in return, forsook Turkey and encouraged the Tsar to expand his domains at her and Sweden's expense. Although the latter constituted Britain's sole remaining ally, she now found herself all but abandoned. Her king, Gustavus IV, was becoming increasingly erratic in his behaviour and, in July 1807, repudiated the Pomeranian ceasefire. This provoked a French attack, which, assisted by the withdrawal of the British contingent, culminated in the garrison's defeat and the capture of Stralsund. Russia was to declare war on Britain in November 1807, and on Sweden the following February. This spawned a bizarre situation in which British forces declined to resist Russia's invasion of Finland, yet contested her navy's bid to control the Baltic.[92] Indeed, Sweden was eventually alienated to the point where she too commenced hostilities against Britain.

If the latter's conduct towards Sweden was determined by a policy of self-preservation, then neutral Denmark was seen as meriting treatment that was still more ruthless. She found herself in an invidious position between the warring factions. As a significant maritime power, while suffering economically because of their respective sanctions, she was regarded by both sides as a potential accession of strength. Lest her ships might fall into hostile hands, 'Perfidious Albion' diverted the troops evacuated from Stralsund into an amphibious, pre-emptive attack on Denmark in August 1807. After a bombardment of Copenhagen, which destroyed one third of the city, killing 2000 civilians, the Danish fleet was effectively eradicated.[93]

Needless to say, this propelled Denmark into Napoleon's embrace. But the dilemma she faced was one common to all of Europe's minor powers. As Portugal was about to discover, they had to choose between being the enemies or allies either of France or of the other leading states.

Notes

1. Quoted in J.J. Sheehan, *German History, 1770–1866* (Oxford, 1989), p. 247.
2. See Sheehan, *German History*, pp. 244–53.
3. Sheehan, *German History*, p. 235.
4. See M. Finley, *The Most Monstrous of Wars* (Columbia, SC, 1994), pp. 13–14.
5. C.D. Hall, *British Strategy in the Napoleonic War, 1803–15* (Manchester, 1992), p. 133.
6. Hall, *British Strategy*, pp. 136–7; J.H. Rose (ed.), *Select Despatches from the British Foreign Office Relating to the Formation of the Third Coalition against France, 1804–5* (London, 1904), *passim*.
7. Baron M. de Marbot, *The Memoirs of Baron Marbot* (London, 1988), I, pp. 193–5.
8. F.L. Petre, *Napoleon's Conquest of Prussia* (London, 1972 edition), pp. 1–6 (hereafter cited as *Prussia*).
9. See H. Schoeps, *Preussen: Geschichte eines Staates* (Frankfurt, 1966), pp. 108–9.

10. Petre, *Prussia*, p. 8. Also see *Augenzeugenberichten*, pp. 62–3.
11. See, for example, *Augenzeugenberichten*, pp. 54, 59–61; P. Foucart, *Campagne de Prusse, 1806* (2 vols, Paris, 1887), I, pp. 1–8; O. von Lettow-Vorbeck, *Der Krieg von 1806 und 1807* (4 vols in 3, Berlin, 1891), I, pp. 1–37.
12. See Marbot, *Memoirs*, I, pp. 215–16.
13. See Petre, *Prussia*, pp. 42–3; Sheehan, *German History*, p. 295.
14. See, for instance, *Augenzeugenberichten*, pp. 107–8.
15. See *Augenzeugenberichten*, p. 114; Lettow-Vorbeck, *Der Krieg*, I, pp. 38–85.
16. K.O. von Aretin, *Heiliges Römisches Reich 1776 bis 1806* (2 vols, Wiesbaden, 1967), II, p. 275.
17. Petre, *Prussia*, p. 68; *Augenzeugenberichten*, pp. 113–14.
18. See NC, XIII, pp. 193–4, 213, 296; Lettow-Vorbeck, *Der Krieg*, I, pp. 86–171; Foucart, *Campagne*, I, pp. 9–157.
19. See NC, XIII, p. 217.
20. See NC, XIII, pp. 292–6; Lettow-Vorbeck, *Der Krieg*, I, pp. 140–71.
21. NC, XIII, pp. 309–10; Foucart, *Campagne*, I, pp. 165–393.
22. See Petre, *Prussia*, pp. 99–102; C. Parquin, *Napoleon's Army: The Military Memoirs of Charles Parquin*, ed. B.T. Jones (London, 1987 edition), pp. 36–8; Lettow-Vorbeck, *Der Krieg*, I, pp. 191–220.
23. See Foucart, *Campagne*, I, pp. 466–74; Lettow-Vorbeck, *Der Krieg*, I, pp. 221–65; Petre, *Prussia*, pp. 91–9; *Augenzeugenberichten*, pp. 116–21.
24. NC, XIII, p. 348. Also see Foucart, *Campagne*, I, pp. 570–613; Lettow-Vorbeck, *Der Krieg*, I, pp. 303–39.
25. L.N. Davout, *Opérations du 3ᵉ Corps, 1806–7: Rapport du Maréchal Davout* (Paris, 1896), pp. 30, 220; Foucart, *Campagne*, I, p. 586.
26. J. Coignet, *The Note-Books of Captain Coignet, Soldier of the Empire 1799–1816* (London, 1985 edition), pp. 131–2; Marbot, *Memoirs*, I, p. 226.
27. Marbot, *Memoirs*, I, p. 223.
28. See Petre, *Prussia*, p. 111.
29. *Augenzeugenberichten*, pp. 122–3, 126, 128–9; Lettow-Vorbeck, *Der Krieg*, I, pp. 284–339.
30. Petre, *Prussia*, pp. 117–18.
31. Petre, *Prussia*, pp. 124–5.
32. Petre, *Prussia*, p. 126; Foucart, *Campagne*, I, pp. 614–99.
33. Davout, *Opérations du 3ᵉ Corps*, p. 30.
34. See Petre, *Prussia*, pp. 171–4; A. Palmer, *Bernadotte: Napoleon's Marshal, Sweden's King* (London, 1990), pp. 133–4; Foucart, *Campagne*, I, pp. 586, 604–6, 694–7.
35. Marbot, *Memoirs*, I, pp. 226–7.
36. See *Augenzeugenberichten*, pp. 141–6.
37. Details of Auerstädt from: Davout, *Opérations du 3ᵉ Corps*, pp. 30–56; Foucart, *Campagne*, I, pp. 672–94; P. Bailleu, 'Die Schlacht bei Auerstädt', *Deutsche Rundschau*, 101 (1899), pp. 382–99; Lettow-Vorbeck, *Der Krieg*, I, pp. 377–407.
38. Petre, *Prussia*, p. 130.
39. Petre, *Prussia*, p. 132.
40. See, for example, M. Howard, 'Men Against Fire: The Doctrine of the Offensive in 1914', in P Paret (ed.), *Makers of Modern Strategy* Oxford, 1986), pp. 510–26; and P. Bressonnet, *Études Tactiques sur la Campagne de 1806* (Paris, 1909).
41. F.N. Maude, *The Jena Campaign* (London, 1909), p. 156.
42. Carl von Clausewitz, *On War*, ed. M. Howard and P. Paret (Princeton, 1976), p.155.
43. See *Augenzeugenberichten*, pp. 132–41.
44. See Petre, *Prussia*, pp. 189–91.
45. Petre, *Prussia*, pp. 191–2. Also see *Augenzeugenberichten*, p. 71.

46. Details of Jena from: Foucart, *Campagne*, I, pp. 614–71; Lettow-Vorbeck, *Der Krieg*, I, pp. 340–76; F.E.A. von Hopfner, *Der Krieg von 1806 und 1807* (2 vols, Berlin, 1850–1), I; H. Kohl, *Der Untergang des alten Preussen* (Leipzig, 1913); C. Kopfleisch, *Die Schlacht bei Iena nach den besten Quellen und Schriften* (Jena, 1862); E. Leidolph, *Die Schlacht bei Jena* (Jena, 1896). Prussia's military archives relating to the Napoleonic Wars were destroyed in 1945. However, Hopfner's study reproduces many important documents concerning the 1806–7 campaign. French archival sources include: ASH, C2 236 'Correspondance du Maréchal Augereau'; C2 253 and 391 5 'Correspondance du chef de l'État-Major'; C2 246 'Rapports de généraux du corps d'armée de réserve de cavalerie'; C2 476, 478, 480–5 'Situations'; and C2 18–57 'Correspondance: Grande Armée'.
47. NC, XIII, p. 357.
48. Lettow-Vorbeck, *Der Krieg*, II, pp. 101–13; Foucart, *Campagne*, II, pp. 99–106.
49. See *Augenzeugenberichten*, pp. 166–71, 176–7; Lettow-Vorbeck, *Der Krieg*, II, pp. 218–94.
50. See Lettow-Vorbeck, *Der Krieg*, II, pp. 166–217, 308–16; Petre, *Prussia*, pp. 236–55; Foucart, *Campagne*, II, pp. 154–731, reproduces the orders relating to the French pursuit.
51. Lettow-Vorbeck, *Der Krieg*, III, pp. 336–86; Palmer, *Bernadotte*, p. 135; *Augenzeugenberichten*, pp. 197–215.
52. See Palmer, *Bernadotte*, pp. 136–7.
53. *Augenzeugenberichten*, p. 96.
54. Marbot, *Memoirs*, I, p. 234; Coignet, *Note-Books*, pp. 134–5.
55. See *Augenzeugenberichten*, pp. 234–7, for details.
56. See M. de Bourienne, *Memoirs of Napoleon Bonaparte* (3 vols, London, 1836), II, p. 3; M. Handelsman, *Napoléon et la Pologne, 1806–7* (Paris, 1909); F.L. Petre, *Napoleon's Campaign in Poland, 1806–7* (London, 1907), pp.12–15 (hereafter cited as Petre, *Poland*).
57. See, for example, D. Chlapowski, *Memoirs of a Polish Lancer* (Chicago, 1992 edition), pp. 149–50; and R.M. Wilson, *Napoleon's Love Story: Napoleon and Marie Walewska* (London, 1933).
58. Coignet, *Note-Books*, pp. 138–9; T.J. Aubry, *Souvenirs du 12ème Chasseurs, 1799–1815* (Paris, 1889), p. 70 . Also see Sir R. Wilson, *Campaigns in Poland, 1806 and 1807* (Felling, Tyne and Wear, 1995 facsimile edition), p. 17.
59. See Davout, *Opérations du 3ᵉ Corps*, pp. 130–43; Wilson, *Campaigns*; Marbot, *Memoirs*, I, pp. 246–7; P. Foucart, *Campagne de Pologne* (2 vols, Paris, 1882), I, pp. 458–502.
60. Petre, *Prussia*, p. 223.
61. For details of the Russian army see: Wilson, *Campaigns*, pp. 1–54; Petre, *Poland*, pp. 28–39.
62. Petre, *Poland*, pp. 23–6; H. Lachouque and A.S.K. Brown, *The Anatomy of Glory: Napoleon and his Guard* (London, 1978), p. 85.
63. Lettow-Vorbeck, *Der Krieg*, IV, pp. 59–61; Wilson, *Campaigns*, pp. 88–9; Palmer, *Bernadotte*, pp. 139–40.
64. See Marbot, *Memoirs*, I, pp. 254–6.
65. R.A.P.J. Montesquiou-Fezensac, *Souvenirs Militaires de 1804 à 1814* (Paris, 1863), p. 145.
66. See R.G. Richardson, *Larrey: Surgeon to Napoleon's Imperial Guard* (London, 1974), pp. 112–13; J.H. Dible, *Napoleon's Surgeon* (London, 1970), p. 72.
67. Wilson, *Campaigns*, p. 101; Marbot, *Memoirs*, I, p. 257.
68. Marbot, *Memoirs*, I, pp. 257–8, 262–7.
69. Wilson, *Campaigns*, p. 257.
70. Lachouque and Brown, *Anatomy of Glory*, p. 88.
71. Wilson, *Campaigns*, p. 257.
72. See Petre, *Poland*, pp. 195–6.

73. Wilson, *Campaigns*, p. 198.
74. Montesquiou-Fezensac, *Souvenirs Militaires*, p. 149. For further details of Eylau see: C. Langlois, *Relation de la Bataille d'Eylau* (Paris, 1844); F.V. Schachtmeyer, *Die Schlacht bei Preussisch-Eylau* (Berlin, 1857); Lettow-Vorbeck, *Der Krieg*, IV, pp. 95–120.
75. Petre, *Poland*, pp. 219–25.
76. Hall, *British Strategy*, pp. 155–7; Finley, *Most Monstrous of Wars*, p. 100.
77. See Hall, *British Strategy*, pp. 136–7, 153–5; Petre, *Poland*, pp. 250–3, 259–61.
78. For details of the siege see: L.A. Picard, *Le Siège de Danzig en 1807* (Paris, 1910); Chlapowski, *Memoirs*, pp. 21–8.
79. See Hall, *British Strategy*, pp. 144–6.
80. Hall, *British Strategy*, pp. 141–2.
81. Hall, *British Strategy*, pp. 142–3.
82. See Lettow-Vorbeck, *Der Krieg*, IV, pp. 444–54; Petre, *Poland*, pp. 269–70.
83. Petre, *Poland*, pp. 270–8.
84. Petre, *Poland*, pp. 285–98.
85. Wilson, *Campaigns*, pp. 149–50.
86. See Lettow-Vorbeck, *Der Krieg*, IV, pp. 290–381.
87. Wilson, *Campaigns*, p. 150.
88. Details of Friedland from: NC, XV, pp. 334–5; Lettow-Vorbeck, *Der Krieg*, IV, pp. 348–81; V. Derode, *Nouvelle Relation de la Bataille de Friedland* (Paris, 1939); Marquis A. de Grouchy, *Mémoires du Maréchal de Grouchy* (Paris, 1873–4), III; L.M. Poussereau, *Histoire du Maréchal Lannes* (Nevers, 1910); Comte M. Dumas, *Précis des Événements Militaires* (Paris, 1818–26), V; C. von Plotho, *Tagebuch während des Krieges zwischen Russland und Preussen einerseits und Frankreich anderseits in den Jahren 1806 und 1807* (Berlin, 1811).
89. See Wilson, *Campaigns*, p. 170 (note); Lettow-Vorbeck, *Der Krieg*, IV, pp. 399–42; P.K. Grimsted, *The Foreign Ministers of Alexander I: Political Attitudes and the Conduct of Russian Diplomacy, 1801–25* (Berkeley, CA, 1969), pp. 160–1.
90. Sheehan, *German History*, p. 260.
91. Quoted in Sheehan, *German History*, p. 252. Also see H. Schoeps, *Preussen*, pp. 115–31.
92. See Hall, *British Strategy*, pp. 162–6.
93. See R. Muir, *Britain and the Defeat of Napoleon, 1807–15* (New Haven, CT, 1996), pp. 23–5; R.N. Buckley (ed.), *The Napoleonic War Journal of Captain Thomas Henry Browne, 1807–16* (London, 1987), pp. 45–64; anon., *The Authentic Account of the Siege of Copenhagen by the British, in the Year 1807* (London, 1807); C.T. Atkinson (ed.), 'Gleanings from the Cathcart Manuscripts: The "Conjoint" Expedition to Copenhagen, 1807', *Journal of the Society for Army Historical Research*, 30/122 (1952); A.N. Ryan (ed.), 'Documents Relating to the Copenhagen Operation, 1807', in N.A.M. Rodger (ed.), *The Naval Miscellany*, vol. 5 (London, 1984), pp. 297–324; A.N. Ryan, 'Causes of the British Attack on Copenhagen in 1807', *English Historical Review*, 68 (1953); P.W. Schroeder, *The Transformation of European Politics, 1763–1848* (Oxford, 1996 edition), pp. 327–9.

5

The Reformists

Just as France's defeat in the Seven Years War led to intense intellectual analysis of the reasons for her failure and, in time, an innovative programme which sought to rectify the defects within her military machine, so too did Napoleon's victories of 1805–7 act as a catalyst for reform among the beaten armies of his opponents. Of these, Prussia was the most profoundly affected. Jena–Auerstädt and Tilsit had left her not only vanquished and dismembered but also tottering on the brink of extinction at Napoleon's hands. Such abject decline, it was perceived by some, could only be reversed with drastic measures. The success of the French armies in recent years could not be accounted for exclusively in narrow military terms; what was evidently of equal significance was the political changes which enabled France to mobilize her resources more completely and efficaciously than her adversaries. If Prussia was to survive, she too would have to undergo not just military but also social, economic and political reform.

German thinkers, notably Gerhard von Scharnhorst and Adam von Bülow, had been attempting to analyse the reasons for France's growing martial prowess since before the turn of the century. In 1797, Scharnhorst had published a 'Development of the General Reasons for the French Success in the Wars of the Revolution', which, written with a friend, Friederich von der Decker, argued that France's victories could only be explained by a range of factors including her transformed sociopolitical structure.[1] Similarly, in *The Campaign of 1800, Militarily and Politically Considered*, Bülow, building on ideas he had first espoused in the 1790s, stressed the role of Revolutionary France's social and political strengths in accounting for the defeat of Austria.[2] Scharnhorst founded the *Militärische Gesellschaft* in Berlin in 1801, whereby he came into contact with Johann Yorck, Hermann von Boyen and other theorists. However, it was his relationship with the young Carl von Clausewitz, a cadet at the Berlin Institute for Young Officers, of which Scharnhorst was director, which bore the most intellectual fruit. Clausewitz became Scharnhorst's *protégé*, adopting his enlightened theoretical outlook as the basis for his own work, the summation of which was to be *On War*.

All of these men were caught up in the ruination of Prussia's army in 1806. But although they had discerned the need for change before Jena and Auerstädt, it was not until after them that they were in a position to bring it about. In 1807, Frederick William's principal adviser was the Francophobic Karl von Hardenberg. After Napoleon had secured his removal, he was replaced, in October 1807, by Karl Freiherr vom Stein, a professional administrator who had been dismissed only nine months before for insubordination. Stein had served in Prussia's bureaucracy since 1780, accruing vast experience of internal affairs. Like Scharnhorst, he believed that the country's social and political order would have to be transformed if she was successfully to challenge France, a precondition for which was governmental reform.

Stein's views are best articulated in the so-called *Nassauer Denkschrift*, a memorandum of June 1807.[3] He favoured changes in both local and central government: the former was to be made more effective through greater popular participation, which would encourage people to be loyal citizens; the latter was to be entrusted exclusively to professional administrators rather than to the monarch's confidants. Accordingly, in December 1807, provincial *Stände* were convened, and an edict of November 1808 allowed for the election of some local officials and other aspects of popular representation. During the same month Frederick William's privy council was superseded by a body of five ministers, each with responsibility for a distinct department. While the king remained absolute in theory, these functionaries exercised virtual control of policy formulation and enaction.

Whereas the cameralists had limited their aspirations to promoting the 'common good' within the context of increasing state power and prosperity, Stein hoped to give all of Prussia's subjects a sufficiently large stake in society to make them committed to its defence. This called for social mobility and economic liberalization. Indeed, Stein's aim was to create a 'free people'. But this ineluctably conflicted with the interests of the *Junker*, the guilds and other privileged groups. The principle of equal opportunity, for example, threatened the nobility's prerogatives with regard to the obtaining of military commissions. 'If your Royal Highness deprives me and my children of our right,' Yorck remarked to Prince William, the king's youngest brother, 'what is the basis of yours?'[4] Nor could emancipation benefit most of those at the bottom of the social ladder in any tangible way. Rights and privileges were the very essence of relationships within a feudalistic country like Prussia. Thus, whereas the nobility lost its legally defined status, it benefited from economic liberalization. The peasantry, by contrast, were released from their hereditary servitude and became legally free, but continued to be socially and economically reliant on their erstwhile lords.

Predictably, the implications of Stein's reforms were provoking anxiety both inside and outside Prussia when, in September 1808, French agents linked him with factions advocating a renewal of the war with France. Not content with his dismissal from office, Napoleon deemed him an international criminal and had his Westphalian lands confiscated.[5] Stein fled first to Austria and, following her defeat, to Russia, where he became part of Alexander's coterie. By December 1812, his vision was to encompass the absorption of Prussia and the other Germanic states by a new entity. 'I have but one fatherland, and that is Germany,' he was to write. 'I am completely indifferent . . . to the fate of the dynasties . . .'[6] His fall was, in the meantime, greeted with relief by many Prussian conservatives. Although his immediate successors, Count Dohna and Karl Altenstein, did not reverse his initiatives and even furthered them in a few instances, they lacked his passion and failed to satisfy the advocates of change. On the other hand, the supposed beneficiaries of reform, the population at large, were discontent as well. Not only was the notion of giving them an interest in the future of the social order proving impracticable, there was also no real affinity between the lower orders and the idealists within the ruling elite. The former lacked sufficient political consciousness or sense of national identity to relate to Stein's ideology and evinced little interest in the *Stände*, which became the focal points for conservative opposition to reform.

In June 1810, Hardenberg returned to the helm, his new title of *Staatskanzler* officially designating him as Prussia's first prime minister and highlighting the encroachment of bureaucratic rule. Although he was to dabble in representative politics through the establishment of an assembly of notables, which proved ephemeral, and an 'Interim National Representation', which was elected by local government assemblies and was convened in 1812 and 1814 to advise the executive, Hardenberg's concept of 'democratic principles in a monarchical government' was enunciated in a lengthy memorandum he composed at Riga in 1807, the *Rigaer Denkschrift*, and boiled down to economic and social emancipation of the individual in so far as was compatible with the preservation of untrammelled state control of public affairs.[7] His immediate problem was Prussia's impoverishment as a result of her defeat in 1806. Economic liberalization would, Hardenberg hoped, create more wealth which, together with the ending of tax exemptions, would bring more money into the state coffers. Predictably, he was obliged to compromise with the enraged *Junker*; he restored some of their tax immunities, came to an accommodation with them, at the expense of the peasantry, over land tenure, and abandoned a bid to bureaucratize the government of rural districts. On the other hand, ecclesiastical lands were nationalized, the emancipation of Jews was furthered, and the control of economic activity transferred from the guilds and municipal authorities to the state.

The motive behind all these domestic reforms was *Realpolitik*. The goal of Stein, Hardenberg and the other innovators was the revitalization of Prussia in order that she could regain her international standing and sovereignty. Her defeat in 1806 had made change both possible and indispensable – the objective of that change being an improvement in the state's ability to mobilize its resources for war. So far as alterations to the army itself were concerned, the initial vehicle was a Military Reorganization Committee[x] headed by Neithardt von Gneisenau, one of the few officers who had distinguished themselves in the war. Set up by Frederick William immediately after Tilsit, the commission included among its members Boyen and Scharnhorst. It began its work by applying the same criteria of responsible professionalism to the army which Stein had used in transfiguring Prussia's central government. All of 208 officers, among them 17 generals, were purged from its ranks. In 1808, the old cadet schools were replaced by training institutes for subalterns and an academy in Berlin which provided outstanding candidates with a solid grounding in staff work. At the end of that year, a war ministry was also established, which took responsibility for all aspects of military affairs. Scharnhorst served as its *de facto* head – a minister was not appointed until 1814. But what mattered was that a distinct administrative apparatus now existed which would coordinate military and political decisions.

In reforming the officer corps, the commission also applied the principle of equality of opportunity. Here again, however, theory and practice diverged because of the need to accommodate the concerns of the *Junker*. Under the regulations of August 1808, the nobility lost its legal monopoly on commissions but retained effective control over appointments, with the result that relatively few untitled officers were installed.[9] There were other compromises, too. Whereas Scharnhorst wanted to bring the people and the military into a 'more intimate union' through the creation of a *Volksarmee*, this was resisted by Frederick William and Hardenberg because of the threat it posed to the sociopolitical order, the monetary costs involved and fears about provoking France into a pre-emptive attack. By the Treaty of Paris of September 1808, Prussia was not only compelled to pay an indemnity of 140 million francs to France but also undertook to limit her army to just 42 000 men for the next 10 years. She might, moreover, be called upon to place many of these troops at Napoleon's disposal in the event of him becoming embroiled in a war with Austria.[10] Thus, while Frederick William did accede to some alterations to the way his army was recruited, ideological and practical considerations circumscribed the scope for change. Scharnhorst attempted to circumvent the Paris Treaty's stipulations by constantly discharging trained soldiers and replacing them with raw recruits – the so-called *Krümpersystem*. Although this created a clandestine reserve, the number of troops involved was unavoidably small, leaving the total strength of the Prussian Army well short of the reformers' ideal figure.

As it was, Napoleon had ample grounds for being suspicious as to Prussia's intentions in the light of her reforms. In 1810, he successfully pressed for Scharnhorst's removal from office and, by 1812, the remaining innovators had been thoroughly disillusioned by the trend of Hardenberg's foreign policy. Far from embarking on the war against France which they craved and which, they believed, Prussia's people would support, the *Staatskanzler* concluded an alliance with Napoleon and provided him with troops for his impending invasion of Russia. For some two dozen officers, this was too much. Subordinating their sense of allegiance to their monarch to their patriotism, they resigned from the army, several, like Clausewitz, departing for St Petersburg. When Boyen also left his post at the War Ministry, Scharnhorst suggested that another of his *protégés*, Karl von Tiedemann, should replace him. Tiedemann, however, preferred to leave with Clausewitz and duly submitted his resignation, too. Scharnhorst, torn between 'the duties of the citizen' on the one hand and those of 'a moral man' on the other, could only empathize. 'I cannot condemn your decision,' he told Tiedemann, 'because everyone must first see that he remains true to himself.'[11]

Frederick William was neither as understanding nor as forgiving. Deeply offended by these acts of defiance, he had the property of those officers who had gone to Russia sequestered. Although he was grudgingly, if belatedly, to pardon Clausewitz in the light of subsequent events, the bright young Tiedemann was lost to him for ever; he perished near Riga while resisting the Franco-Prussian X Corps of *La Grande Armée*.

Like Gneisenau and others within the Prussian military reform movement,[12] Tiedemann had been fascinated by the part played by light troops in France's recent victories. The flexibility of her infantry's tactics stood in stark contrast to the Frederician doctrine's rigid, geometric formations and, as we have seen, had baffled and overwhelmed Prussia's finest regiments in 1806. Liberating soldiers from the physical constraints of eighteenth-century drills was thus identified as a key component in the emulation of the French. But the use of aimed fire and attacks *en dabandade* were not sufficient by themselves to produce success; skirmishing and the other facets of *la petite guerre* had to be integrated into a comprehensive operational plan which exploited the synergy between light and heavy forces and between units from different arms. Not only did this point to the abandonment of unitary structures in favour of combined-arms divisions and *Armeekorps* capable of semi-autonomous action, but also to the standardization of drills and procedures in order that units could, at the tactical level, operate harmoniously together. So far as the footsoldiery was concerned, this also necessitated the blending of light and heavy infantry skills to produce all-purpose troops. Moreover, if this was to be effective, the skirmisher's attitude of self-reliance would have to be cultivated among the infantry as a whole, suggesting training which was as psychological as it was mechanistic.

So it was that, alongside the few battalions of specialist *Jäger* and other units dedicated to *petite guerre* operations, a new generation of line troops arose which, to a degree at least, had been coached in open-order tactics. Although, given the speed of their mobilization, many conscript units were barely proficient in rudimentary procedures and evinced little tactical finesse,[13] in the campaigns of 1813–15 the better Prussian regiments were able to deploy up to a third of their strength as skirmishers – a far greater proportion than ever before.[14] In order to help engender a mental state more appropriate to this *modus operandi*, soldiers were treated more like human beings and less like automatons. Corporal punishment was largely done away with as education and *esprit de corps* replaced the lash and cane as the instruments by which men were motivated to fight. Predictably, this rankled many a *Junker* who believed that exemption from flogging was a privilege, not a right, and resented the implicit elevation of common soldiers, many of whom were ex-criminals, to the status of free, thinking men. In any case, in both the Prussian Army and elsewhere, many officers felt that, given war's brutalizing nature and the unpromising material from which their units were formed, a more relaxed approach to discipline was inappropriate, however well intentioned. Long after the Napoleonic Wars, Wellington, for instance, testified to a royal commission that he had 'no idea of any great effect being produced on British soldiers by anything but the fear of immediate corporal punishment'.[15] Indeed, it is striking that the most successful application of Enlightenment reasoning to military discipline occurred in distinct light infantry units, such as the *Jäger* battalion commanded by Yorck, where such thinking did not conflict with the ethos that prevailed in most line regiments.

This was also Britain's experience. Here, military reform was not accompanied by the political and social changes seen in Prussia. Shielded by her geography and naval supremacy from the type of warfare that served as a catalyst for drastic modification elsewhere in Europe, Britain could continue to rely largely on eighteenth-century practice so far as the tactics of her army were concerned, even if its size and organization underwent appreciable change. Indeed, for the first few years of the Napoleonic War Britain's endeavours were almost wholly maritime. While she gained mastery of the waves, she looked to the armies of Austria and Russia to confront the French by land. Not until Maida in July 1806 did British and French troops meet in a sizeable encounter; and even this was a trifling affair when compared with the battles which had occurred at Ulm and Austerlitz and were shortly to take place at Jena, Auerstädt, Eylau and Friedland. In fact, as late as August 1813, when the Peninsular War was all but over, Wellington's army still included no more than 60 000 redcoats at a time when 800 000 French, Prussians, Russians, Austrians and Swedes were squaring up to one another in Central Germany alone.

Although Britain mobilized scores of thousands of militia and regulars in the course of the war, nearly all of these were committed to home and colonial defence and never saw a shot fired in anger. This had three principal repercussions. First, Britain's army never suffered the massive and almost incessant attrition experienced by the continental powers' land forces. Second, this, together with the sedentary life imposed on most of her units by their defensive missions, allowed a high level of training to be maintained. One of the ironies of Napoleon's threat to invade Britain is that it necessitated the permanent basing of large numbers of troops in Ireland and in southern and southeastern England especially. With no enemy to fight, these soldiers, scattered in camps of which the most famous is unquestionably the one at Shorncliffe, Kent, where Sir John Moore and Colonel Kenneth Mackenzie trained what was to become the nucleus of Wellington's celebrated Light Division,[16] had little to do other than perfect the tactical skills they were subsequently to employ so effectively against Napoleon's forces in the Peninsula. Third, because the armies Britain could field on the continent were relatively small, while unitary structures were rejected, the largest integrated units were divisions; there were no semi-independent corps. Indeed, it was feasible for one man to command the army, which is what, for the most part, Wellington insisted on doing. Although as much as a centralizer as Napoleon, he was spared the dependence on subordinates that the latter inevitably suffered from as the scale of his operations expanded.

While both the scarcity of soldiers and tonnage for their transportation circumscribed the size of any British expeditionary force, conveyed and supplied by the Royal Navy, troops could, weather permitting, be deposited at or retrieved from almost any point on the European littoral. By exploiting the sheer flexibility of maritime power, Britain could more or less choose when and where to initiate land operations. Regions of difficult terrain where the French would be deprived optimal conditions for their method of waging war and where the British could offset their comparative weakness in cavalry and guns were favoured, Italy and Spain being the obvious examples. Under Wellington's skilful guidance especially, small but highly disciplined British forces capitalized on their own strengths while taking advantage of chinks in their opponents' armour. Again, the importance of efficacious light infantry had been recognized by the early 1800s and, timely steps having been taken by the commander-in-chief, the duke of York, to ensure that the army was well provided with such troops,[17] from their very first engagements in the Napoleonic Wars British commanders were able to sheath their battle-lines with numerous riflemen and other skirmishers who kept the *tirailleurs* at bay. Similarly, the formidable French artillery, either held at long range or denied worthwhile targets by terrain features, notably ridges, which were used to screen the British forces from fire and observation, was effectively neutralized. Nor, on precipitous slopes and other rugged terrain, was there much scope for an attacker to employ horsemen. Thus, unsupported French heavy infantry too often had to assail naturally strong positions without their defenders having been subjected to preliminary bombardment and sniping. Moreover, concealed on the reverse slopes of hills and safeguarded against prying hostile light troops by their own, the British forces' main positions were often impossible to descry. Consequently, at Bussaco, for example, Reynier, thinking it was their flank, attacked their centre, while, at Salamanca, Marmont was to make a similar error.

Time and again, French columns would penetrate the British skirmisher screen only to find themselves confronted with an intact and unshaken wall of heavy infantry. With insufficient time and space to deploy into line, the French were at an obvious disadvantage. A columnar formation could not match the firepower of a linear one at the best of times, but the British, unlikely to be molested by cavalry, tended to maximize their frontage by deploying in just two ranks – a structure which, under most conditions, would have been dangerously flimsy. The line could hardly fail to triumph. Often pushing its wings forward to enfilade the column, it engulfed it with fire. If the French endeavoured to charge, they were shot into the ground, while attempts to change formation were asking more than flesh and blood could withstand. Describing a typical incident, one British soldier who was actually in the firing-line recalls how he saw

> their gallant officers vainly using every effort to deploy ... [their men] into line. Sometimes a company or more filed out; but [our] ... fire ... was so severe, that they ran back into the column as to shelter. After several abortive efforts, the attempt to move them was given up ...[18]

It should not be thought, however, that there was anything magical about the British line *per se*. What distinguished it from the Frederician line which had failed so disastrously at Jena–Auerstädt was the context in which it was used. (Indeed, the British 1792 *Regulations*, which were utilized throughout the Napoleonic Wars, had been derived from Prussian drill manuals.) In their campaigns of 1808–15, the British seldom faced the sort of coordinated, mixed-arm operations that the French had employed to crush other opponents. On the other hand, Britain was able to refine her army's tactics with selective but key reforms inspired by the French example, notably the introduction of formidable light infantry forces. In other regards, however, her insularity shielded her from the need to indulge in innovations of an actual or potentially revolutionary kind.[19] She was not obliged to raise massive armies through universal conscription, with all the political and social ramifications that this would have entailed; her territory was never ravaged by invasion; and, while there were some who advocated peace with Napoleon,[20] her population never had to choose between collaborating with an occupying power or resisting it. On the contrary, the sustained threat from an external enemy did much to promote unity among the diverse peoples of the British Isles.[21]

For the continental states, by contrast, the Napoleonic Wars not only imperilled the stability of their governments, societies and economies but also jeopardized the very existence of the international order as they knew it. Such a challenge, Archduke Karl, Austria's pre-eminent military figure, believed, called for the revamping of not just her army but also the whole machinery of government, a task which could realistically only be undertaken in peacetime. Indeed, it was begun within months of the Lunéville Treaty of February 1801. The old *Staatsrat*, the privy council, which had had no responsibility for foreign affairs and had tended to deal with domestic matters in a disjointed fashion, was abolished and replaced by a *Staats und Konferenz Ministerium* which was to coordinate external, internal and military policy. Similarly, the *Hofkriegsrat* lost its direct access to the *Kaiser* and was subordinated to a new war ministry. While Karl became *Kriegs und Marine Minister*, his nominee, Matthias von Fassbender, a trusted functionary, was appointed *Presidial Hofrat* and *Staats- und Konferenzrat*.

Although Karl's innovations did streamline the military administration appreciably, among other structural problems, the empire's financial difficulties stultified many of his endeavours. The expenses incurred through lengthy wars interrupted only by precarious peace devoured much of Austria's dwindling military budget, while inflation eroded the purchasing-power of officers' salaries. This, together with seemingly poor prospects, deterred many promising candidates from entering the army, leading to a shortage of good officers. An attempt to fill the gaps with cadets drawn from the middle and lower classes was hampered by such fundamental shortcomings as illiteracy. This, in turn, ruled out the wholesale removal of inept or unprofessional officers; while Karl did secure the creation of a permanent if embryonic general staff and strove to improve the morale and training of the officer corps in its entirety, he had to tolerate the widespread selling of commissions which, along with nepotism, led to the appointment of many unsuitable men to positions of command.

Over other issues, a personal reluctance on the part of the *Kaiser* or Karl himself even to try to change Austria's established ways and structures manifested itself. Francis had all but forsaken the attempts at reform begun by Joseph II in the 1780s and Karl was conservative if enlightened. As Joseph had discovered to his cost, the fractious, polyglot Habsburg Empire was far from malleable. The Hungarians especially insisted on concessions from Vienna in return for recruits and money. Indeed, Karl argued with the diet for two years before settling for just part of what he had originally requested.[22] In order to mollify opposition to the draft, the archduke endeavoured to reduce the period of service for conscripts from life to eight years. This, however, foundered on the nobility's concern that discharged soldiers might furnish popular revolts with expert leadership.[23] Again, a compromise had to be reached, with troops being required to serve for a minimum of 10 years. More will be said elsewhere about Austrian views on the creation of a *Volksarmee* to resist Napoleon, but, for a mixture of ideological and financial reasons, conscription was to remain highly selective, with exemptions being granted to, among others, those seen as being in economically important occupations.

Austria's attempts at reform fall into two distinct phases, the first of which ran up to the eve of Austerlitz, while the second occurred in the period between that battle and Wagram. When, in early 1805, the *Kaiser* was contemplating joining the Third Coalition and Karl counselled caution in view of the army's unpreparedness, the archduke's political opponents seized their chance to undermine his position. Francis was persuaded to restore the authority and autonomy of the *Hofkriegsrat*, to impose Mack as head of the general staff and to elicit Fassbender's resignation. Although Karl remained minister of war and the ministry itself survived until 1806, real power was shifted elsewhere. Decisions were again taken by privy-council cronies rather than by professional bureaucrats, and the coordination of policy suffered accordingly. Even after the Austerlitz *débâcle*, the *Kaiser* resisted Karl's calls for the *Hofkriegsrat* to be made subservient to the supreme military commander or the war minister, eventually agreeing to a compromise whereby Karl was created

Generalissimus and given command of all forces in wartime and a supervisory role of the whole military establishment, including the *Hofkriegsrat*, in peace. Needless to say, this treated the symptoms of the problem, not its cause. Throughout the 1809 war, Karl was to face interference and criticism from his adversaries within the Imperial court, eventually being toppled by them after his defeat at Wagram.

As to the organization and tactics of the Austrian Army, at the start of the Napoleonic War Frederician structures, formations and training remained standard. There had actually been a cut in light infantry units in the aftermath of Lunéville, implying that little had been learnt about the French *modus operandi*. Mack, however, sought to rectify this shortcoming by issuing interim regulations at the inception of the 1805 campaign which suggested that the line's third rank might be deployed as skirmishers. Although the army's unitary organization was preserved, Mack also changed the size and number of sub-units in individual regiments. These and some of his other innovations were sensible enough. Indeed, they were to be incorporated into the *Exercier-Reglement* issued by Karl in 1807. However, the timing of their introduction – just days before war commenced – was foolhardy. Karl was to commit a similar blunder in 1809 when, on the eve of hostilities, he organized his forces into *Korps*, leaving them no time to accustom themselves to the new structure and the demands it imposed.

That said, most of the measures introduced during the second reform period proved beneficial in the main. The infantry's drills were simplified somewhat and, besides the traditional linear formation, columns were accorded great significance. Indeed, so-called 'masses' – closely packed battalion columns – were recommended as an alternative to squares in resisting cavalry attacks. The 1807 manual also made provision for skirmishing and open-order manœuvres by line troops. Several new *Feldjäger* battalions were also created. However, Austrian skirmishers, stifled by the stringent control of their superiors and by training which emphasized mechanistic techniques far more than psychological aptitude, proved a poor match for the French. Nor did the Austrian horse develop the ethos and capabilities necessary for it to function as an independent strike force. Cavalry was deployed in small packages, primarily as an infantry support arm, rather than *en masse*. Even its attached artillery was neither equipped nor trained to back cavalry charges; mostly the *Kavallerie Batterien* operated as mobile field artillery. Indeed, Austrian ordnance was generally lacking in manœuvrability and, although Karl organized it with the provision of concentrated fire and combined-arms operations in mind, few of his gunners could or would make the mental leap necessary to incorporate the artillery fully into integrated battle plans. Powerful and numerous enough though its individual pieces were, the Austrian ordnance was rarely used to optimum effect.[24]

The impact of reform was also marginal in the Russian Army. By 1806 it had abandoned its unitary structure in favour of 18 standardized if rather cumbersome divisions, each of which comprised: 18 infantry battalions; 82 guns, split into positional, light and horse batteries; and 10 squadrons each of light and heavy cavalry.[25] Defeat at Friedland prompted Tsar Alexander to instigate an attempt to render both the Russian military machine and the state bureaucracy more efficient. Mikhail Speransky, an interior ministry official of great talent and humble origins, was appointed virtual head of the privy council, which, composed of eight ministers, each responsible for a functionally defined department, constituted Russia's central government. In 1809, Speransky drew up a 'Statute of State Laws' that, while only partially implemented, created a new council of state, to which the reformed council of ministers was subordinated. Besides improving the training of functionaries and seeking to make the administration more professional, he also endeavoured to tackle Russia's economic backwardness and spiralling financial difficulties. Moreover, he introduced a legal code. Like reformists everywhere, however, Speransky made enemies among those whose interests he attacked. Jealous boyars and die-hard obscurants, notably General Alexei Arakcheev, the Frederician-school war minister who, in 1810, was replaced by Mikhail Bogdanovitch, Baron Barclay de Tolly, had strong reasons for resenting Speransky, whose admiration for and emulation of Napoleon's reforms made it easy for his opponents to isolate him once the Franco-Russian alliance began to unravel. Not only did the Tsar's favourite sister, the Grand Duchess Catherine, detest Speransky, but also Alexander himself, a *poseur* more interested in appearing enlightened than being it, feared that his state's secretary's radicalism might erode the Crown's powers. Sure enough, in March 1812, Speransky was arrested and exiled.

In his capacity of minister of war and commander-in-chief, Barclay concentrated on organizational and quantitative improvements to the army. Every foot regiment was given at least two front-line battalions as well as a depot unit, while all cavalry regiments were provided with additional squadrons. Similarly, the artillery was increased to no fewer than 44 heavy, 58 light and 22 horse batteries. The large divisions of earlier wars were restructured and distributed among *corps d'armée*. Again, however, attempts to imitate the French were constrained by both practical and psychological factors: the very qualities which made Russians formidable line troops prevented them being good skirmishers, even though dozens of regiments were designated as light infantry; the transport, commissariat and medical services all lacked resources and were poorly organized; many officers were unprofessional, illiterate or indolent, even the general headquarters' staff lacking adequate training; and there was little conceptual thinking to underpin the use of forces in action.[26]

Lastly, we should mention the case of Spain. Here, the monarch's auto-cratic first minister and favourite, Manuel de Godoy, tried to overhaul the state during the last quinquennium of the eighteenth century. Again, much of the impetus for change stemmed from defeat in war, namely that of the First Coalition. Yet, in his anxiety to rebuild Spain's land forces, for example, Godoy soon encountered resistance to his recruitment schemes and other measures. After the brief conflict with Portugal in 1801 high-lighted how little had actually been achieved in terms of improving the army, Godoy embarked on what was intended to be a root and branch modernization programme. Once more, however, the will to alter things outran the means: the officer corps remained unprofessional and queru-lous; there were insufficient artillery, cavalry and support units; and tacti-cal and strategic doctrine barely evolved at all. Nevertheless, through a combination of his attempts at innovation and his irritating personality, Godoy incurred the wrath of various vested interests both within court cir-cles and across Spain as a whole. Savage reductions in the royal guard and his tinkering with the armed forces in general strained their loyalty, while his relationship with the royal family was as provocative as it was scan-dalous in the eyes of those nobles who scorned the upstart favourite. Although the king and queen diluted his 'ministerial despotism' in a bid to appease his opponents, as the events of March 1808 were to prove, his – and, consequently, their – position remained precarious.

Throughout continental Europe, then, what political, social and eco-nomic reform did occur was inspired not by enlightened altruism but by *Realpolitik* – by the inescapable need for states to mobilize more of their resources if they were successfully to confront the Napoleonic challenge. If Britain could evade much of the pain involved and Spain, ultimately at the cost of reliance on her, was never firmly to grasp the nettle, in Prussia, Austria and Russia sufficient was done to achieve the survival of the state without jeopardizing the established hierarchy.

Notes

1. Gat, *The Origins of Military Thought* (Oxford, 1989), p. 163; P. Paret, *Yorck and the Era of Prussian Reform, 1807–15* (Princeton, 1966), p. 230.
2. Gat, *Origins*, pp. 84–5.
3. See J.J. Sheehan, *German History, 1770–1886* (Oxford, 1989), p. 298.
4. Quoted in Paret, *Yorck*, p. 131.
5. See G.S. Ford, *Stein and the Era of Reform in Prussia, 1807–15* (Gloucester, MA, 1965), pp. 151–8.
6. Quoted in Sheehan, *German History*, p. 320. Also see Ford, *Stein*, pp. 307–8.

7. Sheehan, *German History*, pp. 304–7.
8. See Paret, *Yorck*, pp. 122ff.
9. See Paret, *Yorck*, pp. 132, 265–6.
10. Ford, *Stein*, pp. 150–1.
11. See Sheehan, *German History*, p. 310; Paret, *Yorck*, p. 172.
12. See Paret, *Yorck, passim.*
13. See Paret, *Yorck*, p. 209.
14. Paret, *Yorck*, p. 97.
15. Quoted in D. Gates, *The British Light Infantry Arm, c. 1790–1815* (London, 1987), p. 134.
16. See Gates, *British Light Infantry*, pp. 111–28.
17. See Gates, *British Light Infantry*, pp. 10–94.
18. Quoted in Gates, *British Light Infantry*, p. 167.
19. See I.R. Christie, *Wars and Revolutions, 1760–1815* (London, 1982).
20. See J.E. Cookson, *The Friends of Peace: Anti-War Liberalism in England, 1793–1815* (Cambridge, 1982).
21. See L. Colley, *Britons: Forging the Nation, 1707–1837* (New Haven, CT, 1992). Also see C. Emsley, *British Society and the French Wars* (London, 1979).
22. G.E. Rothenberg, *Napoleon's Great Adversaries: The Archduke Charles and the Austrian Army, 1792–1814* (London, 1982), p. 71.
23. Rothenberg, *Great Adversaries*, p. 72.
24. Rothenberg, *Great Adversaries*, pp. 113–16.
25. F.L. Petre, *Napoleon's Campaign in Poland, 1806–7* (London, 1907), pp. 36–7.
26. Even the staunchly Russophile Sir R. Wilson is critical of the Tsar's army in these respects. See *Campaigns in Poland, 1806 and 1807* (Felling, Tyne and Wear, 1995), pp. 49ff.

6

The Rise and Fall of the Fifth Coalition

In the 10 months following the conclusion of the Tilsit Treaty, Napoleon's domination of Europe seemed to go from strength to strength. His entente with Russia, the feebleness of Austria and the prostration of Prussia had left him with no immediate concerns about his empire's eastern flank, and he had swiftly turned his attention to matters elsewhere. Britain's enmity was unwavering, but the ramifications of her continental allies' defeat rumbled on, deepening her predicament: Denmark had to be disarmed, Sweden shored up, and Russia contained yet, if possible, not overly antagonized. The remorseless extension and intensification of the Continental System severely constricted the commerce that was Britain's life-blood and, as we have seen, compelled her to seek new markets outside Europe. However, Lieutenant-General Whitelocke's gory repulse at Buenos Aires in July 1807 shattered dreams of lucrative trade with South America, while the clash between HMS *Leopard* and the USS *Chesapeake* shortly before brought London and Washington to the verge of war. This crisis, besides highlighting the perils surrounding the Royal Navy's attitude to neutral shipping, put a further strain on Britain's over-stretched forces in that it necessitated the reinforcement of the garrisons in Canada. Simultaneously, Turkey's ongoing hostility, and the French occupation of Corfu and Cattaro, jeopardized British interests in the Levant. Overtures were made to the Porte in the summer of 1807, but it was not until the start of 1809 that peace was formally concluded. Long before then, Portland's cabinet had had to take the decision to rely on economic and diplomatic instruments to influence Turkey's behaviour. Major-General Fraser's position in Egypt was judged untenable and, by September 1807, his force had been evacuated from Alexandria. This, however, was just part of a general British withdrawal from the eastern Mediterranean.[1] Henceforth, the emphasis was to be placed on retaining

Gibraltar, Capri, Malta and Sicily as bastions from which forays against the Spanish and Italian coastlines could be mounted.

Yet there were even times when Britain's grip on these outposts appeared shaky. Ever since their defeat at Maida on 4 July 1806, the French had been slowly but surely reasserting themselves in Calabria. Once the bulk of the British expeditionary force had withdrawn to Sicily, the insurgents lacked the backing of a regular field army, and their ferocious guerrilla war against King Joseph's troops and supporters was gradually contained if not suppressed.[2] Key centres of resistance were systematically reduced: Gaeta fell on 17 July 1806; Amantea in February 1807; and Cortone the following July. This left just the fortresses of Reggio and Scilla on the Messina Strait in Allied hands. However, once the Tilsit accords were signed, Napoleon was at liberty to double the size of his forces in Calabria to all of 25 000 men. The British, given their relative weakness and strategic priorities, were already reluctant to get embroiled in further operations on the mainland[3] – a policy which seemed to be vindicated by the rout of a Sicilian expeditionary corps at Mileto in late May 1807 – and a successful offensive now looked out of the question for the foreseeable future. In fact, as the French not only took the toeholds of Reggio and Scilla in early 1808 but also captured Capri the following October, there were some fears for the security of Sicily. So long as they held that and Malta, however, the British felt safe enough. The Mediterranean was less vital to them than the Baltic and the waters surrounding their homeland.[4] After Tilsit, a French descent on England was again regarded as a possibility, while, as we have seen, the Baltic was greatly imperilled.

Indeed, British anxiety about the security of that region had led to more soldiers being sent there following the Russian declaration of war on Sweden in early 1808. After the raid on Copenhagen, London had recalled its troops, much to the chagrin of Gustavus IV, who already felt betrayed by the British withdrawal from Stralsund. He refused to negotiate a position of neutrality *vis-à-vis* the warring powers, yet could neither offer much support against Napoleon nor adequately protect his own possessions from Franco-Russian encroachments. London was thus obliged to furnish him with £1 200 000 in subsidies each year and send some 11 000 men, under Sir John Moore, to try to safeguard crucial harbours, notably Gothenburg, in conjunction with Admiral Saumarez's fleet. Increasingly unbalanced, Gustavus proved a difficult partner and was scornful of the British forces' circumscribed participation in the war. He eventually ordered Moore's arrest, but the general escaped and promptly withdrew his entire command to Britain.[5]

Although this left the Royal Navy as the sole guardian of British interests in the Baltic, this was sufficient. The war with Russia was essentially cosmetic, while Napoleon was increasingly distracted by events elsewhere. Throughout the summer of 1807, the emperor had intensified the pressure on Britain's oldest continental friend, Portugal. He warned that, if her ports were not closed to British trade by 1 September, France, together with Spain, her ally, would invade Portugal and confiscate any British property and merchandise.[6] By August, he was insisting that Lisbon actually declare war on Britain and was assembling a corps under General Junot to implement his threats of invasion. Like Denmark before her, neutral Portugal was in a dilemma. If she acceded to Napoleon's demands, Britain would inevitably retaliate by seizing her colonies and trade. As early as September, London had its eye on Madeira as a potential haven for its shipping, while the fate of Portugal's mainland harbours and battlefleet was an issue of paramount concern.[7] But, if Portugal did not do as he wished, Napoleon fulminated at a reception attended by Lisbon's ambassador on 23 September:

> The House of Braganza will not be reigning in Europe in two months' time. I will no longer tolerate a single English envoy in Europe; I will declare war on any power that has one two months from now. I have 300 000 Russians at my back, and with this powerful ally I can do anything. The English declare that they will no longer respect neutrals at sea; I will no longer recognize them on land.[8]

While the Portuguese vacillated, Napoleon and the British acted. France declared war on 20 October, as Junot's troops, already in Spain, marched on Lisbon. On the 27th, the emperor and Godoy, Spain's corrupt prime minister, concluded the Treaty of Fontainbleau, which envisaged the partition of Portugal.[9] Although the Portuguese responded by closing their harbours to British trade, at the same time their ambassador to London accepted a pact whereby Portugal's navy and royal family would be removed to Brazil. The British government, determined to see this agreement implemented, ordered a flotilla under Rear-Admiral Smith to proceed to the Tagus and, if necessary, seize the Portuguese fleet by force. Lisbon's endeavours to run with the hare and hunt with the hounds culminated in Portuguese batteries firing on a Royal Navy frigate on 5 November. However, with Smith blockading the Tagus and Junot nearing their capital, the Braganzas finally threw in their lot with Britain. When, on 30 November, the French entered Lisbon, they found that every seaworthy Portuguese vessel had accompanied the royal family on its flight to Brazil.[10]

By Christmas 1807, Britain's forces had secured Madeira, too, while Portuguese colonies in South America were beginning to open up to her

trade. On the other hand, the Continental System had expanded throughout the Iberian Peninsula, and there was no sign of the pressure on British
commerce abating in Europe. Indeed, on 17 December, the Milan Decrees
were promulgated, formally outlawing all neutral shipping which entered
any British port or submitted to inspection by the Royal Navy on the high
seas. By the issuing of *lettres de marque*, privateers were also encouraged
to attack British merchantmen. Furthermore, Napoleon contemplated an
ambitious scheme aimed at menacing Britain's interests in the Levant and
Orient: one French army, supported by Russian and, perhaps, Austrian
units, would threaten India by an advance through Constantinople into
Asia, while a second would take Gibraltar, cross the Straits and conquer
the Barbary kingdoms. Sicily would also be seized in order to deprive the
Royal Navy of its last substantial outpost in the Mediterranean, trans-
forming it into a French lake. Franco-Spanish squadrons could then be
amassed for attacks on Britain's remaining possessions around the
globe.[11]

While little came of this grandiose plan, it does illustrate the dimensions of Napoleon's strategic vision and the lengths to which he was prepared to go to try to subdue the 'Nation of Shopkeepers', who, despite
everything, remained implacable. As Canning observed towards the end
of 1807, another ephemeral peace was not Britain's objective:

> Our interest is that *till* there can be a final settlement that shall last, every
> thing should remain as unsettled as possible: that no usurper should feel
> sure of acknowledgement; no people confident of their new masters; no
> kingdom sure of its existence; no spoilator secure of his spoil; and even the
> plundered not acquiescent in their losses.[12]

At this juncture, given their irreconcilable aims, a durable peace between
Britain and France was scarcely likely, but, on the other hand, neither
was the infliction of a decisive blow by either side. However,
Napoleon's latest attempts to consolidate the Continental System were to
pave the way for direct British military action in a manner and place that
promised to prove very damaging to his position overall. Although
London had earnestly considered deploying a substantial force in
Portugal on several occasions in the preceding 10 years, France's invasion of that country seemed to offer a particularly auspicious opportunity
in this regard, particularly when Napoleon went on disastrously to mis-
judge the popular mood in Spain the following spring. As early as
January 1808, the British cabinet was contemplating seizing Cueta and
attacking both Port Mahon and Lisbon, where Admiral Siniavin's
Russian warships had taken shelter.[13] The implementation of these
schemes was delayed by bad weather and, thereafter, they had to be

modified in the light of various complications and unfolding events, notably the incipient collapse of Spain. Fearful that a new regime might cede Napoleon virtual or actual control of Spain's possessions in South America, Britain decided to encourage these colonies to break away from their motherland with a fresh bout of military intervention: large expeditions to Mexico and Montevideo were envisaged.[14] Again, however, London's plans were to be overtaken by developments. During May and June a popular insurrection spread across the Iberian Peninsula, and both the London government and its local military commanders were approached by the Spaniards for help. The notion of assisting them appealed to both the Pittites' pragmatism and the Whigs' ideology, and much of Britain was engulfed by a wave of enthusiasm.[15] There was, Canning told the Commons, 'the strongest disposition . . . to afford every practicable aid' to the rebels. 'We shall proceed upon the principle, that any nation of Europe that starts up with the determination to oppose . . . [France], whatever may be the existing political relations of that nation with Great Britain, becomes instantly our essential ally.'[16]

Although Spain had been France's ally since the Treaty of Basle in 1795, Napoleon had good reason to be suspicious of her and the venal, duplicitous Godoy. The emperor knew that he had been plotting with the Prussians at one point in 1806;[17] and, after their defeat, a large troop contingent, under the Marquis of La Romana, was exacted from Spain to serve with Napoleon's forces on the Baltic and demonstrate Spain's goodwill. However, by the end of 1807, the emperor was exploiting the unscrupulous Godoy's unpopularity among elements at the Spanish court – notably Ferdinand, Prince of the Asturias, and his coterie – to further his own ambitions in the Peninsula. The crown prince's machinations against Godoy had culminated in the so-called 'Affair of the Escurial', in which, on King Charles IV's orders but at Godoy's instigation, Ferdinand had been accused of treason and arrested.[18] Although he was pardoned by his father, Ferdinand's hatred for Godoy had only been exacerbated by this episode, while Charles was left suspicious and resentful. Napoleon skilfully manipulated these internecine rifts within Spain's ruling elite, while preparing his next move. Having, on the pretext of supporting the operations in Portugal, accumulated troops at key points throughout Spain, he was poised to seize control whenever he judged it propitious. That moment came in mid-February 1808, when, through a blend of trickery and force, these soldiers wrested Pamplona, San Sebastian, Barcelona, Figueras and other nodal forts and towns from their astonished garrisons.[19] In the next few days, dozens more French units poured over the Pyrenees with impunity, until there were no fewer than 118 000 Imperial troops on Spanish soil. In the political turmoil that ensued, the royal family attempted to leave for the Americas, but were stopped at Aranjuez by riotous crowds of citizens and soldiers. Rebellion quickly engulfed Madrid, too, and Murat, commander of Napoleon's forces in Spain, occupied the capital, ostensibly to restore order. By this time, however, an unholy alliance between the mob and disaffected aristocrats had ended the *antiguo régimen*: Godoy had been deposed and Charles, desperate to appease the rioters, had abdicated in favour of the undeservedly idolized Ferdinand.[20]

This revolution alarmed Napoleon, however. Seeing himself as the successor to Charlemagne, he was eager to transform Spain into a modern state which would be both politically and socially compatible with France and her other vassals. This would entail the kind of reforms already exported to Germany and Italy: the introduction of the *Code Napoléon*; secularization; the creation of a new ruling elite based primarily on meritocracy; the abolition of feudal rights and provincial customs barriers; and the establishment of new political institutions. Bent on ousting the corrupt, incompetent Bourbons altogether, he now had to find some way of dislodging Ferdinand from the throne without, if possible, resorting to force. Luckily, Charles insisted that his abdication, obtained under duress, was invalid, while his wife, Maria Luisa, Godoy's longstanding lover, accused her own son of treachery and demanded that he be executed. Even Napoleon was shocked by her vindictiveness: 'She filled me with horror!', he admitted.[21] She evidently did the same to Ferdinand, too, for when Napoleon invited the whole quarrelsome family to Bayonne to discuss the matter he returned the crown to his father without much ado.[22] As Charles had already surrendered his own rights to Napoleon, this left the emperor free, on paper at least, to dispose of the realm as he saw fit. He promptly issued a decree proclaiming his brother Joseph, the disillusioned ruler of rebellious Naples, king of Spain and the Indies.

This transfer of power was completed by 6 May and, apart from Ferdinand, who was kept a virtual prisoner at Valençay, the deposed royal family left for a life in exile. By then, however, their former kingdom was descending into pandemonium. Tension had been rising for some time and, on the 2nd, Madrid's inhabitants had turned on Murat's troops. As Goya's celebrated paintings graphically show, the rising was put down pitilessly. Yet this was only the beginning of a general insurrection which quickly spread across the entire country. Although its revolutionary aspect dismayed many officials within the military and the civil bureaucracy, and most of the ruling classes questioned the wisdom of challenging France's military might, the tide of popular feeling could not be stemmed. Napoleon could place Joseph on the throne, but he could not give him the people's support. While the institutions of the *antiguo régimen* hesitated, improvised provincial Juntas began orchestrating a revolt. Thousands of ordinary Spaniards took up arms in the name of the captive Ferdinand, '*El Deseado*', to fight for him, their motherland and their Catholic faith.

Nevertheless, while they were ready to accept British gold, arms and munitions,[23] the exchange of former prisoners of war,[24] and the assistance of the Royal Navy not only in transporting troops from the Balearic Isles to the mainland but also in spiriting away most of La Romana's corps from Denmark,[25] the Spaniards' pride and suspicions ruled out the widespread deployment of British soldiers on their territory. Mindful of Gibraltar, they were particularly reluctant to see the redcoats occupy key fortresses, notably Cadiz. Accordingly, the British focused their efforts on Portugal, which, besides offering them useful harbours and a toehold on the continent, would, if it could be liberated, form a bulwark for the Spanish, too; their strategic rear and flanks would be free of the enemy. An army, initially commanded by Sir Arthur Wellesley (subsequently Wellington), was duly assembled at Mondego Bay in Portugal during early August 1808, and, on the 15th, assailed one of Junot's divisions at Roliça in overwhelming strength. Its commander, General Dellaborde, fought a masterful rearguard action and escaped to rejoin Junot's main body.[26]

Since the end of May, that general had faced mounting difficulties. He had but 26 500 men to hold down a country of 76 000 square kilometres with two million inhabitants. Initially, this had not proved impossible. First, the precaution of removing the regular Portuguese Army to France had been taken. Second, Portugal had no really large towns other than Lisbon, which contained one tenth of the population and formed the administrative and military heart of a highly centralized state; the few arsenals, for instance, that existed were concentrated here. With Lisbon firmly under French control, a countrywide insurrection of the type seen in Spain was impracticable; there was no way of mobilizing, concentrating and equipping sufficient manpower. However, once news of the Spanish revolt arrived, Junot's position became considerably more precarious. Although he managed to disarm and imprison one of the Spanish divisions allocated to the partition of Portugal by Godoy, the other two escaped, stirring up disorder as they went. A largely ineffectual yet troublesome rebellion flared up around Junot's beleaguered forces, compelling him to detach numerous flying columns and garrisons. Nor could he secure any help from Siniavin's 6000 seamen and marines. Though technically Napoleon's allies, the Russians were unwilling to do anything – even guard the 6000 Spanish prisoners or Lisbon – other than fight the Royal Navy, should it enter the Tagus.[27] While this seemed improbable to Junot, he could not be sure where the British amphibious force known to be hovering off the coast might strike. Indeed, no sooner had he set out to succour Dellaborde on 15 August than false rumours of a British landing at Cascais sent him hurrying back towards Lisbon.[28]

The outcome of all of this was that, at Vimiero, on the 21st, Junot had but 13 000 men to oppose to 16 700 British and 2000 Portuguese ensconced in a formidable position. This was bad enough, but he also committed his forces in scattered and uncoordinated assaults. He sustained 2000 casualties and was repulsed.[29] However, Wellesley was prevented from exploiting this success by the intervention of Sir Harry Burrard and Sir Hew Dalrymple. Just arrived from Britain, these generals, both senior to Wellesley, were daunted by the prospect of further fighting and readily accepted Junot's suggestion of a negotiated settlement. Thus was born the notorious Cintra Convention, whereby Junot and his remaining men, with all their equipment (and plunder), were repatriated by the Royal Navy. Thereafter, they would be free to return to Spain. Similarly, Siniavin and his crews were also returned to their homeland, where they would be at liberty to fight the Swedes, Britain's allies.[30] Although the Russians had to surrender their vessels, this curious arrangement is indicative of the true sentiments of these putative foes and of the complex nature of Anglo-Russo-Swedish relations.

The Cintra Convention also showed scant regard for the sensitivities of the Spaniards and Portuguese. Nevertheless, it was signed on 30 August and enacted over the next few weeks. Long before then, however, the French army's position in Spain had also been severely compromised. While Marshal Bessières crushed a Spanish offensive in Old Castile at Medina de Rio Seco on 14 July,[31] in Andalusia a corps of some 20 000 men under General Dupont was encircled by twice as many Spaniards and, having failed to break out in a battle at Bailen on the 19th, compelled to capitulate.[32] This was the first defeat and capture of a French army in the field since the Revolutionary Wars began, and the reverse did tremendous damage to the reputation for invincibility acquired by Napoleon's legions. Indeed, it horrified King Joseph, who had only arrived in Madrid on 20 July, to such an extent that he ordered a general retreat to the Ebro, thus compounding the impression of a French *débâcle*.

Certainly, the British government was both exhilarated and inspired by this development. 'How glorious to England it would be, after recovering Portugal, by her Command of the Sea,' enthused Castlereagh, 'to meet the Enemy at the Foot of the Pyrenees, and to forbid his return to France.'[33] It was already being assumed that Wellesley would overwhelm Junot's isolated army; and the tidings of Roliça and Vimiero did nothing to dim that expectation. When news of the Cintra Convention began to arrive, however, the euphoria and unanimity generated by the Peninsular venture waned sharply. All the same, the cabinet had already committed itself to moving 20 000 troops from Portugal into northern Spain, where they would unite with La Romana's corps and 10 000 more redcoats. Moore, recently returned from the Baltic, was to lead the new expedition and was granted considerable discretion as to precisely how he expelled the French from Spain. British forces had seen little service in that country for roughly a century, and there was a lack of up-to-date maps and other basic intelligence material, including reliable information as to the dispositions of the French. Nevertheless, it was assumed that the fielding of a substantial British army alongside the Spanish corps in northwestern Spain would encourage insurrections in the regions straddling Joseph's communications and, with luck, culminate in his isolation and destruction.

This calculation failed to allow for Napoleon's speedy reaction to developments in the Peninsula. Dismayed and shocked by Joseph's withdrawal to the Ebro, by mid-August the emperor had 130 000 men marching for the Pyrenees. Whereas most of the troops initially sent to the region had been conscripts with only rudimentary training, most of these were veterans drawn from the forces in Italy and Germany. After reaffirming his pact with Russia at a glittering conference held in Erfurt, Napoleon left to assume personal command in the Peninsula, arriving on the Ebro in early November. The Spaniards, who had overestimated the damage done to Joseph's forces and had sluggardly followed them northwards as though the conflict was all but over, were suddenly confronted by a vigorous counteroffensive. Routed at Gamonal, Espinosa and Tudela – on 10, 11 and 23 November respectively – they recoiled. Madrid fell and, by mid-December, the French were fanning out across the interior and preparing for an advance on Lisbon.

Having collected his forces at Salamanca on 5 December, Moore, largely unaware of the details of developments, notably of the sheer size of the hostile army before him, now sought to deliver a riposte by striking at Soult's corps around Burgos. It was a risky venture: 'If the bubble bursts,' he acknowledged, '. . . we will have to run for it.'[34] Indeed, Napoleon, glimpsing an opportunity to corner the redcoats, suspended the march on Lisbon and wheeled much of his army northwards, hoping to sweep behind Moore at the Esla. However, the British, together with La Romana's troops, now went into precipitant retreat, the former heading for Corunna, the latter for Orense. Toiling over mountain tracks in atrocious weather and constantly pressed by their pursuers, they suffered terribly. Soult's attempts to prevent Moore embarking his ragged columns climaxed in an unsuccessful assault on Corunna on 16 January 1809.[35] Nevertheless, though extricated, the British expeditionary force had lost all of 8000 men, among them Moore himself, who, buried at Corunna, was, in Charles Wolfe's words, 'left alone with his glory'.

Prior to his departure for Spain, Moore had been warned by Canning that his force comprised most of Britain's disposable army.[36] That now lay in ruins. Had Moore not perished, it seems probable that he would have been relieved of his command by a dissatisfied government.[37] As it was, his heroic death prevented him from being openly blamed for the campaign's failure. Nevertheless, coming so soon after Cintra, this defeat deepened the rifts in British society concerning the Peninsular enterprise in particular and continental entanglements in general. On the other hand, Moore had distracted Napoleon at a crucial moment and, by so doing, saved Portugal from reconquest. Britain's continental foothold remained secure, and Portland's cabinet boldly resolved to continue exploiting it. Moreover, while there was much criticism of the Spaniards' handling of the conflict, their defection from Napoleon's cause had transformed the overall situation. First, it virtually ended the danger of an attack on Britain's overseas interests, allowing surplus resources to be switched to the all-important European theatre. Yet, between 1808 and 1811, Britain's colonial expansion at her rivals' expense reached its zenith: besides Martinique and Guadeloupe in the Caribbean, Bourbon and Mauritius in the Indian Ocean were captured without any additional forces having to be allotted to fulfil these objectives; local units proved sufficient. Second, the Spanish rebellion was constantly to menace the western flank of Napoleon's empire when new threats were looming to the east as well. Whereas the Calabrian revolt had proved vexatious to the French, it was essentially a xenophobic, parochial affair, revolving around opposition to French taxation, anticlericalism and conscription. As we shall see, a similar rising was to occur in the Tyrol during 1809. Consequently, the Calabrian insurrection never possessed the strategic potential of that seen in the Iberian Peninsula, contrary to what one recent study has suggested.[38] The British realized that it was not going decisively to influence the outcome of the struggle against Napoleon in a way that the nationalist *Guerra de la Independencia* promised to. As Lord Liverpool observed in early 1809, in Spain: 'The people were unanimous in their resistance to the invader; and it was the only instance since the French revolution in which a whole people had taken up arms in their own defence.'[39] Nor were the British alone in noticing this. Napoleon's troubles in Spain had obliged him to weaken his forces in Germany – a development which the Austrians were about to exploit.

The Austrian campaign of 1809

As we have seen, throughout his campaigns of 1806–7, Napoleon was fearful that Vienna might recommence hostilities. The measures he took to safeguard against such an eventuality, combined with Austria's preoccupation with her own internal difficulties and weaknesses, ensured that this did not occur. However, peace between the two empires was unlikely to prove enduring. As Chancellor Stadion concluded: 'Napoleon wants to destroy us, because our principles and size are incompatible with a single, universal hegemony.'[40] The erosion of her standing in the international order was something that Austria was not prepared to acquiesce in; under the Pressburg Treaty alone she had lost some three million subjects and 48 000 square kilometres of territory. Another war might be delayed, but was practically unavoidable.

In order to strengthen his forces in Spain, Napoleon had had to weaken those in Germany. However, this shift in the numerical military balance was not the only ramification of the Peninsular conflict, for it also spawned attempts by his adversaries to mimic Napoleon's exploitation of popular sentiment. The Spanish insurrection caught the imagination of literati throughout Germany, giving fresh impetus to the evolution of European thought and inspiring those who hoped to throw off the shackles of French rule. Despite extensive censorship, newspapers quickly disseminated the tidings of the Spanish rising. Long accustomed to Frederick the Great's methods and, more recently, the short, decisive but essentially conventional wars of Napoleon, most Germans found the notion of civilians engaging in combat as anarchic as it was alien. Just 20 years before, '*Alter Fritz*' himself had stressed that his subjects were forbidden to take up arms even in self-defence during an enemy invasion, warfare being exclusively the sovereign's prerogative.[41] Between 1807 and 1813, however, Germany witnessed a steady stream of writings and public lectures, which, composed against the backcloth of Napoleonic domination, were devoted to the themes of political philosophy, patriotism and the nation in arms. Besides the poetry and prose of such prominent artists as Ernst Arndt, Heinrich von Kleist, Georg Hegel, Theodor Körner, Johann Fichte, Friedrich Jahn and Joseph Görres, less celebrated but none the less significant pieces appeared. Among these were Karl Venturini's two volumes on the *Geschichte der spanisch-portugiesischen Thron-Umkehr und des daraus entstandenen Krieges* (1812–13); Adolf Baurle's *Spanien und Tirol tragen keine fremden Fesseln* (1808); Friederich Stagemann's *Kriegsgesange aus den Jahren 1806–13* (1813); *Der Krieg Napoleons gegen den Aufstand des spanischen und portugiesischen Volkes* (1813); and *Der Feldzug in Portugal, 1810–11* (1811).

This last work was actually commissioned by the British government and then smuggled into Germany during 1811. But the idea of inciting insurrection there had first occurred to London with the start of the rebellion in the Iberian Peninsula.[42] From its outset, many within the German intelligentsia were to draw on the image, if not the reality, of the fearless, patriotic guerrilla leaders when contrasting their own submissive *Volk* with the defiant Portuguese and Spaniards.[43] In Austria, as in Prussia, some statesmen and soldiers also hoped to arouse and exploit nationalistic or patriotic sentiments as a weapon against French hegemony; the Archdukes John and Karl joined with Stadion in realizing that the forces unleashed by the French Revolution might be channelled against Napoleon. Indeed, the cultivation of a citizen–soldier ethos within society appeared as vital as the need for tactical and structural reform within the military itself.

This, however, posed a conundrum: what was the point in protecting feudal societies from revolutionary change if, in order to do so, one had to transform them anyway? Moreover, in Germany, where geographical, linguistic, cultural and political variables complicated endeavours to identify a nation, there were commensurate difficulties in objectively defining what 'nationalism' constituted. Usually, nations are forged by political, social or cultural struggles during which association with 'national' values or causes is exploited as a means of combating enemies at home or abroad, as was to occur in the case of Britain during the Napoleonic Wars.[44] Yet not all German nationalists were opposed to French influence: Goethe and Hegel, for instance, fascinated by Napoleon's strong leadership, felt that it might reinvigorate German society; and whereas Stadion hoped that the restless peoples of the Habsburg Empire might be rallied by a 'nationalist' war against France, for others, notably the philosopher Johann Fichte, an ardent believer in the French Revolution's ideals, patriotism could be as good a vehicle as cosmopolitanism when it came to spreading humanitarian values. Although his *Reden an die Deutschen* of 1807–8 might encompass the elements from which German national consciousness was elaborated, and were regarded by many intellectuals as patriotism in its simplest form, he was unsure as to the details of Germany's political future; French power, he feared, might jeopardize Germany's cultural identity unless the states protected their political liberties.

On the other hand, peoples and civilizations rarely abandon their historic aspirations because their ruling institutions alter. Rather, ruling institutions are replaced or revamped because they are failing to satisfy those ambitions. Through the establishment of the *Rheinbund*, France had been the supporter or instigator of important and often popular changes which had reconstructed Germany, while, even in Prussia and Austria, emulating her politically was acknowledged to be a precondition for defeating her militarily. Robust, largely autonomous states, created at the expense of the *Reich*, *Kleinstaaterei* and *Herrschaft*, were the principal products of this process, not nationalism. Certainly, most Germans, even those able to read, remained unmoved by the minority of patriotic and nationalistic agitators among the literati.[45] While one exploiter was much the same as another in the common people's eyes, Napoleon's policies eventually proved too burdensome for too many. That is why, if at all, they resisted the French occupation – not out of any devotion to some vague notion of a fatherland.[46]

In fact, the few localized and limited risings that were to occur across Germany during 1809 had the hallmarks of civil war in so far as Germans fought against their own compatriots as much as they resisted the French. During the Tyrol revolt, for instance, locals who had benefited not only from the region's recent annexation by Bavaria but also from the reforms imposed by Joseph II as far back as the 1780s were just as much a target as French or Bavarian troops. Likewise, Germans serving with *Rheinbund* contingents in the Peninsula soon shed any illusions they might have had about guerrilla warfare; it seemed to have as much to do with indiscriminate killing, loot, rape and general anarchy as it did with patriotism.[47] Further, although 20 years had elapsed since the French Revolution, that concept, as opposed to allegiance to a local ruler, was still a rather alien one within the Germanic states; and empowering the people – and, more to the point, arming them – seemed too dangerous a policy to many, both in and outside the military and political elites. As Spain was to discover, guerrillas might turn from waging war on an invader to seeking societal change through violence. In any case, for polyglot, autocratic polities like the Habsburg Empire to encourage nationalism or undermine legitimism appeared foolhardy in the extreme. What people like Karl and Stadion envisaged was a restoration of Habsburg power through a return to something more akin to the old *Reich*, not the formation of a nation state in the modern sense of the term.

It was against this background that, in autumn 1808, Vienna began preparations for a new war against France. Britain was approached for financial aid amounting to £2 500 000 to finance Austria's mobilization and all of £5 000 000 for each year that the conflict continued. These were huge sums which, given Britain's resources, her commitments and the restraints imposed by the Continental System, were wholly unrealistic. Indeed, just £1 185 000 could be pledged.[48] The Austrians also pleaded for military diversions in Italy, the Peninsula and northern Germany. Mounting a significant offensive from Sicily was judged impracticable[49] and, given the Allies' experiences in 1805, was in any case unlikely to prove much of a distraction to Napoleon. However, Wellesley, restored to command of the army in Portugal, might be able to exert some pressure through either an invasion of Spain or an attack on Soult's corps which, since Corunna, had advanced as far south as Oporto. Britain was also petitioned to underpin a prospective revolt in northern Germany, which was being organized by a group of Prussian and other activists inspired by the Spanish rising.[50] Although this promised to be of more direct assistance to the Austrians, and Canning was to advocate the sending of weapons and munitions to aid the would-be rebels,[51] considering the existing strains, both military and monetary, on Britain's resources, a protracted, major operation here was out of the question.[52] A *coup de main* against the French naval installations on the Scheldt seemed to have far more to recommend it, and it was to this that Britain was eventually to devote her disposable forces. Always of dubious value to the Austrians, the project actually commenced so belatedly that, as Christopher Hall has observed, they ended up providing a diversion for the British, not the other way round.[53] Nor were the Prussians to provide any help, despite initial intimations to the contrary. Plans by some of his officials to commit 80 000 troops to the recrudescent struggle were cancelled by Frederick William at the last moment. Another defeat, he feared, would result in Prussia's eradication and the end of the Hohenzollern dynasty.[54] The only comfort for the Austrians was the thought that, despite the Tsar's public reaffirmation of his alliance with France at Erfurt, Russia might be relied upon to adopt a position of benign neutrality in the forthcoming war.

Once again, however, the military and diplomatic endeavours of Napoleon's enemies were to be fatally lacking in coordination. As in 1805, the Austrian leadership was divided as to the wisdom of renewing the struggle against him. Archduke Karl, the *Generalissimus*, was doubtful, whereas Stadion, Archduke John and the Empress Maria Ludovica were all in favour of it. Prince Metternich, Vienna's ambassador to Paris, also sent in encouraging reports. Francis himself seems to have vacillated until, like Karl, he was persuaded by the war party and, on 8 February 1809, ordered the army to mobilize. While secondary operations were to be mounted in Italy, the Tyrol, Poland and Dalmatia, Germany was identified as the decisive theatre. A rapid advance here promised to catch the dispersed and weakened French forces unawares, and to provoke both a popular insurrection and the defection *en masse* of Napoleon's *Rheinbund* troops. It might even culminate in an invasion of France itself. Yet no sooner had the Austrians irreversibly committed themselves to taking advantage of Napoleon's preoccupation with the Peninsula through this *Niederwerfungsstrategie* than news began to arrive of the Spanish armies' collapse and Moore's headlong flight. Shortly after, just as reports of French preparations for renewed hostilities in Germany began to circulate, Prussia's promises of help were rescinded, obliging Vienna's plans for an offensive along the Main to be abruptly jettisoned in favour of one up the Danube.

Since Karl had already assembled the main army in Bohemia, matters got off to an inauspicious start; his forces had to shift southwards to the Inn, from where they could march west or cover Vienna as circumstances dictated. This move was not completed until 8 April, giving Napoleon a useful respite which he exploited to the full. Ever since June 1808, when she had unveiled plans to raise 180 000 *Landwehr*, his concerns about Austria had been growing. Returning from the Peninsula in mid-January but not wishing to provoke Vienna – at least not prematurely – he had remained in Paris, leaving Berthier, his chief-of-staff, surreptitiously to prepare the army in Germany for fresh hostilities. Napoleon's stepson, Eugène Beauharnais, Viceroy of Italy, was also given detailed instructions as to the part his forces[55] might play in any new conflict, as was Prince Poniatowski, commander of the 20 000 troops in the Grand Duchy of Warsaw.

As we saw in Chapter 5, the Austrians, bent on *revanche,* had made every effort to enhance their forces' fighting efficiency since their last disastrous encounters with those of the French. However, when hostilities resumed, they still suffered from serious shortcomings. For example, the notion of creating a dependable *Landwehr* and other auxiliary units had proved politically and financially hazardous. Of all the empire's ethnic groups, only Germans were regarded as sufficiently trustworthy; so just a fraction of the available manpower could actually be tapped. Furthermore, while recently organized into *Armeekorps,* Austria's regular land forces had had insufficient time to accustom themselves to operating on this basis. The nominated corps commanders, for instance, had no experience in handling such large bodies of men either on or off the battlefield; they lacked the initiative necessary for the semi-independent role that these new structures were essentially designed for, and failed to exploit the synergy offered by the combination of foot, horse and artillery units.[56] Nor could the general staff efficiently manipulate the army as a whole: there were too few trained staff officers, and the lack of standardized procedures frequently gave rise to confusion. Karl was thus hampered by mediocre subordinates and a flawed command and control system. He also had weaknesses of his own. Though an acknowledged military theorist who had studied Napoleon's politico-strategical principles, he found their implementation difficult. While he escaped from the bonds of Frederician norms more than most Allied commanders during the Napoleonic Wars, his failure to exploit the central position he was to gain at the outset of the 1809 campaign ruined the offensive upon which Austria's hopes rested. Prone to epilepsy and equally debilitating slumps in self-confidence, he was a courageous soldier but, unlike Napoleon, did not possess the talents of both a strategist and a leader of men.

Nevertheless, if no better directed, the Austrian army that took the field in 1809 was appreciably bigger and more proficient than that which had fought in 1805: eight *Armeekorps* straddled the Danube theatre; two, commanded by Archduke John, were in Italy; while another, 35 000 men under Archduke Ferdinand, was in Galicia. Altogether, some 209 000 regulars made up Karl's *Hauptarmee*. John had a further 65 000, while General Stoichewich, in Croatia, could muster around 10 000. In addition, there were several *Freikorps,* which, initially at least, consisted of volunteers, as well as the *Grenzer, Landwehr* and *Insurrectio*.[57] The last of these units mostly comprised peasants whose feudal obligations included local defence service in wartime. Although some 35 000 strong, these militiamen, predominantly Hungarians, Croats and Slavs, lacked equipment, training and motivation. The same problems bedevilled the *Landwehr*. In view of Austria's inability to pay for yet more regular forces, and given 'the inadequacy of the military resources still remaining to [her] . . . after fifteen years of fighting and fifteen years of misfortune',[58] Karl had reluctantly conceded the need to raise a substantial militia. Yet, owing to the Habsburg Empire's thorny internal politics, relatively few men were summoned to the colours; and, of them, only a handful fought enthusiastically. James Arnold might describe the mere presence of *Landwehr* at the Battle of Wagram as 'the manifest spirit of German nationalism, a willingness to risk all in open battle against the world's most formidable war machine',[59] but one can only agree with Gunther Rothenberg's conclusion[60] that the long promulgated image of the 1809 war as a struggle that was popular – in both senses of the term – is a romantic myth.

Nor is it accurate to portray Napoleon's *Grande Armée* of 1809 as 'the world's most formidable war machine'. The casualties incurred in the various campaigns since 1805, together with the distribution of his forces over an area that stretched from Sicily to the Baltic and from Portugal to the Niemen, left Napoleon with comparatively few battle-hardened troops in Germany. In response to Austria's preparations for war, he had hoped to muster 260 000 men here, as well as 123 000 in Italy, by March 1809. This proved too optimistic, however, and, even after calling up 80 000 conscripts *two* years ahead of schedule, he could only count on 255 000 troops when the campaign began. Of these, roughly 80 000 were in Dalmatia and Italy under the command of Generals Marmont and Eugène respectively. Of the remaining 174 000, 54 000 were *Rheinbund* troops. Among these, the Württembergers and the Hesse-Darmstadt infantry were perhaps the most proficient.[61] The three veteran divisions of Davout's III Corps formed the army's nucleus, but these stalwarts of earlier fights were fielded alongside units composed partially if not exclusively of conscripts with varying degrees of training. Indeed, some 47 000 raw draftees were incorporated directly into '*l'Armée d'Allemagne*', making up nearly all of General Oudinot's II Corps and half of Marshal Massena's IV Corps.[62] Notwithstanding their inexperience, however, these youths were imbued with the martial spirit of *La Grande Armée* and, under Napoleon's inspired leadership, were to prove formidable opponents.

So it was that, in April 1809, the emperor set out to confront the might of Austria with, as he put it, just 'his little conscripts, his name and his big boots'. He recognized that, to begin with at least, he would probably have to stay on the defensive, reacting to Karl's movements. Accordingly, Berthier, having received instructions in the form of both dispatches[63] and semaphore messages, was to have assembled *l'Armée d'Allemagne* in a '*bataillon carré*': if the Austrians attacked before 15 April, this was to be located in the triangle bounded by Donauwörth, Ingolstadt and Augsburg; but if, as was anticipated, their offensive occurred on or after that date, then its epicentre was to be at Ratisbon (Regensburg). However, Berthier was more accustomed to disseminating orders than giving them. His aide, Colonel Lejuene, was 'much distressed to see this man . . . so calm in the midst of fire, whom no danger could intimidate, trembling and bending under the weight of his responsibility'.[64] Moreover, the semaphore transmissions were interrupted at a crucial point by bad weather, compounding Berthier's uncertainty as to what his master envisaged.[65] As a result of his bewilderment and consequently inept directives – for which he incurred the wrath of Davout – the army, instead of concentrating in response to the incipient Austrian advance, began splitting into two distinct clumps within the rhomboid formed by Ulm, Munich, Ratisbon and Nuremberg.

Indeed, the maldeployment of *l'Armée d'Allemagne* could scarcely have been more favourable to the Archduke Karl. On 9 April, without any formal declaration of war, he had advised the authorities in Bavaria that he had instructions to advance and treat as enemies all who opposed him. Crossing the Inn the next day, he told his soldiers that: 'The eyes of the world . . . of all who still retain a sense of national honour, are focused on you. . . . Europe looks for freedom under your banners. . . . [Y]our German brethren wait for redemption at your hands.'[66] With two *Armeekorps* descending through the Böhmerwald towards Ratisbon, and another six advancing between it and Salzburg on the Danube's southern side, the Austrians were poised to seize a position in their scattered foes' very midst. Panicking, Berthier sent a pathetic plea to Napoleon at midnight on the 16th: 'In this position of affairs, I greatly desire the arrival of your Majesty . . .'[67]

Within hours, his wish had been granted. The emperor, leaving Paris at 4am on the 13th, reached Donauwörth before dawn on the 17th. His Bavarian allies had already been ejected from Munich and Landshut by Karl's spearheads, while, further afield and unbeknown to Napoleon, the Austrians were making other gains: 12 000 regulars under General Chasteler had been sent into the Tyrol by Archduke John, where a large, prearranged rising had already led to the capture or encirclement of isolated French and Bavarian detachments;[68] Archduke Ferdinand's VII Corps had crossed the Polish frontier and, within the next few days, was to defeat Poniatowski's heavily outnumbered forces at Raszyn, occupy Warsaw and advance on Thorn;[69] while Eugène, rashly attacking John at Sacile on the 15th to parry what he erroneously took to be a pincer movement by the archduke and Chasteler's columns, had been repulsed.[70]

Though weary after his incredibly rapid journey, Napoleon immediately assumed control of *l'Armée d 'Allemagne*. As Berthier had gone off to Augsburg, he had to wade unguided through the correspondence at headquarters in order to ascertain where the various corps had finished up. Marshals Lannes, Bessières and Augereau, as well as General Vandamme's VIII (Württemberg) Corps and many other units – among them the Imperial Guard, which, by forced marches and rides on relays of wagons, was to cover the 2800 kilometres between Valladolid and Vienna in just 70 days – were still *en route* to the front. They were initially directed on Ingolstadt to form a strategic reserve. This left Napoleon with Davout's III Corps, which had an additional infantry division attached, and Lefebvre's VII Corps, comprising three Bavarian divisions, to block the Austrian advance south of Ratisbon. Meanwhile, the II and IV Corps would come up from the Lech Valley and, pivoting on the right of this *masse de primaire*, strike at the enemy's exposed left flank. Although he was unsure as to the Austrian forces' precise strength and whereabouts, Napoleon postulated that Karl was making for Davout's isolated corps around Ratisbon, with a strong flank guard to fend off Lefebvre's Bavarians further south. This was broadly correct, but neither Karl's strike force nor Napoleon's *masse de manœuvre* made its presence felt as quickly as was anticipated. Both sides were reacting to snippets of information which dribbled into their respective headquarters, and each experienced its own peculiar problems. Like the Prussians in 1806, Karl was unwilling to let his columns forage. Encumbered by vast supply trains which, together with their many guns, reduced their mobility, they could cover only about 12 kilometres a day. Massena, too, was tardy in assembling his forces and was not to reach Pfaffenhofen on the Ilm before noon on the 19th.

Dawn that morning saw the Austrian forces distributed along a line

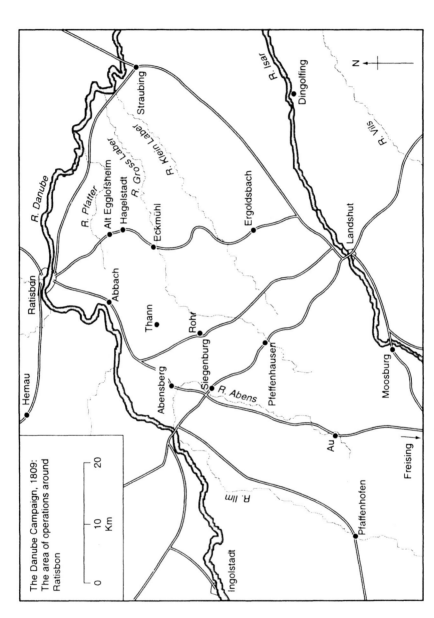

The Danube Campaign around Ratisbon

running from Munich to Au on the Abens and then northwest along the Gross Laber towards the Danube. Small detachments occupied Pfaffenhofen and Hagelstadt, on the left and right of the line respectively, while Karl's main force – roughly 120 000 strong – lay between Pfeffenhausen and Eckmühl (Eggmühl). General Hiller's *Korps* and other detachments – some 42 000 men in all – protected the archduke's left flank. Beyond the Danube, a further 48 000 men under Generals Bellegarde and Kolowrat-Krakowsky were sealing off Ratisbon. At 5am, leaving the 65th *Ligne* to try to hold that town, Davout's corps, skirting the Danube, marched for Abensberg to join up with Lefebvre's Bavarians. A sequence of separate but interconnected fights – known collectively as the Battle of Thann – erupted across the wooded, hilly countryside as the III Corps brushed against the advancing Austrians. Such terrain enabled the French infantry to exploit their aptitude for initiative and nimbleness to the full. Entire battalions were deployed as skirmishers and, despite being grossly outnumbered in most of the actions, repeatedly worsted their opponents until torrential rain curtailed the fighting.[71] Simultaneously, Lefebvre's Bavarians repelled an enemy column east of Abensberg,[72] while Massena and Oudinot, overwhelming the little garrison of Pfaffenhofen, loomed on Karl's left flank.

Having drawn his army together, Napoleon now seized the initiative. Whipping the Bavarians into a frenzy, he launched them into a counter-stroke at Abensberg the next day. Marshal Lannes, who had just arrived from Spain, supported this riposte with his command – a corps improvised out of Gudin's and Morand's infantry and Jacquinot's *Chasseurs* from III Corps, and the heavy cavalry divisions of Generals St Sulpice and Nansouty. The *Rheinbund* troops fought with great *élan*, penetrating deep into their opponents' lines and threatening to cut off the Austrian left wing, the remnants of which recoiled towards Landshut in tremendous confusion.[73] Massena advanced on Freising and Moosburg, seeking to complete their discomfiture. Karl, however, appears to have been more concerned about his right. Although it would seem that he was laid low for several hours by an epileptic seizure, what orders he did issue shifted the balance of his forces not to Hiller's support but across Davout's front towards Ratisbon. Here, the 65th, short of ammunition and fighting against overwhelming odds on two sides, was compelled to surrender that evening.

As the town's exceptionally sturdy bridge had defied demolition, Karl could now combine the troops under his personal direction with the two *Korps* under Bellegarde and Kolowrat, while Hiller's units fell back on the Isar at Landshut, a formidable position. However, mistakenly taking Hiller's fleeing troops for the main Austrian army, Napoleon continued to press them throughout the 21st. That evening, assailed by his pursuers in a fashion that was as audacious as it was furious, Hiller was already facing ruin in the choked streets of Landshut when Massena's column, having forced its way over the Isar at Moosburg, emerged on his left. At this, his shattered command went into precipitant retreat for the Inn, eventually reaching Neuötting late on the 22nd.[74]

Although spectacular, this blow was not as decisive as Napoleon first imagined. While he was directing the battle at Landshut, Davout, with some support from Lefebvre, had moved against what had been dismissed by the emperor as just the northern wing of Karl's army. Cornered before Ratisbon – the fall of which Napoleon could only have learnt of when he was engaged with Hiller at around 2pm on the 21st – this force was evidently not seen as much of a threat, and its retreat to Straubing or Dingolfing was doubtless anticipated.[75] In the ensuing fighting across the dells and hills between Eckmühl and the Danube, however, it soon became apparent that Davout was confronted by the archduke's main force, some 56 000 bayonets and sabres. Again the superior morale and tactics of the French had carried the day, but it was clear that, unless they were reinforced immediately, the VII and III Corps would be overwhelmed; Karl was already bringing up Kolowrat's 20 000-strong *Korps* from beyond the Danube.[76] Accordingly, leaving Bessières with Wrede's Bavarian infantry and General Marulaz's light cavalry division to shadow Hiller, Napoleon turned the bulk of his army about and hurried north.

At about 2pm on the 22nd, Napoleon's breathless vanguard – the head of Vandamme's VIII Corps – came up against the extreme left of Karl's army just south of Eckmühl. From here, the Austrian forces, running parallel to the 35 000 men of Davout and Lefebvre, curled northwards towards Abbach on the Danube. Karl, having dismissed reports of Napoleon's approach, had resolved to crush the hostile units immediately before him by a renewal and intensification of his attack of the previous day. However, marshalling his 74 000 bayonets and sabres for the assault consumed the entire morning, and the battle was barely recrudescent when Napoleon's *attaque débordante* began to make its presence felt.

Karl promptly countermanded his orders for an advance, recalling his right wing to bolster his centre and left. Davout, too, was astir. During the 21st, the heaviest fighting had occurred amidst the ravines, woods and hills just to the northwest of the Gross Laber at Eckmühl. Building on their existing gains, Davout's troops now pressed eastwards here once more, while the Württembergers cleared the enemy from the Gross Laber's southern bank and, with conspicuous courage, stormed Eckmühl in the face of heavy artillery and small-arms fire. Thereafter, Napoleon filtered squadron upon squadron of cavalry over the captured bridge, bending the Austrian left back on itself. A powerful, 16-piece battery, sited on the Bettelberg beyond the reach of Napoleon's own artillery, pinned down the attack's southern pincer for a time. Davout, however, maintained his advance, cutting into the Austrians' centre and all but completing the envelopment of their left wing, Prince von Rosenberg's IV *Armeekorps* and a division of the III under General Vukassovich. At about 3.30pm, 20 squadrons of French, Bavarian and Württemberg horsemen assailed Rosenberg's 22 and, surging up the Bettelberg, finally silenced his grand battery. Threatened on three sides, he endeavoured to execute a fighting withdrawal up the Ratisbon road, but, harried relentlessly, his units steadily disintegrated. By 6pm, they were streaming in panic into Alt Egglofsheim.

In the course of this flight, the fugitives carried away almost all of a combined grenadier division under Prince Rohan. This had been attached to Prince Hohenzollern's command, immediately north of Rosenberg's initial positions. With the collapse of the IV *Armeekorps*, Hohenzollern had been compelled to retreat towards Alt Egglofsheim and the Pfatter Valley, along which Karl was gradually regrouping his forces. However, Napoleon was thrusting towards it, too; and, shortly after dusk, a massive cavalry *mêlée* erupted here, 32 squadrons of Austrians trading blows in the moonlight with thousands of French and *Rheinbund* troopers. Although exhausted after their long march, the French *carabiniers* and *cuirassiers* especially proved more than a match for their opponents; the Austrians were soon routed. Spurring onwards, the jubilant French horsemen trampled down Rohan's remaining grenadiers and very nearly captured Karl himself. Hohenzollern, appearing to the west, also sustained serious losses as he committed his heavy cavalry to the fight in a bid to save his compatriots and secure his own retreat northwards. With Davout's troops snapping at his heels, he eventually fled across the Pfatter, too, bringing the battle to its conclusion.

Although a few Württemberg horsemen raked in some prisoners along the Ratisbon–Straubing road, the bulk of Napoleon's forces were far too tired for further efforts to be made that night.[77] With six days of hard fighting and marching, they had wrenched the initiative from Karl, triumphed in five successive battles, split his army asunder and inflicted some 30 000 casualties. Their own losses were less than half this figure. It was a sensational achievement and one which thoroughly disconcerted the *Generalissimus*. At the outset of the war, he had cautioned that 'The first lost battle is the death sentence of the monarchy and the present dynasty.'[78] He now advised Francis to seek terms and, within a week, was writing directly to Napoleon: 'I shall be equally honoured, Sire, to meet you either with the sword or the olive branch,'[79] he concluded. This peace feeler left the court war-party baying for Karl's blood. Though no response was forthcoming, it doubtless helped persuade Napoleon that Austria's ruling circles were at loggerheads over the conflict and that he was better placed to sustain it than they were.

At 9am on the 23rd, fighting resumed between the two armies as Napoleon's forces, in a colossal semicircle, closed in on Ratisbon. Another massive cavalry *mêlée* ensued on the plain south of the town, during which the Austrians were steadily edged back. Karl, at this juncture, decided to put the Danube between himself and his pursuers by withdrawing his entire army into Bohemia. A garrison of nine battalions clung stubbornly to Ratisbon's decrepit fortifications to cover this retreat but, by 7pm, had succumbed to a determined escalade directed and inspired by Lannes.[80] Nevertheless, by that time, the bulk of Karl's army was well into the Bayerischer Wald, heading for Cham. While the tails of his columns might have been molested, there was scant prospect of manœuvring him into a decisive engagement amid such difficult terrain. Indeed, when Massena reported that IV Corps had reached Straubing but could not cross the Danube as the enemy had destroyed the bridges there, the emperor acknowledged that, for the time being at least, his prey had eluded him.

However, that Karl would endeavour to recross the river further downstream so as to be able to protect Vienna appeared almost certain. Accordingly, though weakened by a slight wound he had sustained at Ratisbon, Napoleon hastily prepared his army for an advance eastwards. The II and III corps were reconstituted, with Lannes being given command of the former, while newly arrived reinforcements, notably the leading elements of the Imperial Guard, were assimilated into the emperor's order of battle. Bernadotte's IX Corps was also hurried southwards from Gera in Saxony; Napoleon wanted it at hand for the climactic battle he anticipated and, in the interim, it could bolster Davout's troops, who were gingerly tailing the Austrian *Hauptarmee*. This, moving with uncharacteristic speed, was to cover some 320 kilometres in 18 days, emerging east of Vienna on 16 May.

Apart from Lefebvre's Bavarian corps, which was directed on Salzburg and the Tyrol to reopen communications with Eugène and guard the right flank, the rest of *l'Armée d'Allemagne* now descended on Vienna via the Danube's southern bank. Napoleon's decision not to pursue Karl directly has been a point of controversy for several generations of historians.[81] Bonnal's *Manœuvre de Landshut*, for instance, which strongly influenced later writers such as Petre, seeks to attribute it to an obsession on Napoleon's part; though his own doctrine identified destroying the enemy's army as strategy's primary objective, he was bent on seizing

Vienna for reasons of political prestige. This is far too simplistic. His doubts about the likelihood of entrapping the archduke aside, Napoleon was beset by other worries. First, given the Austrians' past fixation with Italy, he was unsure what the strength and intentions of their forces there might be. Although he was yet to learn of Sacile – it took a week or more for an *estafette* to travel from Viceregal to Imperial Headquarters – Napoleon was acutely aware of the interdependence of the theatres separated by the Alps and was reluctant to let the centre of his operations stray too far north.[82] Second, even if by menacing his opponent's capital Napoleon did not precipitate a negotiated settlement, he would almost certainly compel Karl, John or both to fall back to save Vienna, which could culminate in a potentially decisive encounter. In fact, this was precisely how the Austrians were to react; and that the climactic battle ultimately occurred not west but east of the city was because of circumstances that neither commander-in-chief could have foreseen. Third, and most importantly, the emperor's critics fail to allow for factors which were exacerbating warfare's inherent intractability. Indeed, the 'fog of war' impeded both sides to an extent rarely experienced before. With their armies scattered along relatively long fronts and functioning not as unitary blocks but as semi-autonomous units, both Napoleon and Karl were highly dependent on their subordinates performing well and on the receipt of accurate intelligence. Neither prerequisite could be taken for granted. Late on the 22nd, for instance, as the Battle of Eckmühl was petering out, Bessières insisted in a report to Napoleon that the Austrian *Hauptarmee* had started retreating on Neumarkt via Dingolfing 24 hours earlier.[83] Similarly, reviewing his battered forces on the 27th, Karl concluded he had just 50 000 men left.[84] Actually, he had close to double this. Moreover, the *Generalissimus* did not know what had become of Hiller's forces, or vice versa, while Napoleon was only to learn of Sacile and the Tyrol revolt at the very end of April. Likewise, conflicting opinions as to Karl's movements in Bohemia complicated the efforts of Napoleon, Davout and Bernadotte to coordinate a response.[85]

It has been said that, in war, victory goes to the side that makes the fewest mistakes. This is broadly true. For all the errors, shortcomings and misapprehensions, the superiority of Napoleon's generalship, staff, subordinate commanders and soldiers had been sufficient to overcome both the enemy and 'friction'. The Austrians had fared less well. Hiller, having gathered perhaps 35 000 men together, was oblivious to Karl's fate until news finally reached him early on the 25th. These tidings came indirectly, via the *Kaiser*, who, meantime, had ordered Hiller to rejoin the *Hauptarmee*. After clashing with Wrede at Neumarkt on the 24th,[86] he duly headed for Linz, wrecking the bridges over the Danube's tributaries behind him. Though hampered by the swollen rivers barring its path, *l'Armée d'Allemagne* was not far behind. As Lefebvre chased General Jellacic's division out of Salzburg and into the Tyrol on the right, Bernadotte replaced Davout on the left, releasing the III Corps for operations on the Danube's southern bank. Simultaneously, Massena and Lannes thrust across the Inn hoping to overtake Hiller, whose intentions were gradually becoming more apparent.

However, Hiller now discovered that three quarters of the *Landwehr* in Upper Austria had deserted at the enemy's approach, and that Karl was still well to the north. Although the *Generalissimus* indicated he would bring the *Hauptarmee* across the Danube, he failed to say when or where.[87] Judging Linz to be indefensible, Hiller demolished its bridge over that river and was in the act of withdrawing through nearby Ebelsberg on the Traun when, on 3 May, Bessières's horsemen and Massena's infantry fell on his rearguard. General Claparede's division pierced the Austrian centre and, intermingled with hordes of fugitives, stormed over the 550-metre bridge that led into Ebelsberg itself. Here, heavily outnumbered, the French grappled with the next line of defenders, who were ensconced in the castle and other buildings lining the steep, narrow lanes, while Austrian guns indiscriminately bombarded the town from the heights beyond. It was a seemingly impregnable position, but as General Legrand's French and Baden infantry gradually picked their way across the corpse-clogged bridge to join the fray, the blazing town was wrested from Hiller's grasp.[88] Lannes, meanwhile, had repaired the crossing at Wells and was poised to threaten the Austrians' rear. Indeed, rumours inaccurately put him as far east as Steyr. With any defence of the Enns seemingly compromised, too, Hiller fell back as far as St Pölten. Here he detached some grenadiers to bolster Vienna's garrison, before finally slipping over the Danube at Krems.

Located on that river's right bank, the Austrian capital had some 35 000 personnel to man its rickety perimeter, many of them *Landwehr* and municipal militia. When Lannes's vanguard appeared before the city on 10 May, however, any fighting spirit evoked by Heinrich von Collin's rousing *Wehrmannslieder* or the *Vaterlandische Blätter für den österreichischen Kaiserstaat* swiftly evaporated. Nor was the garrison's commandant, Archduke Maximilian, any less fickle. Once the French compromised the outer defences and began shelling the city's core, he led most of his troops over the Tabor Bridge to safety. As in 1805, the court, mandarinate and imperial archives had long since been evacuated, but vast quantities of war *matériel* were abandoned to the enemy. Over 2000 regulars and those volunteers still with the colours also surrendered when the city was occupied on the 13th.[89] Far from resisting, most Viennese coexisted quite happily with the invaders. Such was the fraternization between the womenfolk and Napoleon's soldiery that, according to one eyewitness, parts of the city looked 'like Sodom and Gomorrah',[90] while another observer reported that once the inhabitants noticed that the French:

> instead of attacking people's purses with their bayonets, were setting up bivouacs in the main squares and that the soldiers . . . were washing their bodies and shirts in the fountains . . . people dared . . . to go out into the streets again. Within a few hours, everyone was all over the place and . . . the hot sausage vendors were doing their rounds.[91]

Among all of this was Ludwig van Beethoven, whose music was as revolutionary as the times in which he lived. Like many intellectuals, he had welcomed the French Revolution, only to be disillusioned by the corruption of its ideals. Beethoven had dedicated his Third Symphony to Napoleon, but had scratched out the inscription on learning that he had crowned himself emperor. 'With that bastard, I made a mistake,' he mournfully opined[92] – a sentiment that many of his contemporaries would doubtless share. After sheltering in a cellar to protect his faltering hearing from the roar of the explosions during the bombardment of Vienna, Beethoven emerged to find himself surrounded by 'nothing but drums, cannon and human misery of every kind.'[93] Furthermore, as his home was on the city ramparts, which Napoleon was planning to demolish, he discovered a mine had been placed under his windows.[94] A Viennese story, probably true, relates how he shook his fist at the French troops and yelled: 'If I knew as much about military strategy as I do about counterpoint, you'd be bloody for it!' But several years were to pass before Beethoven could avenge himself. In December 1813, during a charity concert for the benefit of Germanic soldiers injured in the *Befreiungskrieg*, he conducted the *première* of his *Battle of Vitoria*, which celebrated Wellington's climactic triumph in the Peninsula.[95]

For the time being, however, Napoleon's star was ascending. On 1 May, Archduke John, confronted on the Adige by a strengthened and reorganized *Armée d'Italie*, conceded that he had lost the initiative and, alarmed by tidings of Eckmühl, began retiring on Carinthia. Eugène, audaciously hurling his army across the Piave under his complacent adversary's nose, attacked him on the 8th. John lost all of 7000 casualties; Eugène well under a third of this figure. The crestfallen Austrians recoiled and, within days, had been swept from Italian soil.[96] Simultaneously, the small but veteran garrison of Dalmatia, under Marmont, blunted an invasion by Stoichewich's command before assuming the offensive. Driving into western Croatia, Marmont annihilated Stoichewich's main force and, by inciting the Bosnians to raid the frontier, too, precipitated the dissolution of his *Grenzer* units; these reservists deserted *en masse* in order to defend their homesteads. Leaving the Croatian borderlands in turmoil, Marmont then marched on Laibach.

With Carinthia and Carniola endangered and Karl urging him to come to the succour of the *Hauptarmee*, John was torn between competing demands on his few resources. He endeavoured to recall all the regulars in the Tyrol – Chasteler's troops and Jellacic's 'lost' division – and to retard Eugène's progress. However, by this time, Lefebvre's intervention was tilting the balance in the savage struggle for the Tyrol in the Bavarians' favour. Chasteler was routed at Wörgl on 13 May, while, 12 days later, Jellacic blundered into Eugène's path near Leoben and lost two thirds of his force. Consequently, relatively few of these troops managed to link up with John's army as it was edged back into Hungary by the closing enemy pincers. Although relinquishing so much territory was unpalatable, Karl reasoned that any decisive encounter would occur on the Danube's banks near Vienna, and he was prepared to sacrifice the various secondary operations in order to strengthen his hand there.

Napoleon was equally eager to concentrate every available unit for this showdown, even at the expense of subordinate undertakings on the flanks and rear of his army.[97] As the majority of Lefebvre's corps was withdrawn from the Tyrol to Linz, the smouldering revolt flared up again. The partisans, still backed by handfuls of Austrian regulars, ejected the few remaining Bavarian troops from their Alpine stronghold and intermittently pillaged the adjacent countryside.[98] Nevertheless, this essentially parochial rebellion posed no strategic threat to either Napoleon's or Eugène's operations and, while irksome, could be adequately contained if not immediately suppressed. Likewise, a few tiny pockets of disorder materialized elsewhere in the *Rheinbund*. On 2 April, Friedrich von Katte, an ex-lieutenant in the Prussian Army, led roughly 300 rebels in an abortive bid to seize Magdeburg. Expecting to provoke a national rising and entice Prussia into the war, Katte found the overwhelming majority of the population unreceptive to his entreaties. Most of his band was arrested in a bloodless scrimmage with some National Guardsmen, while Katte himself fled to Bohemia. Three weeks later, despite this failure, Wilhelm von Dörnberg, an officer in King Jerome's Guard, tried to stage a *coup d'état* in Kassel. Perhaps 5000 people gathered in his support, but very few of them were interested in nationalistic crusades; they were merely dissatisfied with Jerome's domestic policies. His followers dispersed by loyal troops within a few minutes, Dörnberg shared Katte's fate. Lastly, there was the tragic farce instigated by Major Ferdinand von Schill of Prussia's 2nd Brandenburg Hussars. On 28 April, he led some 500 troopers out of Berlin 'on manœuvres' – an invasion of Saxony. Believing

Schill's renegades to be the vanguard of a Prussian army, the Saxon court, with most of its own troops far afield, was plunged into panic. However, rebuffed with a few choice words by Wittenberg's tiny garrison, Schill turned into Westphalia, where, at Dodendorf near Magdeburg, he clashed with a tiny, improvised force of German and French soldiers. After killing one man and injuring 50, his troopers, shunned by the populace and denounced by their own king, resumed their aimless wandering, finishing up near Stralsund. On 31 May, what remained of his band were exterminated in Stralsund's streets by Danish and Dutch troops. Schill was killed and his head, pickled in wine, sent to Holland.[99]

Nevertheless, by 1813 such depictions as Arndt's 'Song of Schill' and Stagemann's *War Songs* had transfigured Schill; he had become a fearless liberator, a martyr for the *Volk*. This was typical of the myths which stemmed from the romantic, patriotic literature of the period. Just as many a European's images of the Great War were to be influenced by the poetry of the 1920s and 1930s, numerous *belles-lettres* of Napoleon's time were exploited as didactic, political tools and coloured the perceptions of subsequent historians.[100] In 1809, however, the exploits and sentiments of Schill and the other patriots had scant if any appeal for the majority of people and posed no real threat to the Napoleonic order in Germany. Nevertheless, the emperor was aware that the Austrians, Prussians and British were all anticipating a Peninsular-style rebellion breaking out. Accordingly, in late April and early May, he strove to improve the internal security of the *Rheinbund* and to guard against the amphibious attack that, it was reported, the British were preparing. A 'Corps of Observation' – deliberately misrepresented for propaganda and counterespionage purposes as 50 000-strong – was assembled at Hanau under Marshal Kellermann, while Jerome was given an assortment of detachments – impressively dubbed the 'X Corps' – with which to quell any disorder between Hamburg and the Main, to protect the coast and to assist the Saxons if and when necessary. A special division under General Beaumont was also created at Augsburg to help Bavaria contain the Tyrol and Vorarlberg insurrections and to safeguard Napoleon's communications in the event of upheaval in southern Germany.[101]

The battles of Aspern–Essling and Wagram

Satisfied that he had done all he could to secure his army's rear and flanks, Napoleon continued his quest for a decisive clash with Karl's *Hauptarmee*. The first obstacle to be overcome was the Danube, the

Austrians having destroyed the Tabor Bridge after abandoning Vienna. Repairing it under their noses was clearly impossible, so alternative, prospective crossing sites were earmarked: one was at Nussdorf, some 5 kilometres north of Vienna, where the Danube was relatively narrow, and a second was identified at Kaiserebersdorf, a similar distance to the southeast of the city. Here the river, though broader, was split into four principal channels by the Island of Lobau and a maze of sandbars. From south to north, these branches were respectively 460, 270, 30 and 80 metres across.[102] Linking the natural piers between them would be a daunting task which, in the interests of secrecy, would also have to be accomplished as rapidly as possible – a point underscored when, on 13 May, the Austrians spotted and captured a party of *voltigeurs* who, ferried across by boats, were endeavouring to secure a lodgement opposite Nussdorf. With further efforts here dismissed as too hazardous, work began on the Kaiserebersdorf crossing.[103] Napoleon's *pontonniers* eventually scraped together sufficient building materials and boats to bridge the four arms and, at 6pm on the 20th, hauled the last section into position. After initially assembling on Lobau Island, Massena's IV Corps and two cavalry divisions, the troopers leading their mounts, promptly began filing across the long, slender, rather rickety bridge that led to the north bank.

The Austrians indubitably had some inkling of what was afoot. Their patrols had skirmished with the units screening the bridges' construction and, from the Bisamberg just north of Vienna, enjoyed a panoramic view of the river valley. Indeed, a semaphore post erected here relayed rapid reports of any French movements. Yet no attempt was made to stop the consolidation of the bridgehead; the vanguard trickled, unimpeded, towards the nearby villages of Aspern and Essling. This puzzled and concerned Napoleon. Aware that Karl had united the *Hauptarmee* with Maximilian's and Hiller's contingents north of Vienna,[104] the emperor was fearful that his adversaries might now double back, pass over the Danube and fall on his communications. The Austrians were known to have several pontoon trains and, on the 17th, a corps led by Kolowrat had attacked an entrenched camp protecting the restored crossing at Linz. Although Kolowrat had been driven off by Bernadotte's approaching troops,[105] another hostile column had made a bid to cross at Nussdorf that very morning. This was evidently a feint, but the potential threat to his rear obliged Napoleon to keep much of his army west of Vienna: besides Bernadotte's IX Corps, Vandamme's VIII was at Linz, while Davout's loitered near St Pölten.

As, on the other hand, either one of the now diverging wings of *l'Armée d'Allemagne* might be attacked by the entire *Hauptarmee*, Napoleon was in a quandary. Yet, curiously, the Austrians seemed quiescent when compared with the elements. After strong winds had delayed its completion by several hours, his flimsy pontoon bridge was jeopardized during the night of the 20th when the onset of spring triggered a thaw across Upper Austria, raising the Danube by a metre. Barely had Napoleon's vanguard gained the far bank when the bridge was broken by a hulk swept along by this freshet. It was 3am before the damage could be repaired and the flow of men resumed. Shortly after, Napoleon discussed the situation with his staff. Bessières reported that the few cavalry that had completed the crossing had encountered nothing but an impenetrable curtain of Austrian horsemen. Lannes, who was accompanying the IV Corps until his own arrived, averred that they were faced by a detachment of 8000 men at most. Massena, after clambering up the tower of Aspern's church to gauge the extent of Karl's forces, concurred; while to the north and northwest the horizon was aglow with the reflected light of campfires, there appeared to be nothing on the Marchfeld, the Danube's floodplain.[106]

In fact, most of the reorganized *Hauptarmee* was just 8–10 kilometres away, behind a chain of hillocks between Wagram and the Danube. It had been ordered into this position at 3pm the previous day, but the greater part of it had received the instruction belatedly and was still in motion when Massena was conducting his reconnaissance. Though there were few campfires for him to see, there were Austrians aplenty: 83 000 infantry, 14 000 cavalry and 292 guns were poised to confront the few thousand unsuspecting Frenchmen around Aspern.

Yet Karl, like Napoleon, was beset by doubts. Ever since Ratisbon he had been toying with the idea of venturing back onto the Danube's right bank. By mid-May, however, he had recognized the advantages offered by remaining on the defensive in his current location. Time was on his side, whereas Napoleon would have to mount an assault sooner or later. Nevertheless, he was not convinced that the crossing downstream from Vienna was not a feint and feared that Napoleon's real blow would be delivered via Nussdorf.[107] Fortifying the bank opposite that place and leaving ample troops to safeguard it, he wheeled the balance of his army southwards to pounce on whatever force debouched onto the Marchfeld, where the open terrain would favour the Austrians' tactical style. Strategically, however, his thinking was more Frederician than Napoleonic. Instead of seeking to drive his opponent's entire army into the Danube, he merely envisaged cutting off and defeating a sizeable portion of the French force in order to confirm the military stalemate. Although Russia had declared war on Austria in compliance with her obligations to France, and Sweden, having deposed Gustavus IV, had finally abandoned her futile struggle against Napoleon, with Spain still defiant, Prussia restless, Britain preparing an amphibious assault and

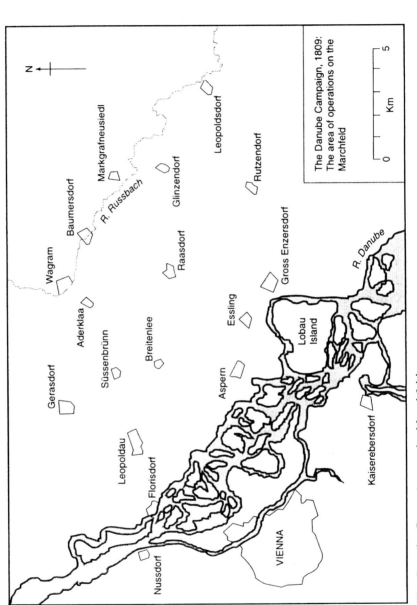

The Danube Campaign, 1809:
The area of operations on the
Marchfeld

Km
0   5

The Danube Campaign on the Marchfeld

disorder flaring up across the *Rheinbund*, the Austrians were pinning their hopes for salvation on strategic Micawberism.

Obscured by dust clouds and a slight ridge some 3 kilometres beyond the enemy's positions, the *Hauptarmee* advanced at noon on the 21st, Whitsunday. Having allowed his prey time to move out onto the Marchfeld, Karl was disgruntled to find that the French had barely ventured beyond their bridgehead. Just 23 000 troops and 44 guns had gained the north bank when, at 12.15pm, the bridge was ruptured west of Lobau, interrupting the flow of men and *matériel*. Struggling to restore this, the French came under attack. Divided into five blocks, Karl's army started a concentric assault: while three of the columns struck at Aspern on Napoleon's left, the other two edged south to storm Essling on his right. Stunned by this development, the emperor initially considered withdrawing but, as the fighting escalated, resolved to cling to the bridgehead. Luckily, both Aspern and Essling had substantial stone buildings – notably the church in the former and the granary in the latter – and enclosures which lent themselves to defence. While Lannes entrenched Boudet's infantry division in Essling, Massena supervised Aspern's occupation by Molitor's four regiments. Arrayed behind the embanked road which rippled across the plain between the two settlements, Bessières' cavalry – 6300 sabres under Lasalle, Marulaz and Espagne – formed the centre.

At 5pm, after having repelled three rather piecemeal and poorly synchronized assaults, Molitor's powder-stained troops were assailed on three sides in an attack led by Karl in person. Western parts of Aspern changed hands six times in furious fighting, but as the evening wore on and more French infantry – Legrand's and Carra St Cyr's divisions – arrived to join the fray, Massena continued to hold out. Meanwhile, Bessières's troopers executed a series of desperate charges against Karl's centre, where scores of guns were pummelling the French lines. In suppressing their fire, and engaging the infantry and cavalry behind them, Bessières's squadrons sustained heavy casualties, among them Espagne. However, they did relieve the pressure on Massena's right flank, besides shielding Lannes's left. That marshal was already under attack from the north, east and southeast as, around 6pm, the Austrian fourth and fifth columns, having completed their circuitous march, joined the battle. Though ravaged by shelling and penetrated three times, Essling remained firmly in French hands.

Both sides spent the night preparing to renew the struggle. Some *cuirassiers* completed the crossing late on the 21st, and the II Corps and the Foot Guards arrived, too. Davout was also summoned with all available troops and munitions. Eager to glimpse the proceedings, many civilians followed his columns out of Vienna to line the Danube's southern bank.

Sporadic skirmishing had persisted in Aspern throughout the night, but, at 3am, the fighting intensified to the levels of the previous evening. The French gained the upper hand and, by 5am, controlled the entire village once more. At Essling, too, the Austrians fared badly. Looming out of the morning mist, they penetrated the village only to be ejected for the fourth time. Although he had just 62 000 men and 60 cannon to pit against Karl's remaining 94 000 troops and 280 guns, Napoleon now thought of switching to the offensive. The Austrian centre was temptingly weak. A thrust northwards here, supported by Davout's corps which had arrived at Kaiserebersdorf, could culminate in Karl's army being split in two and its dregs rolled up against the Danube.

Accordingly, at 7am, Lannes's three divisions moved forward in echelon. Their close-order columns swept by the fire of scores of guns, to which they could reply with just a few, they pressed on despite dreadful losses. Behind them came Bessières's horsemen, who intermittently repeated their valiant charges of the 21st, with similar results. Nevertheless, as the French infantry arrived within musket-range, the Austrians wavered. Karl, summoning reinforcements from his flanks, waded into the midst of the fighting, sword in hand. Heartened by his example, his troops stood fast, trading volleys with their assailants. By 9.30am, the latter, their ammunition almost exhausted, had slithered to a standstill.[108] In any case, the chance of victory had slipped from Napoleon's grasp. Barely had Lannes commenced his advance than the bridge, buffeted by the churning waters and a variety of flotsam, much of it launched into the current by the Austrians, broke once again. No sooner were repairs effected than a vast, floating water-mill, set ablaze and cut from its moorings by the enemy, careered into another span west of Lobau; a large section, bearing the engineers' General Pernetti and several *pontonniers,* was carried several kilometres downstream.[109]

With the influx of fresh troops and munitions stopped for the foreseeable future, Napoleon had no alternative other than to disengage his forces and retreat onto Lobau as soon as was practicable. In the mean time, the bridgehead's perimeter would have to be held, come what may. Lannes was duly instructed to fall back. As he did so, Karl reformed his battered units and returned to the attack. From 10am onwards, pressure on Aspern's and Essling's weary defenders began to mount afresh, while 150 cannon resumed the bombardment of the French centre. At 2pm, Rosenberg's IV *Korps,* supported by a grenadier brigade, finally overran Essling at the fifth attempt; only the granary remained in Boudet's possession. Although a savage bayonet-charge by the Young Guard regained the village and restored the French line here, the remorseless Austrian barrage and infantry assaults soon rendered the position of Napoleon's left and centre untenable. By 4pm, Hiller had stormed Aspern and was probing across the enclosures between it and the Danube. The Austrians, however, proved unable or unwilling to cut across their opponents' rear; they merely maintained their bombardment, gradually pressing the French back into the bridgehead.[110]

Napoleon himself stood amidst the falling shot and shell for some hours until, at the Guard's insistence,[111] he crossed to Lobau to supervise the preparations for the army's withdrawal and recuperation. He was already thinking about the next battle;[112] many others were fighting their last. Among other diarists, Chlapowski, of the cavalry, and Coignet, of the Old Guard grenadiers, luridly convey the effect of the barrage which the French had to endure.[113] Eventually, in order to suppress the enemy's fire, Coignet and his colleagues abandoned their customary role as the army's heaviest infantry and, deployed as snipers, started picking off the gunners. It was an impressive display of their versatility, but it came too late for many. Among the thousands of casualties inflicted by the Austrian fire was Lannes, who, grief-stricken by the death of an old comrade, slumped down by a ditch where a ricocheting ball shattered his knees.[114] After Larrey had amputated the marshal's left leg, Lannes was carried onto Lobau, where a tearful Napoleon hugged his grievously injured friend, smearing his white waistcoat with blood. 'Larrey will save you. . . . Is that not so, Larrey?', the emperor assured him, half-pleadingly.[115] Although he was undoubtedly one of the most knowledgeable and skilled physicians of his time, there was little Larrey could do to combat gangrene and septicaemia. His best endeavours notwithstanding, Lannes died several days later.

The marshal was the most eminent of the 20 000–25 000 men killed or wounded on each side in this terrible battle,[116] which fizzled out after dusk. Largely unmolested, the French, supervised by Massena, began a phased, orderly withdrawal onto Lobau, taking their injured and all but a handful of dismounted guns with them. The bridge was retracted behind them at 3.30am. Despite the fortitude and skill Napoleon's troops had shown, there was no disguising the fact that they had been repulsed. It was the first defeat inflicted on the 'Corsican Ogre' himself, and it was to form the apogee of Karl's career. Yet while the news of Napoleon's defeat rippled across Europe, exhilarating his enemies and shocking his allies, the expectations underpinning Austria's *Ermattungsstrategie* were not fulfilled. Of the anticipated British landing and the hoped-for Prussian intervention there was no sign, while not only had the *Rheinbund* remained loyal to France but also Italy had been lost and Hungary invaded. Indeed, on 2 June, Archduke Joseph was instructed to mobilize the Hungarian *Insurrectio* and reinforce John's mangled army which, detaching a small corps to stiffen resistance to Marmont's advance, was slowly drawing nearer to the *Hauptarmee*. The *Insurrectio* proved predictably apathetic, and only 12 000 joined John at Raab (Gyor), where, on 14 June, he confronted Eugène's pursuing columns. Initially, the Austrians' position, numerical strength and powerful artillery blocked the Franco-Italian attacks. Once his left flank had been turned by cavalry, though, John's line began to buckle; some 10 000 men were slain, injured or captured and the rest fled across the Danube at Komorn.[117] Nor were the tidings from the north more comforting. Archduke Ferdinand had hoped to subdue Poniatowski quickly and then invade Saxony to support the ragbag of soldiers – among them the fugitives Dörnberg and Katte – who were already active along the Bohemian frontier.[118] However, the Poles not only clung to Thorn and other key bastions but also mounted incursions into Galicia, rousing their compatriots there against Habsburg rule. The Russians, too, though preoccupied with their operations against Sweden and Turkey, grasped the opportunity to seize choice pieces of Austrian territory. By late June, Ferdinand was in retreat and badgering the *Kaiser* for reinforcements.

Stadion favoured sending them. Whereas Karl continued to press Francis to seek a negotiated settlement immediately,[119] the war-party still looked either to the wider, international situation or to the prospect of a great victory for salvation. Indeed, Hiller advocated the mounting of a counteroffensive through Pressburg. Karl, however, again unsure of Napoleon's intentions, preferred to await developments and John's arrival while drawing men – including Kolowrat's *Korps* – and *matériel* from Bohemia. By July, the *Hauptarmee* amounted to 534 guns and 161 000 personnel, among them 21 *Landwehr* and 12 *Freikorps* battalions, as well as other reservists who filled gaps in depleted regiments.[120] Of this host, the small V *Korps* was left to safeguard the Bisamberg, while the *Avant-garde*, the VI *Korps* and a few entrenchments secured the Danube's bank near Lobau. The main body, meanwhile, was in two clumps: the first stretched from the river to Wagram, from where the second extended towards Markgrafneusiedl along the Russbach, the Marchfeld's northern edge. John's residual 14 000 troops were still many kilometres distant at Pressburg.

Contrary to Karl's hopes, Napoleon was in no mood to make peace yet. Since his check at Aspern–Essling, he had transformed Lobau into an impregnable base; ringed with a flotilla of gunboats crewed by the Guard Marines, it bristled with heavy cannon dragged from Vienna across solidly constructed bridges. Summoning every available unit of both *l'Armée d'Italie* and *l'Armée d'Allemagne*, he amassed 189 000 person-nel, including 23 000 horsemen, and 617 guns with which to renew the struggle,[121] while scores of improvised workshops produced rations, munitions, clothing and equipment. Napoleon's measures for deceiving his adversaries as to his intentions were equally elaborate. Among ruses aimed at persuading them that he would cross the Danube at the same point as last time was the commencement of four bridges here on 30 June.[122] In fact, the blow was to come from Lobau's eastern side, not its northern edge. Disguised as humble sergeants, the emperor and Massena wandered down to the waterline here as if they intended to bathe. The Austrian sentries paid little heed to such quotidian occurrences, and Napoleon was able to scrutinize the prospective bridgehead at leisure.[123] By 4 July, all was ready. At 9pm the 129 heavy guns on Lobau began a crushing bombardment of the Austrians' forward positions, while boatfuls of infantry disembarked on the Danube's eastern bank. Behind this screen, the first of many bridges was swung into position within minutes, allowing the waiting army to begin streaming onto the Marchfeld. This time, the weather was also on Napoleon's side: tremendous downpours shrouded the proceedings; neither the Austrians' Bisamberg observatory nor most of their picquets discerned the enemy's movements.

In any event, Karl's army was in no position to dispute the crossing. The *Generalissimus* had remained convinced that nothing of significance was impending on the Marchfeld. Indeed, until 7pm on the 4th, when the Bisamberg observatory's last reliable report warned him that even Bernadotte's Saxons were crossing onto Lobau, he was more concerned about possible threats to Pressburg and Bohemia.[124] He promptly sent new orders to John, directing him to leave a small garrison at Pressburg and to edge closer to the *Hauptarmee* so as to be able to protect its left flank if necessary. Only at 5.30am on the 5th did Karl realize what was brewing. Belatedly, he summoned John to the Russbach with all possible speed.

Napoleon had around 85 000 men on the Marchfeld by then. Wheeling northwards, they annihilated several of the stunned Austrian outposts by the Danube before pausing to form up and cover the deployment of the second wave. *L'Armée d'Italie* duly arrived at noon, followed by the Saxons and the Guard. By 5pm, Napoleon's front line curled for roughly 20 kilometres from Leopoldau to Aderklaa and from there along the Russbach as far as Leopoldsdorf. Massena's corps faced the Bisamberg, while Bernadotte's, Eugène's, Oudinot's (who had replaced Lannes) and Davout's troops were approaching the Russbach. Wrede's Bavarian divi-sion and Marmont's small corps had still to come up, but, thanks to Berthier's meticulous planning, 180 000 men with 488 guns[125] had been moved into position with scarcely a hitch.

Karl, meanwhile, had drafted directives to unite his divided army on the Russbach, where he had belatedly ordered the construction of field-works. However, events unfolded so swiftly that his forces not only remained on two axes but also failed to coalesce; the area between Wagram and Gerasdorf, some 5 kilometres across, was almost devoid of troops. While he had been caught off his guard by Napoleon, both com-manders were again groping their way through the fog of war. Their armies were the largest yet seen in European history and were distributed along a commensurately long front. Gleaning dependable intelligence and controlling developments in such circumstances posed unprecedented difficulties. Whereas Napoleon appears to have surmised that the bulk of the *Hauptarmee* was already behind the willow-lined Russbach and that the seemingly paltry, disjointed Austrian forces west of Wagram could be contained by Massena's corps alone, Karl had no fewer than 55 000 men with 190 guns here. On the other hand, Napoleon was overly concerned about the approach of John's army, which had been progressively whittled down. Certainly, he was anxious to gain an advantageous position before the sun set and, glimpsing the chink in Karl's armour about Wagram, ordered an immediate assault on the Russbach.

Just beyond the steep, overgrown banks of that rivulet, along a ribbon of slightly rising ground, 90 000 Austrians with 256 guns were waiting. Napoleon evidently intended his *corps d'armée* to strike simultaneously: while Davout enveloped Markgrafneusiedl, Oudinot and Bernadotte, sup-ported by Eugène, were to thrust at Baumersdorf and Wagram respec-tively. However, because their forces were in differing states of readiness and had varying distances to cover, their attacks began sequentially. Shortly after 6pm, bitter fighting erupted at Baumersdorf. Despite com-mitting two divisions, Oudinot could not master the village, still less its bridges over the Russbach, which would have given his cavalry and guns access to the northern bank. By 8.45pm, he had been repulsed. In the interim, elements of Eugène's and Bernadotte's forces had come into action around Wagram; Dupas's division from the latter wheeled against the settlement itself, while General Macdonald led three divisions from the former across the Russbach to the east. Although Dupas was checked, Macdonald made considerable headway, almost piercing the Austrian lines. Once again, Karl plunged into the thick of the fighting, rallying retreating units and summoning fresh ones. The attackers were halted and, as Oudinot recoiled, the Austrians around Baumersdorf descended on their uncovered right flank. Already wearied and depleted by weeks of fighting and marches, this proved too much for Macdonald's regiments. They fled in panic over the Russbach just as Bernadotte was bringing up 10 Saxon battalions to bolster Dupas's faltering assault on Wagram.[126] In the growing darkness, the Austrians fell on them in turn. Some Saxons, speaking German and clad in white, were mistaken for the enemy and fired on by their own side, too.

By 11pm, Bernadotte had been repelled and had withdrawn as far as Aderklaa, which he abandoned shortly after. He blamed Napoleon for his defeat, alleging that the crossing of the Danube and the subsequent engagement had been mismanaged. Had he been in command, he asserted before several officers, he would have executed a 'scientific manœuvre' which would have compelled Karl to surrender 'almost without a blow'.[127] With the main assault repulsed, Davout also disengaged his troops about Markgrafneusiedl, bringing the battle to a halt.

It was clearly not over, however. Emboldened by his success, Karl resolved to attack at 4am with the fresh forces on his right while pinning the enemy to the Russbach with his left. John, it was hoped, would reinforce the latter as the day wore on. Yet barely had John received the orders issued to him at 7pm on the 4th when Karl started penning him those of 5.30am on the 5th. Arriving at 6pm, these, together with those of the 4th, reversed earlier directives he was still in the process of enacting. Gathering his bewildered units together, he finally set out for the *Hauptarmee* at 1am on the 6th. As even the eastern fringes of the Wagram battlefield were over 40 kilometres away, he had little prospect of arriving in time to influence the impending struggle. There was also a fatal delay in the dissemination of Karl's orders to the component corps of the *Hauptarmee*, with the result that the pinning attack on the Russbach commenced before the right wing's outflanking manœuvre.

Napoleon, meanwhile, had completed the concentration of his forces, tightening their front around a central reserve until Karl's intentions became clearer. When Davout came under attack around Glinzendorf at 5am, the emperor feared that John had already arrived and began to shift reinforcements to bolster his right. Karl, by contrast, baffled by the inaction of his own right wing, which was supposed to initiate the battle, ordered his left back to the Russbach. This reassured Napoleon, who now sent Davout in pursuit, directing him to envelop the enemy's position while Eugène and Oudinot assailed it frontally. As the Austrian units here braced themselves, those further west found Aderklaa unoccupied and promptly seized it. This development, which was as avoidable as it was unforeseen, threatened to compromise Napoleon's entire scheme; Eugène had to bend his left back to avoid being enfiladed and to maintain lateral contact with the Saxons, while Oudinot could only mark time. Infuriated by Bernadotte's thoughtlessness, Napoleon ordered the village's immediate recapture. No sooner had this operation commenced, however, than the Austrian VI, III and I *Korps,* debouching from the Bisamberg's foothills, loomed on the plain to the west. Karl's flank attack was finally beginning.

Confronted by an almost continuous chain of hostile units curling from Wagram through Aderklaa and Breitenlee to Essling, the relatively few troops on Napoleon's left were in danger of being overwhelmed and his communications with the Danube severed. The emperor was alerted to this danger at around 9am and immediately hurried over from the right wing. He arrived to find the Saxons, who had been caught in a withering crossfire between the enemy guns at Wagram and Aderklaa, in headlong rout. Bernadotte, trying to stop them, suddenly came face to face with his master. 'Is that the scientific manœuvre by which you are going to make the Archduke lay down his arms?', Napoleon enquired sarcastically. 'I remove you, sir, from the command of the army corps, which you handle so badly. Withdraw at once, and leave the Grand Army within 24 hours; a bungler like you is no good to me.'[128]

Though rallied by the emperor, the Saxons were incapable of renewing the savage struggle for Aderklaa; *l'Armée d'Italie* would have to plug the gap in the line here. Napoleon needed time to organize this and to counter the burgeoning threat to his left flank. As at Eylau, he looked to his cavalry to buy it. Accordingly, Bessières deployed the two *cuirassier* divisions from the reserves and stemmed the Austrian onslaught with a series of furious charges. In the interim, Boudet's division, left to guard the bridgehead, strove to block the enemy's progress at Essling, while Massena, hurriedly extricating the rest of his infantry from the fighting around Aderklaa, marched for Breitenlee.[129] To cover this manœuvre and support Bessières, Napoleon filled the void caused by Massena's departure and the retreat of the IX Corps with an immense battery comprising 112 guns drawn from the Guard and Macdonald's corps. Its fire, together with the cavalry's valiant charges, robbed the Austrian advance of its momentum. By noon, it had ground to a standstill; Karl had shot his bolt.

Davout, meanwhile, had made slow but steady headway against the archduke's left wing; enveloped in artillery fire, the Austrians were gradually ousted from Markgrafneusiedl and rolled up towards Baumersdorf. Glancing over his shoulder, Napoleon gauged the extent of Davout's progress from the pall of gunsmoke that accompanied his movements and, at 12.30pm, judging the battle to be 'ripe', ordered the delivery of the *coup de grâce*. Emerging on the grand battery's left, across wheatfields swept by fire, strewn with dead and injured and set ablaze in places by shells and burning wadding, Macdonald's 30 weak battalions, deployed in a huge, box-like formation, comprising columns on the sides and rear and lines at the front,[130] tramped, with shoulders hunched and heads bowed against the enemy's fire, towards the stalled Austrians between Breitenlee and Aderklaa. Arrayed on Macdonald's right- and left-rear respectively were Walther's Guard cavalry and Nansouty's battered *cuirassiers*. Simultaneously, Eugène and Oudinot thrust across the Russbach, while, to the south, Massena, aided by the heavy batteries on Lobau, swept General Klenau's VI *Korps* from Aspern. Plunging into the enemy's midst, Macdonald found, as he had anticipated, Austrian cavalry lapping against both his flanks. His columns formed squares and repelled the Austrian horsemen, only to be engulfed by hostile infantry supported by cannon around Süssenbrünn. Nansouty appears to have been too far back to give timely assistance, while Walther pleaded that he had no orders to intervene; Bessières had been wounded, leaving the French cavalry lacking overall direction.[131] Although Macdonald's comments about his losses have been misinterpreted by many past historians, Broussier's division, which he accompanied, certainly lost half its strength, as did most of his other units.[132] Only when reinforced by Wrede's Bavarians and the Young Guard could he press on and take Süssenbrünn.

Rather than risk his army's destruction, Karl now ordered a retreat towards Bohemia. In this, the largest battle yet seen in the gunpowder age, he had sustained approximately 42 000 casualties. Napoleon's forces lost some 37 500 men. However, a far higher percentage of the latter were killed or wounded rather than taken prisoner.[133] Nor could the French, exhausted and with their cavalry temporarily paralysed, exploit their breakthrough with a determined pursuit. Indeed, Napoleon could not even be confident that battle would not be rejoined the next day; Karl's army was beaten, but not routed.

The archduke, however, now regarded peace as essential and had no intention of risking another engagement save to preserve his forces. After a sequence of rearguard actions, he acknowledged the situation to be hopeless, signing an armistice at Znaim on the 12th. This virtually ended the conflict. The war faction, still dreaming of perpetuating it, was incensed. Cast as a scapegoat, Karl was stripped of the rank of *Generalissimus* and resigned as commander of the *Hauptarmee* on the 23rd. But his successor was no more able to repair either the psychological or the material damage it had sustained. Although the *Kaiser* refused to endorse the armistice until 18 July, and continued to haggle over peace terms until mid-October, resuming the war was fundamentally impracticable.

The British, too, were as reluctant to accept this unsavoury fact as they were to abandon the cherished hope that the sporadic outbreaks of disorder in corners of the *Rheinbund* would develop into a massive, popular revolt. The endeavours of the secret societies and the outpourings of the patriotic literati notwithstanding, this was never really likely, as

Dörnbergs, Kattes and Schill's abortive rebellions demonstrated. Yet if their failures were not proof enough, then that of the Duke of Brunswick-Oels should have convinced both Britain and Austria that their lingering expectations in this regard were not going to be fulfilled. As the Battle of Aspern–Essling was beginning, the duke – who had been dispossessed of his estates under Tilsit, following the death of his father at Auerstädt – issued a proclamation, urging the people of Germany to unite in a war for their 'lawful freedom' and fatherland. With a little band of dark-clad volunteers, popularly known as 'The Army of Vengeance' or the 'Black Corps', he participated in the Austrian forays into Saxony from Bohemia during June. Although they enjoyed some momentary success, even capturing defenceless Dresden, a derisory 300 Saxons 'of doubtful aspect' joined the duke's followers, who, behaving more like brigands than liberators, were dismissed as such by most of the population. Whereas the Austrians retreated at the approach of Jerome's X Corps and, with the signing of the Znaim armistice, ceased hostilities altogether, Brunswick bolted for the North Sea, embarking his remaining men for England on 7 August.[134]

Nevertheless, clutching at the hope that Franco-Austrian hostilities might be rekindled, Britain had belatedly commenced the Walcheren landing just days earlier. Long after that enterprise's disastrous culmination, a toehold was still being retained on the island, not merely because of its strategic importance to Britain but also to encourage Vienna to take up the sword again, to try to provoke a rebellion in Holland and to endeavour to postpone the fall of Portland's stumbling government.[135] That inevitably followed the expedition's demise, and a new ministry was eventually formed under Spencer Perceval. By then, however, Austria had conceded defeat. Stadion was replaced by Metternich, who was to remain at the helm of state for four decades. Precisely how long he anticipated France's hegemony in Europe would persist is unclear, but, in 1809, he resolved to replace Russia as her principal ally through a process of 'tacking, and turning, and flattering. Thus alone', he contended, 'may we possibly preserve our existence, till the day of general deliverance.'[136] Part of this disagreeable policy was the marriage of Francis's daughter, Marie-Louise, to Napoleon. Under the Schönbrunn Treaty, Austria also agreed to pay a crippling indemnity, limit the size of her army and cede still more territory not only to France, Bavaria and the Grand Duchy of Warsaw, but also to Russia. Although the news of this humiliating settlement was greeted with cheers in Vienna's streets,[137] the terms were lenient when compared to the treatment Napoleon had meted out to Prussia in 1807. Above all, the Habsburgs had secured their principal objective, the continuation of their dynasty.

The Tyrolian rebels were less fortunate. After Znaim, the greater part of the VII Corps was gradually diverted to their subjugation. The Bavarians were held at bay throughout the summer, prompting Napoleon to replace the hesitant Lefebvre with General d'Erlon. He launched a new, concentric offensive as soon as Austria's capitulation was formalized. Adapting his troops' tactics to the demands of mountain warfare, he seized the Alpine valleys to deprive his opponents of food and intelligence. By mid-November, the insurrection had been quelled.[138] Andreas Hofer, the most prominent of the rebels' leaders and another figure whose depiction in the romantic literature of the period bears little resemblance to his real nature and exploits,[139] was betrayed and executed.

Napoleon's triumph appeared complete. However, in contrast to his previous wars, conquering Austria had proved a protracted, troublesome affair; at Aspern–Essling he had suffered his first significant repulse and even his victory at Wagram had not secured the total destruction of Karl's army, which had fought with skill and heroism. All of this suggested that future conflicts, if they could not be avoided, might be more difficult to win. In fact, while the emperor was to prevail in numerous engagements during the next six years, he would never again conduct a victorious campaign.

Notes

1. C.D. Hall, *British Strategy in the Napoleonic War, 1803–15* (Manchester, 1992), p. 166; R. Muir, *Britain and the Defeat of Napoleon, 1807–15* (New Haven, CT, 1996), p. 27; P. Mackesy, *The War in the Mediterranean, 1803–10* (Cambridge, MA, 1957).
2. See M. Finley, *The Most Monstrous of Wars* (Columbia, SC, 1994), *passim.*
3. Finley, *The Most Monstrous of Wars*, pp. 70–2; Hall, *British Strategy*, pp. 87–8, 155–7.
4. Hall, *British Strategy*, pp. 87–8.
5. See Hall, *British Strategy*, pp. 163–6; and R. Carr, 'Gustavus IV and the British Government, 1804–9,' *English Historical Review*, 60 (1945), pp. 36–66.
6. NC, XV, p. 433. Also see C. Oman, *A History of the Peninsular War* (7 vols, Oxford, 1902–30), I, pp. 6–7.
7. See Hall, *British Strategy*, p. 167.
8. Quoted in D. Gates, *The Spanish Ulcer: A History of the Peninsular War* (London, 1986), p. 7. Also see NC, XV, p. 433.
9. See Oman, *History*, I, pp. 9–10.
10. Hall, *British Strategy*, pp. 167–8.
11. D.G. Chandler, *The Campaigns of Napoleon* (London, 1966), pp. 600–1.
12. Quoted in Muir, *Britain and Napoleon*, p. 6.
13. Muir, *Britain and Napoleon*, pp. 27–8, 35; Hall, *British Strategy*, p. 169.
14. See Hall, *British Strategy*, pp. 98–170; Muir, *Britain and Napoleon*, p. 35; C. Mullet, 'British Schemes against Spanish America in 1806', *Hispanic American Historical Review*, 27/2 (1947); J. Lynch, 'British Policy and Spanish America, 1783–1808', *Journal of Latin American Studies*, 1/1 (1969); W. Kaufman, *British Policy and the Independence of Latin America, 1804–28* (London, 1967).
15. See Oman, *History*, I, pp. 22–3; Muir, *Britain and Napoleon*, pp. 37–9.

16. *Parliamentary Debates from the Year 1803 to the Present Time* (31 vols, London, 1803–15), XI, cols 890–1.
17. See Oman, *History*, I, pp. 4–5; Lovett, *Napoleon and the Birth of Modern Spain* (New York, 1965), I, p. 115.
18. See Oman, *History*, I, pp. 16–23.
19. See Oman, *History*, pp. 36–8.
20. See Lovett, *Modern Spain*, I, pp. 88–100. Also see R. Herr, 'Good, Evil and Spain's Uprising against Napoleon', in R. Herr and H. Parker (eds.), *Ideas in History* (Durham, NC, 1965); J. Lynch, *Bourbon Spain, 1700–1808* (Oxford, 1989); R. Herr, *The Eighteenth-Century Revolution in Spain* (Princeton, 1958).
21. Quoted in Herr, *Revolution*, p. 118.
22. See Herr, *Revolution*, pp. 116–19.
23. See Hall, *British Strategy*, pp. 173–4; Muir, *Britain and Napoleon*, p. 63.
24. See A.D. Berkeley (ed.), *New Lights on the Peninsular War* (British Historical Society of Portugal, Almada, 1991), pp. 231, 236, 239.
25. For details of this astonishing escape see: Oman, *History*, I, pp. 367–75; J. Stewart, 'The Stolen Army' *Army Quarterly*, 66 (1953), pp. 24–31; and J. Robertson, *Narrative of a Secret Mission to the Danish Islands in 1808* (London, 1863).
26. See Oman, *History*, I, pp. 229–41.
27. Oman, *History*, p. 244.
28. Oman, *History*, pp. 242, 245.
29. Oman, *History*, pp. 245–62.
30. For details of the Convention and reactions to it, consult: Oman, *History*, I, pp. 263–300; and Muir, *Britain and Napoleon*, pp. 50–9.
31. See Oman, *History*, I, pp. 163–72.
32. See Oman, *History*, pp. 176–205.
33. Quoted in Muir, *Britain and Napoleon*, p. 53. Also see Hall, *British Strategy*, p. 172.
34. J. Moore, *A Narrative of the Campaign of the British Army in Spain Commanded by . . . Sir John Moore* (London, 1809), pp. 92–3. Also see Oman, *History*, I, pp. 473–538.
35. See Oman, *History*, I, pp. 539–96.
36. J.F. Maurice (ed.), *The Diary of Sir John Moore* (2 vols, London, 1904), II, p. 360.
37. See Muir, *Britain and Napoleon*, pp. 76–7.
38. Finley, *Most Monstrous of Wars*, p. 72.
39. Quoted in Hall, *British Strategy*, p. 174.
40. Quoted in J.J. Sheehan, *German History* (Oxford, 1989), p. 285.
41. See C. Duffy, *Frederick the Great: A Military Life* (London, 1985), pp. 295–6. Also see H. Delbrück, *History of the Art of War* (Westport, CT, 1985), pp. 249–51.
42. See W.H. Collins, *George Canning* (London, 1973), p. 215.
43. See O.W. Johnson, 'The Spanish Guerilla in German Literature during the Peninsular War', Berkeley (ed.), *New Lights on the Peninsular War*, pp. 347–56; and R. Wohlfeil, *Spanien und die Deutsche Erhebung, 1808–14* (Wiesbaden, 1965), *passim*.
44. L. Colley, *Britons: Forging the Nation, 1707–1837* (New Haven, CT, 1992). Also see H. Rothfels, 'Grundsatzliches zum Problem der Nationalität', *Historische Zeitschrift*, 174 (1952); E.N. Anderson, *Nationalism and the Cultural Crisis in Prussia, 1806–15* (New York, 1939); W.C. Langsam, *The Napoleonic Wars and German Nationalism in Austria* (Columbia, SC, 1930); H. Kohn, *Prelude to Nation-States: The French and German Experience, 1789–1815* (New York, 1967); H. Schulze, *The Course of German Nationalism: From Fichte to Bismarck, 1763–1867* (New York, 1985); H. Segeberg, 'Germany', in O. Dann and J. Dinwiddy (eds.), *Nationalism in the Age of the French Revolution* (London, 1988).
45. For a fuller discussion of their impact, consult Sheehan, *German History*, pp. 358–88; H. Kohn, 'Romanticism and the Rise of German Nationalism', *Review of Politics*, 12 (1950).

46. See N. Donath and W. Markov, *Kampf um Freiheit: Dokumente zur Zeit der deutschen Nationalerhebung* (Berlin, 1954), *passim*.
47. Consult, for example, *1808–14: Badische Truppen in Spanien* (Armeemuseum Karlsruhe/Deutsche Wehr am Oberrhein, Karlsruhe, 1939); R.M. Felder, *Das Deutsche in Spanien, oder Schicksal eines Wurttembergers während seines Aufenthaltes in Italien, Spanien und Frankreich* (Stuttgart, 1832–5); J. Schuster, *Das Grossherzogliche Würzburgische Infanterie-Regiment in Spanien 1808–13* (Munich, 1909); J. Walter, *A German Conscript with Napoleon* (Lawrence, KS, 1938).
48. J.M. Scherwig, *Guineas and Gunpowder: British Foreign Aid in the Wars with France, 1793–1815* (Harvard University Press, 1969), pp. 208–9, 212–13.
49. See P. Mackesy, *War in the Mediterranean*, pp. 311–34; Hall, *British Strategy*, pp. 176–7.
50. For details of these secret societies and their activities, see: *Augenzeugenberichten*, pp. 338–48; O. Dan, 'Geheime Organisierung und politisches Engagement im deutschen Bürgertum des frühen neunzehnten Jahrhunderts: Der Tugendbundstreit in Preussen', P.C. Ludz (ed.), *Geheime Gesellschaften* (Heidelberg, 1979); J. Voigt, *Geschichte des sogenanten Tugenbundes oder des sittlichwissenschaftlichen Vereins* (Berlin, 1850).
51. See Scherwig, *Guineas*, pp. 174–211; Collins, *Canning*, p. 215.
52. See Muir, *Britain and Napoleon*, pp. 89–90; Hall, *British Strategy*, p. 177.
53. Hall, *British Strategy*, p. 177.
54. F.L. Petre, *Napoleon and the Archduke Charles* (London, 1976 edition), pp. 13–14; G.E. Rothenberg, *Napoleon's Great Adversaries* (London, 1982), p. 123.
55. For details of *l'Armée d'Italie*, see S. Bowden and T. Tarbox, *Armies on the Danube, 1809* (Chicago, 1989), pp. 130–5.
56. Rothenberg, *Napoleon's Great Adversaries*, pp. 127–9; Petre, *Charles*, pp. 45–7.
57. Rothenberg, *Napoleon's Great Adversaries*, pp. 116–19, 126, 129; Petre, *Charles*, pp. 26–32; Bowden and Tarbox, *Armies*, pp. 16–17, 76–83.
58. Quoted in H. Rossler, *Österreichs Kampf um Deutschlands Befreiung: Die deutsche Politik der nationalen Führer Österreichs, 1805–15* (2 vols, Hamburg, 1940).
59. J.R. Arnold, *Napoleon Conquers Austria: The 1809 Campaign for Vienna* (London, 1995), p. 119.
60. Rothenberg, *Napoleon's Great Adversaries*, p. 139. Also see G. Rothenberg, 'The Archduke Charles and the Question of Popular Participation in War', CREP (1982).
61. For details of Napoleon's German allies during this campaign, consult G.H. Gill, *With Eagles to Glory* (London, 1992).
62. For details of the Austrian forces, see: Petre, *Charles*, pp. 18–21; Bowden and Tarbox, *Armies*, pp. 44–8.
63. Notably NC, XVIII, pp. 403ff. Also see C.G.L. Saski, *Campagne de 1809 en Allemagne et en Autriche* (3 vols, Paris, 1899–1902), II, pp. 122–4.
64. L.F. Lejeune, *Memoirs of Baron Lejeune*, ed. A. Bell (2 vols, London, 1897), I, pp. 215–16.
65. See Petre, *Charles*, pp. 78–82. For French archival sources relating to the 1809 campaign, see: ASH, C2 445–8 '*Campagne de 1809*'; C2 88–100 '*Correspondance: Armée d'Allemagne*'; and C2 673–83 '*Armée d'Allemagne*'.
66. Quoted in Rothenberg, *Napoleon's Great Adversaries*, p. 131. Also see Sheehan, *German History*, pp. 286–7.
67. Saski, *Campagne*, II, p. 162.
68. Consult J. Hiru, *Tirols Erhebung im Jahre 1809* (Innsbruck, 1909 and 1983); F.G. Eyck, *Loyal Rebels: Andreas Hofer and the Tyrolean Uprising of 1809* (New York, 1986); Gill, *Eagles*, pp. 321–84.
69. See Rothenberg, *Napoleon's Great Adversaries*, p. 146; Petre, *Charles*, p. 316; Gill, *Eagles*, pp. 279–82.

70. See R.M. Epstein, *Napoleon's Last Victory and the Emergence of Modern War* (Lawrence, KS, 1994), pp. 74–85.
71. For details see C. Binder von Krieglstein, *Der Krieg Napoleons gegen Österreich 1809* (2 vols, Berlin, 1902–6), I, pp. 194–206; Saski, *Campagne*, II, pp. 255–65; Petre, *Charles*, pp. 106–28.
72. For details see Petre, *Charles*, pp. 121–5; Gill, *Eagles*, pp. 81–6.
73. For details of Abensberg, see Binder von Krieglstein, I, pp. 226–49; Saski, *Campagne*, II, pp. 276–99; Gill, *Eagles*, pp. 81–6; Petre, *Charles*, pp. 106–28.
74. See Binder von Krieglstein, *Der Krieg*, I, pp. 256–67; Petre, *Charles*, pp. 146–54.
75. There is some controversy regarding Napoleon's view of this force, but it is difficult to accept Petre's reading of the situation. Compare: Petre, *Charles*, pp. 146–7, 155–6, 167; H.G. Bonnal, *La Manœuvre de Landshut* (Paris, 1905), pp. 163–5, 170, 226; Epstein, *Modern War*, p. 68; Rothenberg, *Napoleon's Great Adversaries*, p. 134; Gill, *Eagles*, pp. 93–5, 141; and Lejeune, *Memoirs*, I, pp. 221 and 239.
76. See Gill, *Eagles*, pp. 94–7; Petre, *Charles*, pp. 154–64.
77. For details of Eckmühl consult: Lejeune, *Memoirs*, I, pp. 226–32; Saski, *Campagne*, II, pp. 332–75; Binder von Krieglstein, *Der Krieg*, I, pp. 282–309; Gill, *Eagles*, pp. 141–4; Petre, *Charles*, pp.167–85.
78. Quoted in Sheehan, *German History*, p. 287.
79. See O. Criste, *Erzherzog Karl von Österreich* (Vienna, 1912), III, pp. 79–80.
80. See Binder von Krieglstein, *Der Krieg*, I, pp. 309–18; Baron M. de Marbot, *The Memoirs of Baron Marbot* (London, 1988), I, pp. 384–93; Lejeune, *Memoirs*, I, pp. 233–7.
81. See note 75 above.
82. See, for example, Eugène de Beauharnais, *Mémoires et Correspondence Politique et Militaire du Prince Eugène*, ed. A. du Casse (10 vols, Paris, 1859), V, pp. 150–2, 156–7.
83. Saski, *Campagne*, II, p. 368.
84. Binder von Krieglstein, *Der Krieg*, I, p. 319.
85. See Petre, *Charles*, pp. 209–11.
86. See Saski, *Campagne*, III, pp. 11–12.
87. Rothenberg, *Napoleon's Great Adversaries*, pp. 137–8.
88. For details consult: Lejeune, *Memoirs*, I, pp. 239–45; Petre, *Charles*, pp. 231–42; Rothenberg, *Napoleon's Great Adversaries*, p. 138; Gill, *Eagles*, pp. 190–3.
89. See Rothenberg, *Napoleon's Great Adversaries*, p. 139.
90. Binder von Krieglstein, *Der Krieg*, II, p. 163.
91. F.A. von Schonholz, *Traditionen zur Charakteristik Österreichs* (ed. by G. Gugitz, Munich, 1914), I, p. 194ff.
92. F. Kerst, *Die Erinnerungen an Beethoven* (2 vols, Stuttgart, 1913), II, p. 192.
93. J. Schimdt-Gorg and H. Schmidt (eds.), *Ludwig van Beethoven* (London, 1970), p. 175.
94. See H.C. Robbins Landon, *Beethoven* (London, 1970), p. 222.
95. Robbins Landon, *Beethoven*, p. 272.
96. For details see Epstein, *Modern War*, pp. 86–96; Rothenberg, *Napoleon's Great Adversaries*, pp. 141–5.
97. See, for example, NC, XIX, p. 24.
98. See Gill, *Eagles*, pp. 338–46.
99. For more details of these incidents see: H. Heitzer, *Insurrektionen zwischen Weser und Elbe* (Berlin, 1959); F. Thimme, 'Zu den Erhebungsplänen der preussischen Patrioten im Sommer 1808', *Historische Zeitschrift*, 86 (1901); R. von Katte, 'Der Streifung des Karl Friedrich von Katte auf Magdeburg im April 1809', *Geschichtsblatter für Stadt und Land Magdeburg*, 70–1 (1935–6); G. Baersch, *Ferdinand von Schills Zug und Tod im Jahre 1809* (Leipzig, 1860); *Augenzeugenberichten*, pp. 349–73; Gill, *Eagles*, pp. 424–34.
100. See, for instance, O.W. Johnston, *The Myth of a Nation: Literature and Politics in Prussia under Napoleon* (Columbia, SC, 1989); R.F. Arnold and K. Wagner,

Achtzehnhundertneun: Die politische Lyrik des Kriegsjahres (Vienna, 1909); S. Heit, 'German Romanticism: An Ideological Response to Napoleon', CREP, 1 (1980).
101. Petre, *Charles*, pp. 225, 245–6; Gill, *Eagles*, pp. 427–8.
102. Kriegsgeschichtliche Abteilung des K. und K. Archives, *Krieg 1809: Kriege unter der Regierung des Kaiser Franz* (4 vols, Vienna, 1907–10), IV, p. 335.
103. See J.J.G. Pelet, *Mémoires sur la Guerre de 1809 en Allemagne* (4 vols, Paris, 1824–6), III, pp. 434–5.
104. See Petre, *Charles*, p. 268.
105. Gill, *Eagles*, pp. 275–9, 282–6.
106. *Krieg 1809*, IV, p. 377.
107. *Krieg 1809*, IV, pp. 353–4.
108. Binder von Krieglstein, *Der Krieg*, II, pp. 214–17; D. Chlapowski, *Memoirs of a Polish Lancer* (Chicago, 1992), pp. 71–2.
109. P. de Pelleport, *Souvenirs Militaires et Intimes du Général Vicomte de Pelleport de 1793 à 1853* (2 vols, Paris, 1857), I, pp. 272–3; Lejeune, *Memoirs*, I, pp. 279–80; E. Gachot, *Histoire Militaire de Massena* (Paris, 1913), p. 173; Pelet, *Mémoires*, III, pp. 318–21; P. de Ségur, *Histoire et Mémoires* (Paris, 1887), III, p. 351.
110. See Rothenberg, *Napoleon's Great Adversaries*, p. 155; Binder von Krieglstein, *Der Krieg*, II, pp. 218–24.
111. J. Coignet, *The Note-Books of Captain Coignet, Soldier of the Empire 1799–1816* (London, 1985 edition), p. 176; Lejeune, *Memoirs*, I, p. 272.
112. See, for instance, NC, XIX, pp. 32–3.
113. Coignet, *Note-Books*, pp. 176–80; Chlapowski, *Polish Lancer*, pp. 72–5.
114. Marbot, *Memoirs*, I, pp. 433–4.
115. P. Triare, *Napoleon et Larrey* (Tours, 1902), p. 309; Chlapowski, *Polish Lancer*, p. 75; Lejeune, *Memoirs*, I, p. 292; Marbot, *Memoirs*, I, pp. 434–6; J.H. Dible, *Napoleon's Surgeon* (London, 1970), pp. 111–12, 114–15.
116. *Krieg 1809*, IV, pp. 700, 786.
117. See Epstein, *Modern War*, pp. 136–43; Rothenberg, *Napoleon's Great Adversaries*, p. 157; Petre, *Charles*, pp. 310–14; Bowden and Tarbox, *Armies*, pp. 153–8.
118. See Gill, *Eagles*, pp. 436–7, 347–50.
119. See, for example, *Krieg 1809*, I, pp. 578, 581–2.
120. Bowden and Tarbox, *Armies*, pp. 203–9.
121. Bowden and Tarbox, *Armies*, pp. 183–96.
122. For a more detailed summary of Napoleon's preparations, see Petre, *Charles*, pp. 329–43; and Binder von Krieglstein, *Der Krieg*, II, pp. 241–302.
123. Marbot, *Memoirs*, II, p. 7.
124. See Binder von Krieglstein, *Der Krieg*, II, pp. 358–61; Petre, *Charles*, p. 343; Gill, *Eagles*, pp. 291–4.
125. Bowden and Tarbox, *Armies*, pp. 183–96.
126. C. Rousset (ed.), *Recollections of Marshal Macdonald* (2 vols, London, 1892), I, pp. 329–30, 332–4.
127. Marbot, *Memoirs*, II, p. 30.
128. Marbot, *Memoirs*, pp. 30–1.
129. See Chlapowski, *Polish Lancer*, pp. 83–4.
130. Pelet, *Mémoires*, IV, p. 222; Lejeune, *Memoirs*, I, pp. 321–2.
131. *Recollections of Macdonald*, I, pp. 338–42.
132. Compare Chandler, *Campaigns*, p. 728; Chlapowski, *Polish Lancer*, pp. 86–7; C. Parquin, *Napoleon's Army: The Military Memoirs of Charles Parquin* (London, 1987), pp. 102–3; E. Gachot, *Napoleon et Allemagne* (Paris, 1913), p. 280; J.B.F. Koch (ed.), *Mémoires de Massena* (7 vols, Paris, 1848–50), VI, p. 427.
133. Rothenberg, *Napoleon's Great Adversaries*, p. 168.

134. See G. von Kortzfleisch, *Des Herzogs Friedrich Wilhelm von Braunschweig Zug durch Norddeutschland im Jahre 1809* (reprint of 1894 edition, Krefeld, Olmes, 1973); M. Exner, *Die Anteilnahme der Königlichen Sächsischen Armee in Sachsen im Jahre 1809* (Dresden, 1894), pp. 58–67; Gill, *Eagles*, pp. 438–55.

135. Hall, *British Strategy*, pp. 178–9; Muir, *Britain and Napoleon*, pp. 102, 105–7. For details of Walcheren, see G. Bond, *The Grand Expedition: The British Invasion of Holland in 1809* (Athens, GA, 1979); C.A. Christie, 'The Royal Navy and the Walcheren Expedition of 1809', in C.L. Symonds *et al.* (eds.), *New Aspects of Naval History* (Annapolis, 1981).

136. C. von Metternich, *Memoirs, 1773–1815* (2 vols, New York, 1970), II, p. 365; E. Kraehe, *Metternich's German Policy* (2 vols, Princeton, 1963–84), I, p. 104.

137. Rothenberg, *Napoleon's Great Adversaries*, p. 171.

138. See L. Harford, 'Napoleon and the Subjugation of the Tyrol,' CREP (1989); Gill, *Eagles*, pp. 350–84.

139. See Petre's comments in *Charles*, p. 224.

7

Trade Patterns and Resource Constraints

Politics has been defined as 'the art of the possible'; and war as 'the continuation of policy by other means'. Axiomatic though it might be, it is frequently overlooked that, in the pursuit of a given objective, the availability of resources often determines what can and cannot be attempted. Seldom have armed services in particular been wholly content with the personnel, equipment and supporting infrastructure at their disposal; some qualitative or quantitative improvement is almost always seen as desirable, if not essential, to meet this or that contingency, to bestow a supposed advantage, or to offset a perceived weakness. But whereas the demand for resources is potentially limitless, their supply is finite. Those that are available have to be allocated in the light of identified priorities; and, while, in war, the application of triage is perhaps at its most glaring in the treatment of wounded, difficult choices are ubiquitous.

Coming hard on the heels of those of the French Revolution, the Napoleonic Wars posed as many financial and political challenges to the belligerents as they did military ones. Although a far cry in many respects from the 'total' wars of the twentieth century, the struggle with France which dominated European affairs for some 25 years surpassed anything that had gone before in terms of its scale and costs. This resulted in, among other things, a far greater degree of state interference in the lives of individuals and across a much broader swathe of economic activity than had hitherto been the case. While the ruling dynasties of Europe had often been prepared to foster certain industries which were regarded as central to the preservation of state power, such as mining and the manufacture of armaments, this was essentially a byproduct of *Realpolitik* rather than part of a wider attempt to orchestrate their countries' economic development. In Frederick the Great's Prussia, for instance, military considerations dictated that economic self-sufficiency be developed as far as possible. Thus, agricultural reforms were aimed at securing an adequate supply of homegrown foodstuffs, while the Crown established a state bank, shipyards and its own agencies for the marketing of basic commodities such as salt, timber and iron ore. Although some private enterprise was encouraged through the provision of cheap supplies of materials from the royal monopolies, with protective tariffs, or with licences to engage in state-controlled activities, this was only done in so far as it was compatible with the Crown's aspirations; where it existed at all, interest in economic development as a modernizing power was governed by the creeds of cameralism.

Such state-regulated mercantilism contrasted with the thinking of Adam Smith and other *laissez-faire* theorists who believed that each individual was the best judge of his own interests and, if left to pursue them, would by so doing promote the wellbeing of all the members of society. Indeed, in some regards, libertarian attitudes constrained the interference of the state in the lives of individuals and of the population as a whole. Property was largely seen as sacrosanct. Similarly, the imposition of a graduated tax system was politically unthinkable and would in any case have sorely tested most government bureaucracies. While Pitt introduced a general income tax for the war against France,[1] it is doubtful whether, prior to the French Revolution, any government in the Europe of the eighteenth century could have contemplated, let alone levied, a graduated surtax, leaving low, flat-rate exactions as the only alternative.

Historians remain divided over the role played by such economic factors as taxation policies in the causes of the French Revolution. What appears to have been of significance, however, was not the burden of tax *per se* but rather its distribution: because of the vagaries of assessment and various exemption privileges, direct taxes fell primarily on the middle bands of the social spectrum, leaving the very poor and extremely rich comparatively unscathed. In fact, as a share of *per capita* output, the tax burden in Britain was significantly heavier than that in France at the time of the Revolution and had been for some 60 years.[2] Nevertheless, France's bankruptcy was the immediate cause of the Revolution, and her new, republican government was quick to introduce more uniform taxes as well as abolishing some aspects of feudalism, notably dues and tithes.

Other parts of Napoleon's legacy from the Revolutionary period also merit consideration, above all the land settlement. As the republic dared not risk alienating the lesser peasantry by engaging in the sort of grand teneurial reforms which would have revitalized French agriculture economically speaking, it sought to distribute land confiscated from the Church and nobility in a fashion which would both slow the peasantry's inevitable decline and give it a stake, however tiny, in the new order. The result was a patchwork of farmsteads, many too small to be efficient, and the preservation of some feudal practices. Strip farming and common grazing were still encountered, together with the concomitant customs of leaving land fallow and limiting crop rotation. Indeed, enclosure was often impracticable owing to a combination of the expense involved and the fragmentary nature of holdings; with millions tied to nugatory pieces of land, both labour and capital were largely immobile.

But in many areas the lesser peasantry were not the cardinal beneficiaries of reform. Whereas numerous peasants who began with no holdings actually remained landless, those who already had some property acquired more. Although this led to a net increase in the number of peasant proprietors, it strongly consolidated the position of the *bourgeoisie rurale*, the moderately wealthy peasants who formed the most conservative faction among French agriculturalists and who saw their holdings not as capital assets to be exploited but as patrimonies which endowed their families with a degree of independence.[3] Given the mutually reinforcing mentalities and structures that thus emerged within France's rural communities, they were unable and unwilling to make a direct contribution to the wider economy, unlike their counterparts in some other countries. The profit margins of the innumerable small and medium-sized plots were inevitably slim, generating little in the way of taxes or capital surpluses for investment, while low returns gave producers few incentives to venture beyond self-sufficiency. Not only did this mean that internal trade was stifled but also that peasants became entrenched in a sedentary, parochial life style, rendering manpower immobile and thereby depriving the industrial–urban sector of the economy of much-needed labour.

These trends, begun by the republic, could scarcely be reversed by Napoleon without dire political consequences for his regime. Indeed, he had to confirm them in some instances as he strove to reconcile opposing factions within French society. Whereas, for example, primogeniture had been outlawed during the Revolutionary epoch, equal inheritance, which had been a peasant custom, was formalized by him. Thus, handkerchiefs of land continued to shrink still further as they were divided up within families.[4] The outcome was that in 1815, and for decades thereafter, French agrarian society was to be much as it had been in 1789, while, across the country as a whole, the family unit had been firmly established as the cornerstone of economic activity.

This latter development can also be partly attributed to another aspect of the Revolution's legacy, the growth of individualism throughout French society. While this was to yield some benefits in the military field, notably in the initiative shown by the rank and file, which made them naturally adept at skirmishing and other activities where the onus fell on the individual soldier, so far as economic enterprise was concerned it was frequently a drawback. Not only did labourers exhibit a profound preference for individual work, they also shunned, and were rather inefficient in, collaborative, large-scale ventures. These tendencies manifested themselves at both the macro and the micro level. To the peasant, remaining on his morsel of soil and pursuing his own chosen life style seemed far more attractive than joining the faceless masses who toiled in urban employment. In proclaiming the gospel of liberty, equality and fraternity, the governments of the 1790s also shared this distaste for grand capitalism, be it in the guise of farmers, manufacturers or merchants, which exploited workers and turned inequality into profits. Despite ideological enthusiasm for free trade among the revolutionary leaders, they were suspicious and fearful of unfettered enterprise. Equally, manufacturers sought to safeguard their companies against reliance on capital from banks or the state, against merger, and even against expansion in order to retain their autonomy. As Clive Trebilcock has concluded:

> French-style individualism bred a passion for independence, and that, logically, required economic self-sufficiency, which in turn entailed a preoccupation less with risk-taking than with security. And security, under nineteenth century conditions, correlated readily with thrift. Little farms with gold coin bricked into their mantels or small firms 'drowning in their own liquidity' could be constructed with thrift, but not industrial empires or 'transformed' manufacturing sectors.[5]

A developed, unitary state, second only in population to Russia and with considerable natural resources, France was already one of the leading European powers on the eve of the nineteenth century. However, in his attempts to unlock more of her latent strength, Napoleon was to be thwarted by intractable structural problems. Above all a pragmatic rationalist, a child of the Enlightenment, who subordinated rights to efficiency where necessary, he strove to create an environment in which enterprise might flourish: French law in its entirety was codified; logical, versatile weights and measures, the metric system, were imposed; the Bank of France was established to support business credits and regulate government finance; international industrial exhibitions were staged; and, while the national bank was permitted to issue some notes in Paris, a metal-based currency – with the franc fixed at five grains of silver – replaced the Revolutionary *assignats*. Napoleon also centralized the control of education, concentrating, in contrast to the Revolutionary legislators who had favoured mass education instruments in general and primary schools in particular, on elitist secondary schools, the *lycées*, which drew their pupils principally from middle-class families and prepared them for a life of public service as doctors, functionaries and officers. Again, uniformity was stressed, both to ensure the maintenance of standards – the *baccalauréat* was introduced in 1809 – and to help foster a sense of national identity.[6] By 1813, the *lycées* were arguably the finest secondary schools in Europe, producing, among other state servants, that generation of bureaucrats who, amid the political instability which bedevilled France for so much of the nineteenth century, consistently served their country well.

As the empire expanded and the demand for qualified officials grew, however, Napoleon had to look to his vassals to provide some of them. Since the bourgeoisie was insufficiently developed in many countries to be used in this regard, local notables had to be employed, few of whom were of the same quality as the *lycée* graduates. Moreover, Napoleon had to curb his reforming zeal so as not to antagonize them; they were often allowed to retain their traditional, feudal privileges.[7] In other regards, too, in the light of local circumstances, pragmatism overrode principle, with the result that the *Code Napoléon*, though conceived as a set of universal principles founded on reason, was applied unevenly beyond France's frontiers. Moreover, although Napoleon's reforms created an environment conducive to economic opportunities, he could not guarantee that it would be exploited. Indeed, more use was made of the apparatus he forged in parts of Germany, notably in the Rhineland, where his imported system of government 'was in close harmony with the needs of a buoyantly industrialising economy',[8] than in France itself.

While still consul, Napoleon realized that France's military power needed adequate economic roots for its nourishment; although he could and did exact indemnities from her vanquished foes, war could never entirely pay for war. Accordingly, he sought to put France's public finances on a sturdy footing,[9] a task in which his reform of her governmental apparatus assisted greatly; for with an improved bureaucracy, a rigorous cadastral survey was a practical proposition, leading to a fall in the incidence of tax evasion. More efficiency within the state's administrative machinery also yielded considerable savings. At the same time that revenue collection was becoming more businesslike and productive, increased or new levies were also introduced: more indirect taxes were imposed, as was a 25 per cent surcharge on personal and property taxes. The result of all of this was that the public debt was kept firmly in check – it still only amounted to 60 million francs in 1814 – and Napoleon was able to count on annual tax receipts of between 430 million and 500 million francs.[10]

Impressive though this income was, it constituted but a fraction of the amounts raised by the great paymaster of the anti-French coalitions, Britain. Whereas almost all of the continent was, at best, at the proto-industrialization stage of development, she had been experiencing the effects of the Industrial Revolution for some time. This had sparked off significant increases in foreign trade, boosting yields from indirect taxes which were already being levied before the French wars even began. To these were added new measures, such as the introduction of an inheritance tax in 1796, the suspension of the paper pound's convertibility in 1797 and the imposition, two years later, of a graduated tax on all incomes exceeding £60. Together with a rationalization of stamp duty regulations and other efficiency savings, these steps increased revenue dramatically without choking the economic activity that generated it or provoking dangerous internal dissent. Thus, returns from customs and excise duties alone rose from £13.57 million in 1793 to just under £45 million in 1815, while, between 1806 and the Napoleonic Wars' end, £142 million in income tax was wrung from a population of around 18 million people – two thirds that of France.[11]

Nevertheless, government expenditure regularly outstripped income by between 25 and 30 per cent. Military spending alone climbed from £29 million in 1804 to nearly £113 million in 1815, while, over the whole of the 'Great War with France', it underwent a tenfold increase.[12] Indeed, estimates of the total costs incurred by Britain during the hostilities of 1793–1815 range from £1500 million to £1657 million. Since any shortfalls in the public finances had to be made good by borrowing, Britain's creditworthiness was central to her capacity to go on fighting. In the period 1811–13, for instance, her annual loans more than doubled to £38.4 million.[13]

But, for over 100 years, Britain had regularly used advances to pay for her wars. Indeed, this had been the primary consideration behind the establishment of the Bank of England, around which a network of strong and sophisticated finance houses gradually formed, headed by people such as Alexander Baring and Henry Hope. Ably assisted by these international bankers and underwriters, Pitt was able to borrow money at advantageous rates to fund the war against Revolutionary and Napoleonic France. Further, the alterations to property rights and the disruption of established trade patterns that occurred in the wake of the French Revolution and were perpetuated and extended during the course of the Napoleonic Wars not only transformed international commerce but also did so in a fashion which benefited Britain. In 1789, the stability which had prevailed on foreign exchanges since 1721 began to break down, as French and Dutch nobles and merchants started liquidating their assets and transferring the realized capital abroad. These *émigrés* made particular use of London's international merchant bankers, with the result that vast sums of money were moved there. Whereas in 1794 France's government had expropriated all French-owned foreign assets and their proceeds to finance the war against Austria and Britain, the latter responded with legislation which was both more just and politically expedient: any money owned by residents in France, 'or in any country, territory or place' under French control, and which was 'in the hands of His Majesty's subjects' was not confiscated but sequestered, thus securing it for Britain's use while simultaneously preserving the owner's legal entitlement to it. The funds were then deposited with the Bank of England and, administered by commissioners, were used to help finance the national debt. As Napoleon's empire expanded, the assets of citizens of other European countries were encompassed by this scheme, as were those of Americans following President Jefferson's imposition of an embargo in 1808. As early as 1806, not less than 8 per cent of Britain's national debt was being financed by such means.[14]

Together with millions of pounds in Bank of England deposits and accrued dividends which were effectively forfeited because their owners had died intestate,[15] these sequestered monies helped give Britain the capital injection she required as investment in agriculture and heavy industry gathered pace to meet the demands imposed by the war effort. The costs of increased land cultivation and enclosure at a time of tremendous industrial expansion and diversification were thereby alleviated. In turn, this process generated yet more demand for power, machinery and labour. The production of pig-iron, for example, a good indicator of economic activity, almost doubled to 244 000 tons in the period 1796–1806. Moreover, investment in new infrastructure – toll roads, canals, docks and so on – reached new heights, with Parliament approving record amounts of legislation to permit such projects to proceed.[16]

Given the way in which the war against Napoleon was paid for, all of this was of considerable importance. Since the 1680s Britain had financed forces on the continent through trade credits based on bills of exchange. These, purchased by the Exchequer from merchants in London, were forwarded to the army and used to pay for provender, foodstuffs, equipment and mercenaries. The suppliers then exchanged the bills for British merchandise, notably coveted colonial produce. So long as demand for this and other British goods existed, foreign traders were content to treat the bills as if they were specie and to accumulate credits in London, effectively investing in Britain's industries.

This system operated throughout the wars of the eighteenth century and Pitt depended on it in the early years of the struggle against Napoleon.[17] This did not escape the emperor's attention and, apparently influenced by the Chevalier de Guer's 1802 survey of Britain's finances, *État de la Situation des Finances de l'Angleterre et de la Banque de Londres*, he realized that, if markets could be closed to Britain's trade, either through conquest, diplomatic agreements, or a combination of the two, the mercantilist circle on which she depended to finance her own war effort and subsidize continental allies could be broken.[18]

Thus was born the concept of the Continental System, which was turned into reality by Napoleon's extensive conquests and concomitant alliances of 1806–10. So far as capital flows are concerned, until its introduction, record amounts of money were being transferred to Britain from the European mainland. However, the implementation and enlargement of Napoleon's blockade threatened to undermine Britain's capacity to pay for the war, particularly from 1808 onwards, when, in addition to having to find sufficient funding to subsidize her various alliances with Austria, Russia, Sweden and Prussia,[19] she took on protracted and substantial commitments in the Iberian Peninsula. Not only did she give financial support to Portugal and Spain, she also fielded an army which grew to 60 000 troops.[20] Indeed, the annual cost of the conflict in Portugal alone tripled to over £9 million in 1810, precipitating a crisis in Britain's public finances. While the government warned Wellington that the war in the Peninsula could not be sustained for much longer,[21] he responded with complaints that the shortage of specie might necessitate the dissolution of his Portuguese units and prevent him being able 'to take advantage of the enemy's comparative weakness in this campaign for sheer want of money'.[22]

So serious did the financial situation appear that, as early as August 1809, William Huskisson, Perceval's Secretary to the Treasury, was calling for substantial economies. During the Portland ministry, the cost of the war had climbed from an average of £37 million in 1805–7 to £44 million by 1809.[23] Yet, over the same period, tax receipts had faltered as attempts to impose new money-raising measures had failed to gain Parliament's endorsement. With little latitude for reducing the national debt, the capital and fixed-interest repayments on which amounted to some 6 per cent of the principal sum – which, by January 1807, had already exceeded £550 million[24] – the only way Huskisson could see of balancing the budget was savage reductions in expenditure: £1.5 million from the Navy, £2 million from the Army, £1 million from the Ordnance and £2 million from transport costs. Even if all these cuts were made, further loans and increases in taxation would be necessary, but, Huskisson maintained, these would be more acceptable politically in the light of the cabinet's determination to master public expenditure. Above all, confidence in the underlying robustness of Britain's economy, upon which the government's continuing ability to raise money depended, would be preserved.[25]

In the event, the spending reductions suggested by Huskisson proved unnecessary. Despite the additional problems caused by the USA's embargo of 1808,[26] during 1809 and 1810 the British economy proved more vibrant than anticipated. Rampant evasion notwithstanding, tax revenues increased without the introduction of new measures, and huge amounts of foreign capital were locked into Britain. Not only were the assets of overseas depositors converted into inexpensive loans to the Bank of England through sequestration, but also foreign merchants, caught between Britain's Orders-in-Council, Napoleon's Continental System and an unfavourable exchange rate, could neither realize their investments in British merchandise nor safely import the goods they had paid for; they effectively made interest-free loans to British industry.[27]

In short, even when Napoleon's System affected the physical flow of British products, it could not prevent capital streaming into London's coffers so long as European merchants were prepared to go on accepting British bills.[28] By so doing, they signalled their faith in the eventual triumph of Britain and her allies and in the resumption of her exports to the continent. It helped, of course, that Britain intermittently found new *entrepôts* to compensate for those lost elsewhere and that, because of her naval dominance, she could not only eliminate economic competitors by blockading their home ports and capturing their once-protected colonial markets but was also able to alter the direction of her trade with much greater ease than countries dependent on overland transport. For instance, no sooner had Spain's fleet been destroyed at Trafalgar than British merchants were able to commence infiltrating the markets of her Latin American possessions. Following the Iberian revolts against France in 1808, a treaty regulated Anglo-Portuguese commercial relations, while Spain, though refusing to formalize any arrangements, had to acquiesce in the continuing influx of British goods into South America. Between 1807 and 1812, the value of such imports rose from £1.2 million to £2.7 million. Trade with the Iberian Peninsula itself was still more lucrative, its value almost quadrupling from under £1.7 million in 1807 to over £6.7 million in 1809. By 1812, the region was absorbing 19 per cent of all of Britain's exports.[29] Similarly, as markets in Northern Europe were closed by Napoleon's decrees, British exports and re-exports to Southern Europe and the Mediterranean as a whole acquired greater significance. Whereas between 1800 and 1805 their annual value had averaged £4 million, between 1807 and 1812 this soared to over £9 million, accounting for 33 per cent of all Britain's exports.[30]

By means of the Continental System, Napoleon hoped to 'conquer the sea by the power of the land'.[31] Although he never claimed any economic expertise, in common with mainstream physiocratic and mercantilist thinking he concluded that the European mainland, though predominantly still at the proto-industrialization level of development and massively reliant on agriculture, would, because of its superior resources and population, ultimately prevail in any economic contest against a relatively tiny country which depended on its commercial and maritime strengths.[32] By endeavouring not so much to end as to control Britain's trade, he hoped to induce her capitulation; without a favourable trading balance, the 'Nation of Shopkeepers' would face bankruptcy, unemployment and possibly even revolution.[33] His Berlin and Milan Decrees of 1806 and 1807 respectively imposed economic sanctions which far exceeded in scale and complexity anything seen in earlier conflicts. Under the former, those parts of Europe within the System were forbidden to purchase either British goods or neutral cargoes transported in British hulls. In 1807, London retaliated with its Orders-in-Council – decrees issued, in theory, by the monarch without Parliamentary scrutiny – which stipulated that the continent was under blockade and that any shipping heading there must visit Britain *en route*, pay duty on its cargoes and purchase a licence, costing around £13,[34] before proceeding. Again, the objective was to control rather than eliminate trade, though it helped place the neutral powers in an invidious position; for Napoleon now had to tighten the System accordingly, proclaiming, with the Milan Decree, that any vessel complying with the Orders would be liable to seizure.

Between 1802 and 1807, neutral vessels trading out of British ports rose from 28 to 44 per cent of total tonnage.[35] American-flagged ships became ever more prominent as European carriers such as Denmark had their operations disrupted by both France and Britain, and as the tapping of the USA's immense resources boosted her participation in international trade. Indeed, between 1802 and 1810, her merchant marine expanded from 558 000 to 981 000 tons, while the value of her trade climbed from $60 000 000 in 1793 to $250 000 000 in 1807.[36]

Whereas commerce on this scale could only undermine Napoleon's boycott of Britain's merchandise, the British, seeing themselves as being engaged in a crusade on behalf of the rights and freedoms of all mankind, were equally anxious to regulate the USA's dealings with France and her allies. Irritated by America's behaviour, as early as 1805 James Stephen, MP, published a robust defence of Britain's entitlement to interpret the liberties of neutral shipping as she saw fit. In his *War in Disguise, Or The Frauds of the Neutral Flags*, he depicted Britannia as 'the bulwark and safeguard of all nations which the ambition of the enemy [seeks] . . . to conquer or destroy'.[37]

But, where the British talked of right, the Americans spoke of rights. Although both the Orders and Napoleon's decrees affected US shipping, because of the geostrategic situation in Europe it was primarily with

Britain in the form of the Royal Navy that difficulties arose. After diplomatic pleading had failed, President Jefferson tried to exact concessions from the belligerents with the Embargo Act of December 1807, which forbade any US vessel to sail from any home port for any foreign harbour and barred French and British shipping from docking in the USA. However, while this measure effectively reinforced the Continental System – indeed, from Napoleon's perspective it was the next best thing to an American declaration of war on Britain – it largely backfired on the USA. Whereas the porous Canadian frontier became a hotbed of smugglers, and New England's maritime interests and the South's cotton plantations were brought to the brink of ruin, the British, after some initial hardships,[38] secured timely access to Latin America's markets as Portugal and Spain rebelled against France. Consequently, when Washington's ambassador sought to wring concessions from London, George Canning, the foreign secretary, was able to disarm him with a flourish: 'The embargo is to be considered as an innocent municipal regulation which affects none but the United States themselves. His Majesty does not conceive that he has the right to make any complaint of it; and He has made none...'[39] One of Jefferson's last deeds as president was to repeal the Embargo Act.

James Madison succeeded him in 1809 and endeavoured to refine American policy with the passing of the Non-Intercourse Act. This restored commercial relations with the entire world save Britain, France and their respective dependencies. The president was empowered to suspend the operation of this legislation in favour of either belligerent that was prepared to lift its restrictions on American trade. London expressed its willingness to do this, but only in return for specific agreements, notably that the Royal Navy should be authorized to enforce American regulations against France. This was unacceptable to the USA, which, in May 1810, attempted to hone its economic coercion with a new law, Macon's Bill Number Two. This subtly altered the USA's stance from that of seeking to exact concessions to one of offering a virtual alliance in return for indulgences. While global trading links were reopened, Britain was advised that, if she rescinded her regulations, America would respond by imposing non-intercourse measures on France. Conversely, providing France revoked her decrees, the USA would institute sanctions against Britain.

Predictably, Napoleon was quick to grasp the opportunity afforded by this change of policy. In August 1810, the Americans were led to believe that the Berlin and Milan Decrees were being revoked on the understanding that, if Britain did not rescind her Orders, America would act against her. This boiled down to London choosing between the USA becoming an effective ally of France on the one hand and, on the other, Britain relinquishing many of the advantages stemming from her mastery of the seas. It would seem probable that Madison chose to treat this doubtful French promise as genuine in the hope of prising at least some concessions out of London. The British, by contrast, demanded tangible proof of the ending of Napoleon's embargo – a requirement which, incidentally, also featured in Macon's Bill – and thus called Madison's bluff when Congress renewed sanctions against them in March 1811.

With America's ambassador in London insisting that the Berlin and Milan Decrees had been revoked, while his colleague in Paris was vainly beseeching the French for some proof that they had been, the USA's policy became increasingly muddled. In fact, France's spoliation of neutral commerce around this time was actually as bad if not worse than Britain's, and Madison's approach neither appeased nor deterred either of the belligerent powers. Yet, although relations with Britain especially continued to worsen, there was little Congressional support for any attempt to prepare the USA for hostilities. The British, by contrast, responded to the American sanctions by deploying a few warships off New York and other major ports. One, the corvette HMS *Little Belt*, was bombarded on 16 May by the USS *President*, one of America's uncommonly large and heavily armed frigates, on the grounds that the latter had orders to protect neutral shipping from unlawful interference. In reporting the episode, both captains claimed to be innocent victims of aggression.

This had a predictable impact on popular opinion in their respective countries and helped accelerate the drift towards hostilities at a time when the British were, essentially because of domestic problems, edging towards conciliation. During 1810, recession had begun to grip the manufacturing regions of the British Isles, spawning an economic crisis that was to continue until early 1812.[40] With the Continental System at its zenith and most of mainland Europe closed to British trade, the reimposition of America's embargo deepened Britain's predicament. Parliament was soon inundated with petitions from merchants, manufacturers and industrial workers to amend the Orders. After the upheaval caused by Spencer Perceval's assassination by a disgruntled bankrupt in May 1812, Lord Castlereagh, foreign secretary in Lord Liverpool's new ministry, began to assume a more compromising stance. As early as April, the cabinet had announced that, if France would formally rescind her decrees, the Orders would likewise be withdrawn. Napoleon had responded by circulating the so-called Decree of St Cloud, which purported to be a revocation of the Berlin and Milan Decrees dating from April 1811. It was a fabrication of course, but, as it suited its domestic political purposes, the British cabinet accepted it as genuine evidence of repeal. Accordingly, on

23 June 1812 – the day Napoleon's invasion of Russia began – the Orders were, with some qualifications, revoked, Castlereagh commenting that 'One does not like to own that we are forced to give way to our manufacturers.'[41]

Regrettably, Britain's capitulation to the USA's demands came too late to avoid hostilities, for, on 1 June, Madison had persuaded Congress to declare war. Indeed, there were pitfalls in the economic struggle for all concerned. The Continental System, for instance, bred discontent among middle-class consumers especially because colonial products such as tobacco, cotton, tea, spices, coffee and sugar became rare and expensive. Manufacturers had problems obtaining modern machinery, which could only come from Britain, with the result that French technology lagged badly. For example, even the most up-to-date textile machinery in use in 1815 comprised designs which the British had abandoned by the 1790s – and much of this was powered not by steam but by water or horses. In fact, the entire French economy could boast only 65 steam-driven factories as late as 1820.[42] Similarly, the battlefleet and merchant marine had problems procuring supplies, which normally originated in the Baltic, and this, coupled with the crippling British blockade and the loss of colonial markets, drove economic activity off the seaboard. During the early 1800s France's overseas commerce all but disappeared, inflicting lasting structural change on her economy. Once-great ports such as Nantes and Marseilles declined, with external trade not regaining its 1789 levels until 1825.[43]

As French export values sank from 456 million francs in 1806 to 330 million three years later and a run of good harvests depressed grain prices, Napoleon, anxious to avoid rising unemployment, began adjusting the Continental System.[44] During 1809, partly to raise revenue to pay for the Austrian war and partly to further the aim of draining Britain's specie reserves, he authorized the sale of surplus wheat to the British, whose crops had failed.[45] Likewise, in 1810, with measures contained in the Trianon and Fontainebleau Decrees, he tried to combat smuggling, inveigle the USA into joining him against Britain, secure some colonial produce for his acquisitive subjects and revive French exports.[46] Licences, obtainable for a fee, were issued to American merchants especially, who, on condition that they balance their imports with purchases of equivalent amounts of French products, notably silks, were allowed to sell goods in France.

This breaching of his own boycott suggests that, at this juncture at least, Napoleon valued the System more for its wider political impact than any immediate economic effect. He appears to have concluded that, while Britain was too robust to bankrupt directly, by giving French traders preferential treatment at the rest of Europe's expense, he could put indirect pressure on London; economic hardship on the continent and elsewhere would curtail demand for Britain's goods and exacerbate anglophobia, with 'Perfidious Albion' being blamed for the continuation of the war. Indubitably, this policy did conciliate the USA and secure the imposition of American sanctions on Britain in March 1811. That deepened Britain's existing recession, turning it into a crisis. Simultaneously, however, the strain Napoleon's measures put on his relations with Sweden and Russia proved too much; they defected, giving Britain timely access to new markets. After the subsequent Franco-Russian War of 1812, the System all but vanished as Napoleon's allies deserted him and his enemies rolled back the frontiers of French influence.

If Napoleon intermittently modified his boycott of British trade to relax domestic tension, Britain was no less willing to be selective in applying her Orders when circumstances warranted it. The principles of the 1807 regulations notwithstanding, her government issued licences for the import and export of prohibited merchandise, allowed ships to enter and leave ports which were nominally under blockade and even admitted French vessels to her harbours on certain occasions.[47] Whereas her policy could accommodate a degree of flexibility, Napoleon had to be much more consistent in his and, to be successful, close not only Europe's markets to British trade but also those further afield, notably in the USA. After Trafalgar deprived him of any direct means of achieving the latter, he cleverly manipulated Britain's attitude to neutral shipping to bring it about, the resulting American embargo conflating with his own sanctions to bring Britain close to ruin.

If Napoleon occasionally underestimated Britain's economic resilience, then so did her own government. However, he was keenly aware of the costs to France and the rest of the continent that the breaking of British mercantilism entailed.[48] As the warring parties' various sanctions distorted economic activity, businesses and banks were ruined, and the incidence of unemployment, crime and prostitution increased. The wave of company failures which hit the European mainland in 1811 was probably not as large as that in Britain, but it did compel the emperor to implement emergency measures to alleviate hardship, some of which were actually coordinated with London.[49] Indeed, in prosecuting his economic war, he did show some restraint which, with hindsight, might appear imprudent: his pragmatism and mercantilist leanings deterred him from taking action against the international banking system which was crucial to Britain's ability to resist him. Although this was recognized and there was a suggestion that the acceptance, endorsement, discount or payment of any bill to the benefit or credit of any British subject should be outlawed,[50] he declined to act, reasoning that any such step might damage his own as well as Britain's interests. Instead, he hoped slowly to exhaust her credit.

There were other flaws in the thinking behind the Continental System, too. While the embargo turned Britain's attention to markets beyond Europe – a process that was to continue until well into the twentieth century – the interdiction of their overseas trade compelled the other European states to look nearer home for potential customers. Not only did this necessitate the migration of industrial activity from, for example, France's coastline to her northern and eastern reaches, it also led to a growing dependence on land, as opposed to sea, transport, which was palpably less efficient, at least so far as the movement of bulk loads was concerned. For a mixture of economic and military purposes, Napoleon built or improved some 64 000 kilometres of roads and 200 of canals.[51] Impressive though this was, it was inevitably insufficient. However, with both the agricultural and the mercantile sectors of the economy generating little surplus capital, funding for such infrastructure was scarce and costly. Building work was, moreover, labour-intensive, and manpower was in short supply.

It is of course easy to disparage many of Napoleon's policies. One recent study, for instance, has suggested that:

> To the extent that the empire brought reform at all, it did not result from disinterested benevolence, but rather from a desire to exploit the Continent more effectively. Undermined by ... Napoleon's wars ... reform also took second place: where the emperor wanted to win the support of traditional élites, the abolition of feudalism was diluted; when he wanted to reward his followers with great estates, administrative rationalization was set aside; and when schools vied for revenues with armies, it was the latter which won.[52]

These are perfectly valid observations, but the implied disapproval seems incongruous if only because it betrays a lack of empathy. Surely, the essence of imperialism is exploitation. The only remarkable thing about Napoleon's empire from this perspective is that, through the classic methods of military conquest and political and economic subjugation, it applied colonialism to the heart of the developed world. Equally, his preference for soldiers rather than students is uncontroversial. Did *any* European government of the time rate schools above armies? The extent of illiteracy on the continent all of 50 years later attests that they did not.[53] The point here is that it is not just the abundance or scarcity of resources that determines their allocation but also the prevailing *mentalité* of the times. Napoleon's enlightened despotism was derived from the model of the eighteenth century. His domestic policies were broadly consistent with those pursued by other monarchs whose aspirations were shaped by the same forces and tempered by similar constraints. Indeed, with regard to numerous issues, it is hard to see what alternative policies he could have pursued, even if he had wanted to. It is not clear, for example, what coercive instrument he might have substituted for the Continental System.[54]

While there were indubitably European regions which suffered economically under the French *imperium*, others prospered, if only in spite of Napoleon rather than because of him. With French industries starved of manpower by conscription and atomistic individualism and often slow to embrace the economic opportunities stemming from the emperor's reforms, producers elsewhere were effectively shielded from competition at a time when his armies and the millions of consumers within the empire formed a captive market. In Germany, for instance, towns such as Aachen benefited from a surge in textile production, while the Roer Department was transformed from being an almost exclusively agricultural area in 1799 to an industrial centre employing 65 000 workers by 1815. Saxony and the Duchy of Berg also enjoyed such spectacular growth in their textile industries that the latter became known as 'Little England' and the former, despite crude technology and a shortage of capital, not only competed with Britain in some lines but also established a dominant position in the European hosiery trade.[55] Similarly, the exclusion of colonial products from the continent stimulated the quest for alternatives: sugar beet was introduced to offset the loss of cane plantations; chicory was substituted for coffee beans; woad was used in place of indigo; and the French especially learned to make muslins, percales and calicoes, the output of their cotton industry rising fivefold between 1806 and 1812.[56] Likewise, as so much of European industrialization relied upon the diffusion of British 'best-practice' technology, when this process was interrupted the continental states had to look to their own ingenuity. Joseph Jacquard devised a highly efficient loom; Nicholas Appert perfected the art of canning food, which was quickly exploited by the military commissariat; and Lieven Bauwens introduced British methods of cotton manufacture into Belgium.[57]

Other reverberations of the Napoleonic revolution were felt well beyond France's borders. That the application of the *Code* in particular and reform in general was selective, incomplete and only partially successful is hardly surprising. Given the degree of social and regional diversity, vested interests and the turbulent times, there were bound to be gaps between aspirations and accomplishments. Neither were there many resources nor even much time for the enaction of reforms, making what was achieved all the more remarkable. Napoleon's ephemeral intrusion into Germany, for instance, directly and indirectly brought about innovations which were central to the region's future organization, development and prosperity. As his embargoes excluded British products, notably textiles, from the continent, native industries were spawned or, as in the case of Saxony, protected. A new generation of lawyers, manufacturers and functionaries sprang up in German cities and, if the landed aristocracy's resilience and sheer deviousness meant that initially the *Grundherrschaft* was tinkered with rather than dismantled, in the Rhineland especially the peasants were to benefit as seigneurialism gradually faded away. Everywhere, state power and bureaucratic rule were affirmed and consolidated. Nor should the immediate and longer-term impact of Napoleon's victories, notably Jena–Auerstädt, be overlooked. If conflict, or the threat of it, acted as a catalyst for changes in the structure and ethos of military forces, it also helped begin or accelerate a process of economic liberalization and administrative reform.

Views of the Continental System vary. But even if, like Crouzet,[58] one concludes that it was as damaging to Europe's economies as it was ineffective in curbing Britain's trade, it should not be forgotten that it was part of a bigger contest. Both Britain and France sought supremacy by inflicting pain on those caught between them. The former's victories by sea and the latter's by land reshaped international commerce to their advantage alone. Nor were the System's participants the only ones to suffer. Spain, supposedly Britain's ally, was profoundly suspicious of the immense damage inflicted by rampaging redcoats on the great trade centre of San Sebastian when the city was liberated in 1813. Similarly, Britain's ruthless treatment of neutral countries was often seen as having ulterior motives; President Madison, for example, surmised that her spoliation of the USA's commerce was inspired not by a desire to stop France receiving imports, for Britain was quite willing to provide them herself, but to acquire a monopoly on trade and carriage.[59] Given the extent of her naval and industrial supremacy, however, Britain's eventual triumph in any exclusively economic contest was virtually assured. Once the measure of protection afforded by Napoleon's System was removed, businesses and jobs were swept away by a deluge of British imports with which local producers could scarcely compete. One might conclude that this would have occurred anyway; the process was already evident in the 1790s, and Napoleon's attempts to create a monolithic bloc with the wherewithal to resist it only postponed the inevitable.

Although the 30 years straddling the Revolutionary and Napoleonic Wars were inauspicious times for France's economy, Napoleon's fiscal and administrative reforms enabled him to exploit many of the resources that were available with greater effect than his predecessors. Besides equipment, which, until the need to make good the losses incurred during the 1812 and 1813 campaigns imposed demands that were as abrupt as they were huge, was manufactured in adequate quantities, manpower and horses constituted the basic needs of the emperor's armies. Horses were required for the cavalry and for tractive power, both functions demanding trained animals. Just how many of these noble, loyal creatures perished in the course of the Napoleonic Wars is unknown, but the French alone lost scores of thousands just in the Russian campaign. Supplies of colts were usually quite plentiful, but procuring sufficient numbers of mature, trained horses became increasingly problematic and, by 1813, was having a seriously detrimental effect on the operations of the French forces in both Spain and Germany.

Similarly, good-quality personnel became scarcer as almost ceaseless warfare took its toll. By the end of the eighteenth century, most European countries had arrangements for the mobilization of the male population in times of emergency. However, these were cosmetic: besides the constraints imposed by limited administrative capabilities and equipment inventories, there were numerous exemptions from military service, notably for married men, those divorced or widowed with dependants, and those wealthy enough to purchase a substitute. Regular armies were relatively small, and compulsory military service could often be performed in militia or garrison units of some description.

All of this was transformed by the Napoleonic Wars. If the French *levée en masse* of 1793 was the conceptual precedent, it was during the early 1800s that the expansion of armies to unheard-of sizes really occurred. *La Grande Armée* with which Napoleon struck into Germany in 1805 amounted to 200 000 troops, while he was to assemble all of 600 000 men for the Russian campaign. His opponents had no choice other than to mobilize their own manpower on a similar scale. Thus, at Leipzig, 570 000 troops were engaged in the largest battle Europe had ever seen. War theatres also expanded commensurably; French armies ranged as far as Moscow and Lisbon in search of victory.

This type of warfare took scores of thousands of young – and some not so young – men far away from the life they had known. They intruded into the lives of others, often with ruinous consequences. Frequently, a dozen or more soldiers might be billeted with some wretched, frightened householder and his family.[60] Everywhere, war brought destruction in its wake. As a British sergeant discovered while marching with his unit from Stralsund to the Elbe in September 1813:

> The country had been overrun with troops, alternately friendly and hostile; but (whether one or the other) draining [the settlements] of their resources, driving away their cattle, and producing the utmost desolation; so that

though the inhabitants of the villages were extremely kind to us, it was not in their power to furnish us with any provision, even for money. The only inhabitants indeed remaining in the villages were old men and women, and young children, no cattle, no horses, sheep, pigs or poultry.[61]

Here, as elsewhere, the able-bodied men had been incorporated into the various armies. Some volunteered, but most were conscripted, often ahead of their time. Although large numbers managed to evade the draft, in France for instance Napoleon made it far more efficacious than it had been in the Revolutionary epoch, when only one third of those summoned to the tricolour ever materialized. In the period 1799–1805, two million men became eligible and 1.25 million were called up, roughly 25 per cent of whom were rejected on health grounds. Throughout Napoleon's reign, some 2.1 million Frenchmen were mobilized.[62]

By 1809, the attrition caused by incessant wars was leading to a marked deterioration in the quality of his forces. Whereas *La Grande Armée* of 1805 had consisted of seasoned, professional, well-drilled troops, the army fielded in Germany during 1809 contained substantial numbers of inexperienced conscripts who were incapable of performing sophisticated tactical evolutions. Napoleon sought to offset this weakness by bolstering his infantry with more artillery. In any event his opponents were fielding ever larger numbers of guns, with the result that subsequent battles, notably Wagram and Borodino, were dominated by huge artillery duels.

The deadly effects of this firepower were reflected in massive casualty lists. But, for all the armies of the period, strategic consumption tended to pose a bigger threat than battle itself; thousands of men were lost through desertion, straggling, exhaustion, malnutrition and disease. This was seen at its starkest during the Russian campaign of 1812, when both sides suffered dreadfully. That campaign, however, virtually destroyed every trace of Napoleon's original *Grande Armée*. The forces he fought with thereafter had to be created at short notice and lacked equipment, experience, training and officers.

As the search for manpower became more desperate, draft evasion worsened and the cost of substitutes rose from 1500 francs in 1805 to 15 000 in 1812.[63] Not even affluent nobles and bourgeoisie were always willing or able to pay such sums, and their numbers in the military steadily grew. Napoleon simultaneously sweetened the pill and exploited their vanity by allowing them to join his Horse Guard, providing that they furnished 1000 francs each year for their upkeep and paid for their own mounts and equipment. This led to the creation of several 'Guards of Honour' units at a time when the army's cavalry arm was fatally weak.[64]

Along with the selling of commissions, such practices were to be indulged in by the other belligerent states, too, all of which had their own peculiar resource problems. Britain, for example, nominally introduced compulsory military service for all men with the Levée-en-Masse and Training Acts of 1803 and 1806 respectively. However, given that life in His Majesty's services was far from alluring, that the state bureaucracy was incapable of implementing mass mobilization and that such a step, had it been practicable, would have been politically unacceptable, little actually came of this. While the regular army increased from approximately 150 000 personnel on 1 January 1804 to a peak of 260 000 in late 1813, no fewer than 54 000 men were overseas recruits such as French *émigrés*, Caribbean slaves, Hannoverians and Brunswickers.[65] Further, many of these troops had to be used to stiffen the militia and volunteer units whose cardinal functions were safeguarding the homeland and preserving law and order. As late as 1811, for instance, some 56 000 regulars were stationed in Britain, 17 000 of them in Ireland.[66] A further 76 000 were needed to garrison Britain's colonial possessions, while securing Sicily and other outposts consumed several thousand more. When a further allowance is made for wastage – 17 000 men per annum between 1803 and 1807, and 24 000 thereafter[67] – it becomes apparent why the British were chronically short of troops for operations on the European mainland. Indeed, in late 1809, with expeditions simultaneously underway in the Peninsula and at Walcheren, the British still had fewer than 80 000 men on the continent.

Although Napoleon failed in Spain and Russia largely because of a lack of resources and a viable long-term plan for their employment, within our period there is no better illustration of the interaction of trading concerns, limited means and military strategy than the Anglo-American conflict of 1812–15. Preoccupied with the struggle in Europe, Britain suddenly found herself obliged to divert precious forces beyond the Atlantic. Few could be spared. This heavily circumscribed the type of warfare that could be prosecuted. Even if substantial numbers of troops had been available, vessels to transport them were not. In any case the War of Independence had underscored the futility of trying to acquire and retain territory on the American continent; a few relatively inexpensive blows against carefully selected targets would have to suffice. Britain's mostly encouraging experience with amphibious operations seemed to have much to offer from this perspective; although Walcheren had been a serious setback, time and again the fundamental efficacy and flexibility of maritime power had been demonstrated in operations along the Spanish coastline especially. As the USA was a democracy in which the people, as electors, were deemed to have at least some responsibility for their government's policies, attacks on towns were singled out as being both legitimate and potentially decisive. Bold *coups* by enterprising naval squadrons, their reach and hitting-power enhanced by a few thousand marines, might spread panic and division among the population, persuading the American leadership to sue for terms lest its own electorate might turn against it.

For their part, the USA's tiny armed forces were quite incapable of safeguarding her vast littoral. Moreover, the country was divided over the War's aims and necessity: the northern, maritime states were favourably disposed towards Britain and, it was feared, might make a separate peace or even secede from the Union; for various economic and strategic reasons, the south, by contrast, was eager to annex Florida; while the west, which was suffering from recession, blamed Britain's interference with American exports and perceived confrontation with the Royal Navy and expansion at the expense of Canada to be a solution to its ills.

While American privateers joined the *guerre de course* and harassed British shipping far and wide, the Royal Navy soon sealed off the US coastline and, despite the occasional loss of a minor vessel in one-to-one engagements, secured almost total naval supremacy. American exports, which had stood at $45 million on the eve of the war, plummeted to $25 million in 1813 and only $7 million in 1814.[68] Meanwhile, incendiarism, Britain's sole available stratagem, was enthusiastically applied to the settlements of the Chesapeake and Delaware Bays, and an attempt to invade Canada was checked. Nevertheless, when asked by the cabinet in early 1814 how Britain might deliver 'some blow which might immediately bring the war . . . to an honourable termination', Wellington replied that 'I do not know where you could carry on . . . an operation which would be so injurious to the Americans as to force them to sue for peace, which is what one would wish to see. . .'.[69] Equally, however, the Americans were incapable of dealing a conclusive blow. Although they demonstrated the limitations of the British amphibious raids with their staunch defence of Baltimore, they had few real gains to show for their efforts. With the military situation virtually deadlocked, both sides eventually settled for peace without victory.

Before news of the conflict's end could be fully disseminated, the British were to launch another major raid, this time on New Orleans. Unable to exploit their superior manœuvrability or to deploy adequate artillery support because of the terrain, they were obliged to attack entrenched defenders head-on. Repelled with heavy losses, they retreated to their ships. Resource constraints had determined their overall strategy and, on this occasion, imposed tactical limitations which proved disastrous. Nevertheless, given the cabinet's circumscribed objectives and the need to minimize the commitment of men and *matériel* to the American theatre, the amphibious operations were the most cost-effective means available of conducting the war.[70]

Notes

1. See A. Hope-Jones, *Income Tax in the Napoleonic Wars* (Cambridge, 1939).
2. C. Trebilcock, *The Industrialisation of the Continental Powers, 1780–1914* (London and New York, 1981), pp. 112–21.
3. G. Lefebvre, *Les Paysans du Nord* (Lille, 1924), pp. 498–504.
4. Trebilcock, *Industrialisation*, pp. 133–5; R.B. Holtman, *The Napoleonic Revolution* (New York, 1967), p. 93.
5. Trebilcock, *Industrialisation*, p. 137.
6. Holtman, *Revolution*, pp. 139–62.
7. Holtman, *Revolution*, p. 110.
8. H. Kisch, 'The Impact of the French Revolution on the Lower Rhine Textile Districts', *Economic History Review*, 15 (1962), p. 326.
9. A. Cunningham, *British Credit in the Last Napoleonic War* (Cambridge, 1910), pp. 13–14.
10. See Holtman, *Revolution*, pp. 100–3; L. Bergeron, *L'Épisode Napoléonien: Aspects Intérieurs, 1799–1815* (2 vols, Paris, 1972), I, pp. 52–62; G. Thuillier, *La Monnaie en France au début du XIXe Siècle* (Geneva, 1983), pp. 92–106.
11. N.J. Silberling, 'The Financial and Monetary Policy of Great Britain during the Napoleonic Wars', *Quarterly Journal of Economics*, 38 (1923–4), 214–33; E.B. Schumpeter, 'English Prices and Public Finance, 1660–1822', *Revue of Economic Statistics*, 20 (1938), pp. 21–37; J.M. Sherwig, *Guineas and Gunpowder* (Cambridge, MA, 1969), p. 352.
12. See B.R. Mitchell and P. Deane, *Abstract of British Historical Statistics* (Cambridge, 1967), pp. 288–96.
13. Schumpeter, 'English Prices'.
14. See L. Neal, *The Rise of Financial Capitalism* (Cambridge, 1993 edition), pp. 206–11.
15. Neal, *Rise*, p. 214.
16. Neal, *Rise*, p. 216.
17. Sherwig, *Guineas*, p. 18.
18. See Cunningham, *Credit*, pp. 32, 85–146.
19. See C. Emsley, *The Longman Companion to Napoleonic Europe* (London, 1993), pp. 135–6.
20. C.D. Hall, *British Strategy in the Napoleonic War* (Manchester, 1992), p. 212; R. Muir, *Britain and the Defeat of Napoleon 1807–15* (New Haven, CT, 1996), p. 154.
21. See WSD, VII, pp. 69–70.
22. WSD, VII, p. 318. Also see WD, V, pp. 434, 536; WSD, IX, p. 266; Cunningham, *Credit*, pp. 72–5.
23. Muir, *Britain and Napoleon*, p. 111.
24. Neal, *Rise*, p. 211. It stood at £563 million in 1802 and was to reach £834 million in 1815.
25. Muir, *Britain and Napoleon*, pp. 110–12.
26. See J.A. Frankel, 'The 1808–9 Embargo against Great Britain', *Journal of Economic History*, 42 (1982).
27. See J.M. Herries, *Review of the Controversy Reflecting the High Price of Bullion and the State of our Currency* (London, 1811), pp. 44–5.
28. For example, a substantial part of the subsidy paid to Spain in 1808 consisted not of specie but of Treasury bills. Similarly, in 1809, £466 000 was transferred in specie, but £2 174 000 was raised locally through the sale of bills. In 1810, the figures were £679 000 and £5 382 000 respectively. See Hall, *British Strategy*, p. 174; Muir, *Britain and Napoleon*, p. 118.
29. Hall, *British Strategy*, pp. 93–4.
30. Muir, *Britain and Napoleon*, p. 165. Also see Emsley, *Napoleonic Europe*, pp. 132–3.

31. Quoted in Holtman, *Revolution*, p. 58.
32. Cunningham, *Credit*, pp. 46–55.
33. Holtman, *Revolution*, pp. 59–60.
34. G. Lefebvre, *Napoleon* (2 vols, London, 1969), II, p. 109.
35. Lefebvre, *Napoleon*, II, p. 5.
36. B. Perkins, *Prologue to War: England and the United States, 1805–12* (Berkeley, CA, 1968), p. 29.
37. Quoted in K. Caffrey, *The Lion and the Union* (London, 1978), p. 91. Also see W. Galpin, *The Grain Supply of England during the Napoleonic Period* (New York, 1925), p. 51.
38. Direct exports to the USA fell by roughly 50 per cent, while the re-exportation of colonial produce also slumped owing to the importance of American carriers in this trade. Bread prices rose and there was a short-lived manufacturing crisis.
39. Quoted in H.L. Coles, *The War of 1812* (Chicago, 1965), pp. 8–9.
40. See Lefebvre, *Napoleon*, II, pp. 131–41.
41. See C.J. Bartlett, *Castlereagh* (London, 1966), p. 111.
42. Trebilcock, *Industrialisation*, p. 132.
43. Tribilcock, *Industrialisation*, p. 130; D.M.G. Sutherland, *France 1789–1815: Revolution and Counter-Revolution* (London, 1985), pp. 423–4. Also see Emsley, *Napoleonic Europe*, pp. 143–5.
44. Lefebvre, *Napoleon*, II, pp. 120–1.
45. Galpin, *Grain Supply*, p. 111.
46. Lefebvre, *Napoleon*, II, pp. 126–8.
47. Lefebvre, *Napoleon*, II, pp. 108–9.
48. See Lefebvre, *Napoleon*, II, p. 132.
49. Lefebvre, *Napoleon*, II, pp. 142–5.
50. Lefebvre, *Napoleon*, II, pp. 132–3.
51. Holtman, *Revolution*, p. 111.
52. C.J. Esdaile, *The Wars of Napoleon* (London, 1995), p. 98.
53. See Trebilcock, *Industrialisation*, pp. 446–7.
54. See Cunningham, *Credit*, pp. 15–31.
55. Cunningham, *Credit*, pp. 29–37; Holtman, *Revolution*, p. 115.
56. Trebilcock, *Industrialisation*, p. 140.
57. Holtman, *Revolution*, pp. 115, 106.
58. F. Crouzet, 'The Impact of the French Wars on the British Economy', in T.H. Dickson (ed.), *Britain and the French Revolution* (London, 1989); F. Crouzet, *L'Économie Britannique et le Blocus Continental, 1806–13* (2 vols, Paris, 1958); F. Crouzet, 'War, Blockade and Economic Change in England, 1792–1815', *Journal of Economic History*, 24 (1964). Also see E.F. Heckscher, *The Continental System: An Economic Interpretation* (Oxford, 1922); G. Hueckel, 'War and the British Economy, 1793–1815', *Explorations in Economic History*, 10/4 (1973); A. Gayer, W. Rostow and A. Schwartz, *The Growth and Fluctuations of the British Economy, 1790–1850* (Oxford, 1953); Cunningham, *Credit*, pp. 78–83; J. Tulard, 'L'Empire Napoléonien', in *Le Concept d'Empire* (Paris, 1980); A. Sorel, *Europe and the French Revolution* (London, 1969); E. Driault, *Napoléon et l'Europe: Le Grand Empire* (Paris, 1924).
59. Coles, *War of 1812*, p. 24.
60. See, for example, the tables listing the thousands of troops billeted in Dresden during 1813 in Baron E.O.I. von Odeleben, *A Circumstantial Narrative of the Campaign in Saxony in . . . 1813* (2 vols, London, 1820 edition), II, pp. 391–2.
61. T. Morris, *The Napoleonic Wars [Recollections of T. Morris]*, ed. J. Selby (London, 1967), p. 19.
62. Holtman, *Revolution*, p. 46.
63. Holtman, *Revolution*, p. 46.

64. NC, XXIV, p. 379.
65. Muir, *Britain and Napoleon*, p. 14; Hall, *British Strategy*, pp. 1–10.
66. Hall, *British Strategy*, p. 8.
67. Muir, *Britain and Napoleon*, p. 14.
68. Coles, *War of 1812*, p. 89.
69. WSD, VIII, p. 547, and WD, XI, pp. 525–6.
70. For more details of the war of 1812, consult: H. Adams, *A History of the United States in the Administrations of Jefferson and Madison, 1801–17* (9 vols, New York, 1889–91); F. Beirne, *The War of 1812* (New York, 1949); A.T. Mahan, *Sea Power in its Relation to the War of 1812* (2 vols, Boston, 1905); J.C.A. Stagg, *Mr Madison's War* (Princeton, 1983); D.R. Hickey, *The War of 1812* (Urbana, IL, 1989); Coles, *War of 1812*.

8

The Peninsular War

Napoleon's intervention in Spain and the rising which ensued in May 1808 served as a catalyst for upheaval that extended far beyond the relatively few parts of the country which, at that juncture, were occupied by French troops. This was to give rise to an extremely complex domestic political backdrop against which *La Guerra de la Independencia* was played out.

As evinced by the ousting of Godoy and the fall of Charles IV, powerful elements of Spanish society were already sufficiently disgruntled with the *antiguo régimen* openly to assail it even before Napoleon had sought to replace the Bourbons with his brother Joseph. Indeed, disenchantment was practically ubiquitous. In the course of the previous 16 years, Godoy's attempts to modernize Spain's economic, political, administrative and military structures and to curb the influence of the Pontiff within the Hispanic Church had alienated virtually all of his countrymen and women one way or another.[1] At the same time the comparative prosperity of the 1780s had, largely as a result of military reverses for which Godoy's foreign policy was blamed, given way to economic stagnation.[2] Allied to France and consequently at war almost constantly with Britain from 1793 until 1808, Spain had seen her navy all but annihilated, her ports blockaded and her commerce plundered. Not only did this end the crucial flow of wealth from her overseas possessions, but also those that were not actually seized by her enemy, notably her Latin American colonies, started to edge towards independence once contact with the motherland was broken.[3]

So it was that, in the revolution of May 1808, besides Godoy himself, across the length and breadth of Spain civil and military authorities, which were largely dominated by his appointees, found themselves the victims of popular wrath. Several prominent officials were murdered and others imprisoned as the Spanish people, seeking to fill the vacuum caused by their monarch's removal, overthrew the established order and replaced it with provincial Juntas.[4] United solely by a common hatred of

Godoy and his ilk, the motives of the revolutionaries were diverse in their details. Yet they all plainly expected some benefit to flow from their actions and were intent on enacting change accordingly.

However, this was easier said than done. The tangible manifestation of popular rebellion, the Juntas contained not only representatives of the traditional cornerstones of the *antiguo régimen* – nobles, military figures, clerics and bureaucrats – but also the landed and commercial classes, all of whom now regarded themselves as the voice of the people. Beneath a veneer of unity they had palpably conflicting if not irreconcilable interests. Moreover, between the Juntas there was rivalry and prejudice, which evinced itself in, above all, protracted disputes over whether a commander-in-chief should be appointed to coordinate their respective military endeavours. In fact, this issue was not to be resolved until the end of 1812, when, despite ongoing opposition from numerous Iberian generals, Wellington was to be chosen for the post.

Indeed, securing a degree of political cooperation between the various Juntas and their fractious military hierarchies proved problematic enough, and it was to be the September of 1808, weeks after King Joseph, '*El Rey Intruso*', had abandoned Madrid in the aftermath of Bailen, before they could agree to establish a 'Supreme Central Government Junta of Spain and the Indies', the *Suprema*.[5] This was an interim measure, for, after publishing an adumbrative reform programme which was sufficiently nebulous to be all things to all men, the *Suprema* invited suggestions as to the form that a new, national assembly should take.

This body, the *Cortes*, was eventually convened in Cadiz in September 1810 and, for a time, imposed a semblance of order on the Spanish political scene, virtually all of its members advocating at least some degree of reform in order to protect the sovereignty of the people from a return to the 'ministerial despotism' experienced under Godoy. Just as many Germans believed that their country had, in the Middle Ages, enjoyed a golden age of prosperity, social order and unquestioning religious faith, many delegates in the *Cortes* had a somewhat quixotic view of medieval Spain. The liberties Spaniards had, it was perceived, enjoyed then had been eradicated by despotism and the infectious desire for change which the French Revolution had spawned. Those basic freedoms, dormant in inherited laws, should now be restored through a combination of circumscribing the power of the Crown on the one hand and, on the other, resisting trends which might jeopardize the social framework, notably those that affected the status of the Church or aristocracy, such as regalism or reform concerning entail or lands held in mortmain.[6]

These legitimist deputies represented those who had orchestrated the fall of Godoy and Charles IV at Aranjuez. They had thrown their weight behind the feeble Ferdinand, Prince of the Asturias, in the expectation that under him the monarchy would be more malleable. Napoleon's interference in Spain's affairs jeopardized this ambition and, in resisting it, the medievalists both regarded and depicted the struggle as a holy crusade on behalf of the throne and altar. Alongside Generals Cuesta and La Romana, José Palafox, a young officer in the Royal *Guardias de Corps* who had participated in the Aranjuez mutiny and went on to inspire the defence of Saragossa when the city was besieged during the summer of 1808,[7] is probably the best known of the prominent soldiers who subscribed to the traditionalist school of thought. In fact, he seems to have hoped that, having established himself as *generalissimo* in Aragon, all of Spain would rally behind him. While this was precluded by the rise of the provincial assemblies during the revolution, the traditionalists' continuing intrigues against their political rivals was to culminate in the demise of the *Suprema* in January 1810 and its replacement by a regency under the virtual leadership of General Castaños, the victor of Bailen.[8]

Alongside the medievalists within the *Cortes* were the more numerous liberals, whose basic premiss was that the early successes against Joseph's imposed regime had been achieved by the people, fired by the desire for reform, and not by their ruling elites, who had brought Spain to the brink of disaster in May 1808. Indeed, the nation had turned on the invader to regain its own freedom rather than perpetuate absolutism. Mesmerized by the insurrectionists' perceived triumph, contemptuous of the regular Army, which they regarded as an economically burdensome tool of despotism,[9] and influenced by the Enlightenment's rationalism and vision, the *liberales* believed that the momentum of reform had to be maintained, with social equality and more economic freedom being identified as the keys to contentment. Of course, such objectives, together with their desire to forge a unitary state, ineluctably put them at variance with other factions and institutions within Spanish society, which, if their aims were to be accomplished, would need extensive renovation. The liberals, moreover, an educated, cultured minority, could scarcely empathize with the masses they purported to represent. Many of them had bourgeois antecedents and, under Godoy, had accumulated appreciable wealth, using it to acquire land and social standing. Ongoing reform promised to consolidate and extend their gains, essentially at the expense of the peasantry and Church. Fearful of the mob which had toppled the *antiguo régimen* and determined to develop a modern, enlightened society, they, as has been said of the British reformers of 1832, sought to secure the representation and dominance of the middle classes through a property-based suffrage. When it came to devising a constitution for the new Spanish state, they were careful to ensure that the illiterate and the poor were not enfranchised.[10]

Between the legitimists and the *liberales* was a third, looser grouping of deputies who, personified by Gaspar de Jovellanos, held views which overlapped with those of the other two factions. Jovellanos himself, for instance, shared many of the liberals' economic aspirations, but was more conservative so far as the distribution of political power was concerned; he wanted the prerogatives of the Crown, Church and nobility constrained rather than eliminated, much as they were in Britain.[11] Again, however, the corollary of this was support for change, yielding a clear majority within the *Cortes* in favour of reform, as embodied in the vague manifesto published by the *Suprema* and in the constitution which was subsequently passed in 1812. Inevitably more a product of the rationalism of the Enlightenment rather than of traditional thinking, this sought to transform Spain and her institutions: it enshrined the principles of equality before the law and in liability for military service; imposed more equitable and progressive tax-raising arrangements; substituted episcopacy for ultra-montanism; and established a uniform system of local government and administration. Within the new, unitary state, sovereignty was vested in the nation and the monarchy's powers were truncated. Taxation and legis-lation became the prerogatives of the *Cortes*, while the Crown was to be advised by a council of state, behind which stood a governmental appara-tus consisting of several ministries. Ferdinand was, on his return to Spain, expected to swear an oath of allegiance to the constitution, just like every-body else. But, while its authors stipulated that it could not be amended for eight years, little consideration was given in 1812 to what would hap-pen if, should he be released by Napoleon from his gilded cage in Valençay, Ferdinand declined to accept its provisions.

The prevailing mood within Spanish domestic politics inevitably had a major impact on the conduct of the war against Napoleon. At the very start of France's intervention in their country during the winter of 1807 and the spring of 1808, numerous Spaniards had actually welcomed the French troops as the harbingers of beneficial change; Napoleon, it was expected, would depose Godoy, the hated '*Choricero*', arrange Ferdinand's marriage to a French nominee and proclaim him king.[12] This, of course, did not occur, and the great majority of Spain's people utterly repudiated '*El Rey Intruso*'. However, there were some who elected to collaborate with his regime. Largely accepting French dominion as a *fait accompli*, they fell essentially into three groups: those who, shocked and alarmed by the popular insurrection of May 1808, sided with Joseph's new order against the forces of revolution; those who saw cooperation as a potentially more fruitful approach than confrontation; and those who anticipated that the new regime might continue the trend of enlightened reform pioneered by, above all, Charles III between 1759 and 1789.[13]

The last of these factions was dominated by local officials and members of the aristocratic and ecclesiastical hierarchies who transferred their allegiance to the new sovereign[14] and, in many cases, actively assisted attempts to consolidate his position. Others were less committed, either practising passive collaboration or simply endeavouring to coexist with the new regime. Indubitably, for many Spaniards, ideological considerations were transcended by a pardonable desire to survive the conflict between the *Josefinos* and the patriots. This required that they take a very pragmatic view of their own interests, if not those of the nation, and adapt their loyalties according to the circumstances prevailing at the time.[15]

Whatever their motives, all *afrancesados*, once discovered, had to live with the stigma of having failed to resist the invader. Dismissed as *traidores* and *infidentes* who had embraced both 'El *Intruso*' and his heretical creeds, they were rejected by the bulk of the Spanish nation, even if behind the initial clarion calls there lurked a more complex web of reasons for this than the ostensible pre-eminence of 'King, Religion and Fatherland'. Indeed, it is revealing that, whereas the French penetrated only a limited area of both Spain and Portugal in 1807 and 1808, disorder was much more widespread once the Spanish revolution commenced. Furthermore, no sooner had the invaders been obliged to withdraw to the line of the Ebro in the summer of 1808 than many Spaniards lost all interest in the Napoleonic War, as did the Portuguese when Junot, only weeks later, was compelled to evacuate their country under the Cintra Convention.

This combination of parochialism, xenophobia, myopia and divided loyalties, together with the antimilitarism which liberal opinion had done so much to stoke up, made it very difficult for, first, the *Suprema* and, thereafter, the Regency and *Cortes* to orchestrate an efficacious response to the threat posed by the Napoleonic empire to Spain as a whole. After Bailen and the ephemeral retreat of the French forces from Spain's heartland, the *Suprema* called for the mobilization of all of 550 000 men in order to confront any counterstroke that materialized. Yet the Spanish Army, long neglected by Godoy in favour of the Navy, was in a poor state, and the prospects for its improvement and enlargement were not good. Not only had the country succumbed to a debilitating triumphalism, thanks to the general exaltation of the supposed victory of the valiant Spanish people over 'the strongest and most warlike *tercios* of the north,'[16] but also there was insufficient time to raise, equip and train substantial forces, even if the requisite manpower had been forthcoming. However, given fears of a popular backlash, widespread exemptions from military service,[17] the lack of *matériel* and the stranglehold which the provincial Juntas had on recruitment, universal conscription was scarcely a realizable goal; volunteers would have to be relied upon. But, despite attempts to add to their numbers by offering free pardons to various criminals if they would agree to enlist, insufficient volunteers were found to expand the regular forces dramatically. Between May and November 1808, they grew by 84 000 to 215 000 personnel, of whom barely 150 000 were actually at the front in time to meet the counteroffensive mounted by Napoleon in person during the autumn. The rest were either still *en route*, in training, or had been deliberately withheld by their provincial authorities,[18] which were reluctant to furnish forces for operations beyond their own frontiers.

As we saw in Chapter 6, Napoleon routed his opponents with his customary skill and speed. However, his conquest of the Peninsula was interrupted successively by Sir John Moore's expedition and the Austrian war of 1809. The fact that he was so slow to withdraw the Imperial Guard from Spain suggests that the emperor had at least toyed with the idea of returning there, though he evidently felt the conflict, given the utter collapse of the Spanish armies, was nearing its end.[19] However, matters in the East increasingly preoccupied him, and the subjugation of Spain and Portugal had perforce to be left to his subordinates.

As the Peninsula was the British Army's principal arena of operations during the long struggle with Napoleon, events here, at least those which impinged on the campaigns of Moore and Wellington, have been thoroughly explored by writers from the English-speaking world, with numerous publications, including soldiers' diaries, appearing on the subject. The role of the Spanish and Portuguese themselves in this protracted and complex conflict is more unfamiliar, if only because it holds less appeal for the numerous lay readers who take an interest in the period and, it must be said, because of the unduly prejudiced view that many non-Hispanic writers have taken of it in the past.[20]

Had the performance of the Spanish armies in the war been less lacklustre and perceived to be of wider significance, no doubt matters would have been different. Yet not only have their heroic if generally ineffective operations been overshadowed by those of the British and the guerrilla bands which sprang up across the occupied territories, but also the entire conflict in the Peninsula appears, when seen in the context of the Napoleonic Wars as a whole, to be something of a sideshow. Crucial though it was to the British, it was never accorded much significance by either Napoleon or his other enemies. Thus, in April 1811, as Lord Liverpool was writing to Wellington that 'We are determined not to be diverted from the Peninsula to other objects. If we can strike a Blow, we will strike it there,'[21] Metternich was advising the *Kaiser* that even the expulsion of the French from Spain in its entirety would hardly affect 'the main course of affairs'.[22]

Nevertheless, neither he nor the leaders of Russia and Prussia would have welcomed an end to this drain on Napoleon's resources and his latitude for ventures elsewhere. Had the emperor succeeded in either conquering Spain or, as he was belatedly to try with the Treaty of Valençay, neutralizing her, the repercussions for his adversaries elsewhere must have been dire. However, not only did this not come about, for most of the time it was never likely, allowing Napoleon's enemies beyond the Rhine to take the continuation of the Peninsular War for granted. To them, it seemed inconceivable that Portugal and Spain, still less Britain herself, would sign a separate peace with Napoleon, whereas London constantly dreaded that its allies in Eastern and Central Europe, and possibly even Spain, might desert it.

Such problems persisted throughout the Peninsular War and were to climax during the summer of 1813, when the British, striving to make their voice heard in the discussions regarding the terms on which peace might be concluded with France, could only exalt their recent victory at Vitoria and emphasize the importance of the financial subsidies they had paid to underpin their coalition partners' respective war efforts, thereby making it impossible for Napoleon to consolidate his gains undisturbed. Nor were Spain's and Portugal's opinions to be accorded much significance when the greater powers outlined the postwar settlement during the spring of 1814, by which time even Britain's attention had begun turning to those regions of Europe, notably Holland, which had a more direct bearing on her security, although her cardinal military effort was still anchored on the Iberian Peninsula.

So far as the conduct of the war there is concerned, the Portuguese, soon followed by the Spanish, rapidly found themselves playing a subordinate role to the British. After driving Moore's expeditionary corps from the Peninsula at Corunna in January 1809, Soult had moved south, capturing Ferrol and occupying Oporto. Simultaneously, Victor, having quashed Cuesta's Spanish 'Army of Estremadura' at Medellin on 28 March, was probing down the Guadiana with a view to invading Portugal from the south just as soon as he had assimilated some reinforcements he was expecting. The British, meanwhile, had assembled over 23 000 troops in their Portuguese foothold. Whereas Moore had maintained that 'If the French succeed in Spain it will be vain to attempt to resist them in Portugal ... [and] in that event [we must] ... immediately take steps to evacuate the country,'[23] Wellesley took a very different view. 'I have always been of the opinion that Portugal might be defended,' he wrote to

Lord Castlereagh, 'whatever might be the result of the contest in Spain ...' He went on to explain that, even if Spain were to be overrun, the French would require a field army of at least 100 000 men to conquer Portugal and, given their existing commitments both in the Peninsula and further afield, he saw no prospect of them mustering such a force, particularly as Austria was mobilizing for war and hostilities in southern Germany were imminent. Britain should, he argued, seize this opportunity to consolidate her hold on Portugal with 'very extensive pecuniary assistance and political support' for the regency government which had been set up after Cintra. Besides the fielding of a substantial British army, 'The Portuguese military establishments, upon the footing of 40 000 militia and 30 000 regular troops, ought to be revived.' Such a force, he concluded, should both safeguard Portugal from invasion and 'as long as the contest should continue in Spain ... would be highly useful to the Spaniards, and might eventually decide the contest'.[24]

Just as had occurred in Spain, many Portuguese peasants, steadily disadvantaged by some of the reforms which, favouring the nobility and commercial classes, had been implemented since the 1750s by the autocratic ministers Pombal and Manique,[25] had seen the French invasion of 1807–8 as an opportunity to improve their lot. The result was extensive disorder, with alienated peasants, many of them drafted into militia units, proving as eager to attack their local notables as they were to confront the invaders. However, Junot's grip on Portugal was neither strong nor extensive and, broken altogether by the British at Vimiero, proved ephemeral, too. Nor was Soult's occupation of the north in 1809 to be any more durable. As Napoleon prepared to enter Vienna on 12 May, the marshal was attacked by Wellesley at Oporto and was shoved back over the mountains into Galicia, leaving Portugal completely devoid of French troops. Although some central parts of the country were to be temporarily affected by Massena's invasion in the winter of 1810–11, 15 months elapsed before this even began, during which time the British were not only free to construct a huge series of concentric defences to safeguard Lisbon and its environs, the Lines of Torres Vedras, but were also able to augment their own forces with Portuguese regiments. These, raised and trained under the direction of one of Wellesley's generals, William Beresford, also contained British officer cadres, which provided them with dependable leaders while simultaneously reassuring Portugal's jittery propertied classes. Thus, the danger of internal revolt was obviated, while, the French occupations of her territory being as short-lived as they were limited, Portugal was never subjected to Napoleon's reforming zeal and all the upheaval that tended to generate.

Having secured Portugal as his base of operations, at the start of July

1809 Wellesley led his field force into Estremadura to join with Cuesta's rallied army and another Spanish column under General Venegas in a concerted advance on Madrid. The task of pinning down the bulk of the opposing French forces while Wellesley and Cuesta overpowered Victor's 22 000 men and seized the capital was allotted to Venegas's 'Army of La Mancha', which was supposed to approach Madrid via Aranjuez. However, the *Suprema*, distrustful of Cuesta, who, as part of the legitimist faction, had been involved in plots against it, was anxious to preserve Venegas's forces as a counterpoise to the suspect 'Army of Estremadura'.[26] Venegas was in any case a timid commander and, provided with the perfect excuse by his political masters, failed to pressurize the Imperial forces in and south of Madrid sufficiently to stop them reinforcing Victor. As a result, the French, operating on interior lines, were able to concentrate almost all of their troops in New Castile – some 50 000 men – against the advancing columns of Wellesley and Cuesta. The latter quickly lost his nerve when he realized the strength of the enemy and, hotly pursued, scurried to join Wellesley. Fierce fighting ensued on 27 and 28 July as King Joseph's army hurled itself against the Allied positions at Talavera. Kept at bay, the French sustained some 7200 casualties, but their opponents' losses were nearly as heavy, most of them falling on Wellesley's redcoats, which lost a quarter of their strength in the largest and toughest battle fought by a British army in 16 years of war. So numerous were the Allied wounded that the tiny medical corps was overwhelmed. Indeed, amid the atrocious roads and barren countryside of Estremadura, Wellesley's logistical arrangements had all but collapsed and his divisions were on the brink of starvation.

This had already brought the Anglo-Spanish offensive to a standstill when Soult, having rallied his battered forces and augmented them with the French forces in Galicia, marched southwards with all of 50 000 men, seeking to sever Wellesley's communications with Portugal. In this, he almost succeeded. Warned in the nick of time, the Allies fled across the Tagus at Arzobispo, suffering grievously in a gruelling retreat over mountainous terrain. They escaped destruction, however, and Soult, denied permission to thrust towards Lisbon, sullenly halted on the Tagus.[27]

Although the opportunity to jeopardize Britain's hold on Portugal was thus allowed to slip, Joseph, his western flank secured for the time being at least, now turned on Venegas, destroying his army at Almonacid on 11 August. The damage done to Anglo-Spanish relations by the abortive Talavera campaign was scarcely less severe. 'In the distribution of their forces,' Wellington grumbled about the *Suprema*, 'they do not consider ... military operations so much as political intrigue and the attainment of

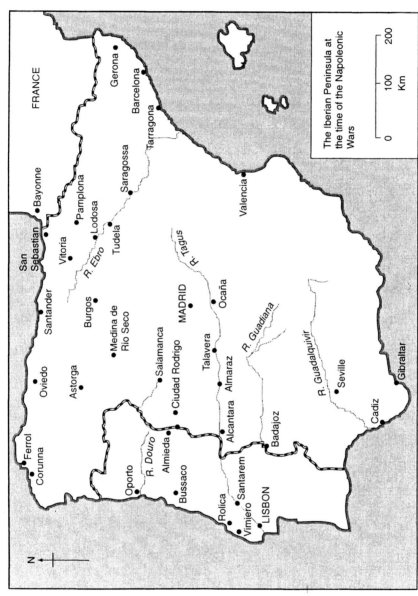

The Iberian Peninsula

petty, political objects.'[28] Henceforth, he insisted, collaboration with them would be kept at a diplomatic arm's length until:

> The evils of which I think I have reason to complain are remedied: till I see magazines established for the supply of the troops and a regular system adopted for keeping them filled; [and] till I see an army on whose exertions I can depend, commanded by officers capable and willing to carry into execution the operations . . . planned by mutual agreement . . .'[29]

The *Suprema* was largely incapable of fulfilling these not unreasonable demands. As the French discovered, too much of Spain was insufficiently fertile to support sizeable armies, and so well-organized convoys and depots were essential. Yet there was a chronic shortage of transport vehicles and dependable drivers, as well as satisfactory rations and equipment. Much of the latter had to be provided by Britain, whereas the former could only be obtained from local sources. Amid the turmoil of war and revolution, however, harvests were frequently disrupted and yields fell. Produce, if purchased, was expensive, while requisitioning carried a heavy political price.[30]

Plainly, the French invasion and the revolution's ramifications greatly circumscribed the ability of the *Suprema* to tap Spain's material and human resources in a comprehensive fashion. But many of its difficulties were of its own making. Having failed to use the respite gained by Moore's daring diversion and the heroic defence of Saragossa to raise, train, equip and field adequate regular forces, it had then proceeded to fritter away many of the troops it did have to hand in the ill-considered offensive operations of 1809. These, as Wellesley complained, were largely motivated by domestic political considerations. From a military perspective, a defence anchored on the as-yet unconquered rim of the Peninsula would have been more prudent, particularly if harmonized with the insurrectionists' activities. The mere proximity of Spanish regular forces would have made it difficult for the French to focus their efforts against the partisans, just as their harassment tactics would have impeded any bid to confront the regulars. However, the offensive ardour which gripped so many of Spain's generals in the heady days after Bailen was slow to evanesce and, fused with the public's expectations, which the *Suprema* itself did much to raise,[31] led to caution being thrown to the winds. On several occasions, rather than risk being condemned as traitors or cowards and perhaps lynched by their own troops or the local populace,[32] army commanders were effectively coerced into accepting battle under unfavourable circumstances, with predictable results.

The news of Austria's defeat and the Znaim Treaty reached Wellesley as he retreated from Talavera. He realized that this would release huge

numbers of Imperial troops, and possibly Napoleon himself, for operations in the Peninsula. Nevertheless, it would, he reasoned, be some
time before any French reinforcements could cross the Pyrenees and, he
reported to Perceval's new cabinet, in London[33] 'I conceive that till
Spain shall have been conquered . . . the enemy will find it difficult, if
not impossible, to obtain possession of Portugal . . .'. Stressing that the
enemy had 'neither the means nor the intention' of crossing the
Portuguese frontier at this point, he concluded that, by the time they
would be sufficiently strong to try, he would have prepared defences,
notably the Lines, which, supplied and supported by the Royal Navy,
would thwart them.[34]

Although the ill-fated Walcheren expedition had sapped Britain's
strength and the Talavera campaign had revealed the Spaniards to be troublesome and unreliable allies,[35] the cabinet, heartened by the optimism of
Wellesley – shortly to be dubbed Viscount Wellington – and lacking any
other arena in which they might continue to exert direct pressure on
Napoleon's legions, resolved to strengthen their forces in Portugal. The
Suprema, meanwhile, confronted by a growing clamour for its replacement by the national *Cortes*, had also recognized that Austria's defeat
would lead to the reinforcement of the French armies in the Peninsula.
Anxious to strike before this could occur and convinced that a military triumph would revitalize its flagging political fortunes, it decided to stake its
remaining regular forces, which had regrouped and been enlarged with
new levies, on another offensive against Madrid during the autumn of
1809.

General Areizaga's 50 000-strong 'Army of La Mancha' duly converged on the capital from the south, while General Del Parque, with
50 000 more troops, advanced on it from Galicia. Simultaneously, another
10 000 soldiers under the duke of Albuquerque approached from the
southwest. Initially, things went well. Del Parque defeated part of Ney's
VI Corps at Tamames on 18 October[36] and liberated Salamanca. However,
on 19 November the French inflicted one of the most crushing defeats of
the war when, although heavily outnumbered, they routed the 'Army of
La Mancha' at Ocaña; barely 24 000 of Areizaga's men escaped the disaster.[37] Nine days later, at Alba de Tormes, Del Parque also came to grief.
Smarting from a vicious riposte, his army disintegrated as it recoiled into
the *sierras* between Ciudad Rodrigo and Plasencia. Here, cold, disease
and malnutrition continued the destruction started by the French; soon,
Del Parque could muster no more than 17 000 languid soldiers.[38] Before
the year was out, the fall of Gerona – which had managed to withstand
two sieges and had come to rival Saragossa as a symbol of resistance to
Napoleon – had dealt the Spaniards another bodyblow.[39] Moreover,

90 000 fresh French troops now joined the forces already in Spain, quelling the insurgents in Navarre and Old Castile.

So disastrous did the Spaniards' defeats appear that even Wellington's sanguine expectations regarding Portugal's defence were eclipsed. 'Will 10 000 men more, which will distress our means, supposing that Great Britain can afford to supply them, compensate for the loss of these Spanish armies?', he wrote. 'If the Portuguese do their duty, I shall have enough to maintain . . . [their freedom]; if they do not, nothing that Great Britain can afford can save the country.'[40] However, in the aftermath of Ocaña, Joseph found Andalusia's vulnerability too tempting to resist. Eager to acquire a reputation as a conqueror in his own right[41] and disregarding the views of Marshal Jourdan, his chief-of-staff, who wanted to eradicate the British Army rather than squander his forces' strength by occupying 'the whole surface of Spain',[42] he ordered 70 000 men to cross the Sierra Morena.

They encountered little resistance. In fact, Joseph enjoyed a fleeting period of popularity as many Andalusians, disheartened by the recent defeats and disillusioned with the *Suprema*, gave him a genuinely cordial welcome, evidently hoping for 'a new era of happiness and glory'.[43] Given the realities of French dominion, this goodwill could scarcely have persisted for long, but it was dissipated within weeks by the news that Napoleon, alarmed by the financial costs of the Peninsular conflict, had placed all of the territories north of the Ebro under military rule with a view to using the revenue from them to subsidize the army. This virtual partition of their country alienated many of Joseph's new-found supporters and, although numerous Andalusians continued to collaborate with his regime, overall the province turned implacably hostile.

Nor had the Imperial troops managed to occupy all of it. The extensive mountain ranges were perfect sanctuaries for guerrillas, while the island fastness of Cadiz, which had been secured in the nick of time by Spanish regular forces and became the seat of the *Cortes*, was to prove a gigantic thorn in Joseph's side. Although invested on its landward side, it lay beyond the range of all but the most powerful artillery pieces and was practically impregnable unless attacked by sea as well. Lacking naval support, the French siege corps, in operations which were to last all of two years, could barely incommode the garrison, which steadily grew in size. Nor was this all: the beleaguering forces constituted a tempting target for Allied ripostes and were to fall victim to a daring if ultimately unsuccessful Anglo-Spanish amphibious raid in March 1811.[44]

The sustained exploitation of natural bastions, often supplemented with manmade defences, was a prominent feature of the Allies' *modus operandi* in the Peninsula and posed difficulties for the French of a kind seldom encountered elsewhere during our period. Military campaigns in the eighteenth century had tended to centre on depots, usually located in fortresses, occasioning a good deal of siege warfare. However, the handful that occurred during the Calabrian insurrection and that of Danzig in 1807 aside, prior to the conflict in the Peninsula, full-blown sieges were unheard of in the Napoleonic Wars. The emperor's whole strategic doctrine was founded on brisk manœuvre aimed at the destruction of an adversary's army, with geographical points serving more often than not as mere hinges; the seizure of territory was a means to an end, not an end in itself. Moreover, the culmination of his strategic manœuvres, his decisive battles, were just that: the enemy's will and means to resist were shattered, and an end to hostilities assured. Napoleon would then secure any territorial concessions he wanted at the peace-talks, which were of course conducted with the recognized – and recognizable – sovereign authority of the opposing state. Having cowed its leadership, Napoleon had to do no more.

In Spain and Portugal, however, all of this broke down. First, while French troops might put Joseph on the throne, they could not gain him popular support; Napoleon's military and diplomatic policies were out of step. Second, there was a failure of strategic doctrine, as, if only from a geographical perspective, the Peninsula was an environment quite unsuited to the French way of war. Bounded, by definition, on three sides by water – a medium over which Napoleon's forces had lost all control – it was largely underdeveloped, with vast tracts of barren, mountainous or otherwise inhospitable terrain and few good roads or navigable rivers. In addition to hampering communications and effectively compartmentalizing the theatre, making unitary command impracticable, however desirable, this rendered the movement and concentration of forces highly problematic. As living off the land was frequently an impossibility for all but the most exiguous units, armies had to take convoys containing sufficient supplies with them, to keep moving, or to disperse in order to forage across as large an area as possible. Once spread out, they were easier to feed, but very vulnerable to attack. On the other hand, protracted concentrations, as was unavoidable in the case of sieges, incurred the risk of starvation. Marshal Marmont was to complain in 1812 that, whereas the Anglo-Portuguese Army, which could always look to the Royal Navy for logistical support, was

> always concentrated and can always be moved, because it has adequate supplies of money and transport . . . we do not have four days' food in any of our magazines, we have no transport, [and] we cannot draw requisitions from the most wretched village without sending thither a foraging party 200 strong; to live from day to day, we have to scatter detachments to vast distances, and always be on the move. . .[45]

Thus, in place of the swift and decisive manœuvre warfare to which they were accustomed and geared, the French forces found themselves bogged down in the ponderous, step-by-step business of acquiring forward depots and accumulating supplies as a prelude to each and every move. A prerequisite for wider success, it not only involved the reduction of fortified towns, a time-consuming and often gory affair, but also, because the countryside was aflame with rebellion, the occupation of any territory that was captured.

This latter obligation siphoned off scores of thousands of troops who would otherwise have been available for service against the Allies' regular forces. Indeed, *la petite guerre* against the irregulars who harried the French at every opportunity was little in name alone. Although the mass rising of 1808 fizzled out in many areas as the invaders withdrew or the insurgents began to coalesce into distinct *partidas*, few corners of Spain were left untouched by insurrection and its ramifications. Predominantly composed of armed peasants, in some instances the guerrilla bands were organized and led by regular soldiers, such as Villacampa, Eroles, Porlier and Renovales, who often strove to mould them into conventional units. Others congealed around civilians who distinguished themselves as warriors, such as Espoz y Mina, Juan Martin Diez and Julian Sanchez. Still more were gangs of cut-throats who, joined by deserters from all of the armies serving in the Peninsula, practised indiscriminate banditry.

Throughout the war successive Spanish governments endeavoured to impose their authority on the guerrillas and subordinate them to their regular forces. Initially, when much of Spain was still unoccupied, and again as the conflict's end drew nigh, they enjoyed some success in this respect. For much of the intervening period, however, many partisans did essentially as they pleased. After all, a cardinal attraction of insurgent warfare was the freedom it offered when compared with the ordered, stifling and harsh life style of regular units, not to mention the latitude for personal enrichment. The *Suprema* having proclaimed that the spoils of *la guerrilla* could be retained by its participants as their legitimate possessions, besides any motivation they derived from patriotism or a simple desire to avenge some injury or insult, the members of the *partidas* had strong material incentives for chipping away at the French occupation of their country. This was, moreover, something they could do with comparative ease and in their own neighbourhoods, whereas service in the regular army could take them far from home and exposed them to the full might of Napoleon's legions in a style of warfare which was much more to the latter's advantage. Too often the outcome was, as we have seen, abject, catastrophic defeat.

So considerable were the attractions of guerrilla warfare that the army found its difficulties in recruiting sufficient manpower compounded by competition from the *partidas*. Retaining soldiers was equally arduous. When on the march, few Spanish troops could rival the stamina and discipline of the French, and defeat in battle frequently resulted in the dissolution of entire armies. Thousands of men, having deserted at the first opportunity, returned to their homes, while others joined, or were impressed by, local partisan chieftains. By 1812, between 35 000 and 50 000 guerrillas were at large.[46] Indeed, if the *partidas* made life difficult for the French and the *afrancesados*, their conduct was frequently as bothersome for other Spaniards, including the official government. Exacting contributions of money, men and other necessities, they terrorized huge areas of the country, reducing them to virtual anarchy and preventing the tapping of their human, financial and other resources by the authorities in Cadiz. This, in turn, helped preclude the recovery of these territories, for the incessant loss of *matériel* and personnel to the *partidas*, coupled with the shortfalls in recruitment and the inability to feed, equip and clothe many of the men who were enlisted, crippled Spain's attempts to create and maintain regular armies of appreciable size. Following the annihilation of what forces were available during late 1809 and early 1810, the only substantial body of regulars left to the Allies in the Peninsula comprised Wellington's Anglo-Portuguese units, which were thrown onto the defensive. Thus, in Spain, the *partidas* were left to hold the ring virtually unaided, a mission they were neither interested in nor capable of fulfilling. Guerrilla raids in isolation could only impede the French, not inflict a decisive defeat upon them. Devoid of artillery and unable to stage large-scale operations, the partisans might make a thorough nuisance of themselves, but the capture of French bastions or the challenging of robust forces, particularly mixed-arm units, was completely beyond them. In fact, for all the problems experienced in terms of supply, force-to-space ratios, the division of command between Paris, Madrid and local military governors, inadequate resources and the hostility of the populace, the French steadily gained the upper hand in the course of 1810 and 1811. Besides losing Andalusia, the Spanish forces were driven back to the very periphery of their country, as immense areas of territory and dozens of major towns and fortresses – ranging from Lerida, Tortosa and Tarragona in Catalonia, to Astorga and Badajoz in Galicia and Estremadura respectively – fell to Imperial troops. Simultaneously, the inchoate disintegration of Spain's empire in Latin America, which, as we have seen, Britain had deliberately fomented, accelerated, denying her much-needed revenue and proving a dangerous distraction from the struggle for the motherland itself.[47]

Profoundly anti-militarist, the *liberales* refused to acknowledge the crucial contribution made by regular forces to the successes of 1808 against the French. Both Vimiero and Bailen were won not by partisans but by regulars – the latter by the troops of the *antiguo régimen*, the former by those of His Britannic Majesty. The notion that the nation in arms had triumphed was a myth, albeit an alluring one, later relayed by Goya in his depiction of the fighting at the Puerta del Sol on 2 May 1808, between Murat's elite cavalry and *madrileños* armed with little more than knives, pistols and raw courage. But the ultimate futility of this sort of resistance to Napoleon's war machine is highlighted by Goya's other familiar canvas portraying the executions which ensued on Mount Principe Pio after the suppression of the Madrid rising. While armed peasants, led by local nobles and clerics, regularly found the bravery to confront French troops in open combat, more often than not heroism proved insufficient grounds for success. In one action after another, they were crushed by their opponents' superior discipline and firepower. If, as liberal thinkers perceived, through partisan warfare the people were striving to regain their political freedom from not only the French but also a despotic monarchy and to assert their right to control their own destiny, few members of the lower orders saw the struggle in such terms. There was no sense of modern political consciousness among the Spanish masses any more than there had been, or was to be, any evinced in other countries during the Napoleonic epoch; popular resistance to the French appears to have been predominantly the product of a blend of dynastic and provincial loyalties, sociocultural and economic concerns and simple xenophobia.

What is certain, however, is that, in contrast to their campaigns elsewhere, Napoleon's legions found themselves locked in a dispiriting, morally unjustifiable, protracted and unimaginably brutal struggle in which the distinctions between combatants and noncombatants were all but obliterated; 'War to the knife' ineluctably consisted of a pitiless spiral of atrocity and retaliation.[48] King Joseph had no chance of winning the goodwill of the Spanish if only because his generals, sometimes capriciously but usually of necessity, resorted to ever more ruthless expedients in a bid to damp down the insurrection. Yet, although they enjoyed appreciable success, a decisive victory, and thus peace, eluded them. So long as the fighting persisted, the human, monetary and political costs continued to climb; and, while Napoleon was prepared to provide large numbers of troops and some financial subsidies, he expected Joseph to make good any shortfalls from his kingdom's own resources.[49] Thus taxation had to increase, and attempts were made to recruit soldiers locally. Predictably, however, the former measure antagonized an already sullen population, while the latter yielded no more than a few regiments of *juramentados*. Consequently, the king's frustrating reliance on his brother's military might went on, while some of the *guardia civica* and *brigadas de escopeteros* raised to protect communications, neighbourhoods and communities of *afrancesados* proved as much of a liability as an asset. One volunteer counterinsurgency unit, led by a certain Martin de Llanos and based at Berja in Granada, perpetrated such savage, indiscriminate violence against the locals that it was actually more feared than the French themselves.[50]

Plainly, if it was not to prove counterproductive, this type of warfare called for a mixture of political and military skills; the end had to determine the means.[51] Marshal Suchet, whose troops gradually gained control of much of southeastern Spain, appreciated this more than most French commanders in the Peninsula and sought to create conditions in which the locals could adopt a position of benign neutrality at least. Yet it was an uphill struggle. The tax burden; insensitivity to customs and religious beliefs; capricious violence; inconsistent penalties for misdemeanours; requisitions and plundering; the widespread loss of loved ones in sieges and other battles: all of these helped turn many Spaniards into irreconcilable foes who, while frequently horrified by the guerrillas' behaviour as well, were more likely to side with them than the French, if only becuase the latter seldom afforded adequate protection, still less rewards, for the few *afrancesados* who did come forward.

Coincident with and influenced by the rout of the Spanish regular armies in the winter of 1809–10 was the fall of the *Suprema*, which also marked a watershed in the Anglo-Spanish alliance. From early 1810 onwards, Britain had to shoulder most of the burden of maintaining resistance to the French in the Peninsula. The Spanish were losing ground everywhere and so fearful for the safety of Cadiz that they even reversed their policy of not permitting British troops to enter it; on London's orders, some 10 000 redcoats were ultimately brought in by sea to bolster the Spanish garrison.[52] Wellington saw this as something of a waste, for he was anxious to commit every available man to the defence of Portugal. Nevertheless, the apparent ease with which the French overran the rest of Andalusia alarmed him, and he took the precaution of seeking clarification from London as to the circumstances in which he might evacuate Portugal if the French were to advance in overwhelming strength.[53]

They were not to. Although in the course of 1810 Napoleon increased his forces in the Peninsula to over 300 000 troops, the need to hold down the conquered territories prevented the French employing their numerical advantage; the garrisons in Andalusia alone amounted to 70 000 men. Nor was the emperor free to direct the invasion of Portugal in person as he had intended; his divorce and remarriage preoccupied him among other things, so he handed the task to a rather unwilling Massena.

Having besieged and taken the fortresses of Ciudad Rodrigo and Almeida,[54] Massena advanced into the Portuguese interior at the head of 65 000 troops. To oppose him, Wellington had 44 000 British and 45 000 Portuguese regulars, supported by roughly 70,000 militia. The country-side in the path of the invaders had been 'scorched' and, unknown to the French, Lisbon had, as we have seen, been ringed with elaborate defences.

Resisting pressure from the Portuguese to make a determined stand in the north, Wellington withdrew his field army before the advancing foe, stopping only to give battle on the awe-inspiring ridge at Bussaco. His new Portuguese regiments performed well in this, their baptism of fire, and the French infantry, denied cavalry and artillery support by the adverse terrain, were repelled with heavy casualties.[55] The next day, how-ever, Massena discovered a way past the Allied position and Wellington was obliged to continue his retreat towards Lisbon.

Although he and his political masters exalted the victory at Bussaco,[56] the seemingly inexorable progress of the French caused some concern, not least among those Portuguese who anticipated that the British would abandon the country. But, on 11 October 1810, Massena found himself brought to a halt by the Lines of Torres Vedras. He quickly judged them to be impregnable and, pulling back to Santarem, dallied there until March in the hope that Wellington might be tempted into attacking him. This did not occur, however, and Massena, lacking fresh orders from Napoleon and with his army on the brink of starvation, retreated towards Almeida, gingerly shadowed by the Allies.[57]

The next few weeks saw clashes along the Portuguese–Spanish frontier at Sabugal and Albuera as the Allies advanced to encircle Almeida and Badajoz respectively.[58] Massena, having rested and replenished his forces, strove to relieve the former in May, but was checked by Wellington in a bitter, two-day battle at Fuentes de Oñoro.[59] Having secured the Leon bor-der for the time being at least, Wellington besieged Badajoz, only to be chased off by relief columns under Soult and Marmont (who had super-seded Massena).[60] However, switching his attention back to the north, he invested Ciudad Rodrigo on 8 January 1812, and stormed it just 11 days later before Marmont could assemble his army and react.[61] Although he sustained heavy casualties, this gave Wellington control of the gateway to northern Spain, to which he added mastery of the southern corridor when, just weeks later, he finally seized Badajoz in similar style.[62] Should an opportunity present itself, the Anglo-Portuguese forces were now ready and able to mount an offensive into Spain's heartland.

Such a chance was not long in coming. The fortunes of the French were now firmly on the wane, if only because the impending Russian campaign meant that no reinforcements would be available for operations in the Peninsula. In the Tyrol and Calabria, it will be recalled, popular revolts had, in time, been smothered through the application of overwhelming military power. By 1812, the Imperial forces had come very close to accomplishing this in Spain, too; despite heavy losses in their attritional contest with the partisans, they had made considerable headway and the Spanish were palpably feeling the strain. For just how much longer they would have proved able to continue the struggle without active British and Portuguese assistance must remain a moot point; but their ancestors had fought the Romans for 200 years and the Moors, as one beggar observed to a cocksure French captain, for 800.[63] As early as 1810 the conflict's financial costs alone were troubling Napoleon, while the ongoing fighting continued to encourage his adversaries elsewhere. Indeed, the preservation of his empire as a whole was imposing burdens which France could not carry for much longer.

But if the Peninsular game was not worth the candle, how was it to be ended? Abandoning his own brother would have done little for Napoleon's credibility with his other allies, and any admission of defeat would have badly tarnished his own military and political prestige. In any event, while Portugal steadily lost interest in the war as the French menace receded from her frontiers, not only was an end to hostilities with Spain unlikely so long as Imperial troops occupied her territory, but also it was unclear with whom Napoleon could negotiate an enforceable settlement. For, whereas his earlier wars had all been neatly terminated by accords with the relevant dynasties, in Spain's case the *Cortes* insisted that sovereignty resided in the people and had arrogated the monarch's prerogatives to itself. In fact, when Napoleon did eventually conclude the Treaty of Valençay with the captive Ferdinand, the *Cortes* was to reject it precisely on these grounds.

On this, the deputies were to exhibit a unanimity that had become all too rare. For as the legislative programme of the *liberales* steadily revealed a determination to further the sociopolitical changes begun by the *antiguo régimen*, popular opinion hardened against it. Particularly controversial were measures which undermined the Church's position, such as the extirpation of the Holy Office, attempts to curb the re-establishment of religious orders destroyed in the war and the ending of censorship. However, the fundamental problem was that the lower strata of society derived no benefits from the 1812 Constitution whatsoever; at their expense, it advanced the interests of the middle class *and* effectively protected many of the rights of the *señores*.

The result was a cataclysmic backlash against the liberals and those associated with them.[64] By the time of the Inquisition's abolition in 1813, a distinct traditionalist party – the *serviles*, 'the servile ones', as their political opponents dubbed them – had emerged in the *Cortes* and begun linking liberalism with the heresies and anticlericalism of the French revolutionaries. Nobles were alienated by the reformers' attacks on their seigniorial privileges, while many peasants, penalized by the loss of benevolent local monasteries and convents and by fiscal and land reforms, resorted to open rebellion; they withheld their dues, occupied estates, rioted and even murdered landlords and entrepreneurs. It became, as one French officer remarked, 'a war of the poor against the rich',[65] with the *Cortes* responding to the disorder by authorizing the creation of municipal guards. Not only did this underscore another schism, that between those Spaniards who inhabited the countryside and those who dwelt in urban areas, it also inflamed the tensions between patriots and *Josefinos*. However inappropriate, liberalism's adversaries found it all too easy to equate it with Bonapartism. Besides any similarities between the Bayonne Constitution devised by Napoleon for Spain – the first document of its kind in the country's history[66] – and that of 1812, the typical *afrancesado* was a bourgeois town-dweller.

Owing to a combination of the liberals' reforms and the incipient collapse of the French occupation, all this internecine strife gradually intensified, with guerrilla *partidas* turning their attention from the retreating French to milking local communities.[67] Moreover, as its unpopularity grew, the liberal faction within the *Cortes* became ever more concerned about the regular Army's loyalty, which, through its antimilitarism and general neglect, it had progressively undermined.[68] Not only had Spanish professional soldiers to endure the appointment of Wellington as their commander-in-chief in September 1812, they also had to suffer the humiliation of watching him and his Anglo-Portuguese divisions take the lead in liberating their country. Yet such were the accumulated weaknesses within the Spanish forces and so suspicious were the *liberales* of his efforts to rectify them that not even the talented Wellington could achieve more than a marginal improvement. Consequently, he was only able to allot the Spaniards a subordinate role in the decisive battles of 1813–14.[69]

Predictably, all this compounded Spain's mounting Anglophobia, while Wellington, who detested the liberals, was encouraged to overthrow them by the British cabinet. This would just exacerbate matters, he concluded, though he did resign the unenviable office of generalissimo at one point.[70] Some Spanish officers, by contrast, were more unscrupulous. General Ballesteros, in reaction to Wellington's designation as commander-in-chief, 'pronounced' against the government. He was arrested and replaced by Del Parque, one of the grandees who, initially, had joined the *afrancesados* only to change sides after Bailen,[71] subsequently proving his loyalty in a dozen engagements. Ballesteros's example, however, was to be followed by others – and with greater effect. On the return of Ferdinand, General Francisco Elio was to initiate the mutiny which brought down the *Cortes* and, with it, the 1812 Constitution.[72] His successful *pronunciamiento* was the first of many which both Spain and her former colonies were to witness over the next 170 years.

The loss of Badajoz and Ciudad Rodrigo spelt the beginning of the end for the French occupation of Spain. Having first destroyed the great bridge over the Tagus at Almaraz in order to sever the communications between Soult's army in Andalusia and Marmont's in Leon, Wellington launched an offensive against the latter, scattering it at Salamanca on 22 July 1812.[73] He then thrust deep into the interior, compelling Joseph to relinquish Madrid for the second time in four years and pressing on to besiege Burgos. Evacuating the south and bringing his 60 000 troops abreast of the 53 000 in Castile, Soult retook the capital and helped drive off Wellington's startled forces. Burgos was relieved on 22 October – two days after Napoleon began his fateful retreat from Moscow – and, by mid-November, Wellington's army had been swept back over the Huebra.[74] However, the following May he returned with overwhelming forces, entered Burgos on 13 June and, on the 21st, inflicted a decisive defeat on Joseph and Jourdan at Vitoria.[75]

Having pushed the French in northern Spain back as far as the Bidassoa, obliging Suchet to evacuate Valencia and Aragon into the bargain, Wellington set about reducing the strongholds of San Sebastian and Pamplona. News of his victory at Vitoria reached Central Europe just as Napoleon, having negotiated a ceasefire with Prussia and Russia, was seeking to persuade Austria not to join the coalition against France. Alarmed by the collapse of the Peninsular front, the emperor dispatched Soult to take command of the battered divisions on the Pyrenees and, between 25 July and 31 August, the marshal launched a determined, if ultimately unsuccessful, counterstroke.[76] Subsequently dislodged from positions on the Bidassoa and Nivelle, by February 1814, his army, depleted by battles, desertion and detachments being withdrawn for the eastern front, had retreated as far as the Gave du Pau, leaving a garrison in Bayonne. Narrowly defeated at Orthez,[77] as the Allies occupied Bordeaux and invested Bayonne, Soult fell back on Toulouse, where he and Wellington were to fight one last battle.[78] Unknown to them, Napoleon had abdicated several days before and the war had officially ended.

Meanwhile, Suchet had been obliged to relinquish all but a few strongholds in Catalonia; and Prince Ferdinand, having signed the Valençay Treaty, was on his way home. Several of the French garrisons were duped into capitulating by the Spaniards, and, promised that they would be released, Suchet trustingly allowed '*El Deseado*' to proceed. However, Ferdinand intended neither honouring this agreement nor accepting the constraints imposed on the Crown by the liberals' constitution. On nearing Valencia, he was met by Cardinal de Borbon, President of the Regency, to whom he extended his hand in order to receive the customary, deferential kiss. The cardinal, aware of his office and that the king had yet to swear the constitutional oath, hesitated. 'Kiss!', hissed Ferdinand, thrusting his hand into Borbon's face. The president obeyed.[79]

Thus commenced the restoration of absolutism and the demise of the 1812 Constitution. Ferdinand entered Valencia in triumph and, within days, General Elio's *pronunciamiento* against the Cadiz *Cortes* occurred. A royal proclamation declared the *Cortes* and its decrees 'nil and of no value or effect, now or ever, as if such acts had never taken place'.[80] All prominent liberal deputies and reformers were arrested; mobs destroyed memorials, statues and other symbolic tributes to national sovereignty; and known *afrancesados* were lynched, summarily executed, jailed or ostracized. The clock was turned back, and Spain descended into an era of reactionary, counter-revolutionary terror.

Notes

1. G.H. Lovett, *Napoleon and the Birth of Modern Spain* (New York, 1965), I, pp. 22–3.
2. Lovett, *Modern Spain*, pp. 34–5.
3. See: W. Kaufman, *British Policy and the Independence of Latin America* (London, 1967); J. Lynch, 'British Policy and Spanish America, 1783–1808', *Journal of Latin American Studies*, 1/1 (1969); E.J. Hamilton, 'War and Inflation in Spain, 1780–1800', *Quarterly Journal of Economics*, 59/1 (1944); J. Barbier and H. Klein, 'Revolutionary Wars and Public Finances: The Madrid Treasury, 1784–1807', *Journal of Economic History*, 41/2 (1981); T. Anna, *Spain and the Loss of America* (Lincoln, NB, 1983).
4. Lovett, *Modern Spain*, I, pp. 167, 169–72.
5. Lovett, *Modern Spain*, pp. 290–7.
6. Out of Spain's 11 000 000 inhabitants, 403 000 were nobles and 170 000 clergy. Together they owned roughly two thirds of the land. See Lovett, *Modern Spain*, I, p. 38.
7. See Lovett, *Modern Spain*, I, pp. 233–63; Oman, *A History of the Peninsular War* (Oxford, 1902–30), I, pp. 140–61.
8. See Lovett, *Modern Spain*, I, pp. 161–2, 336–45, 357–9; C. Esdaile, *The Spanish Army in the Peninsular War* (Manchester, 1988), pp. 127–32, 134–6.
9. See Esdaile, *Spanish Army*, pp. 169–70.
10. See M. Artola, *La Burguesia Revolucionara* (Madrid, 1973).
11. See J. Polt, *Gaspar Melchor de Jovellanos* (New York, 1971). Also see C.W. Crawley, 'English and French Influences in the Cortes of Cadiz', *Cambridge Historical Journal*, 6/2 (1939); B. Hamnett, 'Spanish Constitutionalism and the Impact of the French Revolution, 1808–14', in H.T. Mason and W. Doyle (eds.), *The Impact of the French Revolution on European Consciousness* (Gloucester, 1989).
12. Lovett, *Modern Spain*, I, pp. 89–90.

13. See, for example. O. Hufton, *Europe: Privilege and Protest, 1730–89* (London, 1994), pp. 260–71; Lovett, *Modern Spain*, I, pp. 1–4.
14. See Lovett, *Modern Spain*, II, pp. 419, 517, 554–609.
15. See M. Artola, *Los Afrancesados* (Madrid, 1953).
16. Quoted in Esdaile, *Spanish Army*, p. 125.
17. See Lovett, *Modern Spain*, I, p. 36.
18. Lovett, *Modern Spain*, I, p. 299; Esdaile, *Spanish Army*, pp. 125–6.
19. See NC, XVIII, p. 237.
20. The finest general history of the Peninsular War in English is Oman's, which is comprehensive and gives due weight to the role of the Spaniards and Portuguese. Other large-scale works are: W.F.P. Napier, *History of the War in the Peninsula and in the South of France* (6 vols, London, 1876); and J. Gomez de Arteche, *Guerra de la Independencia: Historia militar de España de 1808 a 1814* (14 vols, Madrid, 1868–1903). Among more concise and accessible studies is D. Gates, *The Spanish Ulcer: A History of the Peninsular War* (London and New York, 1986). French archival material on the Peninsular War is to be found in ASH, C7 1–29 and C8 1–473.
21. WSD, VII, pp. 104–5.
22. C.S.B. Buckland. *Metternich and the British Government from 1809 to 1813* (London, 1932), p. 173.
23. British Library, Sir John Moore Papers, Add. MS 57544: 'Memorandum on the Defence of Portugal', 25 November 1808.
24. WD, V, p. 261.
25. See, for instance. O. Hufton, *Privilege and Protest*, pp. 271–83.
26. Esdaile, *Spanish Army*, p. 139.
27. Oman, *History*, II, pp. 463–596.
28. WD, V, p. 108.
29. WD, V, p. 258.
30. See, for example, Lovett, *Modern Spain*, II, p. 536.
31. For some of the rather rash propaganda ploys of the *Suprema* and its military commanders, see Esdaile, *Spanish Army*, pp. 137–8.
32. This is exemplified by the fate of General San Juan in December 1808. See Oman, *History*, I, p. 471.
33. For details of the formation of the Perceval ministry, see R. Muir, *Britain and the Defeat of Napoleon 1807–15* (New Haven, CT, 1996), pp. 105–10.
34. WD, V, pp. 268–77. Also see WSD, VI, pp. 350–3; and WD, III, pp. 477–8.
35. See J. Stampa, *La Crisis de una alianza: La campaña del Tajo de 1809* (Ministry of Defence, Madrid, 1996).
36. Oman, *History*, III, pp. 74–80.
37. Oman, *History*, III, pp. 91–6.
38. Oman, *History*, III, pp. 98–101.
39. Oman, *History*, III, pp. 19–66.
40. WD, V, pp. 413.
41. See Lovett, *Modern Spain*, II, p. 527.
42. See J.B. Jourdan, *Mémoires Militaires: Guerre d'Espagne* (Paris, 1899), p. 294.
43. See Lovett, *Modern Spain*, II, pp. 527–9.
44. See Oman, *History*, IV, pp. 91–130.
45. A.F.L.V. de Marmont, *Mémoires du Maréchal Marmont, Duc de Raguse de 1792 à 1841* (9 vols, Paris, 1857), IV, pp. 346–7.
46. See Lovett, *Modern Spain*, II, pp. 683; Esdaile, *Spanish Army*, p. 161.
47. See: M.P. Costeloe, *Response to Revolution: Imperial Spain and the Latin-American Revolutions* (Cambridge, 1986); J. Lynch, *The Spanish American Revolutions, 1808–26* (London, 1973); Anna, *Spain and the Loss of America*; B. Hamnett, 'The Appropriation

of Mexican Church Wealth by the Spanish Bourbon Government: The Consolidation of the *vales reales*, 1805–09', *Journal of Latin American Studies*, 1/2 (1969).

48. For some details of this gruesome conflict, see Lovett, *Modern Spain*, II, pp. 666–752.
49. See, for example, NC, XX, p. 146.
50. Lovett, *Modern Spain*, II, p. 574.
51. See D.W. Alexander, *Rod of Iron: French Counter-Insurgency Policy in Aragon during the Peninsular War* (Wilmington, DE, 1985), *passim*.
52. Muir, *Britain and Napoleon*, p. 115.
53. See Muir, *Britain and Napoleon*, pp. 116–17.
54. See D.D. Howard, *Napoleon and Iberia: The Twin Sieges of Ciudad Rodrigo and Almeida* (Tallahassee, 1984); Oman, *History*, III, pp. 231–81.
55. See Oman, *History*, III, pp. 544–89.
56. Muir, *Britain and Napoleon*, pp. 133–6.
57. See Oman, *History*, IV, 1–90.
58. Oman, *History*, IV, pp. 131–205 and 247–87.
59. Oman, *History*, IV, pp. 288–348.
60. Oman, *History*, IV, pp. 404–60.
61. Oman, *History*, V, 157–86.
62. Oman, *History*, V, pp. 217–64.
63. See Lovett, *Modern Spain*, I, p. 203.
64. Lovett, *Modern Spain*, II, pp. 415–90.
65. Quoted in R. Carr, *Spain, 1808–1975* (Oxford, 1982), p. 109.
66. See Lovett, *Modern Spain*, I, p. 126.
67. Esdaile, *Spanish Army*, p. 166.
68. See Esdaile, *Spanish Army*, pp. 154–85.
69. See Esdaile, *Spanish Army*, pp. 168–71.
70. See WSD, VIII, pp. 16–18; WD, VI, pp. 559–60, 594–5; WD, XII, p. 27. Also see C. Esdaile, *The Duke of Wellington and the Command of the Spanish Army, 1812–14* (London, 1990).
71. Lovett, *Modern Spain*, II, pp. 565–70.
72. Lovett, *Modern Spain*, II, pp. 828–9.
73. Oman, *History*, V, pp. 335–82.
74. Oman, *History*, V, pp. 475–518 and VI, pp. 1–166.
75. Oman, *History*, VI, pp. 299–545.
76. Oman, *History*, VI, pp. 557–740.
77. Oman, *History*, VII, pp. 356–75.
78. Oman, *History*, VII, pp. 465–95.
79. Lovett, *Modern Spain*, II, pp. 827–8.
80. Quoted in Lovett, *Modern Spain*, II, p. 830.

9

The Road to Moscow: The Demise of the Franco-Russian Entente

By the beginning of 1810, Napoleon presided over the greatest empire seen in Europe since Roman times. Although, on the periphery of the continent, his armies still faced implacable foes in the form of the Spanish, Portuguese and the Calabrian insurrectionists, all of whom were actively underpinned by British forces, subsidies and supplies, both he and his enemies were aware that these conflicts were very unlikely to prove decisive in themselves.[1] Indeed, once the emperor was sufficiently free from other distractions to commit enough troops to the job, the revolt in the south of Italy was snuffed out just as that in the Tyrol had been.[2] In the Iberian Peninsula, too, his legions appeared to be gaining the upper hand. As we have seen, Napoleon's plans for the subjugation of Spain and Portugal had been disrupted at a crucial juncture by Vienna's preparations for a renewal of the war in the East. Austria's subsequent defeat released thousands of Imperial troops for the completion of that task and, during 1810, with the wily Massena at their head, they were to advance to the very outskirts of Lisbon, driving the Anglo-Portuguese army before them. Although Wellington was able to give Massena a bloody nose at Bussaco and, thanks to the Lines of Torres Vedras, which he had had the foresight to build, ultimately retain Britain's foothold on the Peninsula,[3] his political masters in London realized that only Prussia, Austria and Russia possessed the military potential to deal the Napoleonic empire a decisive blow. But, with the first of these crushed and the other two actively collaborating with France following her recent victories over them, there seemed little prospect of this occurring. Moreover, the relentless extension of the Continental System was gravely affecting patterns of international trade, causing, if only intermittently, serious economic hardship in

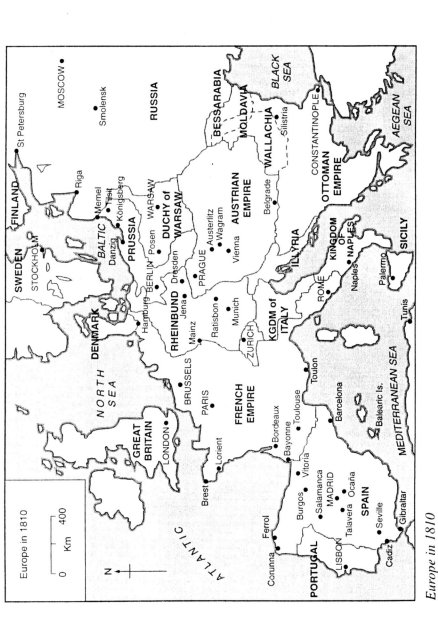

Europe in 1810

Britain's manufacturing regions. This coincided with a run of poor harvests,[4] necessitating the import of costly French and Dutch wheat during the winters of 1808 and 1809.[5] Equally, the Royal Navy's enforcement of the Orders-in-Council was generating more than a few adverse results. Besides the strain that maintaining a protracted, continent-wide blockade imposed on the fleet itself, the USA, like other neutrals before it, was being progressively alienated by the constraints that British policy imposed on her merchantmen, the Orders being perceived by the American government as a 'measure of commercial rivalry' designed to prevent their country's trading relations interfering 'with the monopoly which [Britain] ... covets for her own commerce and navigation'.[6] Indeed, the deepening strategic stalemate was evidence enough of Britain's inability to tackle Napoleon without the aid of continental allies. Mastery of the seas might have been a necessary condition for the defeat of France, but it was not a sufficient one. In the absence of any viable peace overtures from her, the cabinet neither knew how the war was to be ended in the longer term nor actively prosecuted in the interim. Napoleon, however, had no real vision of what form a satisfactory settlement with Britain might take.[7] He only knew what he was opposed to: 'I do not want a peace which ruins ... [France's] trade as ..... Amiens did,' he insisted. 'For peace to be practicable and lasting ... [Britain] has got to be convinced that she can count on no help from the Continent.'[8] To be sure, the Royal Navy could continue to seize the enemy's colonial possessions with virtual impunity. Yet without markets for their produce these could prove more of a liability than an asset and, in the absence of any overall peace settlement, could not even be used as bargaining chips. As evinced by the Louisiana Purchase, Napoleon had in any case long since written many of them off as either indefensible or not worth protecting.

It was against this bleak background that a chain of events began which, among other things, was to lift the drooping spirits of the British and promised to give them the continental allies they were so sorely in need of. Ever since Napoleon's triumph at Tilsit, his relations with Russia had been slowly deteriorating. There were numerous factors which contributed to the unravelling of the Franco-Russian entente, but the following stand out as the most significant.

First, while Napoleon genuinely sought to placate Alexander, each of them was first disappointed and then antagonized by the conduct of the other. For his part, Napoleon strove to tread carefully so far as Romanov interests in Eastern Europe were concerned: in the main, the bulk of *La Grande Armée* was kept at a very respectful distance from Russia's western frontier; the Tsar was encouraged to expand his domains at the expense of Sweden and Turkey; and, recognizing that the region was a traditional sphere of Russian influence, Napoleon held back from seeking to restore the ancient kingdom of Poland, even going so far as to offer the Tsar a convention to that effect. Periodically, suggestions for joint military ventures also emanated from Paris. Although Turkey, Persia and India were the ostensible targets, Napoleon primarily regarded these expeditions as a means of indirectly menacing Britain – an objective of which London was only too well aware. For his part, Alexander was eager to acquire Constantinople and, it will be recalled, had attacked the Turks in a bid to conquer the Danubian principalities. But, while he talked of dismembering the Ottoman Empire, Napoleon was no more keen to see an increase in Romanov influence in the Balkans than the British, who were becoming understandably wary of French and Russian expansionism towards the eastern Mediterranean. As the Tsar strove to wrest Wallachia and Moldavia from the Turks, Napoleon, having already acquired Dalmatia after Austerlitz, added Illyria to his gains in the wake of Wagram, severing Austria from the Adriatic with a cordon of French possessions that extended from the Kingdom of Italy as far as Cattaro on the fringe of the Ottoman Empire. In response to these developments, the British took the precaution of seizing all of the Ionian Islands save Corfu, where the French garrison proved indomitable.[9] Realizing that the situation was becoming disadvantageous, and with more important concerns elsewhere, Napoleon shirked from fully supporting the Russians, effectively encouraging the Porte to stand up to them. His behind-the-scenes endeavours to restrain Alexander in this fashion inevitably appeared duplicitous, generating appreciable suspicion and resentment.

Sweden became another source of Franco-Russian strife. Under the enlightened despot Gustav IV, she had played only a minor part in the Napoleonic Wars so far, vainly struggling to retain Pomerania and Finland as she became embroiled with not only France but Russia and Denmark as well. However, imminent defeat in war was not so much the cause as the occasion of Gustav's downfall. His far-reaching reforms having alienated the traditional power-brokers in Sweden, he was arrested by his own guards in a palace *coup* in March 1809 and exiled, his ageing uncle Charles succeeding him as king. It was not unlike the revolution that had toppled the *ancien régime* in Spain. The disaffected nobles who had overthrown Gustav – the so-called 'men of 1809' – strove to restore their feudal privileges at the expense of not only their emancipated peasants but also the bourgeoisie and the monarchy, all of whom were seen as potential threats to the old order.[10] A constitution that protected their interests was rammed through the *Riksdag*, and their nominee, Prince Christian August, was elected as heir to the throne.

Racked by political schisms and militarily weak, Sweden was easy prey for her assailants. Having tried unsuccessfully to conciliate them, her new rulers had to accept harsh peace terms, ceding Finland to Russia and joining the Continental System. When Prince Christian died suddenly in May 1810, however, various groups within Swedish society glimpsed a chance of salvation. If a Frenchman were to follow Charles as king, Napoleon might take Sweden under his arm. She might be granted some relaxation of the restrictions on her trade, as well as some degree of protection from Russia; indeed, Finland might even be returned. The Swedish Army, disheartened by years of decline, saw obvious benefits in a closer association with the great conqueror, while, entranced by the social and political reforms that followed in his wake, many members of the middle and lower classes hoped for a liberalization of the constitution that would result in them wielding more influence.

Mindful of his kindly treatment of their soldiers captured at Lübeck in 1806, in the eyes of many Swedes the obvious French candidate for the crown was Marshal Bernadotte, who had further enhanced his popularity during a lengthy stint as governor of the *Hansestädte* in the wake of Tilsit.[11] As we have seen, he was publicly dismissed from *La Grande Armée* at Wagram, but had since redeemed himself somewhat by his performance in the face of the British landing at Walcheren.[12] With King Charles in poor health, Bernadotte, having received an apprehensive Napoleon's grudging consent, arrived in Sweden in October 1810 to become crown prince and virtual regent. Though once a Jacobin, he had no intention of satisfying the Swedish liberals' aspirations; even before he ascended the throne in 1818, he made it apparent that he was neither going to reverse the social and economic reforms introduced by Gustav IV nor be constrained by the noble faction which had deposed him. Bernadotte was bent on ruling as an enlightened absolute – and, moreover, one as free from French control as possible.[13]

Predictably, however, the Tsar saw all of this in a more sinister light, as did the British. With the enlarged Duchy of Warsaw barring any Romanov expansion westwards, Austria trying to supplant Russia as France's closest ally, and Napoleon plotting with the Porte, the apparent spread of French influence throughout Scandinavia looked ominous; Russia was being encircled. Napoleon, too, had grounds for feeling uneasy. His meeting with the Tsar at Erfurt in September 1808 had taken place under circumstances very different from those which had prevailed at Tilsit just 14 months earlier. Anxious to stop Napoleon overreaching himself, Talleyrand had secretly encouraged Alexander to stand up to his master. In any event, Napoleon, already perturbed by events in Spain, had no choice but to treat the Tsar as an equal partner; he needed Russian help lest Austria might turn on him while he was preoccupied with the

Peninsula. Yet if, at Erfurt, Alexander was quick to shake off his subservience to his 'cousin', he was rather slower to act when the Austrians finally struck. Indeed, he contented himself with the occupation, for purely selfish reasons, of parts of Austrian Galicia, while continuing with his bid to take territory from the Swedes and Turks.

So far as the British are concerned, throughout 1810 and 1811 the inscrutability of both Sweden's and Russia's foreign policy further muddled what was already a perplexing situation. Nominally at war with both these countries, the British had established a *modus vivendi* with the former in particular. In return for discreetly avoiding confrontation with her garrisons and gunboats, the Royal Navy was permitted unofficial access to supplies and anchorages.[14] In 1811, however, this phoney war threatened to take a more serious turn when the Swedes impounded large quantities of British merchandise which were being transported in neutral vessels. The Carlshamm Cargoes affair, as it is known, was ultimately resolved through lengthy negotiations, but it did little to ease Britain's suspicions of Bernadotte. Separated from the land mass of Central Europe by the Baltic, which was dominated by the Royal Navy, Sweden lay beyond the reach of Napoleon's armies, if not those of his Russian and Danish allies. Nevertheless, despite her relative geographic isolation, like Denmark and Portugal before her she could not expect to remain aloof from the struggle between the great powers indefinitely. Sure enough, Napoleon was soon bawling at the Swedish Ambassador to Paris that:

> Neutrality no longer exists. Britain doesn't recognize it, neither can I. You're suffering? Don't you think I suffer, that France, Bordeaux, Holland and Germany are suffering? That's why there must be an end to it. . . . Open war, or else reliable friendship. Choose now.[15]

Similarly, just a year after Bernadotte's election as crown prince, London's sense that the Prussians and, perhaps, the Russians might be tempted into a new anti-French alliance spawned diplomatic efforts to force the Swedes off the fence. The existing state of relations between London and Stockholm could not be allowed to persist, Bernadotte was warned, since it was 'deeply injurious to the interests not only of Great Britain, but of every power excepting that of Bonaparte'.[16]

At this juncture, Bernadotte was pardonably reluctant openly to align his adopted little country with either side. But the onset of the Baltic winter ruled out any British military action against Sweden for the time being and, in any case, London's hopes regarding the construction of a fresh coalition were to dribble away, letting Bernadotte off the hook. During May 1811, Prussia, anxious to avoid any further erosion of her standing and territory, had secretly approached France for an alliance.

However, uneasy about the impact such a development might have on his relations with Russia, Napoleon had disregarded this overture and, interpreting his failure to respond as a harbinger of impending French encroachments on her domains, Prussia had begun sounding out Britain, Russia and Austria as to the prospects of them coming to her aid. When Napoleon finally did reply to Prussia's entreaty, he demanded that she cease her preparations for war forthwith or face reoccupation. She was also either to join the *Rheinbund* or to conclude an unconditional, offensive–defensive pact with France. Moreover, the emperor insisted, details of these exchanges were to be published in both Berlin and St Petersburg.[17] Unprepared to contemplate another ruinous confrontation with Napoleon, Frederick William yielded, dissipating Britain's dream of a new, powerful coalition. Several Prussian officers left for Russia in disgust, while the poet and publicist Heinrich von Kleist, whose *Hermannschlacht*, though ostensibly about the battle between ancient Rome and the Germanic tribes, mirrored the contemporary struggle against Napoleon, was plunged into despair; already badly depressed by Austria's defeat in 1809 and by the inadequacy of his political invective, he took his own life.

Coincident with and of influence on all of this was a plan hatched by the Tsar to mount an offensive which would overrun the Grand Duchy of Warsaw and provoke a rebellion across northern Germany. By proclaiming the restoration of their ancient kingdom, albeit under Russia's tutelage, Alexander hoped to win over the Poles, giving him an additional 50 000 troops and simultaneously depriving Napoleon of the same number. Prussia and Denmark were also expected to rally to his cause. However, Polish mistrust of Russia and loyalty to France joined with Prussian apprehensiveness and Austrian alarm to smother the scheme in its infancy.[18] The Tsar slowly abandoned any thought of offensive action and the spectre of war receded for the time being at least. Nevertheless, the plot deeply shocked Napoleon, and he promptly embarked on a programme of precautionary measures; key German and Polish fortresses were strengthened, and more troops were deployed across the eastern reaches of his empire.

Although he sought simultaneously to reassure Alexander of his friendship,[19] in among the conspiracies, real and imagined, there were other issues which continued to sour the personal and political relations between the two men.[20] Pre-eminent among these were Napoleon's attempts to extend, refine and enforce the Continental System. Bent on combating smuggling, on 13 December 1810, he abruptly annexed Holland, Hamburg, the old *Hansestädte* and the entire north German littoral, including Oldenburg. Not only had the integrity of this enclave been recognized at Tilsit, but also the Tsar's favourite sister, Catherine, happened to be the wife of the heir to the duchy.

However, tidings of this occurrence had not yet reached St Petersburg when, on New Year's Eve, Alexander issued an *ukase* which greatly increased tariffs on all imports arriving overland, while reducing those on goods brought in by sea. Russia had been deliberately neglecting the enforcement of some of the Continental System's regulations for some time. The Baltic trade in timber, flax, hemp and grain was cherished by numerous boyars and merchants, and Napoleon's restrictions on this prof-itable commercial intercourse were commensurably resented.[21] Equally, the Russian government could ill afford the concomitant loss of customs revenue. While it is questionable whether the impact of Napoleon's decrees did much more than compound Russia's existing economic woes, undermining his prohibitions clearly had a domestic political appeal as well as any mercantile benefits. Certainly, the *ukase* was primarily designed to counter his attempts to secure France a 'veiled monopoly' on the importation and distribution of colonial produce.[22] More has been said about the ramifications of this elsewhere, but, given the continental coun-tries' enforced dependence on overland communications as a conse-quence of Britain's stranglehold on maritime trade, whereas Russia's imports of French brandy, wine and textiles were hard hit, she became an *entrepôt* for 'neutral' merchandise, much of it British. This made a mock-ery of the System and, sooner or later, Napoleon would have to put a stop to it. Although his attempts at Britain's economic strangulation were being thwarted all over the continent by smugglers, acquisitive consumers and malversation, brazen defiance by a major power like Russia could not be seen to be tolerated.

The other great inflammatory issue was Napoleon's quest for an heir to his throne. Although he had acquired a stepson, Eugène, through his wife Josephine, she had failed to provide him with his own children. Since Napoleon had fathered at least two illegitimate offspring, it was con-cluded that the empress, now in her mid-40s, was no longer fertile. As early as the Erfurt conference Napoleon, concerned about the succession, had first enquired as to the possibility of him marrying one of Alexander's sisters, the Grand Duchess Anna. Although the Tsar prevaricated over the matter for months thereafter, he was palpably offended when he heard of Napoleon's somewhat brusque decision to take the Austrian Marie-Louise as his bride instead. While the suddenness of the announcement and the inherent slight upon his sister might have offended Alexander's rather eclectic sense of protocol, one suspects that the move's political signifi-cance is what really disturbed him; the marriage was, after all, as much an instrument of Austrian foreign policy as it was French. In any case,

Napoleon had sensitivities of his own, and seems to have interpreted the Tsar's hesitancy to provide him with a bride as a snub which was both personal and political. The emperor promptly retaliated, in January 1810, by declining to ratify the Franco-Russian convention on Poland's future which he had first proposed.[23]

Throughout the following two years, as the various events outlined above added to both sides' sense of disillusionment, betrayal and insecurity, relations between them steadily deteriorated.[24] In August 1811, during a diplomatic reception, Napoleon openly stated that, while he was not seeking war with the Tsar, he regarded Russia's conduct as provocative.[25] Indeed, over the next few months, he took the precaution of bullying Prussia into concluding an alliance with France. According to the pact that was finally ratified in March 1812, she was to submit to the occupation of much of her territory by Imperial troops and, in the event of a conflict with Alexander, furnish a contingent of 20 000 men and huge quantities of *matériel*. The emperor had, by this time, already circulated a list of his grievances against Russia, calling on his vassals to make similar contributions of soldiers and supplies to '*La Grande Armée de la Russie*'. Whereas Berlin had little choice other than to be obeisant, Vienna enjoyed rather more leverage and managed to curb Napoleon's rapacious demands for Austrian resources, eventually providing a single corps of 30 000 men. Although Prussia and Austria secretly contacted the Tsar to plead that their participation in the impending war against him was a necessary evil and in no sense indicative of their true feelings, Alexander was predictably less than wholly persuaded, bearing in mind the way these powers had responded to his plans for a war against Napoleon in 1811; if he had some sympathy for Prussia in her dilemma, he was more sceptical regarding Metternich's assurances.

But Russia's own diplomatic and military preparations for a conflict with France were, at this stage, well in hand. If the Tsar's desire to take the offensive in 1811 had outrun his means, by early 1812 he was confident that his powerful army, enlarged and reorganized by Barclay de Tolly as we have seen, would make good use of the vastness of his realm in the event of a French invasion. He seems to have been inspired and encouraged by Wellington's successful defence of Portugal against Massena, which had shunned the fighting of potentially decisive battles in favour of the luring of the invader deep into the country's heartland, where his advance could be blocked by prepared defences and 'scorched-earth' tactics.[26] Although in general this was to be the strategy followed by the Russians, the details of their plans were to be compromised from the very outset by, above all, a failure to appreciate the sheer size of Napoleon's forces. This, given the competing demands being made on his resources by the Peninsular War and the need to protect his empire, was estimated to be 250 000 troops at most, when Napoleon had actually gathered what was probably the largest army Europe had ever seen. Its leading echelons alone comprised 600 000 men, 80 000 of them cavalry, with some 1400 guns, 25 000 vehicles and around 170 000 draughthorses, ponies and oxen.[27]

By the time this host had been worn down to a more manageable size, so much territory had had to be yielded that the Tsar's Fabian policy had become politically unsustainable and his generals had been obliged to risk a major battle. So to what extent Russia's military strategy was the product of farsightedness or improvisation is a moot point. As far as her diplomatic preparations for the conflict are concerned, however, her endeavours were both timely and fruitful. Having ended hostilities against Sweden in September 1809, she had turned to wooing her. Aware of this and anxious to secure the left rear of *La Grande Armée*, Napoleon seized Pomerania in March 1812, providing a good pretext for the Russo-Swedish alliance which followed on 5 April. The conflict with Turkey that had been under way since late 1806 was also terminated through the Treaty of Bucharest (May 1812), the Russians thereby releasing Tschitschagov's army on the Danube for operations against Napoleon. Similarly, although at this stage St Petersburg made no approaches to London – the British not being seen as in a position to offer much military assistance, while the Russians were fearful of precipitating hostilities with France[28] – both Bernadotte and the Tsar were formally to end their respective wars with Britain within two weeks of Napoleon commencing his invasion of Russia. While these conflicts had, as we have seen, been largely cosmetic, this development not only paved the way for a new grand coalition – the Sixth – but also permitted its members to focus their efforts on the struggle against their common enemy. Britain encouraged Bernadotte to mount a diversion in northern Germany, while both she and Russia were to aid Sweden in her bid to wrest Norway from the Danes. Finally convinced as to Bernadotte's loyalty, Alexander also felt able to divert 15 000 troops from garrisoning Finland into holding Riga against the French, an operation in which they were to be ably supported by the Royal Navy.[29]

Comforted by the favourable trend of developments on the diplomatic front, in April 1812 the Tsar issued Napoleon with a virtual ultimatum: he was to evacuate Pomerania and Prussia and compensate the duke of Oldenburg as a prelude to any further talks. Unwilling to back down, the emperor rallied his allies at a splendid reception in Dresden,[30] while *La Grande Armée* was stealthily assembled along the Duchy of Warsaw's eastern edge. Finally, on 22 June 1812, Napoleon, having joined his forces, issued a stirring proclamation. Russia, he insisted, had broken the pledges she had made at Tilsit and had thus compelled France to choose between dishonour and fighting. The 'Second Polish War', as he termed it, would, he assured his soldiers,

> bring as much glory to French arms as did the first. But the peace treaty we shall conclude this time will carry its own guarantee; it will put an end to the fatal influence which Russia has exercised over Europe for the past fifty years.[31]

Without any formal declaration of hostilities, his vanguards duly began crossing the Russian frontier the next day. Three years had elapsed since he had taken the field in person.

The sheer size of Napoleon's army and the meticulous care he had taken in preparing for the coming campaign are testimony to both his awareness of the immensity of the geostrategic problems he was likely to encounter and his respect for his adversaries' martial capabilities.[32] Contrary to popular myth, he fully appreciated the implications of the climate and relative barrenness of the Russian borderlands, and had endeavoured to furnish his forces with sufficient logistical support. 'We can hope for nothing from the countryside', he cautioned Davout, 'and accordingly must take everything with us.'[33] Painful past experience had repeatedly demonstrated what slippery and resilient opponents the Tsar's soldiers could be, and Napoleon realized that, given the opportunity, the Russian armies might well be disposed to trade space for time. The key to victory lay in catching them quickly and as far west as practicable, for, if they *did* manage to evade him, it was only to be anticipated that they would withdraw all the way to the Rivers Dvina, Berezina and Dnieper, which formed a colossal arc stretching from Kiev to Riga. According to intelligence reports, these cities' defences were being strengthened and, at various points along the waterways between them, fortified camps were under construction, notably at Dunaburg, Drissa and Borisov.[34] It was, therefore, imperative that the foremost Russian forces be overtaken and destroyed cleanly and swiftly. Accordingly, Napoleon devised a way which, he calculated, would take just three weeks to fulfil and would require his army to venture no further east than Smolensk.

Geographically, Russia's western frontier was broken up into three distinct sections, with the huge Pripet Marshes separating two regions of more easily traversable terrain: to the south was the rolling, lush countryside of Volhynia; to the north a great crescent of sandy, undulating plains, pitted with lakes and swamps, extended from the Duchy of Warsaw through Lithuania and Courland towards Minsk. Although it would take his army over lands which, being comparatively infertile and sparsely inhabited, would offer little scope for foraging, Napoleon concluded that this northern avenue of approach had most to recommend it. Largely populated by (Catholic) Poles and Lithuanians who were reluctant subjects of the Tsar, it was seen as a more secure route than those further south which were too close to unreliable Austria for comfort. Moreover, once across the broad Niemen at Kovno, the army, advancing astride the tolerably good road through Vilna and Vitebsk, would encounter few waterways that the Russians might readily defend, since the western sides of most rivers dominated their eastern banks. Most importantly, this route would bring *La Grande Armée* into a central position. With its right wing refused, it would wheel towards Vilna, dissecting the main enemy forces under Barclay and severing the bulk of them from St Petersburg. When Napoleon's offensive began, Barclay's 127 000 bayonets and sabres were separated by some 200 kilometres from Bagration's Second Army, which, amounting to 48 000 men, was cantoned due south of Grodno, between the Niemen and the Bug, mesmerized by French feints towards Volhynia. Indeed, Napoleon hoped that these would pin Bagration to his position while the pivoting *Grande Armée* swung behind him and Barclay, pressing the Russians into the pocket formed by the Pripet, Bug and Narew. The closing of the pincers would see all of 400 000 Imperial troops converging 'on one point'[35] for a climactic battle which, in all probability, could only end in the annihilation of the two Russian armies.

A large-scale replica of the strategic envelopment that had obliterated Mack's forces at Ulm, this scheme was as breathtaking as any ever devised by Napoleon. However, *La Grande Armée* of 1812 was not that of 1805, nor could western Russia be compared with southern Germany. The emperor acknowledged that 'in such an extended theatre of action, success may only be gained through a well-conceived plan in which all the component parts are in full harmony'.[36] But this, given the technology of the day, was becoming ever harder to achieve. During the conflicts of the eighteenth century it had become apparent that the practical problems involved in not only supplying but also directing and controlling forces effectively circumscribed the size of armies; in the absence of semi-independent sub-units, there was little point in assembling many more than 60 000 troops at any one point. This also tended to make engagements relatively compact affairs. As we have seen, the semi-autonomous structures of *corps d'armée* and divisions as pioneered by Napoleon and gradually copied by his adversaries transformed all of this. Once unitary armies, such as that of Prussia at Jena, gave way to modular ones, forces, battlefields and theatres of war all expanded until at Wagram, for instance, over 300 000 men were locked in combat on a 20-kilometre front. Commanding generals, no longer able to keep a watchful eye on developments everywhere, became increasingly dependent on their subordinates, coordinating their actions from a central headquarters which was ineluctably remote from sectors of the fighting.

In Russia in 1812,[37] the entire system was stretched to new limits. The area of operations became truly enormous as *La Grande Armée*, its communications anchored on Poland, tapered towards Moscow some 1000 kilometres away. Yet though the theatre's dimensions dwarfed them, the components of Napoleon's army were unprecedentedly large. Davout's I Corps alone comprised 70 000 personnel[38] – double the size it had been in earlier campaigns – while its infantry regiments, swollen to five battalions each, had an average strength of some 3700 bayonets – much the same as an entire division had amounted to in 1805. The tremendous influx of new recruits diluted the quality of the French forces in several respects. First, Davout opined that single battalions of close to 1000 men were tactically unmanageable; he would have preferred to see a larger number of smaller, more flexible battalions.[39] Second, in order to provide the freshly created units with a kernel of seasoned soldiers, veterans from the long-established battalions had to be exchanged for draftees in the new ones.[40] This process undermined the capabilities of the force as a whole. Not only were many units left lacking an adequate proportion of men experienced in combat, but also most conscripts had yet to acquire the foraging and fieldcraft skills that had enabled Napoleon's armies to get by with minimal logistical support. Relatively unencumbered by ponderous supply convoys and obliged to keep moving onto fresh territory in order to sustain themselves, the practice of living off the land accounted for much of the French armies' legendary speed and mobility. Unadept at foraging techniques and unaccustomed to the protracted, gruelling marches, barbarism and deprivations of warfare, thousands of raw conscripts rapidly found the abrupt transition from civilian to military life too much to bear. Of those who did not succumb to the physical threats posed by malnutrition, starvation, dysentery, typhus, diphtheria, blistered feet and the extreme weather conditions – suffocating heat punctuated by torrential downpours and plummeting temperatures – many were stricken by demoralization which manifested itself in bouts of apathy, desertion, indiscipline and suicide.

From the outset, the sheer size of *La Grande Armée* sapped the ability of its leadership to cope with these and other problems. Men who were accomplished at leading corps, divisions and brigades in semi-independent roles found themselves entrusted with what in later wars were to be termed 'army groups'. None of them had any experience of command at this level and only a handful possessed the potential for it. At the other end of the spectrum, the expansion in the size of tactical units spawned an insatiable demand for commissioned and noncommissioned officers. Although Napoleon advocated meritocracy, literacy was as much a requirement among senior soldiers as it was among bureaucrats. Thus, such positions were effectively reserved for the educated if not the practically experienced. Normally, the lower commissioned ranks were occupied by graduates of the Fontainebleau Military School who had at least two years' service under their belts. Promotion was similarly regulated; for a sergeant-major to rise to the rank of lieutenant, for example, he needed eight years' experience. Finding sufficient suitable candidates to fill all the posts created by the army's enlargement proved difficult. Although the Imperial Guard, which had itself expanded to 50 000 personnel, was combed for veterans who might be transferred to more senior positions within line regiments,[41] many units' junior commissioned ranks were filled by soldiers of rather less promise. Too many appointees neither knew nor cared about their charges. Indeed, when coupled with the army's polyglot nature – it contained members of at least a dozen races, including Spaniards, Prussians and others of dubious loyalty – the interchanging of personnel proved very detrimental to the camaraderie which had been a striking feature of Napoleon's army in previous campaigns.

Given all of this, it is perhaps unsurprising that the invasion of Russia started inauspiciously. Whereas Napoleon's leading units, masked by Murat's cavalry, advanced smoothly enough, the rest followed fitfully, impeded by supply wagons that sank into the sandy tracks. It quickly became apparent that logistical problems would arise not from a paucity of nourishment as such, but from an inability to transport foodstuffs to where they were needed and to distribute them among the troops. Fresh water supplies, for instance, were essential. Initially the weather was unbearably hot and, finding little to drink, men and horses perished in droves. Napoleon was soon obliged to have Murat mark time while the army's tail closed up. This, however, not only left the Russians alerted as to the main axis of the French advance but also gave them time to slip away from their forward positions. Seeing Barclay escaping to the northeast, Napoleon strove to retrieve what he could of his plan by descending on Vilna so as to encircle Bagration's forces. Hours after he arrived there, a cold spell and a series of thunderstorms began which lasted five days, turning the roads into mires and paralysing many units. As if this was not bad enough, King Jerome, entrusted with a pivotal part in the enemy's envelopment, failed to pin down Bagration until the trap could be slammed behind him; as late as 3 July, he was still near Grodno while Bagration was making tracks for Minsk. Napoleon was furious: Jerome, he complained, 'has robbed me of the fruit of my manœuvres and of the best opportunity ever presented in war – all on account of his singular failure to grasp the first notions of warfare'.[42] So stung was his brother by this remark that he promptly resigned, leaving his army group leaderless at a crucial juncture.

While Davout trailed after Bagration, and other Imperial forces moved towards Riga and Brest to secure the theatre's expanding flanks, Napoleon wheeled the balance of his army against Barclay, whose forces had retreated beyond the Dvina via the entrenched camps at Drissa and Dunaberg. Notified that Bagration was nearing Orsha on the Dnieper and that Barclay had quitted Drissa and moved east, Napoleon's intuition told him that the two Russian armies were intending to combine at Polotsk. On 19 July he duly began concentrating his forces between these two places. In fact, the Russians were making for Vitebsk, and it was the 21st before Napoleon realized his mistake. Two days later, however, Davout intercepted Bagration at Mogilev on the Dnieper, while, on the 25th, Murat clashed with Barclay's forces at Ostronovo, west of Vitebsk. The Russians recoiled from these encounters, eventually uniting at Smolensk on 4 August. In the mean time, Napoleon had been compelled to give his troops a period to recuperate and reorganize. Even when joined by Davout's column, he found that his central army group, originally 375 000-strong, had dwindled to no more than 185 000 men. Detachments and casualties incurred in the cossack raids and the few minor engagements which had occurred accounted for much of the deficit, but roughly 100 000 soldiers had been lost through sickness and straggling.[43]

So far, Napoleon had twice attempted to bring the retreating Russians to battle by means of a *manœuvre sur les derrières*. Both bids had failed, ruined by the problems involved in the synchronization of movements in time and space.[44] But now Barclay began to think of taking the offensive. Initially, Alexander had accompanied his army, his presence compounding the rivalries within the Russian high command. Barclay, a Livonian, was resented by court conservatives as one of the modernizing 'westerners' under whose spell the Tsar had fallen. To them, his Fabian strategy smacked of cowardice, and Alexander was increasingly urged to replace 'the German' with the elderly Kutusov, 'a true Russian, a disciple of Suvarov'.[45] Certainly there was a growing sense that the time for withdrawal was over and that an active defence should be mounted. Accordingly, urging Barclay to go onto the attack, the Tsar set out on 17 July for Moscow, intent on rallying the nation and raising more funds and manpower.

As in Austria in 1809, there was talk of encouraging the population as a whole to turn on the invaders. The Orthodox Church, like that in Spain before it, denounced the 'godless' French and sought to depict the war as a holy crusade, while Alexander's proclamations ritually assured his subjects that both the Tsar and Providence were with them in combating the aggressor: 'You are defending religion, the country and freedom!'[46] But what manner of people did resist the invaders and why? As in Vienna three years before, a clutch of volunteer units were mustered from among the middle classes, while the Church and boyars predictably provided money and serfs for the war effort. As far as those Russians who did not form part of the Establishment are concerned, however, responses to Napoleon's invasion varied considerably. Together with the cossacks' raids, there were instances of peasants harassing stragglers on the fringes of *La Grande Armée*. Yet much of this can be explained in terms other than a groundswell of patriotic enthusiasm for war. The Bashkirs, Tartars, Cossacks and Kalmucks were all nomadic tribesmen who, judging by virtually all the available eyewitness accounts, were principally motivated by a quest for plunder and were reluctant to engage any but the weakest of opponents.[47] Similarly, throughout the Napoleonic Wars, whenever armies – particularly famished, mutinous ones – passed through settlements there were violent clashes simply because the residents endeavoured to protect themselves and their property from predatory soldiers who seldom discriminated between friends and foe. In 1812, many Lithuanians, for example, who started out sympathetic to Napoleon's cause – he actually raised several regiments from their heartland in the midst of the campaign[48] – were alienated by the antics of marauding troops.[49] Equally, the 'scorched-earth' stratagem was largely imposed on the wretched Russian peasantry by their own army. As Chlapowski noted: 'As the Russians retreated, they were burning . . . the villages and forcing the inhabitants to load up their carts with their pitiful belongings and flee with their livestock. . . . Here and there peasants had made their way back.'[50] There were numerous cases of such people complaining about their rulers and collaborating with the French. Nor were many of the men who entered the Tsar's army in 1812 particularly eager recruits. Although there were some who volunteered for short-term military service, coming mostly from wealthy middle- and upper-class families and fearing that Napoleon the reformer might abolish serfdom,[51] they had an obvious stake in protecting the existing social order. In fact, the great bulk of the manpower raised comprised not volunteers but serfs conscripted for all of 25 years. Indeed, the questionable allegiance of these impressed men highlighted a wider concern among Russia's governing classes. A feudal society like Austria, she could ill afford to risk internal disorder through a general arming of the population. Tellingly, the Muscovite militia were equipped with relatively innocuous pikes, despite there being 60 000 muskets stored in the Kremlin.[52] In short, as had occurred across the Habsburg domains in 1809, what little popular resistance the French did encounter was rarely premeditated, still less inspired by patriotism. As has so often happened, very ordinary people with better things on their minds found themselves embroiled in a ruinous war and played the part that fate had dealt them.

Pricked by criticism of his cautious style, on 6 August Barclay, having amassed 125 000 men at Smolensk, groped towards Vitebsk in search of his pursuers. His counteroffensive rapidly stalled, however, as the bickering within his headquarters all but paralysed the Russian forces. Napoleon, meanwhile, glimpsing another chance to get behind them, stealthily and boldly transferred his remaining 185 000 bayonets and sabres to the Dnieper's southern bank around Orsha, planning to sweep through Krasnoye to Smolensk. At 2.30pm on the 14th, Murat's cavalry screen collided with a solitary division under General Neveroski near Krasnoye, eventually forcing the Russian foot into a vast square six ranks deep. Artillery and musketry would have shredded this formation in minutes, but Murat, behaving more like a trooper than a marshal, led his squadrons in a sequence of clumsy charges which, although it neither stopped the Russians from retreating nor inflicted fatal damage on them, prevented Ney's infantry and cannon from getting to grips with the enemy. Neveroski's men escaped into Smolensk, where they were soon reinforced by Barclay, who had already begun to retrace his steps.[53] On the 15th, Napoleon received reports of Russian activity at Katane on the Dnieper, just west of Smolensk. Hoping that the enemy's main body would venture onto the river's southern bank and that he would be able to ensnare Barclay as he had Bennigsen at Friedland, Napoleon held back the majority of his forces pending developments. Certainly, he wanted a battle on the 15th – there would have been no better way to mark his birthday than a great victory – but the Russians failed to oblige him; no more than a few cavalry appeared at Katane.[54] Indeed, Barclay and Bagration were now scurrying back to Smolensk, augmenting its garrison to 20 000 men with 180 guns.

Twenty-four precious hours thus ticked by before Napoleon resumed his march on the ancient citadel, arriving there at 1pm on the 16th. Its medieval walls were over 3 metres thick and proof against his heaviest field guns; only howitzers were of use. Set ablaze by these, much of the city's inner core was destroyed as, throughout the 17th, the attackers endeavoured to penetrate it.[55] That night, the Russians retreated across the Dnieper, closely pursued by Ney's corps.

Barclay, fearing that Napoleon would seek to cross the river at nearby Prudichevo or Dorogobuzh still further east, now raced towards Moscow. Sure enough, harried by Murat, Davout and Ney, he found General Junot's VIII Corps debouching through Prudichevo to bar his retreat. But by now *La Grande Armée*, including Napoleon, was sinking into torpor, borne down by the cumulative effects of its gruelling advance. Junot's Westphalians failed to press home their assault and the Russians again escaped by the skin of their teeth.[56] Napoleon, sick and exhausted, returned to Smolensk to ponder his next move. Aware that fighting between General Tormassov's Third Army and Schwarzenberg's Austrians had erupted in Volhynia, that Tschitschagov's 'Army of Moldavia' was moving up to support the former, and that Oudinot's II Corps was locking horns with General Wittgenstein's corps around Riga,[57] he was increasingly worried about his communications with Poland. He thought of suspending the campaign, consolidating his position and resuming the offensive in the spring. On the other hand, he dreaded the military and political risks involved in either retreating or remaining so remote from his empire's heartland for much longer. British collusion with Russia and Sweden had turned into an open alliance,[58] and too many of his other vassals could hardly be trusted. Shortly to hear of Wellington's victory at Salamanca, the conflicts in Spain and Russia, he told his staff, were 'two ulcers which ate into the vitals of France and . . . she could not bear them both at once'.[59] There was, therefore, 'no time to be lost', he concluded. 'We must extract peace; it is at Moscow. Besides, this army cannot now stop: with its composition, and in its disorganization, motion alone keeps it together. One may advance at the head of it, but not stop to go back.'[60] Accordingly, on 25 August, *La Grande Armée* resumed its eastward trek.

If Napoleon was nearing the end of his strength then so were his opponents. By now, the luckless Barclay had been superseded by Kutusov, who, despite his misgivings, had succumbed to political pressure to make a stand in Moscow's defence.[61] His army – approximately 120 000 men with 640 guns – duly took up a position straddling the village of Borodino. The right wing ran parallel to the shallow River Kalatsha as far as its confluence with the Moskva; the left extended southwards towards the settlement of Utitza. Intersected by several brooks and speckled with knolls, ridges and woods, the Russian front, just 8 kilometres across, was exceedingly cramped, and its natural defences had been supplemented with several earthworks.

Kutusov's relatively open southern flank seemed a tempting avenue of attack. Once turned here, it has been argued by some,[62] the Russians could have been herded into the angle between the Moskva and the Kalatsha. In fact, Davout suggested allotting 40 000 men to such a venture.[63] Napoleon, however, disposing of only 103 000 bayonets, 28 000 sabres and 587 guns, had insufficient troops both to pin the enemy to their position and to mount a telling, wide sweep round their left. His soldiers were, in any case, too weary for strategic pirouettes, and he was afraid that their

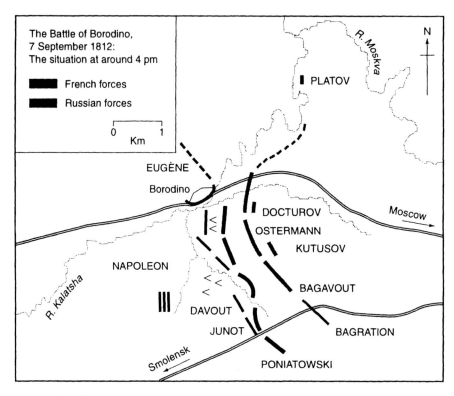

The Battle of Borodino

prey would evade envelopment as had happened so often before. Having sought a conclusive battle for so long, he could neither risk frightening the Russians off nor compromise his chances of victory through an overly complex plan.[64] Moreover, he was unwell, like many of his men, and seems to have been robbed of his customary energy and powers of concentration. For most of the battle he was to remain listless at his command post behind the lines.[65]

Kutusov did largely the same.[66] Indeed, when the French attacked at 6am on 7 September, neither side concerned itself much with tactical finesse. Barely able to manœuvre on the congested field, great blocks of troops tried conclusions with one another as the battle degenerated into an attritional massacre.[67] So numerous were the casualties that, as early as 8.30am, Napoleon had little but the Guard left in reserve, while the Russians were having to draw down units from their right to bolster their left and centre. For four more hours the fighting eddied and swirled around Kutusov's earthworks, with infantry and horsemen struggling to occupy ground won by the lavish quantities of guns on both sides. The Russians resisted with their customary stubbornness, but were eventually ejected from Utitza, Borodino and all of their redoubts. Victory beckoned to the emperor, but he declined to risk his last intact reserves in a final bid to break Kutusov's shaken army. The battle slowly petered out and the Russians retired, unmolested.[68]

Napoleon's decision has attracted much criticism, but he was probably right under the circumstances.[69] Success was far from certain, and he could not know what the future held.[70] His army had in any case been horribly mauled: it had suffered over 30 000 casualties; the Russians half as many again. Yet his failure to triumph in 'the great battle beneath the walls of Moscow' was the campaign's climax; it, if not the war, was now lost. Just as the survival of Karl's army after Wagram had constrained Napoleon's ability to impose terms on Austria in 1809, Kutusov's escape ensured that there would be no dictated peace. The struggle would go on and, as the Tsar had warned the French ambassador on the eve of the war, the Russian winter would enter the fray.[71]

The Russian army made little further effort to bar Napoleon's path to Moscow. Kutusov led his depleted divisions southeast towards Kolomna, while the Muscovites were ordered to abandon their homes by the city's governor, Count Rostopchin, who was planning to set it ablaze.[72] As the first French units marched in late on 14 September, his incendiaries were already at work and, over the next couple of days, most of Moscow was reduced to ashes in a bid to drive out the invaders. Paradoxically, it was as well for the Tsar's cause that this proved unsuccessful. Still able to find ample shelter and food supplies, the remaining 95 000 troops of *La Grande Armée*, together with the few thousand (mostly foreign) civilians who had stayed on, were disinclined to leave the city.[73] Thus, when he should have been thinking of turning against St Petersburg or retracing his steps before the advance of 'General Winter', Napoleon loitered on the Moscva, trusting that his occupation of the Russian heartland would help coerce Alexander into suing for terms.

Certainly, the Russians evinced signs of being as war-weary as the French[74] and, as we have seen, had already abandoned their Fabian strategy because it had become politically unsustainable. Borodino was, predictably, proclaimed a victory, but Metternich at least regarded the fall of Moscow as a sign of Russia's incipient collapse.[75] Nevertheless, the Tsar proved obdurate, rejecting Napoleon's overtures which, as the days ticked by, became ever more supplicatory. Meanwhile, reinforcements of men and *matériel* poured into the Russian army's camps,[76] tilting the strategic balance in favour of Kutusov and his colleagues, who, by early October, were planning a counteroffensive. After spending several more days agonizing over his options, none of which was without great risks or costs,[77] Napoleon finally decided on retreat; on 19 October, *La Grande Armée* would set out for Smolensk via Kulaga.

By this time, Murat's cavalry outposts, notably those at Vinkovo,[78] were already being probed by Russian troops and, as Napoleon's columns headed southwest, they were shadowed by the whole of Kutusov's army. At Maloyaroslavets during the third week of October, the Russians made the first of several attempts to hamper the retreat. They were repulsed after a hard fight, but Napoleon, who was nearly captured at one point,[79] seems to have been panicked into relinquishing the hard-won bridgehead on the Lusha's southern bank and, instead of marching west through Medyn, recoiled northwards to Mozhaysk.[80] Thus, *La Grande Armée* found itself back on the corpse-littered, devastated strip of countryside by which it had advanced in the summer. Stalked by Kutusov, it plodded on towards Vyazma, where on 3 November the Russians again sought to dissect the strung-out cavalcade of men, vehicles and guns. Though the assailants were beaten off once more, the plight of Napoleon's column deepened by the day. With swarms of cossacks snapping at its heels, the rearguard, Ney's III Corps, was already entangled with 30 000 stragglers, while demoralization and indiscipline were pervading even the army's finest units.

On 4 November, the first snow fell and, within a month, the temperature was to sink as low as −37.5° Celsius.[81] Unequipped for winter operations, *La Grande Armée* suffered terribly. Benumbed, weary, abject men would linger around bonfires rather than keep moving, their lives flickering out with the embers. Others, unable to manipulate their weapons because of frostbite or because the barrels and metal fittings cleaved to their flesh in the intense cold, proved easy prey for their pursuers. The few remaining horses fared no better than their masters. Lacking ice-studs on their shoes and deprived of even grazing by the snowdrifts, these long-suffering, jaded animals finally succumbed to starvation, heavy falls or utter weariness. Guns and vehicles were abandoned by the score, and few troopers were left with mounts.

Napoleon had calculated that the huge depots at Smolensk would help relieve his army's agony. So great was the disorder within its ranks, however, that these precious supplies, sufficient for two weeks, were squandered in just three days by the thousands of stragglers. When Ney's troops forsook Smolensk on 17 November, *La Grande Armée* had dwindled to just 42 000 effectives.

The Russians, it should be stressed, were also suffering immensely. Kutusov had commenced his counteroffensive with 110 000 men, only 40 000 of whom were to reach Vilna,[82] while Wittgenstein, who was pressing southwards over the Dvina with 40 000 troops,[83] was to lose a quarter of his strength in the process.[84] Relatively few of these casualties were incurred in battle. Kutusov's units normally hovered on the French flanks and rear, content to let their harassment tactics and cold and hunger grind down their adversaries. Indeed, apart from an action at Krasnoye on 17 November, when Napoleon, using the Guard he had insisted on preserving at Borodino, swept aside the enemy's latest attempt to impede the retreat,[85] there was no serious clash between the French main body and the principal Russian forces until the former reached the Berezina. Although Kutusov did make an effort to encircle Ney's trailing command, with astonishing fortitude and adroitness, *'le plus brave des braves'* carved a way through to rejoin his master at Orsha.[86]

Here, some carefully husbanded stockpiles of clothing and rations gave everyone some relief from the cold and hunger. Nevertheless, by 23 November, the jaws of the Russian offensive were closing around the stricken *Grande Armée* as it searched for a way across the Berezina. The strategic flanks of the theatre having long since been punctured,[87] most of Wittgenstein's and Tschitschagov's forces were on the brink of uniting at Borisov, while Kutusov's were bearing down on Napoleon from the east. Assimilating the remnants of Oudinot's corps and various garrisons into his army, the emperor, suddenly recovering his old energy and flair, rose to the challenge. Between the 24th and the 29th, in an operation that was as audacious as it was desperate, his 49 000 remaining effectives, making up with deception, skill and spirit what they lacked in numbers and equipment, outwitted, outmanœuvred and outfought Tschitschagov and Wittgenstein before Kutusov could come to their support. By means of rickety, improvised bridges built and maintained by engineers who selflessly toiled in freezing waters for hours on end, the greater part of Napoleon's forces gained the western bank and hurried towards Molodechno, skirmishing with Tschitschagov's troops as they went. Some 30 000 camp-followers and stragglers who failed to cross before the bridges were torched perished in or alongside the icy Berezina as the cossacks descended upon them.[88]

On 22 October, a deranged General, Claude de Malet, had escaped from a Parisian mental institution and, claiming that Napoleon had perished in Russia, tried to proclaim a republic.[89] Although this bizarre *coup* was quashed within hours, it highlighted the political nervousness engendered by the emperor's prolonged absence from the seat of government. Realizing, too, that his retreat would almost certainly lead to Prussia's defection, Napoleon resolved to return to Paris as soon as possible to prepare for a new war. Accordingly, once he was satisfied that he had done all he could for the remnants of *La Grande Armée*, he handed command to

Murat and, setting out by sleigh on 5 December, sped across Europe, arriving at the Tuileries just 13 days later.

Notes

1. See, for example, Metternich's opinion of 17 January 1811 regarding the war in Spain in C.S.B. Buckland, *Metternich and the British Government from 1809 to 1813* (London, 1932), pp. 172–3.
2. See M. Finley, *The Most Monstrous of Wars* (Columbia, SC, 1994), pp. 114–26.
3. Consult C. Oman, *A History of the Peninsular War* (Oxford, 1902–30), III, pp. 341–89 and 390–437.
4. See, for instance, A. John, 'Farming in Wartime, 1793–1815', in E. Jones and G. Mingay (eds.), *Land, Labour and Population in the Industrial Revolution* (London, 1967); G. Hueckel, 'English Farming Profits during the Napoleonic Wars, 1793–1815', *Explorations in Economic History*, 13/3 (1976).
5. W. Galpin, *The Grain Supply of England* (New York, 1925), p. 111; A. Cunningham, *British Credit in the Last Napoleonic War* (Cambridge, 1910), pp. 75–6.
6. Quoted in H.L. Coles, *The War of 1812* (Chicago, 1965), p. 24.
7. See, for example, P.W. Schroeder, *The Transformation of European Politics* (Oxford, 1996), pp. 385–8.
8. J. Hanoteau (ed.), *Memoirs of General de Caulaincourt, Duke of Vicenza* (2 vols, London, 1935), I, p. 66 (hereafter cited as Caulaincourt, *Memoirs*).
9. P. Mackesy, *The War in the Mediterranean* (Cambridge, MA, 1957), pp. 353–5.
10. See A.H. Barton, 'Late Gustavian Autocracy in Sweden: Gustavus IV Adolf and his Opponents, 1792–1809', *Scandinavian Studies*, 46/3 (1974).
11. See A. Palmer, *Bernadotte* (London, 1990), pp. 143–6.
12. Palmer, *Bernadotte*, pp. 152–5.
13. See Palmer, *Bernadotte*, pp. 172–3. For further information about Swedish affairs during this period, consult: I. Anderson, *A History of Sweden* (London, 1955); F.D. Scott, *Bernadotte and the Fall of Napoleon* (Cambridge, MA, 1935); H. Barton, 'Sweden and the Atlantic Revolution, 1760–1815', CREP (1982).
14. See, for example, A.N. Ryan, *Trade with the Enemy in the Scandinavian and Baltic Ports during the Napoleonic War: For and Against* (London, 1962).
15. Quoted in Paul Britten Austin, *1812: The March on Moscow* (London, 1993), p. 27.
16. Quoted in R. Muir, *Britain and the Defeat of Napoleon* (New Haven, CT, 1996), p. 189.
17. See Muir, *Britain and Napoleon*, pp. 187–90.
18. See A. Palmer, *Alexander I* (London, 1974), pp. 199–203; A. Gielgud (ed.), *Memoirs of Prince Adam Czartoryski and his Correspondence with Alexander I* (2 vols, London, 1888), II, pp. 222–8; A. Fournier, *Napoleon I: A Biography* (2 vols, London, 1911), II, pp. 151–2, 156–7.
19. See Caulaincourt, *Memoirs*, II, pp. 62–8, 84–5.
20. For an overview of the relationship, consult A.C. Niven, *Napoleon and Alexander I* (Washington, 1978); H. Parker, 'Why did Napoleon invade Russia?'' CREP (Bicentennial Consortium, 1989).
21. See A.W. Crosby, *America, Russia, Hemp and Napoleon: America's Trade with Russia and the Baltic, 1783–1812* (Columbus, OH, 1965); M.F. Zlotnikov, *Kontinental'naia Blockada i Rossiia* (Moscow, 1966).
22. See Caulaincourt, *Memoirs*, I, pp. 59–60.
23. See W.H. Zawadzki, 'Russia and the Reopening of the Polish Question, 1801–14', *International History Review*, 7/1 (1985).
24. See Caulaincourt, *Memoirs*, I, pp. 62–8, 84–5.

25. Fournier, *Napoleon*, II, p. 159.
26. C. von Clausewitz, *The Campaign of 1812 in Russia* (London, 1992 edition), pp. 14–26; A. Palmer, *Napoleon in Russia* (London, 1967), p. 26; Caulaincourt, *Memoirs*, I, pp. 68–70.
27. D.G. Chandler, *The Campaigns of Napoleon* (London, 1966), pp. 754–8. Also see ASH, C2–697 '*État du personnel*'. Other French manuscript sources relating to the 1812 campaign include: ASH, C2 522–35 '*Situations*'; C2 120, 122, 134, 286–8, 290, 299, 303–4 '*Grande Armée: Correspondance*'.
28. See Muir, *Britain and Napoleon*, p. 222.
29. Muir, *Britain and Napoleon*, pp. 222–8.
30. See Austin, *March on Moscow*, p. 29.
31. NC, XXIII, p. 528.
32. See, for instance, Chandler, *Campaigns*, p. 757; G.F. Nafziger, *Napoleon's Invasion of Russia* (Novato, CA, 1988), pp. 85–8.
33. NC, XXIII, p. 432.
34. See Nafziger, *Invasion*, pp. 104–5.
35. NC, XXIII, p. 432.
36. NC, XXIII, p. 469.
37. For a statistical analysis of *La Grande Armée* in this campaign, see O. von Pivka, *Armies of 1812* (London, 1977).
38. ASH, C2–525/63.
39. Nafziger, *Invasion*, p. 94.
40. Nafziger, *Invasion*, p. 94.
41. See, for example, J. Coignet, *The Note-Books of Captain Coignet, Soldier of the Empire 1799–1816* (London, 1985 edition), pp. 208–11.
42. NC, XXIV, p. 19.
43. See Pivka, *Armies, passim*; Clausewitz, *1812*, p. 95.
44. For a more detailed summary of the operations on this front, consult: Chandler, *Campaigns*, pp. 767–82; Nafziger, *Invasion*, pp. 114–27, 173–80.
45. Clausewitz, *1812*, p. 136.
46. E. Labaume, *A Circumstantial Narrative of the Campaign in Russia* (London, 1815), p. 28. Also see R. Wilson, *Narrative of Events during the Invasion of Russia by Napoleon Bonaparte* (London, 1860), pp. 46–8.
47. Typical comments regarding the cossacks can be found in Labaume, *Narrative*, pp. 304–5.
48. See Nafziger, *Invasion*, pp. 209–10; B. Dundulis, *Napoléon et la Lituanie en 1812* (Paris, 1940).
49. See, for instance, Austin, *March on Moscow*, pp. 221–9; and Paul Britten Austin, *1812: Napoleon in Moscow* (London, 1995), pp. 94–103.
50. D. Chlapowski, *Memoirs of a Polish Lancer* (Chicago, 1922), p. 115. Also see p. 116 and Clausewitz, *1812*, pp. 179–80.
51. See Napoleon's comments about this in Caulaincourt, *Memoirs*, I, p. 204.
52. See E. Tarle, *Napoleon's Invasion of Russia, 1812* (London, 1942), p. 118; Chlapowski, *Polish Lancer*, p. 122.
53. See Nafziger, *Invasion*, pp. 183–5.
54. See Chlapowski, *Polish Lancer*, pp. 111–12.
55. See Labaume, *Narrative*, pp. 97–8; Nafziger, *Invasion*, pp. 186–95.
56. See Nafziger, *Invasion*, pp. 199–206.
57. See Nafziger, *Invasion*, pp. 129–67.
58. See Muir, *Britain and Napoleon*, pp. 225–8.
59. P. de Ségur, *History of the Expedition to Russia* (London, 1825), I, p. 202.
60. Ségur, *History*, I, p. 252.
61. Clausewitz, *1812*, pp. 142–3.

62. See, for example, C.J. Esdaile, *The Wars of Napoleon* (London, 1995), p. 258.
63. Ségur, *History*, I, pp. 322–4.
64. Ségur, *History*, I, p. 331. Also see Caulaincourt, *Memoirs*, I, p. 195; A.J.B.F. Bourgogne, *Memoirs of Sergeant Bourgogne, 1812–13* (London, 1996 edition), p. 7.
65. Ségur, *History*, I, pp. 333, 341–2, 346.
66. Clausewitz, *1812*, p. 160.
67. See Clausewitz, *1812*, pp. 152–7.
68. For more details of Borodino, consult: Ségur, *History*, I, pp. 313–56; Caulaincourt, *Memoirs*, I, pp. 192–201; Clausewitz, *1812*, pp. 149–74; Chlapowski, *Polish Lancer*, pp. 117–18; Coignet, *Note-Books*, pp. 223–5; Chandler, *Campaigns*, pp. 799–806; Austin, *March on Moscow*, pp. 273–328; Nafziger, *Invasion*, pp. 215–57; Labaume, *Narrative*, pp. 134–9; R. Riehn, *1812: Napoleon's Russian Campaign* (New York, 1991); C. Duffy, *Borodino and the War of 1812* (New York, 1973); A.V. Gerua, *Borodino* (St Petersburg, 1912); A. Brett-James (ed.), *1812: Eyewitness Accounts of Napoleon's Defeat in Russia* (New York, 1966).
69. See Caulaincourt, *Memoirs*, I, pp. 199–200; Ségur, *History*, I, pp. 344–7.
70. See his concerns about 'another battle tomorrow', etc., in Ségur, *History*, I, p. 347; and Clausewitz's comments in *1812*, pp. 168–70.
71. Caulaincourt, *Memoirs*, I, p. 70.
72. See Austin, *March on Moscow*, pp. 338, 347, 349, 351, 356; Clausewitz, *1812*, pp. 188–91.
73. For an examination of the French occupation of Moscow, see Austin, *Napoleon in Moscow*.
74. See, for example, Caulaincourt, *Memoirs*, I, p. 254; Clausewitz, *1812*, p. 192.
75. E. Kraehe, *Metternich's German Policy* (Princeton, 1963–84), I, pp. 169–71.
76. See Nafziger, *Invasion*, pp. 574–6, 582–3.
77. See, for example, Chandler, *Campaigns*, pp. 817–18.
78. See Nafziger, *Invasion*, pp. 261–3.
79. See Bourgogne, *Memoirs*, pp. 59–60; Baron M. de Marbot, *The Memoirs of Baron Marbot* (London, 1988), II, pp. 282–3.
80. See Labaume, *Narrative*, p. 257.
81. Pivka, *Armies*, p. 32. Bourgogne, in his *Memoirs*, p. 80, speaks of 'twenty-seven degrees of frost' and, especially on pp. 74–92, 104–5, 115, 118 and 198, provides an insight into the traumatic experiences of those civilians and soldiers who participated in the retreat.
82. Clausewitz, *1812*, p. 213.
83. See Nafziger, *Invasion*, pp. 271–88.
84. Clausewitz, *1812*, p. 216. Chandler, *Campaigns*, p. 853, estimates Russian losses as at least 150 000 dead, with a further 300 000 wounded or otherwise incapacitated.
85. See Nafziger, *Invasion*, pp. 305–12.
86. See Chandler, *Campaigns*, pp. 830–2.
87. See Nafziger, *Invasion*, pp. 271–98.
88. See Clausewitz, *1812*, pp. 206–11; Chandler, *Campaigns*, pp. 835–47; Nafziger, *Invasion*, pp. 315–24.
89. See G. Artom, *Napoléon est mort en Russie* (Paris, 1969).

10

The German War of Liberation, 1813–1814

By the closing days of 1812, with the full extent of the catastrophe which had befallen Napoleon's *Grande Armée de la Russie* gradually being revealed, yet another diplomatic realignment of the European powers was under way. The precise numbers of men, horses, guns and other pieces of equipment which the emperor had lost on the Russian steppes will never be known, but were certainly immense. One authority puts them at 570 000 personnel, 200 000 cavalry and draught horses, and 1050 cannon.[1] Nor were many of the troops who did survive in any condition to take up arms again. One eyewitness who saw the remnants of some units stagger into Berlin recalls that: 'One saw no guns, no cavalry, only suffering men crippled by frightful wounds, men with hands, arms or feet missing or else completely destroyed by frostbite.'[2] Indeed, of the I Corps, which, it will be recalled, commenced the Russian campaign with 70 000 personnel, only 2281 men could be mustered in mid-January 1813.[3] Similarly, the strength of the Imperial Guard had plummeted from 50 000 soldiers to just 1533, of whom 200 were permanently invalided by amputations necessitated by frostbite or injuries. Of the once superb Old Guard Grenadiers and *Chasseurs à pied,* just 823 men remained, while the Young Guard had all but 'ceased to exist'.[4]

So great were the losses of men and *matériel* that all of Napoleon's gains over the preceding eight years now stood in jeopardy. Just as the emperor had feared, Prussia's defection from his cause began almost immediately. Several prominent officers – including Clausewitz – had been so appalled by the Franco-Prussian alliance of March 1812 that they had left Prussia for Russia, where, together with Stein, they were to the fore in urging the Tsar to sustain the war against Napoleon.[5] In mid-December 1812, as the dregs of *La Grande Armée* crossed the Niemen, Clausewitz was attached to Wittgenstein's forces, which were trying to intercept Marshal Macdonald's X Corps.[6] This was predominantly composed of Prussians under the command of General Yorck and had been stranded in the vicinity of Riga when the French front had finally collapsed. On encountering Wittgenstein's vanguards near Tauroggen, Yorck, following negotiations brokered by Clausewitz, signed a convention which declared the Prussian units to be neutral.[7] (Macdonald's other troops continued their withdrawal to Danzig). Yorck's insubordinate conduct compromised the position of his superiors. Since it was based on realism rather than friendship, neither Frederick William III nor Hardenberg derived any pleasure from their alliance with Napoleon, but it did give them a degree of security which Yorck had now endangered. Fearing the consequences of either a Franco-Russian accord or a resurgence of Napoleon's power, Berlin promptly disowned the convention and issued orders for Yorck's arrest and court-martial. By this time, however, he was appealing to the garrison of Königsberg and to East Prussia's *Landstände*, persuasively arguing that the king was acting under duress and secretly approved of his behaviour.[8] With Stein stirring up the inhabitants of the territories liberated by the Tsar's troops,[9] and with the patriotic intelligentsia and the military reformers imbued with renewed enthusiasm and clamouring for action, Frederick William began to lose control of his kingdom. Civil war or revolution seemed in the air. After Hardenberg had attempted unsuccessfully to get Austria to either side with Prussia and Russia, or to join the former in creating a neutral bloc which might compel Napoleon and the Tsar to come to terms,[10] Frederick William was left with little choice other than to commit himself wholeheartedly to a pact with Russia.

There were hefty actual and potential costs attached to this, however. First, Prussia agreed to field 80 000 regular troops, backed by militia units. Whereas the Paris Convention of September 1808 had stipulated that the Prussian Army was not to exceed 42 000 personnel for 10 years, Scharnhorst's '*Krümpersystem*' had created appreciable, hidden reserves. In August 1811, for instance, Prussia's forces apparently exceeded 74 000 men,[11] while, at the time of its mobilization in 1813, Petre calculates that approximately 34 000 soldiers were instantly added to the standing army from this source.[12] This meant that Frederick William had perhaps 70 000 troops to hand[13] and, in order to meet his obligations to Russia under the treaty, was obliged to resort to mass conscription, a measure which, as we have seen, he had hitherto been wary of because of its inevitable political and social ramifications.[14] Second, while, with Russia's help, the Hohenzollern hoped to see their realm returned to the status and dimensions it had enjoyed in 1806, it was agreed that Prussia's original frontiers were not to be restored. The Tsar envisaged acquiring most of her Polish lands (which had been incorporated into the Duchy of Warsaw) and compensating her at Saxony's expense. Third, and most important, although both Prussia and Russia pledged not to make a separate peace with France, the former was embarking on a course of action which, if unsuccessful, would prove suicidal. In the event of defeat – and, despite the 1812 *débâcle*, Napoleon was still rightly held in awe, even if his army had been obliterated – the Tsar might withdraw to his homeland, but there would be no sanctuary for Frederick William. This time, Napoleon would eradicate Prussia, bringing the Hohenzollern dynasty to an end.

While still technically her enemy, Prussia hoped to secure some material support from Britain in the impending confrontation with France. Even before the Prussians formally entered the war on 16 March, London had resolved to resume diplomatic relations and was making preparations to provide subsidies and supplies to them as well as to the Russians.[15] Although the long succession of ineffectual coalitions had taught Britain that the continental powers were only likely to exert themselves in pursuit of their own interests, Napoleon's failure in Russia seemed to the British to offer the best chance yet seen of breaking France's European hegemony. They seized upon it accordingly, urging prospective allies to take advantage of France's sudden weakness. While parts of the Parliamentary Opposition argued that, at this juncture, a favourable peace might be extracted,[16] the government, if only because they feared being excluded from any settlement by Austria, Prussia and Russia, was intent on fighting on. There were those who anticipated that Napoleon might be obliged to evacuate the Iberian Peninsula in order to bolster his forces in Eastern Europe. 'The most formidable army ever collected by Bonaparte has been substantially destroyed,' Lord Liverpool wrote to Wellington on 22 December 1812. 'Under these circumstances the question naturally occurs whether he will leave the French army in Spain? . . . Whatever it may cost Bonaparte to abandon Spain, I think he will prefer that alternative to the loss of Germany.'[17] In fact, while Napoleon was to withdraw 20 000 soldiers to furnish the new regiments he was raising with officer *cadres* and a leaven of seasoned soldiers, he had judged the risks involved in forsaking his own brother's kingdom to be too great. The British, like their Allies, were slow to realize this, however, and some thought was given as to where at least part of the peninsular army might most usefully be transferred. Wellington protested and, as the battle for Spain continued, managed to thwart most of the attempts to take troops from him.[18] Nevertheless, there was a price attached to this: unable to commit a substantial force to the war in Germany, Britain could only look on as the other great powers struggled for supremacy at the heart of Europe.

Indeed, with little to offer prospective allies other than subsidies,

Britain's ministers found themselves in a position which was as difficult as it was peripheral. Enjoying little direct influence over Austria, Prussia or Russia, they strove to make the most of their relationship with Sweden. So far, Bernadotte had proved disappointingly inactive in the conflict with Napoleon – a failing of which the Opposition made much – but there were hopes that, with sufficiently generous treatment, he might still be induced to field an army in Pomerania. Actually, Stockholm was far more interested in wresting Norway from Denmark and, like London, feared that the Tsar might now conclude a second Tilsit with Napoleon, whereby the aggrandisement of France and Russia would continue at the expense of lesser states. After pledging lavish sums of gold to assist the impecunious Swedes in mobilizing their forces, the British formally endorsed an alliance with them on 3 March. Nevertheless, the build-up of Bernadotte's troops in Pomerania proceeded at a snail's pace, partly because of the practical difficulties involved and partly because of heightened concerns about Russian intentions. Backed by Britain over her claim to Norway, Sweden discovered that the Tsar, eager to seduce Denmark away from Napoleon, was prepared to let the Danes retain Norway in return for their support, Alexander's earlier promises to Bernadotte notwithstanding. As the Tsar had even undertaken to furnish him with Russian troops, this both infuriated and shocked Bernadotte, who now realized that, unless Sweden quickly made a substantial contribution to the struggle with France, far from gaining territory she might lose some.

For Alexander was bent on, as he saw it, delivering Europe from Napoleon, even though Kutusov and other prominent members of the Russian hierarchy were satisfied with having cleared their motherland of the invader and felt that the Tsar should, at most, content himself with taking a few provinces in Poland and East Prussia. This disagreement can be partially explained in terms of the atavistic debate between those who, on the one hand, wanted to push Russia's frontiers deeper into Europe and expose her to modernizing, Western thinking and practices, and those who, on the other, were more eastward-looking and conservative. But, at this juncture, Kutusov at least also feared for the European balance of power. There is some evidence that, in the closing stages of the 1812 campaign, he deliberately held back from pressing the retreating French too hard. 'I am by no means sure that the total destruction of the Emperor Napoleon and his army would be such a benefit to the world,' he stated candidly to General Wilson, the British liaison officer; 'his succession would not fall to Russia or any other continental power, but to that which already commands the sea, whose domination would then be intolerable.'[19]

This suspicion of Britain was widespread among the continental peoples and their governments. Whereas London had always asserted that it was engaged in a noble battle for survival against Napoleon's tyranny, a struggle which, it was claimed, would determine the liberty and prosperity of every nation, many who had been compelled to subordinate their interests to Britain's as part of this supposed crusade took a less charitable view of her motives. All of the continental states had, unlike Britain, which had consistently waged war on her for 20 years, been partners of France at some point. Under Metternich, Austria had, as we have seen, been seeking to maximize her leverage over Napoleon ever since 1809, and Vienna now glimpsed an opportunity to bring about a general pacification. Although Austria now declared herself to be neutral, Schwarzenberg concluding a ceasefire with the Russians on the Galician front on 24 January 1813, Metternich feared an expansion of Romanov influence more than domination by Napoleon. He had counted on the latter securing another triumph in 1812 and, taken aback by the emperor's defeat, was not only anxious for his own position as the architect of the Franco-Austrian alliance but also anticipated conflicting demands now being made on Vienna by the other great powers. Sure enough, Russia, Prussia and Britain endeavoured to enlist Austrian support for the war against France, with Britain especially failing to comprehend Metternich's preference for peace. But the chancellor realized that, if fighting continued, Austria would almost certainly be dragged into it. Not only was her army far from ready to take the field but also she had been brought to the brink of bankruptcy by the burdens of the 1809 war and the indemnity she had thereby incurred. Another conflict might ruin her financially as well as jeopardizing her political future. Britain, by contrast, appeared to be inciting the continental powers to go on tearing one another apart while she capitalized on their misfortunes. Ideally, Metternich wanted to counterbalance France and Russia and restore Austro-Prussian hegemony in Germany.[20] Among other things, this would entail both winning over as many of the *Rheinbund* princes as possible and preserving residual French power. Thus, British objectives, such as the ending of Napoleon's influence in Spain and Holland, were incompatible with the chancellor's grand plan.[21]

Indeed, Metternich's hopes for an overall settlement gradually crumbled as the belligerents' armies took the field. Apart from their encircled garrisons in Danzig, Thorn and Glogau, the French had been swept from Poland and, by mid-February 1813, Russian light troops and irregulars were across the Oder. One cossack column even lunged at Berlin on the 20th. This thoroughly disconcerted Viceroy Eugène, who had superseded Murat as commander of what remained of *La Grande Armée*, and, in early March, he needlessly withdrew almost all his forces beyond the Elbe, much to his stepfather's annoyance.[22] With Berlin left unoccupied, the

Prussians finally activated their hitherto secret accord with Russia and declared war. Saxony, having averred her loyalty to France, was immediately invaded by Allied forces. Dresden was occupied and, while the commandant of Torgau was ordered to hold that fortress against all comers,[23] his sovereign hastily concluded a pact with Austria, only to revert to his alliance with Napoleon when the emperor loomed on the horizon at the head of a new army.[24] Bavaria, too, was momentarily tempted by Metternich's vision, while Denmark, as we have noted, was contemplating an offer from the Tsar. The King of Württemberg and the Grand Duke of Würzburg, by contrast, were quick to affirm their allegiance to Napoleon,[25] as was the great majority of the *Rheinbund*.

Eugène's feeble resistance to their advance lulled the Allies into a false sense of security; he appeared neither able nor prepared to try to confront them. While, phoenix-like, a new French army rose in the vicinity of Mainz, Kutusov's front-line forces, which amounted to no more than 70 000 men, moved forward on a front which extended 400 kilometres from Hamburg to Dresden. It was in this latter city that, on 25 April, a British delegation was to table London's proposals for subventions in return for Russia and Prussia fielding 160 000 and 80 000 troops respectively. Britain also agreed to cover the maintenance costs for the Russian fleet, which, as a gesture of reassurance and to keep it beyond Napoleon's grasp, had wintered in English ports. All in all, the sums of money were huge,[26] particularly given London's existing obligations to Sweden and the Iberian states. The incipient demise of the Continental System, however, promised to give Britain more scope for financial flexibility. In any event, only by proffering specie in lieu of troops could she retain any control over her partners, her only other safeguard being the clause, ritually incorporated into every treaty of alliance, by which the signatories pledged not to conclude a separate peace with France.

So it was that the Sixth Coalition's lengthy gestation ended and the German War of Liberation, *der Befreiungskrieg*, got under way. In analysing the events of the winter of 1812–13, many historians have been struck by the apparent degree of popular participation and have drawn parallels between the Spaniards' *Guerra de la Independencia* and the *Befreiungskrieg*. Petre, for instance, whose engrossing 1912 study strongly reflected the views of German writers such as Rudolf Friederich and had such an impact on later writers in the English-speaking world, opined that, in 1813:

> The whole character of the war against Napoleon had changed. He found himself no longer opposed to dynasties, but rather to whole peoples, encouraged to rise *en masse* against the tyranny of the oppressor.[27]

Likewise, in an eloquent and magisterial analysis of Napoleon's campaigns which bears the imprint of Petre's writings, David Chandler entitles his chapter on the 1813 war in Germany 'The Struggle of Nations', and goes on to remark that:

> Since Jena, the regenerating political activities of the statesman Stein, the military reforms of Scharnhorst, the patriotic influence of Arndt and Körner, and the pervasive, secret power of the Tugenbund or League of Virtue, had between them produced an entirely new popular atmosphere, and by 1813 Prussia was ripe for revolt.[28]

Although there is a kernel of truth in the above perspectives, they are misleading. Stein, in a letter to Gneisenau in August 1811, wrote that: 'How a people which revolts energetically and fights courageously should feel and how it should be constituted we are taught by . . . the Tyrol, Spain [and] Austria.'[29] But, as we have seen, the romantic, popular image of the Franco-Austrian war of 1809, including the Tyrol rebellion, was as deceptive as it was alluring; few Austrians were motivated by a sense of patriotism or nationalism, the Tyroleans still less so. While, besides Stein, there were German intellectuals and political and military reformers, notably in Prussia, who, simultaneously inspired and embarrassed by the Spaniards' example especially, sought to incite their own *Volk* into throwing off the French yoke, they were few and far between. Frederick William's apprehensiveness, which was shared by Hardenberg, has already been noted, and, according to Boyen, who was an enthusiast, there was little support for a national uprising among Prussia's military elite either: 'In the army, too,' he acknowledged, 'with the exception of Blücher, Yorck and Gneisenau, the great majority was against a guerrilla war, in so far as now and then something was heard about it.'[30] Similarly, the agitation of the patriotic intellectuals continued as before, but they remained a clique within the German intelligentsia as a whole, the venerable Goethe, for instance, scornfully telling Körner and Arndt to 'rattle your chains, you will not break them; the man [Napoleon] is too big for you'.[31]

Indeed, the degree of popular participation and the role of nationalist passions in the war effort were as constrained in the case of Prussia in 1813 as they had been in Austria in 1809. Nor can the exhortations of the patriotic Romantics have affected more than a tiny portion of a predominantly rural society where illiteracy was widespread and where news was often disseminated via the church pulpit. It is extremely doubtful whether most of their contemporaries would have known or cared who Arndt and Körner were, let alone what they stood for. Ineluctably set aside from their wider communities, such *Universitätsleute* were scarcely representative of the populace as a whole, any more than were the secret societies they established and dominated; it is noteworthy that not even Fichte, let alone such prominent members of the reform movement as Scharnhorst or Stein, participated in the *Tugenbund*. To this day, a handful of rather arcane *Studentenverbindungen*, which have their roots in medieval guilds, can be found in the nooks and crannies of traditional, conservative German and Austrian society, their few members, in between downing prodigious quantities of alcohol and singing time-honoured *Volkslieder*, practising swordsmanship and bearing the scars thereby incurred with intense pride. One is struck by the similarities between these very exclusive and somewhat eccentric organizations and Jahn's gymnastic *Deutscherbund* or the *Tugenbund*, which, besides combining paramilitary drills with athletic exercises, conjured up spurious links with the Teutonic knights and other 'glorious memories' of Germany's perceived past.

During the Nazi era of the twentieth century, this sort of propaganda was to be carried to new heights; its influence could and did permeate a far broader swathe of German society.[32] But in 1813 its impact was largely confined to the men of letters who strove to propagate it, a small but vociferous minority who were ideally placed to shape the perceptions of future generations if not their own. Some of them volunteered for service with the *Freikorps*, notably that commanded by the Prussian Major Adolf Freiherr von Lützow. Indeed, Jahn was a prominent and influential member of this unit, while Körner was to meet his death in its ranks. Many Germans, however, saw the presence of such figures as a disincentive to enlist. One prospective volunteer, for example, whilst not doubting that the aims which Herr Jahn advocated were 'very praiseworthy', was so put off by the 'unpleasant impression which this man and his soppy, boyish behaviour' made upon him that he declined to have anything to do with any force in which he held sway.[33] Likewise, Wilhelm von Gerlach, another volunteer who *did* enrol in Lützow's '*Schwarzes Korps*', seems to have regretted it. He confided to his mother that, of the best among his comrades, 'one cannot say anything better than that they are stupid boys. I will probably be selected as an officer,' he continued. 'Being chosen by this bunch is no great honour; the best thing about it is that I will no longer have to stand *next* to them, for I see clearly that I do not belong there.'[34]

The intellectuals who volunteered for military service were a minority within a minority. No more than 12 per cent of the men who fought in *die Freiwilligen* came from the groves of Academe. These units consisted overwhelmingly of artisans and labourers who were motivated by more mundane things than patriotic and nationalistic poetry.[35] Inevitably, however, in the main it was their belletristical comrades' views and recollections of the *Befreiungskrieg* which were recorded and handed down to future generations. As James Sheehan has concluded:

In memoirs and stories, paintings and pageants, festivals and scholarly histories, the war against France assumed a central role in the emergence of
national consciousness. It was, people came to believe, a time when nation
and state had joined in a single struggle, inspired by the same goals, acting
together until victory was theirs.[16]

In reality, it was nothing of the kind. In Prussia in 1813, just as in
Austria in 1809 and in Russia in 1812, volunteers did come forward to
fight against Napoleon. Yet they were predominantly young men from the
middle classes who, armed and equipped at their own or their localities'
expense, would have been conscripted had they not volunteered. The size
and designation of their combat units are also revealing. By August 1813,
when Prussia's mobilization was nearing its zenith and close to 300 000
men – some 6 per cent of the population – had been summoned to the
colours, these 'volunteer *Jäger*' amounted to no more than 10 000 soldiers.[37] There was also a handful of *Freikorps* consisting of mercenaries,
disaffected Germans from outside Prussia and other foreigners. These
units included the 'Schill' Hussars and the Elbe Regiment, but most were
eager to be denoted as *Jäger*, too. In 1807, an official memorandum on
how the army might be improved had argued that, in most recent conflicts,
'love of honour and ambition' had been more important than patriotism
when it came to motivating armed forces.[38] Similarly, Gneisenau conceded that: 'The world is divided into those who, willingly or unwillingly,
fight for Bonaparte's ambition, and those who oppose him. . . . Nationality
seems less significant in this struggle than basic principles.'[39]

In short, the individual's perspective was of greater significance than
esprit de nation, as was *esprit de corps*. Whereas during Frederick the
Great's time light infantry had largely been dismissed as *chair à canon*,[40]
by the start of the Napoleonic War this branch of the army was acquiring
greater esteem and tactical significance. Nevertheless, the high percentage of commoners within its officer corps testified to the disdain with
which many *Jünker* still regarded the service.[41] Even the *Feldjäger*
Regiment, whose distinguished combat record made it one of the army's
elite units, was viewed superciliously by most line officers; and Yorck,
who became its colonel in 1803, was one of the few commanders with
noble antecedents who did not find mingling with bourgeois comrades
unpalatable.[42] At his instigation, in 1808 a Guard *Jäger* battalion was created and, with the widespread adoption of skirmishing and open-order
tactics throughout the army, the prestige of the light service rose appreciably. Plainly, when it came to attracting callow young men who, if not
imbued with the ideals of duty, honour and service to the Fatherland, were
certainly seeking adventure, units styled as '*Jäger*', with their connota-
tions of panache, heroism, initiative and dash, had far more to offer than

seemingly staid and ponderous line regiments – so much so in fact that, although they were obliged to pay for their own equipment and horses, some soldiers from each battalion of foot took advantage of special provisions which allowed them to transfer to the *Jäger*.[43]

All of this perhaps at least partly explains why, as Professor Sheehan puts it, 'a talented young man like Körner would want to waste his time galloping around the countryside playing soldier'.[44] There were others who were keen to join him, too. However, the fact remains that, a few pockets of disorder – notably in Hamburg – aside, a national rebellion along the lines of that seen in Spain did not materialize; as in 1809, Napoleon was again to be confronted primarily by organized armies directed by ruling dynasties. True, in his proclamations, notably *An Mein Volk*, of 17 March 1813, Frederick William argued that 'every son of the Fatherland' would have to struggle and prevail in order to remain German. Yet it is evident that he was appealing, not to the pan-Germanic cultural entity on behalf of which Arndt, Görres, Körner and the other patriotic intellectuals saw themselves as fighting, but to his own subjects, his 'Prussians, Silesians, Pomeranians and Lithuanians'.[45]

It would have been interesting to see just how many of the troops raised for the *Befreiungskrieg* would have come forward had they not been acting under compulsion. Genuine volunteers were, as we have seen, few and far between, with the overwhelming majority of men being furnished by conscription. For in February 1813, Frederick William had begun issuing decrees which all but abolished exemptions from military service 'for the war's duration' and established not only *Landwehr* but also *Landsturm* units for local defence. The former comprised men aged between 17 and 40; the latter all remaining able-bodied males up to the age of 60.[46] By autumn 1813, these measures had yielded field forces alone totalling 300 000 men. Indubitably, many Germans had been alienated by the policies and presence of the French in the region. The damage inflicted on local economies by the Continental System, with its tariffs and other restrictions which, in many instances, were deliberately designed to favour French producers and merchants; the conscription of young men for the army and navy; the burden of taxation, in both blood and money, resulting from bloated military establishments and seemingly interminable wars; the incessant demands of Napoleon's commissariat for foodstuffs, horses, fodder, billets and other necessities which, in 1812, as *La Grande Armée* headed for Russia, had reached intolerable levels; French anticlericalism, which offended both Protestants and Catholics; the loss of land, feudal rights and privileges as a consequence of reforms which, imposed or inspired by the Napoleonic *imperium*, swept away the *Reich*, enhanced the *Mittelstaaten* and restructured the *Herrschaft*, the foundation of German society and politics; larceny, the sexual molestation of women, damage to property and all the other evils which intermittently arose whenever military forces and civilian communities came into close contact with one another: all of these, in combination or isolation, gave numerous Germans good grounds for resenting Napoleon, his legions and his *régime*. Particularist loyalties might also have been a factor in some cases and, in a few others, embryonic concepts of patriotism and nationalism. Nevertheless, if only because life for the lower classes had seldom been easy and, as highlighted by outbursts of opposition to the conscription measures,[47] one exploiting master was seen as being much the same as another, few Germans were prepared to transform anti-French rhetoric into active, still less violent, resistance. The great shibboleth still associated with 1813 is *'Das Volk stand auf, der Sturm brach los'*. But as Heinrich Heine sardonically observed during the 1830s, in the *Befreiungskrieg* his countrymen and women 'were told to be patriots, and we became patriotic because we always do what our princes tell us'.[48]

Those rulers were, however, in an invidious position. We have already noted the dilemma of Saxony in particular and, as the Russians and Prussians approached, Napoleon's other German allies feared that he was no longer strong enough to shield them. On 25 March, in a bid to intensify the pressure in the *Rheinbund* states, Alexander and Frederick William issued a 'Proclamation to the German People and Princes', in which they expressed the hope that none of the latter would fail to support their cause and thereby risk 'destruction through the strength of public opinion and the power of righteous arms'.[49] Yet apart from Mecklenburg, whose ruler was related to the Tsar, all of the *Rheinbund* adhered to Napoleon, who, acutely aware that the parties within the coalition ranged against him would have contrasting and potentially conflicting objectives, was bent on turning the tables on them.

By dint of truly extraordinary efforts, by mid-April, in addition to Eugène's 58 000-strong *'Armée de l'Elbe'*, which was spread out between the Harz Mountains and Magdeburg, he had fielded a new force of 120 000 men, *'l'Armée du Mein'*, which was assembling between the Harz and the Main. A *sénatus-consulte* of September 1812 had called up 137 000 conscripts ahead of their time, and a further trawl of France's manpower pool had yielded another 78 000. National Guard *cohortes* had been transferred bodily to the regular army, and the navy's resources had also been tapped, some 20 000 gunners and naval infantry being formed into field artillery and other units. Eventually, Napoleon hoped to replace *La Grande Armée* lost in Russia with a fresh one comprising all of 656 000 troops.[50] Although he was to come close to meeting this target, there was no way that the army of 1813, extemporized as it was from a *mélange* of novices, near-invalids, old soldiers and partially trained reservists, could match the proficiency and experience of its predecessors. Picked veterans from each battalion and cavalry regiment serving in Spain were used to reconstitute the Imperial Guard, and by means of similar transfusions most of the newly created line regiments were given a nucleus of seasoned troops. However, as in 1812, finding sufficient junior officers posed enormous difficulties. 'You are sending me young people coming from schools who have not been to St Cyr,' Napoleon complained to Clarke, the Minister of War. 'They do not know anything, and it is in the new regiments that you are placing them.'[51] By means of rather liberal promotions – a hundred corporals were elevated to sub-lieutenancies, for instance[52] – sufficient junior and noncommissioned officers to satisfy immediate requirements were eventually found, but there was no cushion against wastage. 'I find myself on the battlefield without officers,' the emperor was to grumble to Clarke on 5 May.

> Moreover, the campaign will use up many of them; it is necessary to have a lot of replacements, without making promotions too rapidly, which does not meet the objective anyway. . . . If you need officers . . . the Army of Spain is an inexhaustible nursery; I authorize you to bring them in from there.[53]

There were other shortcomings, too. If morale in the new army was astonishingly good,[54] its material foundations were less solid. It was badly lacking in logistical support, for example, much valuable equipment, such as pontoons and field forges, having been lost in Russia, together with large numbers of skilled technical staff. For the same reason there was an acute shortage of mature, trained draught horses to haul guns and vehicles. Priority was accorded to fulfilling the needs of the *train d'artillerie*, but this left few resources available for other purposes, notably the transportation of rations; soldiers had to cram what they could into their packs, making them excessively heavy, or extract their needs from their surroundings. However, the inexperience and physical immaturity of many of the conscripts of 1813 precluded either of these solutions; they were simply not strong enough to carry large burdens at speed, nor did they possess the requisite fieldcraft skills to live off the land.

As the legendary mobility of Napoleon's armies largely depended upon the eschewing of cumbersome supply trains in favour of foraging, this was to exacerbate what, from the outset, was a major problem. As we have seen, rapid manœuvre lay at the heart of Napoleon's style of waging war. Time and again he had used it to offset the numerical inferiority of his forces by exploiting interior lines, or to fall on the flanks and rear of his opponents. But in 1813 many of his infantry lacked the stamina necessary to perform forced marches for days on end; with little medical care to hand, most of the surgeons and orderlies having perished in Russia, they soon succumbed to malnutrition, exhaustion or blistered feet. Nor were things much better in the cavalry. Following the losses in 1812, there was a dearth of trained, mature chargers capable of executing the intricate, close-order drills inherent in Napoleonic combat, while many of their riders, being novices, were wholly deficient in equestrian skills and, even if they managed to stay on their unwieldy mounts, had little notion of how to care for them properly; numerous horses became lame or died through unintentional neglect.

Patently, fighting on horseback was particularly taxing, but the demands made on the infantry of the period should not be underestimated either. Such was the haste with which the army of 1813 was created that there was little time for training the new soldiers, be they horse or foot, and much of the instruction that was provided had to be undertaken as units made their way to the front. Inevitably, it was rudimentary. Recognizing the weaknesses in his own cavalry, Napoleon was profoundly alive to the dangers that the Allies' formidable bodies of horsemen would pose to his infantry especially. Accordingly, he emphasized the need for them to acquire a capacity to deal with this threat. His directions to Marshal Ney regarding training are typical of those issued in this respect:

> Have a lot of live-firing exercises at targets. You should also have a lot of manœuvres, practising moving in and out of columns of attack . . . and battalion squares, making sure that the battalion commanders can promptly change into . . . [the latter] formation when charged by cavalry.[55]

Indeed, given his paucity of dependable horsemen, the emperor anticipated that the tactics he had employed to good effect against the Mamelukes in Egypt during 1798 would have to suffice.[56]

These had been based on a stout infantry defence closely supported by artillery; the few French cavalry had played a purely subordinate role.[57] Sure enough, this was to prove the case in much of the fighting in 1813, too. However, the feebleness of Napoleon's mounted forces in the German campaign was to have both tactical and strategic repercussions, for success on the battlefield could not be consolidated and exploited by the sort of pursuit *à outrance* he had so frequently staged in the past. The Allies, too, had their problems of course. While the Prussian Army contained an inner core of well-drilled professional infantry, many of its conscripts had received only elementary training if any. Likewise, the quality of most of the Russian units had been diluted by the influx of green draftees and the heavy losses of seasoned soldiers over the preceding months.

Thus, apart from the advantages stemming from their superior cavalry, the Allied forces were fairly evenly matched with those of Napoleon so far as their performance on the battlefield was concerned. The campaign of 1813 was waged by what were basically massive, conscripted armies which fought with comparatively little tactical finesse. Indeed, it was essentially on the strategic level that it was decided. As had occurred in 1809 and 1812, the sheer size of the belligerents' armies and the theatre of operations deemed that devolution be applied to the system by means of which forces were commanded and controlled, with crucial responsibility again falling on those subordinates who were entrusted with independent or semi-autonomous roles. Though ineluctable, this *modus operandi* plainly presented the Allies with an opportunity to concentrate their strength against Napoleon's weak spots and thereby offset his undisputed genius for war. 'With you,' the Tsar had observed to General Caulaincourt, the French ambassador to St Petersburg in 1812, 'marvels only take place where the Emperor is in personal attendance; and he cannot be everywhere.'[58] The awesome implications of this simple fact were to be accentuated by Marshal Marmont in the midst of the 1813 campaign: 'I fear greatly', he warned Napoleon, 'that on the day on which your Majesty has gained a victory and believe you have won a decisive battle, you may learn that you have lost two.'[59]

Napoleon initially envisaged commencing his operations with a bold thrust involving over 300 000 men. While feint attacks focused the enemy's attention on the Dresden area, the emperor would traverse the Elbe at Havelberg and press on through Stettin to Danzig, assimilating their garrisons into his army as he advanced. With one fell swoop, he would threaten Prussia's heartland and the Russians' communications.[60] This scheme, however, soon proved impracticable. Conceived in early March and scheduled for implementation at the start of May, it was too ambitious given the number of troops actually available. Moreover, the politico-strategical situation changed appreciably in the interim, with Prussia declaring war on 16 March, Saxony and Bavaria wavering in their loyalty to Napoleon, and the beleaguered French garrisons of Thorn and Spandau capitulating on 18 and 21 April respectively. So it was that, in early April, with the Allies' vanguards probing towards Magdeburg in the north and the upper Saale in the south, the emperor recast his plan, devising one which mirrored his blueprint for the Jena campaign. This time, however, he intended focusing on his adversaries' right rather than their left flank: while a covering force detained the relatively small hostile corps around Magdeburg, the Allied main body would be encouraged to continue its advance through Saxony towards Bayreuth, whereupon

Napoleon would thrust through Leipzig to Dresden, cutting behind his prey and severing it from Prussia.[61]

Accordingly, while the bulk of Eugène's *Armée de l'Elbe* shifted southwards towards Merseburg, Napoleon, at the head of *l'Armée du Mein*, moved through Weimar towards Naumburg. Together, they had approximately 200 000 men with 370 guns, but the cavalry amounted to just 15 000 sabres. The eyes and ears of the army, its weakness was already hampering the gathering of intelligence and the masking of Napoleon's movements. 'I would find myself in a position to finish matters very quickly', he wrote to the king of Württemberg, 'if only I had 15 000 more cavalry.'[62] There was a good deal of frustration in the Allied camp, too. Kutusov, old and sick, died on 28 April and the Tsar insisted on appointing Wittgenstein in his stead. This provoked such dissent on the part of two of the four corps commanders, Generals Miloradovich and Tormassov, that Alexander had to divide control of the army between himself and Wittgenstein, the latter being given direct responsibility for no more than the principal Prussian contingent, under Blücher, and General Winzingerode's Russian corps.[63] As at Austerlitz and in 1812, the Tsar's meddling was undermining the authority of his army commanders; and this, together with the innate problems of waging war as a coalition, was to do little to promote harmony in the Allied headquarters.[64]

The last days of April saw the French forces debouching through Weissenfels and Merseburg towards Leipzig. They promptly encountered the outposts of the Russo-Prussian army and a running fight ensued. In these early skirmishes, Marshal Bessières was killed by a cannon shot.[65] A talented cavalry commander, he was the second member of the marshalate to perish in battle, and Napoleon felt his loss keenly; as it was, many of his best subordinates were either dead or otherwise unavailable for the 1813 campaign. On the whole, however, matters proceeded well for the emperor and, by the evening of 1 May, his leading units were poised to enter Leipzig.

But the Allies had other ideas. Having concentrated 69 000 men and 418 pieces of ordnance,[66] they were tempted to attack what they took to be an exiguous flank guard in the pentagon formed by the settlements of Kaja, Klein and Gross Görschen, Rahna and Starsiedel, just west of Zwenkau. Once these villages had fallen, they intended cutting the Weissenfels–Leipzig highway at Lützen, pivoting on this village to hustle the French forces to the north into the Elster. However, this flank guard – thought to be 2000-strong – was in fact the whole of Ney's III Corps, no fewer than 45 000 troops. He had been directed to mass all five of his divisions on Kaja but, instead, had left three of them well back, with the other two out on a limb in Starsiedel and Gross Görschen. Nor had he bothered to post any pickets or sweep the surrounding countryside for signs of the enemy. In fact, many of his troops were actually digging up the neighbourhood's potato crop when the Allied onslaught began.

This occurred at about noon on the 2nd. The orders issued by the Allied high command were bewilderingly complex and verbose. Several columns crossed and there were numerous other delays as the Russo-Prussian army struggled to take up its starting positions behind a chain of hillocks southeast of Ney's unsuspecting units. Some of the forces – notably the Russian Guard and two grenadier divisions, which were answerable to the Tsar rather than Wittgenstein – had still to arrive when the fighting commenced. Suddenly looming over the brow of the hill before them, Blücher's cavalry and artillery spearheaded the attack. But, if the French were caught unawares by this development, their assailants were no less startled by the vigorous resistance they encountered. Furthermore, even if tactical surprise was achieved by the Allies, Napoleon had anticipated a strategic riposte and had made his plans accordingly. Galloping over from near Leipzig, he plunged into the fray, personally directing Ney's youthful conscripts in a ferocious struggle which, spiralling in scale and intensity, swayed to and fro within and between the villages. Cries of '*Vive l'empereur!*' resounded everywhere he went. 'Of all of his career this is probably the day on which Napoleon incurred the most personal danger on the battlefield,' recalls Marshal Marmont. 'He exposed himself constantly, leading back to the charge the defeated troops of the III Corps.'[67] 'Scarcely a wounded man passed before Bonaparte without saluting him with the accustomed *vivat*,' observed Baron von Odeleben, a Saxon officer attached to the emperor's staff. 'Even those who had lost a limb, and in a few hours would be the prey of death, paid him that homage.'[68]

Meanwhile, the rest of *l'Armée du Mein* was hurrying to Ney's support. By 3pm, 35 000 more troops were streaming onto the field as the Guard, together with Marmont's IV Corps, came up from the southwest. Shortly after, the rearmost elements of Wittgenstein's army also materialized, whereupon a spirited assault by Yorck's Prussian infantry overran Klein Görschen and Rahna for the third time. A counterstroke mounted by Lanusse's Young Guard brigade recovered the blazing settlements, Scharnhorst, who was mortally wounded, being among the many casualties on both sides. Nevertheless, having drawn on their reserves, the Allies were again gaining the upper hand when, at about 5.30pm, the leading divisions of Eugène's *Armée de l'Elbe* emerged to threaten their right flank and rear, while General Bertrand's IV Corps, which, distracted by some hostile troops around Zeitz, had come up frustratingly slowly, finally began enveloping their left wing.

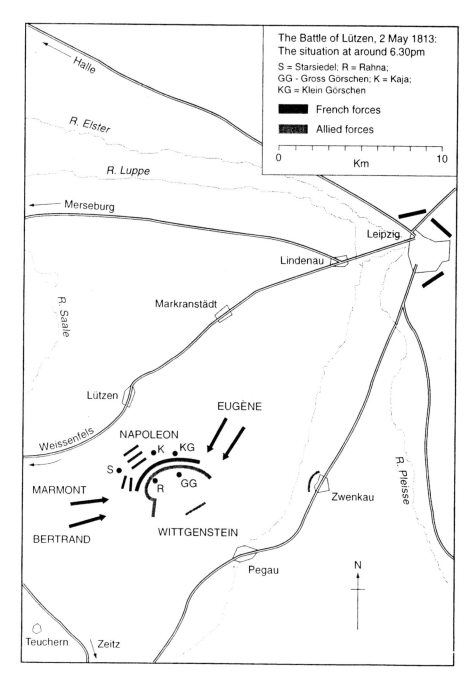

The Battle of Lützen

With all of 140 000 Imperial troops converging on it,[69] the Russo-Prussian army was forced onto the defensive. As dusk fell Napoleon launched the Guards, supported by a formidable battery of 60 guns, against the Allies' centre, while Bertrand's units and Macdonald's XI Corps lapped round their left and right flanks respectively. The French tide sent the Prussians and Russians reeling out of Rahna and Klein and Gross Görschen and back up the slopes beyond. Although Marmont's infantry conducted a limited pursuit until checked by swarms of Prussian horsemen, with few cavalry of his own to exploit this success Napoleon could not prevent the Allies escaping into the darkness. Many of his foot troops were also incapable of further efforts. Owing to incomplete statistics and the large number of men who had already fallen by the wayside prior to the battle, it is difficult to calculate precisely how many were victims of the sanguinary fighting around Lützen. It would appear, though, that at least 18 000 were slain, wounded or captured. The Allies' losses are similarly hard to ascertain, but most estimates put them at 11 500, nearly all of them killed or wounded.

With a victory, albeit a Pyrrhic one, under his belt, Napoleon wasted no time in pressing on after the Allies who were in headlong retreat for the Elbe. Leipzig had been occupied by part of Eugène's forces during the battle of the 2nd, and now the whole of Napoleon's army joined them beyond the Elster. His young troops, however, could barely sustain the rapid tempo of march which the emperor demanded. Although little resistance was encountered, progress was slow and there was an excessive amount of straggling and disorder, as highlighted by an *ordre du jour* of 6 May.[70] Moreover, Napoleon, lacking a pontoon train and expecting his adversaries to try to hold the Elbe, knew he would have to outflank them; part of his force would have to gain the eastern bank by means of one of the fortified bridges that spanned the great river. Fortunately, though invested, all of these remained in friendly hands. Accordingly, Ney, allotted roughly a third of the army as well as some reinforcements which were approaching from Magdeburg and Bernburg, set out to relieve Torgau and Wittenberg, while Napoleon himself continued towards Dresden.

His engineers having repaired the great stone bridge there under covering fire from 80 guns, Napoleon passed 70 000 troops over the Elbe at Dresden on 11 May.[71] That same day, after some delay caused by Saxony's flirtation with neutrality, Torgau opened its gates to Ney, permitting his 45 000 men to cross, too. By now, the Allies, as Napoleon had anticipated,[72] were riven by their conflicting political and strategic priorities. Whereas Wittgenstein and, more predictably, the Prussians feared for Berlin, which was covered by a solitary corps commanded by General

Friedrich von Bülow, the Tsar was anxious to safeguard the Russians' communications, which stretched back through Breslau to Warsaw. All were agreed that the Oder should not be relinquished without a fight lest Lützen might appear a decisive victory, with the result that not only the German princes but also Austria would be dissuaded from turning against Napoleon.

The tidings that the emperor was definitely marching on Königsbruck and Bautzen ended the Allies' dithering, and orders were issued for the concentration of the Russo-Prussian army at the latter place. Its rear-guards crossed swords with Napoleon's spearheads several times, but, by the 15th, the Spree's left bank had been evacuated and Wittgenstein had amassed 80 000 troops in his chosen position. Besides having the river, which, for much of its course, runs through a deeply abraded valley, to its front, this had been prepared by Russian engineers and was studded with redoubts in commanding locations. Its southern tip rested on the village of Binnewitz within 10 kilometres of the Austrian frontier, while its northern extremity nestled amid a network of ponds, bogs and causeways. Although the Spree itself posed less of an obstacle along this sector of the 12-kilometre front, any assault here would be severely hampered by the topography. Furthermore, the marshy Löbauer Wasser, a tributary of the Spree which ran through a parallel valley to the east of the river, presented a secondary barrier to any would-be attacker.

But, unlike at Borodino, where he had lacked the resources for both a pinning operation and an outflanking manœuvre, Napoleon had no intention of taking the bull by the horns. Having sent Eugène back to Italy to safeguard the kingdom against any Austrian invasion that materialized, he had merged the Armies of the Elbe and Main and was planning to tie down the Allies with 119 000 troops while Ney, his forces now amounting to 85 000 men, descended on them from the north. Of all of Napoleon's marshals, Davout would have been the normal choice for such an assignment, but he had been charged with securing Hamburg at the campaign's very outset. Ney was a poor substitute. While a splendid tactician and corps commander, 'the bravest of the brave' had neither the experience nor the aptitude to lead such a substantial force in a semi-autonomous role. Moreover, since his heroic exploits in Russia he had been exhibiting signs of what today would doubtless have been diagnosed as combat fatigue. He never fully understood his crucial mission, and some last-minute changes to his orders[73] compounded his bemusement.

When the two-day Battle of Bautzen finally commenced on 20 May, the Allies had assembled 96 000 men and 622 guns. Although reconnaissance reports suggested that an attack from the north might materialize, this was the one eventuality which their high command failed to allow for. Unlike

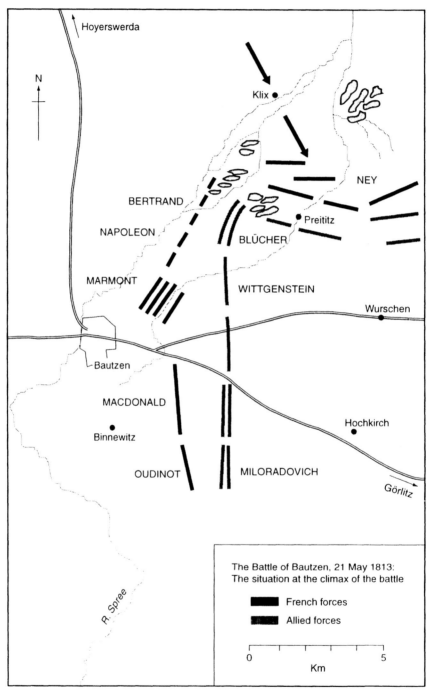

The Battle of Bautzen

Wittgenstein, the Tsar was persuaded that the French would endeavour to cut the Russo-Prussian Army off from Austria, when in fact Napoleon was planning to drive it off its lines of communication and hammer it on the anvil formed by the Bohemian mountains; Austria's neutrality would be violated if the Russians and Prussians crossed her borders and, as yet unprepared for war, she would be likely to side with France. Thus, when, at about 1pm, the three divisions of Marshal Oudinot's XII Corps crossed the Spree southwest of Binnewitz and began molesting the Allied left, the Tsar played right into Napoleon's hands by committing many of the available reserves to shoring it up. Meanwhile, Macdonald and Marmont, backed by a crushing artillery bombardment, bridged the Spree both above and below Bautzen, and Bertrand's corps edged back the Allies' right.

By sunset, the French had fulfilled their initial objectives: the Russo-Prussian army was riveted to its position and a substantial bridgehead had been carved out east of the Spree. Moreover, while all of this was going on, Ney had continued to approach from the north and, by 5am on the 21st, his vanguard was crossing the river, driving in the pickets of Wittgenstein's right wing. Napoleon's last instructions to '*Le Rougeaud*' had stipulated that he should be at Preititz on the Allies' right-rear by 11am. As he was well within reach of that place an hour earlier, however, Ney stubbornly insisted on marking time, eventually sending no more than a division to seize it. In the meantime, Oudinot and Macdonald had succeeded in entangling all of the Allies' left wing and most of their reserves in a bitter fight far to the south. This further unnerved the Tsar, who dismissed Ney's appearance as a diversion. Of course Napoleon intended quite the reverse, but, as the rest of the emperor's army began to advance, seeking to hustle the Allies into the clutches of Ney's *attaque débordante*, the impetuous marshal, instead of pressing on to envelop the enemy, allowed himself to become embroiled in an essentially irrelevant struggle for some heights held by Blücher's troops. Already threatened by Bertrand's corps as it clawed its way forward from the west and south, the grizzled Prussian general withdrew his men just before the French jaws could close on them.[74] At last, the Tsar realized what was afoot and, as Ney's and Bertrand's units collided, the whole of the Allied army executed an orderly, fighting retreat to the east. Although it had sustained some 11 000 casualties, it had again evaded destruction by a whisker.[75]

Once more Napoleon's lack of cavalry prevented him staging an efficacious pursuit and, again, his losses were appreciably higher than the Allies'; at least 12 000 men were killed or wounded in storming the formidable positions along the Spree and the Löbauer Wasser and, as in the days leading up to Lützen, several thousand more were *hors de combat* as a result of arduous marches, often executed in torrential rain. The emperor was also robbed of another close confidant when, as he pursued his quarry towards Görlitz, a round shot mortally wounded Duroc, his chamberlain.[76]

Nevertheless, the Allied forces were very badly shaken by their second defeat in three weeks. Wittgenstein, unable to tolerate the Tsar's constant interference in his plans, used the reverse as a pretext for resignation and was superseded by Barclay de Tolly.[77] He and Blücher promptly fell out over the next move: the Russians favoured a withdrawal into Poland to regroup and recuperate; the Prussians, reluctant to abandon their heartland because of both political and military considerations, wanted to stand and fight. A compromise was eventually brokered by Alexander, and the Allied army retired to Schweidnitz in Silesia.

Here it could maintain contact with Austria. The Allies were still hopeful that the Austrians would join them, but, at this juncture, the signs were not encouraging. Vienna was still mobilizing its forces, and Metternich's dream of rallying Germany's princes behind the *Kaiser* was fading. Frederick of Saxony, it will be recalled, had already returned to the French fold and, on hearing of Bautzen, Max Joseph of Bavaria suspended his negotiations with Vienna. Similarly, Denmark decided to throw in her lot with Napoleon and, by committing 12 000 troops in support of Davout's operations on the lower Elbe, helped the marshal regain both Hamburg and Lübeck.

Further east, however, things did not go quite so well for the French. While Napoleon led the main army over the Katzbach in pursuit of Barclay, Oudinot, detached to threaten Berlin, repelled an attack by Bülow at Hoyerswerda on 28 May, only to throw his advantage away eight days later when, having given his opponent time to regroup his corps in a strong position, he was beaten at Luckau.[78] The day after this, General Woronzow, commander of the Russo-Prussian screen before Magdeburg, led half his force in a daring raid across the Elbe to Leipzig, where he destroyed a trainee cavalry unit, capturing 567 prisoners.

This action was, together with operations in general, brought to a halt by news of an armistice agreed at Pleiswitz. On the eve of Bautzen, Napoleon had dispatched Caulaincourt, who had established a cordial relationship with the Tsar during his time in St Petersburg, to try to get in touch with Alexander and to open secret negotiations with him; it would be in the interests of both France and Russia, Napoleon maintained, to avoid not only further bloodshed but also a situation in which Austria might assume the role of mediator.[79] But Caulaincourt was refused access to the Allied encampment, and thus neither Napoleon nor his adversaries were left with any alternative, so far as finding a diplomatic resolution to the war was concerned, than to accept Austrian arbitration. A congress was duly scheduled to take place in Prague in July.

Napoleon, however, was intensely sceptical about the prospects of a satisfactory outcome. He much preferred the dangers of the battlefield to those of the conference table and had, as he explained to Clarke, only accepted the ceasefire for two, essentially military, reasons: 'This armistice will interrupt the course of my victories,' he acknowledged, but 'two considerations have made up my mind – my shortage of cavalry, which prevents me from striking great blows, and the hostile attitude of Austria'.[80] Indeed, he hoped to deter her from entering the war and, once he had reinforced his cavalry in particular, he would resume hostilities, seeking to exploit the palpable tensions between the Russians and Prussians. If he could achieve no more than to continue edging the former back into Poland, he reasoned, the latter would eventually find the costs of forsaking their homeland intolerable. Yet if they separated from the Russians in order to defend it, the Tsar would feel abandoned and might prove reluctant to venture westwards again. In any case, Napoleon would then be able to contain the Russians with a fraction of his army while he concentrated overwhelming forces against the Prussians. If, in the interim, Austria *did* intervene, he would be in a situation not unlike that in which he had found himself during the Austerlitz campaign. Then, he had crushed the Austrian and Russian armies before the Prussians could intrude; now he would endeavour to annihilate the last of these before the others could make their presence felt.

On 26 June at Dresden, Metternich and Napoleon had a meeting that was as lengthy as it is celebrated, with the emperor doing his utmost to browbeat the wily chancellor and the Austrian doing his to persuade the emperor that compromise was in his own best interests. Having inflicted two defeats on the Allies and driven them far to the east, the latter saw no reason to cede territory. Yet Metternich was seeking sufficient concessions to make a general pacification possible. His minimal demands included the surrender by France of Dalmatia and Illyria, adjustments to the Austro-Bavarian border, the dissolution of both the *Rheinbund* and the Duchy of Warsaw, the relinquishing of all possessions west of the Rhine and the return of Prussia's southern provinces.

It is noteworthy that, in all of this, Metternich evinced little regard for Britain's war aims, which, besides the fulfilment of obligations to Sweden, Sicily, Spain and Portugal, encompassed the preservation of her maritime supremacy, broadly defined, independence for the Low Countries, and the fate of Hannover, Hamburg and northern Italy.[81] Metternich was determined to leave France sufficiently strong to act as a counterpoise to Russia, and viewed many of London's ambitions as jeopardizing both this and the chances of peace. In fact, when he discussed the situation with Prussia's and Russia's representatives in mid-June, he pointedly excluded Britain's delegation from the talks. London had suspended subsidy payments to the Allies for the duration of the armistice and was profoundly concerned that the continental powers might now make peace with Napoleon on terms which were detrimental to British interests. In contrast to Metternich, the British cabinet believed that Napoleon would be left too strong for peace to be a satisfactory or sustainable state of affairs and, while not wishing to incur responsibility for a collapse of the negotiations, entered into them reluctantly. On the one hand, Britain could not remain aloof and chance having to wage war against France almost singlehandedly. On the other, she was loath to acquiesce in the concoction of a settlement which, in time, might prove all too volatile. 'The risk of treating with France is great, but the risk of losing our Continental Allies and the confidence of our nation is greater,' judged Castlereagh.[82] Nor did Britain have many bargaining counters. Although she had donated vast sums of money to finance her partners' war efforts, given her commitments in the Peninsula and those stemming from her conflict with the USA, she had been unable to find more than 9000 Anglo-German troops for operations in Central Europe. Furthermore, while she was prepared to surrender many of her colonial gains in return for concessions elsewhere, her anxiety to protect her naval dominance circumscribed the scope for using some of these acquisitions, especially former Dutch possessions, in this regard; the independence of Holland had to be guaranteed before she could contemplate returning them. Thus, it was realized, all that the British could do was emphasize the pecuniary aid they had furnished over the years and inflate the significance of Wellington's victory at Vitoria on 21 June. If Napoleon were to accept Metternich's outline proposals and serious bargaining began, London would have difficulties imposing its will on the rest of Europe.[83]

On 27 June, following his meeting with Napoleon, Metternich concluded the Treaty of Reichenbach with Russia and Prussia, whereby Austria undertook to join the Allies if France did not meet her minimal terms for peace. This was never probable, and Metternich must have sensed that throughout his talks with the emperor. But even if Napoleon had agreed to Austria's demands, he was but one participant in a complex game and a peaceful outcome was far from assured: Prussia's military commanders were itching to avenge Jena–Auerstädt even if Frederick William was not; Bernadotte was still bent on tackling Denmark and, having built up his forces in northern Germany to 37 000 men, was poised to take a more active part in proceedings; while the Tsar, now free of the restraining hand of Kutusov, had never exhibited any inclination to make peace. Moreover, whether Austria was placated or not, Britain, Russia, Prussia and Sweden might have fought on, for they were not bound by the Reichenbach accord to come to terms with France. In these circumstances, Austria would have had to choose one side or the other, if only to prevent the fate of Europe being decided without her.

In short, none of the great powers regarded the peace talks as anything other than a breathing space in which to prepare their forces for a climactic confrontation. At their meeting on 26 June, Napoleon and Metternich agreed to prolong the ceasefire until 10 August and, as they were eager to enlist Austria's support, the Allies had little option other than to accede to this arrangement. But although he needed time to complete Austria's mobilization for war, Metternich persevered in trying to salvage the negotiations. While, on the one hand, he feared both the strains that the conflict was subjecting German society to and the repercussions of any Allied triumph, on the other his respect for Napoleon's martial skills remained undimmed. If the emperor were to emerge victorious from the impending struggle, who could say what the ramifications would be?[84]

In the absence of a positive response from Napoleon by the stipulated end of the armistice, Austria was left with no alternative other than to declare war. For the first time since 1795 all of Europe's leading powers were now aligned against France. After a good deal of bickering, during which Metternich had to threaten to withdraw Austria from the alliance in order to get his way, Schwarzenberg was appointed as the Allies' commander-in-chief and found himself with the unenviable task of trying to conduct military operations with no fewer than three monarchs looking over his shoulder. Bernadotte demanded a senior role in return for focusing his efforts against France rather than Denmark, and had to be given command of a multinational force styled 'The Army of the North', which amounted to approximately 120 000 troops. The other Allied field forces were divided into 'The Army of Silesia', which was led by Blücher, and 'The Army of Bohemia', which fell under Schwarzenberg's direct control. These contained 95 000 and 240 000 men respectively. Bennigsen was bringing up a further 59 000 Russians through Poland, giving the Allies a front-line strength of just over 500 000 soldiers, with 250 000 more in reserve and garrison units. To these, Napoleon could oppose roughly 473 000 troops divided between the Guard, 13 *corps d'armée* and six of cavalry. Another 61 000 men garrisoned fortresses and other pivotal points across Germany and Poland.[85]

The three Allied armies were arrayed along an arc which ran from the Baltic to Prague. During meetings at Trachenberg north of Breslau in July, their respective commanders had formulated a strategy that, besides allowing them the independence they craved, Schwarzenberg's authority over them being largely nominal, sought to obviate the danger posed by Napoleon's martial ingenuity: whenever forces led by the emperor advanced against one of their armies, it would retire, luring him away while the other two assumed the offensive on his strategic flanks and rear.[86] For his part, Napoleon envisaged making the central stretch of the mighty Elbe, with its various *points d'appui*, into his base of operations. 'What is important to me', he commented, 'is to avoid being cut off from Dresden and the Elbe. I will care little if I am cut off from France.'[87] Planning to exploit interior lines to compensate for his forces' numerical inferiority, he would stand on the defensive in the south with around 300 000 men while Davout, from Hamburg, and Oudinot, from Baruth, were to march on Berlin with 120 000 troops.[88] If, he reasoned, the Army of the North could be defeated and Prussia's core occupied, Sweden might be knocked out of the war and the tensions between Prussia and Russia exacerbated. The temptation simultaneously to wreak revenge on a treacherous former marshal and the duplicitous Frederick William was doubtless a factor in his deliberations too.

Within days of hostilities recommencing, however, the emperor discerned an opportunity to strike at Blücher and, gathering a large force together, moved eastwards. The Army of Silesia, in keeping with the Trachenberg plan, retreated immediately, while Schwarzenberg set his forces in motion towards Dresden. Leaving Macdonald on the Bober to shadow Blücher, Napoleon promptly retraced his steps, regaining Dresden on the morning of 26 August. He arrived in the nick of time, for 170 000 Allied soldiers were already converging on the city's southern suburbs, which were defended by a relatively meagre garrison of 20 000 men under Marshal St Cyr. Over the next few hours, thousands more Imperial troops crossed the Elbe in Napoleon's wake and, after some vicious fighting, all of the Allies' assaults were repulsed with heavy losses. Renewing the battle at dawn the next day, the French, despite incessant downpours and the fact that they were still outnumbered by three to two, went onto the offensive. Parts of the Allied centre held firm, but their left wing disintegrated and the right was driven back some 4 kilometres before the rot could be stopped. Napoleon seems to have captured 23 500 prisoners and 26 guns, as well as inflicting 13 000 other casualties on Schwarzenberg's army. His own losses amounted to just 10 000 men.[89]

It was a triumph and the Allies knew it. During the night they went into precipitant retreat over the execrable tracks that meandered over the Erzgebirge to Bohemia. Now, however, things began to go awry for Napoleon. First, he was 'seized with vomiting, caused by fatigue'.[90] Second, news having arrived that Oudinot had been checked in an action at Grossbeeren[91] and that Macdonald, mounting a needless and poorly cooordinated offensive, had been severely defeated by Blücher on the Katzbach,[92] he was both concerned and distracted by developments to the north and east. As he had hurried back to Dresden to succour St Cyr, he had thought of passing most of his army over the Elbe at Königstein to emerge on Schwarzenberg's right-rear. So hard-pressed had Dresden's garrison appeared, however that the emperor had decided to allot just one corps, the I under General Vandamme, to this enterprise. After some initial success in molesting the fleeing Allies, Vandamme found himself in dire straits as numerically superior columns of enemy troops descended from various directions on his embattled command. Beyond reach of the rest of Napoleon's forces, which were toiling up the muddy lanes in pursuit of Schwarzenberg's disordered army, his units fought a confused and rambling engagement amid the woods and valleys around Kulm until, encircled, half of them were compelled to surrender. Vandamme himself was captured, together with 10 000 others and 82 guns.[93]

Marmont's prophecy was being fulfilled: the setbacks at Grossbeeren, the Katzbach and Kulm cancelled out any advantage Napoleon derived from his victory at Dresden. Dispatching Ney to take control of Oudinot's ruffled army, the emperor began making preparations for a decisive blow against Bernadotte, only to have his plans[94] disrupted once more by the continuing advance of Blücher. Having reinforced Macdonald near Bautzen, Napoleon again discovered that his intended victim had retreated out of striking range, while the Army of Bohemia had begun creeping back towards Dresden.

Dashing to save St Cyr a second time, the emperor arrived in the Saxon capital on the evening of 6 September. He joined the marshal's foremost units the next morning, but was unwilling to attack until he had more troops to hand. St Cyr recollects that Napoleon appeared more bothered about what Blücher and Bernadotte might be up to;[95] and, within 24 hours, the emperor's concerns in this regard were to be justified. News arrived that Ney's 58 000 men had blundered into a battle at Dennewitz near Jüterbog and had been soundly beaten; 22 000 men had been killed, wounded or captured.[96]

Having failed to get to grips with the Allied armies, and with cossacks and other irregulars roving almost at will across his rearward communications,[97] Napoleon now became increasingly concerned about the condition of his army. Those of his men whose feet had not been cut to ribbons because they lacked shoes were being exhausted by ceaseless marches and countermarches. Moreover, the resources of the corridor of land they were distributed along were by now badly depleted. 'The army is not being fed,' he wrote to Daru, the *intendant*. 'It would be an illusion to regard matters otherwise.'⁹⁸ After much of September had been spent in more fruitless manœuvres against Blücher and Schwarzenberg, Napoleon resolved to reduce the theatre of operations to more manageable proportions and to husband what resources he had left for a final confrontation. Accordingly, retaining his bridgeheads along the Elbe, he abandoned all the territory east of the river.

Simultaneously, the Allies also redeployed their forces. Bennigsen's army having finally arrived, it was assimilated into Schwarzenberg's, which now marched not on Dresden but on Leipzig. At the same time, Blücher, skirting the Elbe, moved northwest to unite with Bernadotte. By early October, Schwarzenberg's forces extended from Teplitz as far west as Hof; Bernadotte's were passing over the Elbe between Magdeburg and Wittenberg by means of pontoon bridges; and Blücher, having built a crossing and fought his way over that river at Wartenburg, was moving on Bitterfeld.

Meanwhile, there had been important developments on the diplomatic front. On 3 October Britain and Austria concluded a formal alliance, with the former undertaking to pay the latter £1 million in return for her fielding an army of at least 150 000 men; a new agreement was to be negotiated in April if the war was still in progress.⁹⁹ Of more enduring significance were negotiations regarding the fate of Germany. Following a meeting at Teplitz in September, the Allied sovereigns committed themselves to dissolving the *Rheinbund*. However, in order to reconcile Prussia's greed for territorial acquisitions with Metternich's desire to preserve the German *Mittelstaaten* as a buffer between the West and East, they also pledged to uphold the 'absolute independence of the intermediate states between the frontiers of the Austrian and Prussian monarchies . . . and the Rhine and the Alps'.¹⁰⁰ On 8 October, in pursuance of this policy, Prince Henry of Reuss, commander of the Austrian forces on the Danube, and Wrede, who was at the Bavarian army's head, concluded an agreement at Ried whereby Bavaria left the *Rheinbund* and undertook to devote a minimum of 36 000 troops to the war against Napoleon. In return, the *Kaiser* granted her 'full and entire sovereignty' in both his own name and that of the Allies.¹⁰¹

In the course of the winter, comparable accords were to be struck with Württemberg, Baden, Nassau, Hesse-Darmstadt, Saxe-Coburg and Hesse-Kassel, precluding any restoration of the geopolitical structure of the old *Reich*. The future of at least some of the German polities which Napoleon had fostered was thus assured, even if his own was not. Of course, a truly decisive victory might still have transformed his fortunes. Yet, during the closing stages of the 1813 campaign, so much of his military strategy was subservient to political expediency that it became counterproductive. Although after Dennewitz he seems to have recognized that there was now little chance of him relieving the beleaguered fortresses on the Oder and Vistula, he persisted in clinging to the Elbe's *points d'appui* even though he feared that the war was about to be carried into the Rhineland.[102] While his reluctance to abandon his German glacis and allies without a fight might be understandable, his failure to extricate the substantial garrisons of Dresden[103] and Hamburg at this juncture significantly diminished the likelihood of him prevailing in any climactic battle.

And one finally seemed in the offing. Leaving St Cyr in Dresden and Murat, who had 45 000 men west of the city, to contain Schwarzenberg, Napoleon strove to bring all of 150 000 troops to bear on Blücher. On arriving at Düben on the 10 October, however, he again discovered that his prey had fled, and it was not clear in which direction. In fact, Blücher had raced towards the Salle, where Bernadotte had already taken refuge. After some hesitation Napoleon resolved to abandon the offensive and join Murat, who had already come under attack and been edged back to within 10 kilometres of Leipzig.

It was here that the campaign's climax was reached. On the 16th, as Schwarzenberg closed in from the south with approximately 150 000 troops and Blücher probed up the Elster from Halle with 54 000 more, Napoleon assembled 177 000 to confront them. Erroneously believing Bernadotte and Blücher to have united their armies and extended them so far to the southwest that they had linked up with Schwarzenberg's left wing, he planned to commit the bulk of his forces to an all-out attack on the Army of Bohemia while the rest held a defensive perimeter around Leipzig. Having successfully rebuffed Schwarzenberg's assaults, he commenced his counterthrust at about 11am, making appreciable headway. However, he had counted on drawing down Marmont's VI and General Souham's II Corps from north of Leipzig to clinch the victory and was disgruntled to find that they had become embroiled in heavy – and essentially unexpected – fighting. Denied these essential reinforcements, the offensive gradually lost its momentum, while, 14 kilometres to the north, Marmont's units were dislodged from their positions around the settlement of Möckern and hustled along the Elster towards Leipzig.

The next day saw relatively little fighting, since both sides spent it regrouping. Before the Army of the North wheeled into line between Blücher's and Schwarzenberg's units, cutting the French communications, which still ran via Düben, General Reynier's small corps arrived, increasing Napoleon's forces by 14 000 men. However, the Allies, by contrast, brought up not only Bernadotte's entire army but also Bennigsen's Russian divisions, as well as several smaller detachments,

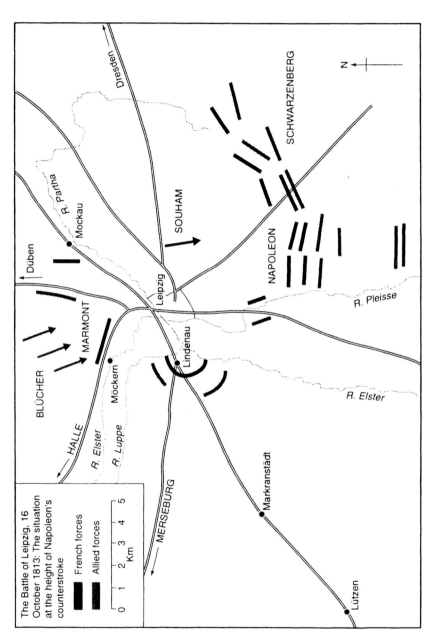

The Battle of Leipzig

Map legend:

The Battle of Leipzig, 16 October 1813: The situation at the height of Napoleon's counterstroke

■ French forces
▬ Allied forces

0 1 2 3 4 5 Km

Labels on map: Dresden, R. Partha, Mockau, Düben, SCHWARZENBERG, SOUHAM, NAPOLEON, R. Pleisse, Leipzig, BLÜCHER, MARMONT, Mockern, Möckern, Lindenau, HALLE, R. Elster, R. Luppe, R. Elster, MERSEBURG, Markranstädt, Lützen, N raising their total regular forces to 256 000 bayonets, 60 000 sabres and 1382 guns. This gave them a numerical advantage of three to two in manpower and two to one in artillery – enough, they believed, to risk a head-on confrontation with the 'Corsican Ogre'.

Arrayed to the east of the Elster in a huge semicircle, the Allies launched six assault columns towards the French outposts at 7am on the 18th. Finally cut off from the Elbe, during the night Napoleon had started making preliminary preparations for a retreat westwards and had formed his forces into a more compact line around Leipzig.[104] While Bertrand's IV Corps carved a path through the few enemy troops beyond the Elster to secure the bridges over the Saale, the rest of the army endeavoured to keep the Allied hordes at bay. They were generally successful. Only in the north and northeast did the attackers make much headway, despite the desertion *en masse* of the remaining Saxon units to the enemy.[105] However, with ammunition running short,[106] casualties mounting and his adversaries closing in, Napoleon now had no alternative other than retreat. Roughly 30 000 men – the remnants of the VII, VIII and XI Corps – were designated as the rearguard and, at 2am on the 19th, the rest of the army commenced withdrawing over the Elster.

At 7am, the whole Allied army began a concentric assault, slowly pushing Napoleon's covering force back through the Leipzig suburbs. The Badeners and Hessians fought with conspicuous determination to retain the Grimma Gate on the city's eastern side, while Poniatowski's Poles disputed every inch of its southern fringe.[107] Nevertheless, by 12.30pm these and the other gallant defenders had been overwhelmed and the fugitives were streaming towards the one bridge over the Elster. This had been mined so that it might be demolished as soon as the rearmost units had escaped over it. Amid the confusion, however, a panic-stricken engineer sergeant detonated the charges lest the crossing might fall into enemy hands.[108] Those men of the rearguard who were not killed by the explosion or, like Poniatowski, failed to swim across the Elster, had to surrender. Among the prisoners was Frederick, king of Saxony.

The Allied victory in the 'Battle of the Nations' was a costly one. They lost at least 54 000 men in killed and wounded alone. The French dead and injured appear to have amounted to 38 000, in addition to which 15 000 were captured.[109] Several thousand sick were left behind in hospitals, most of whom perished from typhus. The epidemic also claimed the lives of many civilians in Leipzig and elsewhere, among them the father of the infant Richard Wagner. Similarly, Fichte was to succumb to the disease, having contracted it from his wife who had been acting as a nurse to stricken soldiers.

Some 5000 Saxons defected to the enemy at Leipzig and the remaining

German troops were soon to follow suit, their states engulfed by the advancing Allied tide. Indeed, Wrede even led his Bavarians down the Main towards Frankfurt, seeking to molest the retreating French. Having posted 30 000 men with 58 guns in a bad position straddling the Mainz road at Hanau on 30 October, he was aghast to find himself confronted by Napoleon in person. The emperor took a cursory look at his former colleague's dispositions and, muttering that he had been able to make Wrede a count but not a general, unleashed the 17 000 troops he had to hand in an attack that swept the Bavarians aside.[110]

With the remnants of Napoleon's army filtering across the Rhine at Mainz, the Allies needed only to reduce the encircled French outposts to complete their victory. Those on the Vistula and Oder, clearly beyond help, capitulated before the year's end. Resistance in the Elbe bastions, on the other hand, mostly lingered on. Davout, evincing his customary valour and skill, clung to Hamburg until the very end of the war. Magdeburg, too, remained defiant. However, Torgau, its garrison swollen by trains and their escorts which, after Napoleon's communications had been severed on 18 October, had been unable to follow him to Leipzig, was to surrender on 10 January 1814, 19 000 of its 24 000 defenders having perished through disease. Wittenberg was also to fall three days later. St Cyr, bottled up in Dresden with 30 000 men, could and did not hold out so long. With his troops and the civilian population suffering appalling deprivations,[111] after one abortive attempt to escape he agreed to capitulate on 11 November, subject to his soldiers being exchanged for Allied prisoners and returned to France. As was to occur in the cases of Danzig and Torgau, however, once the French were outside Dresden and disarmed, the Allies revoked the agreement.[112] Dishonourable though this conduct was, at least St Cyr's men were taken captive. Other French soldiers were less fortunate; one helpless company of artillerymen, for example, was butchered by the Russians to whom it had surrendered.[113]

While all of this was going on, the Allied field armies had descended on France's eastern frontier. Wellington had already crossed her western border a fortnight before Leipzig and, on 12 November, some cossacks, having penetrated into Holland without encountering any serious resistance, surprised and captured Zwolle. Not far behind them were troops under Bülow and Bernadotte. The French evacuated Amsterdam on the 15th and, within days, disorder erupted in The Hague, with a small patriotic faction calling for independence under the House of Orange. The British promptly scraped a little expeditionary force together with a view to seizing the great naval base at Antwerp which, over the years, had caused them so much disquiet. Its departure was delayed by adverse winds, however, and it did not arrive until mid-December.

By that time the French had rallied and the British were to suffer defeats at both Antwerp and Bergen-op-Zoom over the next few weeks. Although afforded some help by Bülow's Prussians, they found that Bernadotte had other fish to fry. He turned aside to tackle the Danes and, by early January, had conquered them. Norway was duly surrendered to Sweden under the Treaty of Kiel and, while Bernadotte's conduct convinced London at least that he was no longer committed to the downfall of France, the British honoured their treaty obligations, instructing the Royal Navy to assist in the disagreeable and politically unpopular task of coercing the Norwegians into accepting Swedish suzerainty.[114]

Indeed, in the wake of Leipzig the diverse aims of the Allies came to the fore once again. Alexander had consistently evaded detailing what his territorial claims might be, for he anticipated that Russia and Austria would clash over Poland's future especially and he wanted to avoid alienating Metternich until Napoleon had been dealt with. For his part, the Austrian chancellor hoped that his disastrous defeat at Leipzig would finally persuade Napoleon to make peace on the basis of France's 'natural frontiers'; and, although the Tsar eventually agreed to such a proposal being made, he seems to have done so in the expectation that it would be turned down, justifying his ambition to invade France and depose his arch-enemy.[115]

Such tensions within the coalition alarmed Britain, More had been achieved within the past year than in the preceding 20, and victory, which only months before had appeared to be decades away, was now on the horizon. But if the peace was not to be short-lived, London insisted, the alliance would have to be kept in being as a guarantee against French recidivism. The Tsar's reluctance openly to declare his objectives was an obstacle to any such agreement and, as Metternich's suspicions as to Russia's intentions grew, threatened to fracture the coalition even before Napoleon could be finally defeated. Equally, Britain feared the imposition of an unsatisfactory settlement by the continental powers despite her own misgivings.

In these circumstances, even if Napoleon were to accept the 'natural-frontiers' proposal, it was doubtful whether Metternich could have persuaded his partners, particularly Alexander and Frederick William, to end hostilities. Indeed, after some vacillation, Napoleon was to instruct Caulaincourt, now serving as foreign minister, to take up the offer, only to see it withdrawn by the Allies.[116] He also endeavoured to make peace with the Spaniards. Since Catalonia was still occupied by 17 000 Imperial troops, and Ferdinand and thousands of Spanish prisoners-of-war were interned on French soil, Napoleon had much with which he could barter. If Spain came to terms, Wellington would have to evacuate his army, releasing the substantial French forces along the Pyrenean front for operations in the east. The Anglo-Spanish alliance had been born of opportunism and had always rested on pragmatism rather than unalloyed amity. Only their common enemy held the parties together and, by the winter of 1813, so strained had relations become that Wellington believed it possible that the *Cortes* would accept the emperor's overtures,[117] thereby pulling the rug from beneath Britain's army. However, if only because of the vagaries of Spain's internal politics, the *Cortes* rejected the Treaty of Valençay which Ferdinand and Napoleon had negotiated.[118] The *liberales*, bent on curbing the monarch's powers, maintained that he had no authority to make peace, while all agreed that he had in any case acted under duress.[119]

The campaign in France, 1814

Although he did transfer some 25 000 seasoned soldiers from this arena to the eastern front, even the release of the whole of the Imperial armies in Catalonia and the south of France – approximately 80 000 troops – for operations against the Austrians, Prussians and Russians could have altered only the details of Napoleon's 1814 campaign, not its outcome. Besides the 80 000 men who had escaped from beyond the Rhine, he still had 50 000 soldiers in northern Italy commanded by Eugène. These, however, were confronted not only by a similar number of Austrians along the Adige but also by a threat to the south; for Murat, anxious to retain his Neapolitan throne, had signed a treaty with Vienna whereby, in return for turning against Napoleon, his claim was recognized. Lord William Bentinck, the British commander on Sicily, though outraged by this development, used cooperation with Murat as a pretext for landing British troops on the Italian Peninsula, where his penchant for reform got the better of him. After Sicily's political instability reached a climax during 1810, with the Crown and nobility clashing fiercely over taxation and feudal privileges, Bentinck had sought to impose order through constitutional change, simultaneously hoping that benevolent, progressive government there would encourage mainland Italy to rebel against French rule. That did not occur, nor did the 'English Constitution' end the political deadlock in Palermo.[120] In 1814, however, none of this deterred Bentinck from trying to rouse Italy or from re-establishing, with a revamped constitution, the ancient republic of Genoa, even though this conflicted with the objectives of both Castlereagh and Metternich.[121]

While Murat's defection might have compounded Napoleon's difficulties in Italy, the situation the emperor faced in France was both more pressing and deadly. Although he sought, just as he had 12 months earlier, to flesh out his skeleton forces through conscription, proclaiming a *levée en masse* that summoned no fewer than 936 000 hoary reservists and immature youths to the tricolour, not only were France's manpower and financial reserves virtually exhausted but also hardly any of the men who were theoretically available could identify themselves sufficiently with Napoleon's cause to fight for it. The professional soldiers he had possessed at the start of the war in 1803 were now all but gone, and the few who remained, most of whom were officers, longed for peace. His marshalate in particular had been growing war-weary for some time, if only because they wanted an opportunity to enjoy the wealth, estates and honours he had heaped upon them. A continuation of hostilities jeopardized all this, just as it endangered the lives and property of so many of his countrymen and women. As consul, he laid down the legal, administrative, financial and religious foundations of nineteenth-century France. By 1814, however, his policies had undermined much of his own support. The Continental System, for example, alienated everybody – producers, traders and consumers – while the middle classes, whose male offspring had largely avoided being drafted into the army by the purchase of substitutes, were being hit hard by the 'blood tax' as well as the fiscal measures which the interminable wars had necessitated. Similarly, aspects at least of the Revolutionary land settlement seemed in jeopardy, as did the concordat of 1801. This had stabilized relations between Church and State, but it had taken a buffeting as Pius VII struggled to assert himself in the face of Napoleon's endeavours to subordinate the Pontiff's authority to his own.[122] While this power struggle probably had a more inflammatory impact on the devout Spanish, the Pope's treatment inevitably offended Catholic opinion everywhere and, in France, spawned a new underground movement, the royalist *Chevaliers de la Foi*, which, together with liberals and die-hard republicans, plotted the subversion of Napoleon's regime and, indeed, was behind Malet's attempted *coup* in 1812.

Of course, there had always been such dissidents, but, by 1814, opposition to Napoleon's policies was even pervading his own administrative apparatus, with some prefects failing to collect taxes or clamp down on draft evasion. In still more instances, the bureaucracy simply failed to cope with the incipient chaos sparked off by the Allied invasion. Moreover, the emperor's attempts to evoke the spirit of 1793 brought back painful memories of the very Revolutionary disorder which he had suppressed: France was convulsed by anticonscription riots, and large numbers of *réfractaires* took not only to the hills and woods but also to crime as their sole means of survival.[123] It has been estimated that, of the

936 000 men who were called up, fewer than 120 000 ever saw service in the ranks.[124]

Thus, the forces that Napoleon could actually field in defence of *La Patrie* comprised a nucleus of veteran troops, supplemented by a hotch-potch of former forest rangers, *gendarmes* and *douaniers*, and a few thousand green conscripts, many of doubtful commitment. The army's by-now familiar problems of insufficient junior officers, incommensurate logistical and technical support and inadequately trained men and horses were worse than ever. There were also crippling shortfalls in basic equipment, roughly 70 000 muskets alone having been lost over the preceding two years.[125] Moreover, whereas Napoleon had lost the resources and services of his erstwhile German vassals, the Allies had gained and exploited them. Indeed, besides Wellington's army in the south, around 230 000 Austrians, 278 000 Russians, 162 000 Prussians, 197 000 other Germans and 20 000 Swedes were on the move against Napoleon's paltry forces.[126]

Against such odds and with such unpromising material, Napoleon, exploiting interior lines to offset his army's numerical weakness, was to conduct one of the most brilliant campaigns in military annals. As we have seen, at times during his recent campaigns, illness, uncharacteristic hesitation, lethargy and carelessness had intermittently impaired his performance, helping to rob his operations of their customary dash and efficacy. But, now, the immense challenge before him had an invigorating effect. After trading some space for time in which to prepare his forces, he regained all of his old verve and, inspiring his troops to make tremendous efforts, went onto the attack, inflicting a string of shocking defeats on his opponents as they tried to penetrate beyond the Marne.[127]

In so doing, he redeemed both his own and the French Army's martial reputation. The French nation, however, largely remained indifferent to the conflict. True, there were some instances of peasants massacring isolated detachments of Allied soldiers,[128] just as some Russian and German civilians had butchered French troops in 1812 and 1813 respectively. But again many of these episodes were rooted not in loyalty to an imperilled ruler but in the indiscriminate pillage and other inflammatory acts perpetrated by unruly, or often desperately deprived, troops. On the whole, those who could stay clear of the war did so. Certainly, the popular rising that Napoleon hoped for[129] and the Allies dreaded might occur failed to materialize, while, paradoxically, the emperor's military successes actually contributed to his own downfall. Besides encouraging him to go on fighting against all the odds in the vain hope of extracting more concessions from his adversaries, his brilliant victories – four of them in five days – during February stiffened the resolve of the Allies at a crucial stage. Having elected to continue negotiations in parallel with their invasion of

French soil, they were at loggerheads over the form that any peace settlement – and, with it, the postwar order – might take. As well as the delineation of territorial frontiers, the future government of France was a vexatious question: the Tsar, having concluded that he no longer needed Austrian help in defeating France, wanted to install Bernadotte, or some other stooge, in Napoleon's stead; Castlereagh, while keen to remove Bonaparte altogether, feared that such a statement of intent might only prolong the fighting, even if British popular opinion demanded one;[130] while Metternich was seeking to thwart Alexander's ambitions and pursue his old policy of preserving France as a counterpoise to Russia. Indeed, as Castlereagh came to share his qualms about the Tsar's intentions, the once-prominent collaboration between London and St Petersburg rapidly cooled and was superseded by an Austro-British axis.

With the powers pursuing increasingly independent and essentially conflicting lines, the coalition was on the verge of being torn asunder when Napoleon's victories jolted the squabbling factions back into cooperating together.[131] The principal manifestation of this was the Treaty of Chaumont, which, signed in March, bound them not only to continue the war but also to extend their collaboration for 20 years after any peace settlement. Thus, the great collective defence structure that would repress French power and which Britain had longed for seemed assured.[132] Metternich, however, was disappointed and concerned that there were no safeguards against revisionism in Eastern and Central Europe.[133] Nor was he alone. As Goethe observed to the historian Heinrich Luden, the Germans had achieved liberation, not freedom. They had become accustomed to expecting dangers to originate in the West. But now, Cossacks and Magyars had been substituted for French and Italians.[134]

Napoleon, having rejected the Allies' final peace offer, soldiered on but, by late March, Schwarzenberg's and Blücher's armies were nearing Paris. Its symbolic significance aside, under the empire the city's position as France's administrative hub had been magnified to the point where its fall would severely compromise the continuation of the country's war effort. Napoleon realized this and, striking at Schwarzenberg's communications, strove to distract him. But the *manœuvre sur les derrières* misfired. Disregarding it, the Allies pressed on and, despite obstinate resistance by Marmont's and Mortier's hopelessly outnumbered troops, reached the French capital on 30 March. The metropolis capitulated and, as its garrison withdrew, the Allied sovereigns entered Paris in triumph the very next morning.

The reception given them by the vast crowds of onlookers was a mixed one, but most people were relieved and thankful that Paris had been spared the fate that had befallen Saragossa, Hamburg, Moscow and so many other European cities over the past nine years. Napoleon, collecting his forces at Fontainebleau, was planning a counterstroke to recover his capital, but time was fast running out for him. Aware of the Chaumont Treaty and its implications, Talleyrand, who had been distancing himself from his master for some time but still occupied the office of Arch-Chancellor and Imperial Grand Elector, had begun making discreet approaches to the Allies, seeking to steer their choice of Napoleon's successor. The very fact that the great powers had persisted in trying to negotiate with the emperor up to the middle of March demonstrates that, among them, there were those who saw him as preferable to Russian domination of Western Europe, or to civil war in France, possibly leading to a Jacobin regime. But, given his inflexibility, a Bourbon restoration was increasingly accepted as a compromise solution. The British cabinet, for instance, viewed this as offering the best chance of peace with security, yet reacted coolly when Bordeaux, occupied by their troops on 12 March, proclaimed its allegiance to Louis XVIII; Napoleon's own experience in Spain cautioned them against trying to impose an unsolicited and unpopular monarch. Metternich, on the other hand, seems to have been persuaded by the Bordeaux declaration that a Bourbon France might act as a counterpoise to Russia as effectively as a Napoleonic one, though he was loath to lose the influence that a regency under Marie Louise would have given Austria. Above all, he feared that Alexander would endeavour to install his *protégé* Bernadotte on the French throne and was immensely relieved when the Tsar, who had taken up residence at Talleyrand's house in Paris, was coaxed by Napoleon's former foreign minister into supporting the Bourbons' return. Having convoked the French senate, or rather the rump of members who echoed his own opinions, Talleyrand succeeded in having Napoleon declared deposed.

The greatest challenge facing any historian is to understand the beliefs and assumptions which held past societies together and shaped the conduct of their affairs. While there are those who have emphasized how Napoleon was betrayed in 1814, they overlook the sheer complexity of the political scene, both domestic and international, the long-term hopelessness of the military situation, and the dilemma in which French soldiers and statesmen, not to mention the population as a whole, found themselves as the empire collapsed about their ears. The author of one recent study, for instance,[135] who perceives conspiracies everywhere, openly confesses his abhorrence for the House of Bourbon[136] and describes Napoleon as the person who embodied 'the unified factions of France',[137] asserts that the emperor had been overthrown not by a resounding military defeat but 'by treason and treachery. . . . A cabal of traitors had foisted a quisling government on his enemy-occupied capital.'[138] There is a smattering of truth in this perception, but it raises far more questions than it answers. Why did Napoleon have enemies and how did they come to be in his capital? Could a military victory in 1814 have brought France the peace with security she needed? His past triumphs had not. And, if Napoleon still represented the 'unified factions of France', why did the French nation not rise bodily and spontaneously in his support as the Spanish had done on behalf of Ferdinand in 1808? Indeed, why were so many Frenchmen doing their utmost to avoid being drafted into his army?

The truth is that, while Napoleon's brilliance as a military commander has rarely been equalled let alone surpassed, by 1812, perhaps because of his phenomenal triumphs, he was losing sight of what war *should* be: the continuation of politics by other means. Success might have vindicated him, but, having elected to live by the sword and been defeated, he exposed his empire and its peoples to the catastrophic consequences of that failure. Nor would he cut his, and their, losses by accepting the peace overtures that were made to him. Although he might not have been exclusively responsible for his defeat, it was he who chose to continue the war, the root cause of his downfall; and, in these circumstances, one might ponder who betrayed whom. Certainly, his marshals saw that the writing was on the wall and, on 4 April, virtually mutinied, Ney, Macdonald, Lefebvre and Oudinot arguing that only Napoleon's abdication would end the crisis. When told by Ney that the army would not march on Paris, the emperor retorted 'The army will obey me!' 'The army will obey its chiefs', replied '*Le Rougeaud*', emphatically.[39] Sure enough, though the loyalty of most of the rank and file remained undimmed, within 24 hours Marmont was to lead his bruised little corps into the Allied lines and order it to surrender.

This rebellion ended all thought of further resistance. Napoleon initially sought to pass the crown to his infant son, but, although briefly tempted by the idea of a regency, the Tsar demanded he abdicate unconditionally. This occurred on 6 April, bringing the First French Empire to a close. Sadly, if the war was over, the killing was not. Before news of the events at Fontainebleau could reach them, on the 14th Wellington and Soult fought a gory battle at Toulouse, while the defenders of Bayonne mounted a foray against the investing Allied forces. Similarly, Generals Habert and Davout, in Barcelona and Hamburg respectively, were to cling to their charges until, long after Napoleon's abdication, they were ordered by the new French government to relinquish them.

Notes

1. D.G. Chandler, *The Campaigns of Napoleon* (London, 1966), pp. 852–3. Also see R. Riehn, *1812: Napoleon's Russian Campaign* (New York, 1991), p. 395; A.A. Lobanov-Rostovsky, *Russia and Europe, 1789–1825* (Durham, NC, 1947), pp. 240–1.

2. Quoted in A. Brett-James, *Europe against Napoleon* (Cambridge, 1987 edition), p. 19.
Also see E. Klessmann (ed.), *Die Befreiungskriege in Augenzeugenberichten* (Munich,
1973), p. 18.
3. ASH, C2 538/75: Davout to Berthier, 8 January 1813.
4. ASH, C3 5: Eugène to Napoleon, 1 February 1813. Also see ASH, C2 537/71; C2 311 and
C2 536–45, 'Correspondance relative au personnel'.
5. See P. Paret, *Yorck and the Era of Prussian Reform* (Princeton, 1966), pp. 171–2.
6. Macdonald, together with Oudinot and Marmont, was made a marshal after the Wagram
campaign.
7. G.F. Nafziger, *Napoleon's Invasion of Russia* (Novato, CA, 1988), pp. 327–30; C. von
Clausewitz, *The Campaign of 1812 in Russia* (London, 1992 edition), pp. 236–45.
8. Paret, *Yorck*, pp. 191–6.
9. R. Friederich, *Die Befreiungskriege 1813–15* (2 vols, Berlin, 1913), I, p. 87. (It should be
remembered that East Prussia had suffered particularly badly from the passage of armies,
rendering the population particularly susceptible to incitation.)
10. Friederich, *Befreiungskriege*, I, pp. 108–9; E. Kraehe, *Metternich's German Policy*,
(Princeton, 1963–84), I, pp. 154–6.
11. According to F. Nippold (ed.), *Erinnerungen aus dem Leben des General-Feldmarschalls
Hermann von Boyen* (3 vols, Leipzig, 1889–90), II, p. 345, the Prussian Army was
declared to have 22 392 effectives in July 1810. However, C. Jany, *Geschichte der
Königlichen Preussischen Armee* (4 vols, Berlin, 1928–33), IV, p. 56, reveals its strength
to have been 74 413 in August of the following year.
12. F.L. Petre, *Napoleon's Last Campaign in Germany, 1813* (London, 1974 edition), p. 22.
13. Petre, *1813*, pp. 21–5.
14. See Paret, *Yorck*, p. 156.
15. See R. Muir, *Britain and the Defeat of Napoleon, 1807–15* (New Haven, CT, 1996),
pp. 248–9.
16. See Muir, *Britain and Napoleon*, pp. 258, 261.
17. WSD, VII, p. 502.
18. D. Gates, *The Spanish Ulcer* (London, 1986), p. 376.
19. R. Wilson, *Narrative of Events during the Invasion of Russia* (London, 1860), p. 234.
20. Kraehe, *Metternich*, I, pp. 148, 153.
21. Kraehe, *Metternich*, I, p. 167.
22. See NC, XXV, pp. 46–51, 88–93.
23. Petre, *1813*, p. 46.
24. See Klessmann, *Befreiungskriege*, p. 23; Kraehe, *Metternich*, I, pp. 169–71.
25. See Klessmann, *Befreiungskriege*, pp. 22, 24.
26. Muir, *Britain and Napoleon*, pp. 253–4; J.M. Sherwig, *Guineas and Gunpowder*
(Cambridge, MA, 1969), pp. 289–95, 301–4.
27. Petre, *1813*, p. v.
28. Chandler, *Campaigns*, p. 870. Also consult, for example, D. Hamilton-Williams, *The Fall
of Napoleon: The Final Betrayal* (London, 1994), pp. 26–7; Friederich, *Befreiungskriege*,
I, pp. 129–32.
29. See E. Botzenhart (ed.), *Freiherr vom Stein: Briefwechsel, Denkschriften und
Aufzeichnungen* (7 vols, Berlin, 1931–7), III, pp. 450–2.
30. Nippold, *Erinnerungen … von Boyen*, II, p. 104.
31. See Klessmann, *Befreiungskriege*, pp. 48–9.
32. See G.L. Mosse, *The Nationalization of the Masses: Political Symbolism and Mass
Movements in Germany from the Napoleonic Wars through the Third Reich* (New York,
1975).
33. Klessmann, *Befreiungskriege*, pp. 41–2.
34. Klessmann, *Befreiungskriege*, p. 46.

35. See R. Ibbeken, *Preussen 1807–13* (Cologne and Berlin, 1970), pp. 405 and 442ff.
36. J.J. Sheehan, *German History* (Oxford, 1989), p. 387.
37. See Petre, *1813*, pp. 23, 25.
38. See R.K. von Scherbening and K. Willisen (eds.), *Die Reorganisation der Preussischen Armee nach dem Tilsiter Frieden* (2 vols, Berlin, 1862–6), I, p. 179.
39. Quoted in F. Meinecke, *The Age of German Liberation, 1795–1815* (Berkeley, CA, 1977), p. 110.
40. See D. Gates, *The British Light Infantry Arm* (London, 1987), pp. 10–35 and *passim*; Paret, *Yorck*, pp. 35–6.
41. See Paret, *Yorck*, pp. 56–7.
42. Paret, *Yorck*, p. 131.
43. Friederich, *Befreiungskriege*, I, p. 119.
44. Sheehan, *German History*, p. 384.
45. E.R. Huber, *Dokumente zur Deutschen Verfassungsgeschichte* (3 vols, Stuttgart, 1956–7), I, p. 49.
46. Friederich, *Befreiungskriege*, I, pp. 122–4. For an exhaustive study of the Prussian Army during this period consult: Kriegsgeschichtliche Abteilung des Deutschen Generalstabs, *Das Preussische Heer der Befreiungskriege* (2 vols, Berlin, 1912–14).
47. See Friederich, *Befreiungskriege*, I, p. 130; F. Meinecke, *Das Leben von Generalfeldmarschalls Hermann von Boyen* (2 vols, Stuttgart, 1869–9), I, pp. 282 ff.
48. H. Heine, 'Die Romantische Schule', in *Beiträge zur deutschen Ideologie* (Frankfurt, 1971), p. 134.
49. Huber, *Dokumente*, I, p. 72.
50. See Petre, *1813*, pp. 10–15; ASH, C2 311 and 536–45, 'Correspondance relative au personnel'.
51. NC, XXV, p. 235.
52. See NC, XXIV, p. 530.
53. NC, XXV, p. 272.
54. See, for example, S. Bowden, *Napoleon's Grande Armée of 1813* (Chicago, 1990), p. 51.
55. NC, XXV, p. 81. Also see pp. 12–13, 132–3, 201.
56. NC, XXV, p. 260.
57. See Chandler, *Campaigns*, pp. 224–6.
58. Caulaincourt, *Memoirs*, I, p. 70.
59. A.F.L.V. de Marmont, *Mémoires du Maréchal Marmont Duc de Raguse de 1792 à 1841* (9 vols, Paris, 1857), V, Book xvii, p. 207.
60. NC, XXV, pp. 61–2.
61. NC, XXV, pp. 189–90.
62. NC, XXV, p. 226.
63. See Petre, *1813*, p. 58.
64. See G.A. Craig, 'Problems of Coalition Warfare: The Military Alliance against Napoleon', in *War, Politics and Diplomacy: Selected Essays* (New York, 1966).
65. Baron E.O.I. von Odeleben, *A Circumstantial Narrative of the Campaign in Saxony* (London, 1820), I, p. 44.
66. Petre, *1813*, p. 65.
67. Marmont, *Mémoires*, V, p. 26.
68. Odeleben, *Narrative*, I, p. 49.
69. ASH, C2 537: parade states. Details of *La Grande Armée* throughout 1813 can be found in ASH, C2 536–45.
70. P. Foucart, *Bautzen* (2 vols, Paris, 1897–1901), I, p. 59.
71. See Klessmann, *Befreiungskriege*, pp. 62–3.
72. See his comments to Ney in NC, XXV, pp. 292–3.

73. See Petre, *1813*, pp. 107–11, 125–7.
74. See Baron von Müffling, *Passages from my Life; Together with Memoirs of the Campaigns of 1813 and 1814* (London, 1853 edition), p. 41.
75. For more details of Lützen and Bautzen consult: Friederich, *Befreiungskriege*, I; Odeleben, *Narrative*, I; Chandler, *Campaigns*; J. Tranie and J.S. Carmigniani, *Napoléon: 1813: La Campagne d'Allemagne* (Paris, 1987); P. Hoffman *et al.* (eds.), *Die Befreiungskriege 1813* (Berlin, 1967); A. von Holleben and R. von Caemmerer, *Geschichte der Befreiungskriege 1813–15* (2 vols, Berlin, 1904–9); T. Rehtwisch, *Geschichte der Freiheitskriege in den Jahren 1812–15* (3 vols, Leipzig, 1908); Foucart, *Bautzen*; R. Lanrezac, *La Manœuvre de Lützen, 1813* (Paris, 1904). Prussia's military archives relating to the 1813 campaign were destroyed in 1945. French archival sources include ASH, C2 35–166, 293, 306–10 'Grande Armée: Correspondance'.
76. Odeleben, *Narrative*, I, pp. 105–9; J. Coignet, *The Note-Books of Captain Coignet, Soldier of the Empire 1799–1816* (London, 1985 edition), p. 248.
77. See M. and D. Josselson, *The Commander: A Life of Barclay de Tolly* (Oxford, 1980), pp. 172–4.
78. G. Nafziger, *Lützen and Bautzen* (Chicago, 1992), pp. 264–7.
79. NC, XXV, pp. 299–300.
80. NC, XXVI, pp. 77–9. Also see Foucart, *Bautzen*, II, p. 174.
81. See Castlereagh to Cathcart, 5 July 1813, in C.K. Webster (ed.), *British Diplomacy, 1813–15* (London, 1921), pp. 6–10. It is interesting to contrast this with Britain's aims at the start of the Napoleonic War given in Webster's appendix 1, pp. 389–94.
82. Castlereagh to Cathcart, 6 July 1813, in Webster, *British Diplomacy*, p. 10.
83. See, for instance, Stewart to Castlereagh, 16 June 1813, in Webster, *British Diplomacy*, pp. 66–9.
84. Kraehe, *Metternich*, I, pp. 188–9; H.R. von Srbik, *Metternich: Der Staatsmann und der Mensch* (3 vols, Munich, 1925–54), I, pp. 157ff; P.W. Schroeder, *The Transformation of European Politics* (Oxford, 1996), pp. 459–76.
85. See Friederich, *Befreiungskriege*, II, pp. 26 and 31; Petre, *1813*, p. 170.
86. See, for instance, Bernadotte's comments in F. Schulze (ed.), *Die Deutschen Befreiungskriege in zeitgenössischer Schilderung* (Leipzig, 1912), pp. 121–2.
87. NC, XXVI, p. 112.
88. NC, XXVI, pp. 37–40.
89. For more details of Dresden, see: Friederich, *Befreiungskriege*, II; Odeleben, *Narrative*, I; Petre, *1813*; Chandler, *Campaigns*; Holleben and Caemmerer, *Geschichte*; K. und K. Kriegsarchiv, *Österreich in den Befreiungskriegen* (10 vols, Vienna, 1911–14), II and *passim*.
90. Coignet, *Note-Books*, p. 251.
91. Friederich, *Befreiungskriege*, II, pp. 158–65.
92. See Friederich, *Befreiungskriege*, II, pp. 103–38.
93. Friederich, *Befreiungskriege*, II, pp. 91–7; *Österreich in den Befreiungskriegen*, IV; Petre, *1813*, pp. 227–49.
94. See his 'Note sur la situation générale de mes affaires', in NC, XXVI, pp. 153–7.
95. L. Marquis de Gouvion Saint-Cyr, *Mémoires pour servir à la Histoire Militaire sous le Directoire, le Consulat et l'Empire* (4 vols, Paris, 1834), IV, p. 137.
96. Friederich, *Befreiungskriege*, II, pp. 175–89.
97. See, for example, Petre, *1813*, pp. 286–7, for a summary of some of the more significant events in this *petite guerre*.
98. NC, XXVI, p. 358. Also see Odeleben, *Narrative*, II, pp. 239–43.
99. Muir, *Britain and Napoleon*, p. 292.
100. Kraehe, *Metternich*, I, pp. 203–4; Schroeder, *European Politics*, pp. 479–81.
101. Friederich, *Befreiungskriege*, II, pp. 378–9. For more details of Bavaria's part in the

Befreiungskrieg, consult: M. Doeberl, *Bayern und die deutsche Erhebung wider Napoleon I* (Munich, 1907); D. Klang, 'Bavaria and the War of Liberation, 1813–14', *French Historical Studies*, 4 (1965).

102. See his instructions to Clarke of 27 September regarding the defence of the Rhine in NC, XXVI, p. 257. Also see Coignet, *Note-Books*, p. 251.
103. By 6 October, Napoleon himself had concluded that Dresden was untenable and had decided to evacuate it – a decision he reversed shortly after. See Gouvion Saint-Cyr, *Mémoires*, IV, p. 185.
104. See, for instance, Coignet, *Note-Books*, pp. 252–5.
105. See Petre, *1813*, pp. 265–6.
106. Coignet, *Note-Books*, p. 255.
107. Odeleben, *Narrative*, II, pp. 30–1.
108. Odeleben, *Narrative*, II, p. 46.
109. For further details of Leipzig consult: Friederich, *Befreiungskriege*, II; Odeleben, *Narrative*, II; *Österreich in den Befreiungskriegen*, V; F.N. Maude, *The Leipzig Campaign, 1813* (London, 1908); R. von Friedrich, *Geschichte des Herbstfeldzuges 1813* (3 vols, Berlin, 1903–6).
110. Friederich, *Befreiungskriege*, II, pp. 379–87.
111. See Odeleben, *Narrative*, II, pp. 280–4.
112. See Friederich, *Befreiungskriege*, II, pp. 400–9.
113. See Klessmann, *Befreiungskriege*, pp. 74–6.
114. See Muir, *Britain and Napoleon*, pp. 309–10; Schroeder, *European Politics*, p. 514; T.I. Leiren, 'Norwegian Independence and British Opinion, January to August 1814', *Scandinavian Studies*, 47 (1975).
115. Kraehe, *Metternich*, I, p. 250; P.K. Grimsted, *The Foreign Ministers of Alexander I* (Berkeley, CA, 1969), pp. 206–8.
116. See Kraehe, *Metternich*, I, pp. 25–63.
117. See WD, XI, pp. 433–4.
118. See Chapter 8, above, pp. 177, 190, 192–3.
119. See C. Oman, *A History of the Peninsular War* (Oxford, 1902–30), VII, pp. 297–313.
120. See J. Rosselli, *Lord William Bentinck and the British Occupation of Sicily, 1811–14* (Cambridge, 1956); H.M. Lackland, 'Lord William Bentinck in Sicily, 1811–12', *English Historical Review*, 42 (1927); H.M. Lackland, 'The Failure of the Constitutional Experiment in Sicily, 1813–14', *English Historical Review*, 41 (1926); Muir, *Britain and Napoleon*, pp. 169–73, 273.
121. Rosselli, *Sicily*, pp. 131–42; Schroeder, *European Politics*, pp. 490, 510–11.
122. See R.B. Holtman, *The Napoleonic Revolution* (New York, 1967), pp. 121ff; E.E.Y. Hales, *Napoleon and the Pope* (London, 1962).
123. See A. Forrest, *Conscripts and Deserters: The Army and French Society during the Revolution and Empire* (Oxford, 1989).
124. Chandler, *Campaigns*, p. 949.
125. D.M.G. Sutherland, *France, 1789–1815* (London, 1985), p. 424.
126. F.L. Petre, *Napoleon at Bay* (London, 1977 edition), p. 12.
127. For more details of the 1814 campaign, see Petre, *Napoleon*; Chandler, *Campaigns*; E.H. Fave, *La Campagne de 1814 dans la Vallée de la Marne* (3 vols, Chalons, 1908–9); I.R. Campana, *La Campagne de France, 1814* (Paris, 1922); A.F. Guesdon, *Histoire des Campagnes en 1814 et 1815* (Paris, 1826); J.B. Koch, *Mémoires pour servir à l'Histoire de la Campagne de 1814* (2 vols, Paris, 1819); J. Thiry, *La Campagne de France* (Paris, 1946); ASH, C2 169–88 and 554–61 'Correspondance: Grande Armée'.
128. See, for instance, Klessmann, *Befreiungskriege*, pp. 233–4 and 228.
129. See A.L. de Caulaincourt, *No Peace with Napoleon!* (New York, 1936).

130. See Liverpool to Castlereagh, 12 February 1814, in C.K. Webster, *The Foreign Policy of Castlereagh* (London, 1931), pp. 520–2.
131. See C.J. Bartlett, *Castlereagh* (London, 1966), pp. 127–9.
132. See Webster, *Foreign Policy of Castlereagh*, pp. 226–9.
133. Kraehe, *Metternich*, I, pp. 303–7.
134. Klessmann, *Befreiungskriege*, pp. 216–18.
135. Hamilton-Williams, *Fall*.
136. Hamilton-Williams, *Fall*, p. 12.
137. Hamilton-Williams, *Fall*, p. 126.
138. Hamilton-Williams, *Fall*, p. 127.
139. Quoted in F. Markham, *Napoleon* (New York, 1966), p. 216.

11

Epilogue: The One Hundred Days

During the night of 12 April 1814, Napoleon attempted suicide by ingesting the poison which, ever since he was nearly captured at Maloyaroslavets in 1812, he had taken the precaution of carrying with him. However, nearly two years old, it had lost its potency and only made him violently sick. Thereafter, for a time at least, he became more resigned to his fate. The Tsar, eager to play the magnanimous conqueror, had promised him the island of Elba, a pension of two million francs to be paid each year by the French government, a small personal guard and the right to retain the title of emperor. Similarly, the Empress Marie Louise was to receive the duchy of Parma. Although Castlereagh and Metternich especially objected to these terms, they were as anxious to remove Napoleon without further delay as they were to avoid a confrontation with Alexander. So it was that the Treaty of Fontainebleau was approved and, on 20 April, after bidding his Old Guard a tearful farewell in the palace's White Horse Courtyard, 'le petit caporal' set out for Elba and exile.

By the end of the following month, following an armistice between the French and Allied armies and the return of Louis XVIII, the Peace of Paris had been concluded whereby France received a far more lenient settlement than she had much right to expect: all of her colonies except the Seychelles, Santa Lucia and Tobago were returned to her, while modest alterations to her western and northern frontiers did more than restore the status quo of 1792, adding around 600 000 people to her population. Although many comparatively minor issues were also resolved in her favour in the interests of securing a lasting peace, so far as substantial adjustments to the map of Europe were concerned the Allies initially intended excluding her from the decision-making process, planning to settle matters between themselves at the congress which was scheduled to take place in Vienna. In their quest for peace and stability, however, they soon concluded that France had an important role to play.

For, as we have seen, Metternich especially had identified the need to balance the powerful states on Europe's flanks – Britain, France and Russia – with a robust centre. All the parties, however, would have to accept this arrangement in order for it to be durable. Above all, the independence of the inner core would have to be ensured. Yet not only was Russia bent on acquiring the Duchy of Warsaw but also Prussia wanted to annex Saxony. It will be recalled that, in 1813, Austria had vainly attempted to encourage a declaration of neutrality by Dresden, while Polish affairs had always had an obvious significance for her. Without British support, which was not forthcoming initially, Saxony could not be preserved. Equally, if Russia was to be restrained over Poland, Austria would need Prussia's backing.

Talleyrand, eager to regain France her voice in international affairs and her influence in Germany and Italy, seized the opportunity presented by the divisions among the Eastern powers. Metternich had been prepared to cede Prussia part of Saxony in return for support against Russia, but Talleyrand now argued that the principles of legitimacy and law, which were central to the durability of any European settlement, dictated that Saxony must be protected and Russia restrained. Britain, too, released from the distracting conflict with the USA by the Treaty of Ghent, took a more active part in resolving the Polish–Saxon question from the beginning of 1815. On 3 January, she, France and Austria signed a pact which committed them to resist Prussia's ambitions regarding Saxony by all necessary means, including war. At the same time, given that little could be done about Poland and in order to complete Prussia's isolation, Austria signalled her acceptance of Alexander's plans for the Duchy of Warsaw. The Tsar duly pressed Berlin to settle for just part of Saxony's territories.

Much has been made of the apparent willingness of Britain, Austria and France to fight over this issue, but their unity needs to be seen in context. Britain knew that France was seeking to capitalize on Austro-Prussian rivalry just as she had done in the past. The alliance was a device to obviate this threat while simultaneously preventing hostilities between the two major Germanic states. War was neither an attractive nor a practical option for either side. Certainly, Prussia was in no position to impose her will on the rest of Europe without Russian support, which was not proffered. Indeed, the situation was indicative of the hegemony which Russia had achieved over Eastern Europe.

The Ried Agreement of 1813 had testified to Austria's inclination to shun any resumption of her old Imperial role of protecting Germany on the upper Rhine. Metternich and the *Kaiser* incurred some criticism for this decision, but they realized that too much had changed in the region to put the clock back. Furthermore, Austria had more pressing problems nearer home to worry about. Nevertheless, the fate of Germany was of immense concern to her and the rest of Europe. Although unification was as unattainable as it was undesirable, some sort of confederation was essential if the various German princes were going to have any chance of peacefully coexisting together and resisting outside influences which might prove destabilizing.

A solution to this problem might have proved harder to come by had Napoleon not decided to make one last bid for power. Separated from his wife and son, bored and still awaiting payment of the pension he had been promised, he observed the trend of events within France with growing satisfaction. The restored Bourbons, hardly popular to begin with, had inherited huge problems stemming from years of war. Although they had secured a speedy end to the Allied occupation of France and her return to the arena of international politics, they could not bridge the chasm between the popular perception of their state's position in the new European order and the reality. For too many of their compatriots, it was too tempting to believe that France had been humiliated and subjected to an unjust peace; that their and their country's woes were due not to defeat in war but to Bourbon maladministration and ideology; and that a return to the heady days of *la gloire* would not only somehow put matters to right but was also an attainable goal. This was, as Paul Schroeder has commented:

> the main problem the allies faced in trying to reintegrate France into Europe: too many French men, rather than the Bourbons, had learned nothing and forgotten nothing. Twenty years of war and a succession of convincing defeats had not destroyed Napoleon's nimbus of glory or the delusions and injured self-view of many in France.[1]

Hoping to exploit the growing disenchantment within France, on 26 February 1815 Napoleon, accompanied by his thousand guardsmen, left Elba, landing near Cannes. If many of the French remained unmoved by his calls to join him, few felt sufficiently strongly about the Bourbons to be prepared to fight for them either. Forces sent to stop him went over to his cause. A large poster appeared in the Place Vendôme bearing the words: 'From Napoleon to Louis XVIII. My good brother, there is no need to send any more troops – I have enough.'[2] On 19 March, the Bourbon court fled Paris for Belgium and, the next day, Napoleon entered the Tuileries in triumph.

These events gave the search for a solution to the German question added urgency, with Metternich seeking consensus on the basis of the

Bundesakte, which envisaged a loose confederation for the German states. By early June, agreement had been reached. Some minor revisions aside, this settlement was to survive until 1866. In fact, in many respects, it lasted until 1919.[3]

On 15 June 1815, only days after it was endorsed, Napoleon began what was to be his last campaign. At the head of 120 000 of the best troops available, he struck through Charleroi into Belgium, driving a wedge between a force of British, Germans and Dutch–Belgians under Wellington and a Prussian army under Blücher further east. On the 16th, while the former was held in check by Ney's wing at Quatre Bras, the emperor fell on the latter at Ligny. Heavily defeated, Blücher retreated, followed by a third of the French forces under the command of Marshal Grouchy. The rest of Napoleon's army, some 72 000 men, turned to try conclusions with Wellington. Grouchy, however, failed to prevent the Prussians manœuvring to rejoin their allies as Napoleon intended, with the result that, as the emperor's troops were locked in battle with Wellington's just south of the village of Waterloo on the road to Brussels, much of the Prussian army appeared on their eastern flank.

As long ago as 1849, one Waterloo veteran, in the introduction to his account of the battle, expressed the fear that potential readers might feel that he could have nothing new to say about it, given the quantity of literature which had already appeared on the subject.[4] Since then, the flow of relevant publications has not slackened, making Waterloo one of the most celebrated engagements in military annals. Indeed, only a couple of points really need to be made about it here. First, as we have seen, tactical success in Napoleonic battles turned very largely on the skilful coordination of artillery, cavalry, skirmishers and heavy infantry. For whatever reasons, on the whole this did not occur so far as the attacks of the French at Waterloo are concerned. With insufficient troops to attempt an outflanking manœuvre, they took the bull by the horns, sending infantry and cavalry forward more sequentially than simultaneously. Wellington had deployed his forces with his usual skill but in an uncommonly compact fashion – he had all of 68 000 men on a front of less than 5 kilometres – producing an in-depth defence which, even under more propitious circumstances, would have proved hard to break. But with Blücher determined to join him, the Allied commanders had done as much on both the strategic and tactical levels as they could to ensure success. Realistically, Napoleon could have expected a Pyrrhic victory at best.[5]

Yet, even if Waterloo had ended in a triumph for France, it is hard to see how this could have brought her lasting peace and security. Napoleon had won battles aplenty without achieving this, essentially because his military and political strategies had long since diverged. So dramatic were his successes of 1805–7 that, one senses, he was taken aback somewhat by their repercussions, notably the opportunities they presented to him. Thereafter, however, he had become obsessed with gaining a total victory over the whole of Europe, which, even if attainable, could not have proved sustainable. A defeat for the Allies at Waterloo could only have led to them making fresh endeavours to restore their ascendancy. That they possessed both the requisite political resolve and sufficient material resources to achieve victory in the long run cannot be seriously doubted; any ensuing campaign would, one suspects, have followed a similar pattern to that of 1813, with the Allies eventually reconquering France and restoring the Bourbons.

Indeed, Napoleon was simply too much of an obstacle to the peace and order Europe sought for his power to be left unbroken. Those among his apologists who argue that France should have fought on in 1815 – and she certainly had the military means to do so, if only for a while – fail to explain what the political objective behind continuing the war would have been. In so doing, they commit the same error as their idol himself. Ironically, this consummate soldier had lost sight of what his art was actually all about. It was not so much military defeat *per se* which ruined Napoleon as war.

Certainly, the Waterloo *débâcle* reopened the rifts within French society. As had happened elsewhere during the course of the Napoleonic Wars, the army had toppled a legitimate government. However, the political foundations of the new regime were shaky, too. Military success might have allowed it to last for a time, but, since it had no viable solutions to the problems facing the French nation, its survival in the longer term was evidently doubtful. Waterloo thus mitigated the internal upheaval caused by Napoleon's *coup d'état*, but it could not obviate it. Whereas the provisions regarding the Bourbon restoration had included an amnesty for those who had supported the Revolution and the empire, his return undermined hopes of national reconciliation. In the course of the 100 days during which he was again in power, anticlerical and anti-seigneurial sentiments among the French peasantry were revived, while royalist rebelliousness steadily mounted. Following his second abdication on 22 June, it exploded into a White Terror. As he left for exile on St Helena, where he was to die six years later, prominent Bonapartists – including Marshals Ney and Brune – were, together with Jacobins and Protestants, persecuted, assaulted or killed in a royalist backlash.[6] France was, moreover, occupied by over a million Allied soldiers. Their subsistence costs, together with a war indemnity amounting to 700 million francs, helped cripple her economy for years to come. Her army was also purged extensively. On the whole, however, she continued to be treated leniently. Although steps were taken to protect her neighbours against any recidivism, the Second Treaty of Paris, endorsed in November 1815, was essentially the same as the First. It, along with the other agreements negotiated within the Vienna Congress, was to provide Europe with a general peace settlement which has rarely been equalled in its success, let alone bettered.

Notes

1.   P.W. Schroeder, *The Transformation of European Politics* (Oxford, 1996), p. 508.
2.   Quoted in D.G. Chandler, *The Campaigns of Napoleon* (London, 1966), p. 1012.
3.   J.J. Sheehan, *German History* (Oxford, 1989), pp. 393–401.
4.   See E. Cotton, *A Voice from Waterloo* (London, 1862 edition), p. viii.
5.   The numerous accounts of Waterloo include: A.F. Beck, *Napoleon and Waterloo* (2 vols, London, 1914); D. Howarth, *Waterloo* (New York, 1968); O. von Lettow-Vorbeck, *Napoleons Untergang 1815: Geschichte der Befreiungskriege 1813–15* (2 vols, Berlin, 1904); J.C. Ropes, *The Campaign of Waterloo* (London, 1890).
6.   See D.M.G. Sutherland, *France, 1789–1815* (London, 1985), pp. 432–7.

12

Conclusion

The more decisive a war is, the longer the period of peace which follows it tends to be. In the course of the 'Great War' with France, the Allied powers experienced the failure of one peace after another, each being followed by an extension of the conflict until it engulfed virtually the whole of Europe. By 1814, Napoleon's adversaries had had sufficient time and experience to realize that not only was concerted action essential for victory but also that, if peace was to be sustainable, if stability was to be restored to international relations, they would have to continue their collaboration, respecting the rights of other states and shunning force as an instrument of policy. While this called for a degree of self-sacrifice, the political equilibrium it created secured peace for a generation, which is perhaps as much as one can expect. Human life is, after all, ephemeral. The challenges facing states over time change just as the individuals and groups who have to confront them do; and yesterday's solutions are not always applicable to today's problems. While much has been written about the alluring subject of perpetual peace, few have acknowledged that its attainment is perforce an endless task.

Certainly, the Congress of Vienna marked the start of a new era in international politics. For all its imperfections, a consensus had arisen, ending the pattern of shifting alliances and frequent conflicts which had dominated relations between the European powers throughout the eighteenth century and into the early years of the nineteenth. One of its products was the 'Pax Britannica'; another, the Austro-Prussian dualism which settled the German question for the foreseeable future.

The price for this period of stability and relative tranquillity was immense, as a glance at the losses incurred by just the two original and most implacable antagonists of the Napoleonic War reveals. Although Britain's insularity, complemented by her naval supremacy, had shielded her from invasion by France – a basic security which none of her allies had enjoyed – and her army had evaded the gory, attritional warfare which the continental powers had had to endure, between 1803 and 1813 there were some 225 000 deaths among her soldiers alone. While only about 10 per cent of the British troops and sailors who perished in the 'Great War' did so as a result of enemy action, and while official figures need adjusting to take account of 'natural wastage' and other discrepancies, Britain lost as many men as a proportion of her population in the struggle against Napoleon as she was to in that against the *Kaiser* 100 years later.[1] Similarly, the Napoleonic Wars are reckoned by one authority to have cost France's armies at least 916 000 dead. For the generation born between 1790 and 1795, this constitutes a mortality rate of 38 per cent, which is 14 per cent higher than the casualties inflicted on the generation of 1891–5 in the First World War, widely regarded as the most devastating conflict in French history.[2] Overall, the Napoleonic Wars resulted in some five million dead, the same proportion of Europe's population as was to be claimed by the conflict of 1914–18.

In many ways, the Napoleonic era gave birth to the modern state. In the war's aftermath, on the whole Europe's ruling elites reversed the reforms they had been compelled to introduce by exigency, retaining only those which strengthened their own position. Thus, measures designed, for example, to centralize power and make governmental machinery more efficient were not done away with. Moreover, after 1815 international treaties became increasingly just that, binding not only monarchs but states, which, through the abandonment of remote enclaves, became monolithic entities. The status of some was transformed, too, notably that of the German polities. Alongside the longstanding powers of Austria and Prussia there arose from the ruins of the *Reich* and its *Kleinstaaterei* a cluster of states which, while still small, were sufficiently large to be economically and militarily significant.

Within these and the other European states, the established hierarchies were strengthened for the time being at least. The Catholic Church, for instance, after suffering decades of attack in which its temporal power had been eroded, was able to reassert itself in the Europe of the Holy Alliance, where princes pledged to deal with each other and their subjects in accordance with Christian teaching. However shallow and opportunistic the commitment of some statesmen might have been to such ideals, the conflation of moral and legal concepts in the principle of legitimacy alone demonstrates the importance of ethics in politics during this period. Much of the basis of this ethical approach was ineluctably derived from shared religious beliefs. Indeed, the Church, both doctrinally and institutionally, was embraced as a means of underpinning the order and peace of Europe, hence the flurry of concordats which formalized its relations with various states.

The price of such order, however, often included the loss of what little political liberty had been gained. Although there is some evidence that rulers accorded greater significance to the opinions of the ruled, definitions of 'the people' remained largely unaltered, as was reflected in the distribution of real power within society. Feudal reforms had benefited the aristocracy more often than not, and Europe's swelling middle classes aspired to join the ruling elites rather than bring them down. Indeed, fear of the masses and revolutionary change was more widespread than ever. Not only was representative government in Napoleon's former satellites, notably Westphalia and Italy, eradicated, but it also vanished in Sicily, for instance, where reform had been imposed by Britain and depended on the presence of her forces for its perpetuation. In Spain, too, the obscurants proved stronger than those who favoured change. Ironically if predictably, several of the guerrilla leaders who had fought for Ferdinand's restoration were to the fore in subsequent rebellions against his absolutism. Juan Porlier was hanged in 1815, a fate which Don Juan Martin Diez was to share in 1825 after he had joined the liberals in the 1820 revolt. Francisco Mina, meanwhile, having participated in both this abortive rising and that of 1814, fled abroad, only returning in 1835 after Ferdinand's death. He, too, died the following year. However, the Peninsular War guerrilla left a terrible legacy. The temptation to use violent means for domestic political ends was to prove irresistible on too many occasions thereafter; and the reverberations of this continue to be felt to this very day.

But it was not just guerrillas who interfered in domestic political affairs. Throughout the Napoleonic Wars, regular armies showed a willingness to turn on their legitimate masters in order to protect their professional interests: Gustav IV of Sweden and Charles IV of Spain were both ousted by their rebellious guards; the Prussian patriots defied Frederick William, culminating in Yorck's acceptance of the Tauroggen Convention; Napoleon's marshals mutinied in 1814 just as Spain's generals revolted against the *Cortes*; and the French Army played the key role in Napoleon's bid to dislodge the Bourbons in 1815. Military revolts of this kind, often headed by so-called 'strong men', became a regular feature of European politics. Indeed, no sooner had Napoleon embarked on the adventure which was to culminate in Waterloo than Murat led his Neapolitan army in a rash invasion of Central Italy, vainly calling on the population to join him in a 'war of independence' against the Austrians. Defeated at Tolentino, he had to flee to Corsica, leaving the Austrians free to restore King Ferdinand of Sicily to the Neapolitan throne. In the October of 1815, however, Murat, hoping to emulate Napoleon's landing at Cannes, returned to Naples, expecting to be welcomed by his erstwhile subjects. Pelted with fruit and stones, he was arrested by some customs

officials, imprisoned, tried and shot. Nevertheless, among the steady
stream of ambitious generals and politicians who were to follow
Napoleon's and Murat's examples was to be another member of the
Bonaparte family. Simultaneously haunted and inspired by the legend surrounding his uncle, he was to embroil France in another catastrophic conflict which not only put paid to the Bonapartist cause but also revealed
more starkly than before the obsolescence of so much of the military
thought which had been predicated on the campaigns of the great
Napoleon.

For to Clausewitz's great intellectual rival, the rationalist Antoine-
Henri de Jomini, who had served with *La Grande Armée* from 1805 until
he deserted to the Allies in 1813, the principles which appeared to underpin the emperor's art of war – particularly the use of interior lines and central positions – had universal and enduring validity. To Clausewitz, by
contrast, who stressed the uniqueness of each and every historical experience and period, the sheer unpredictability of war and the importance of
nebulous factors like morale, the idea of reducing warfare to a set of
immutable rules was absurd. While the objective of Napoleon's battle-ori-
ented strategy certainly reflected the universal essence of war, fighting,
many of the details of his final campaigns, for instance, threw much of
Jomini's reasoning into doubt. Yet it was the latter and his disciples who,
analysing the conduct of war within the conceptual framework pro-
pounded by the Enlightenment, the intellectual environment within which
Napoleon himself had lived, were to hold sway for several decades after
the emperor's final defeat in 1815.[3]

Certainly, Jomini's emphasis on relatively small, professional armies
harmonized well with the ideological and resource constraints of the postwar period. Although Prussia continued to attach some importance to
accumulating reserves of trained manpower in order to be able to expand
her forces in times of emergency, the general trend was to abandon the
conscription measures which had been necessary to match the strength of
Napoleon's armies. Not only were large, conscript forces socially and
economically burdensome, but their level of training made them of questionable military value too. Doubts about the loyalty of mass armies also
persisted. Indeed, once the threat posed to the *ancien régime* by Napoleon
receded, all thought of a 'more intimate union' between military forces
and the societies from which they were drawn was abandoned. European
armies remained as distinct and feudalistic as ever, often serving as the
dependable swords of conservatism both at home and abroad.

The Napoleonic experiment with mass warfare did, however, have
some important repercussions for the future organization of armed forces.
The superiority of mixed-arm units over unitary structures was clearly

demonstrated, with divisions and corps becoming the building blocks of all modern armies. The requirement for dedicated, trained officers capable of mobilizing, administering, manœuvring and meeting the many other needs of complex and substantial forces was also highlighted, leading to the creation of elite academies to prepare such personnel and to the establishment of permanent general staffs which planned for military contingencies in both war and peace. At the tactical level, the development of all-purpose infantry and the massing of firepower also gave a hint of things to come, as did the growing vulnerability of cavalry.

War is the greatest challenge that can confront any human society. How it and its individual members cope with, or fail to cope with, the demands it imposes upon them can not only be a fascinating story, but is also often very moving. If Napoleon's adversaries were a little slow to develop an effective response to his way of waging war, they eventually did enough to emerge triumphant from one of the greatest and most taxing conflicts in the history of humankind.

Notes

1. R. Muir, *Britain and the Defeat of Napoleon* (New Haven, CT, 1996), pp. 14, 377.
2. D.M.G. Sutherland, *France, 1789–1815* (London, 1985), p. 423.
3. See A. Gat, *The Origins of Military Thought* (Oxford, 1989), pp. 106–35; and *The Development of Military Thought* (Oxford, 1992), pp. 1–134.

Bibliographical Essay

Some key manuscript and printed primary sources

Among the more important and reasonably accessible manuscript collections concerning the Napoleonic Wars are the *Premier Empire Cartons* (Classes C1–C17) of the *Service Historique de l'Armée de Terre* at the Château Vincennes, France. These include the manuscripts from which the published (edited) versions of the correspondence of Napoleon and Prince Eugène Beauharnais were compiled, as well as thousands of documents relating to the recruitment, composition, supply and operations of the Napoleonic armies. Similarly, the *Kriegsarchiv* in Vienna serves as a depository for a vast amount of material relating to the Austrian war effort. Among its *Akten* are the unpublished correspondence of such figures as Mack, and the *Militärischer Nachlass* of *Kaiser* Francis I. There are also the *Feldakten* relating to most of the armies' operations, and the papers of the *Hofkriegsrat*.

So far as Britain is concerned, there is an immense amount of relevant material in private and institutional collections. The Public Record Office, Kew, contains Home, Foreign, War Office, Admiralty, Privy Council and Audit Office papers, as well as the correspondence of many prominent politicians, government officials and military figures. The holdings of the British Library are equally impressive and include the papers of Sir John Moore (Add. MSS 57320–57332). Several universities also have important collections. Among these are the Wellington Papers at Southampton, the Pitt Papers at Cambridge and the Portland Papers at Nottingham. Other collections relating to the war can be located by consulting the Historical Manuscripts Commission's *Guide to the Reports on the Collection of Manuscripts of Private Families, Corporations and Institutions in Great Britain and Ireland* (HMSO, London, 1914–38).

Relatively few manuscript collections concerning Prussia's part in the war have survived, many of the relevant military archives having been destroyed by fire at Potsdam in 1945. There are, however, some important holdings at the *Militärgeschichtliches Forschungsamt*, notably the *Nachlass* Scharnhorst.

Moreover, many significant documents concerning the campaigns of 1806 and 1807 can be found, albeit in an edited form in many instances, in works such as F.E.A. von Hopfner, *Der Krieg von 1806 und 1807: Ein Beitrag zur Geschichte der Preussischen Armee nach den Quellen des Kriegsarchivs bearbeitet* (2 volumes, Berlin, 1851–5).

P.K. Grimsted's *Archives and Manuscript Repositories in the USSR* (Princeton, 1972) covers the most significant document collections relating to the Russian war effort. However, although the archives of the former Soviet Union have been opened up more to Western scholars in recent years, the most accessible sources continue to be be printed, edited copies of manuscripts. The most important among these are *Otechestvennaia voina 1812 goda* (21 volumes, St Petersburg, 1900–14) and R.E. Alt'shuller, *Borodino: Dokumenty, pis' ma, vospominaniia* (Moscow, 1962), which cover Borodino and the so-called Patriotic War of 1812 in general.

Turning to Spain and Portugal, the latter's principal manuscript collections are to be found in the *Arquivo Nacional de Torre do Tombo*, the *Biblioteca Nacional*, the *Biblioteca das Ciencias de Lisboa*, the library of the *Palácio Nacional da Ajuda* and the *Arquivo Histórico Militar*. The last of these possesses hundreds of *caixa* containing documents on, among other issues, the raising, equipping, training, organization and administration of the Anglo-Portuguese army during the Peninsular War, as well as the correspondence of such officials as Beresford, Wellington and the Portuguese War Minister. The *Arquivo Nacional* houses the most important single collection of diplomatic and political papers, while the relevant holdings of the *Biblioteca Nacional* are as varied as they are immense, many of them being detailed in C. Ayres de Magalhaes Sepúlveda, *Dicionario Bibliografico da Guerra Peninsular* (4 volumes, Coimbra University Press, 1924–30).

Madrid's *Archivo Histórico Nacional*, *Biblioteca Nacional* and *Servicio Histórico Militar* house huge amounts of material relating to the *Guerra de la Independencia*, though several provincial cities, such as Alicante, Barcelona, Gerona, Oviedo, San Sebastian and Tarragona, also possess significant collections. Among the holdings of the *Servicio Histórico Militar* are the 1008 volumes of the *Fraile* collection, as indexed in *Coleccion documental del Fraile* (Madrid, 1947–50). Another useful publication produced by the Spanish Army's Historical Service is the *Diccionario Bibliografico de la Guerra de la Independencia Española* (3 volumes, Madrid, 1944–52). The 84 *legajos* of the *Archivo Histórico Nacional* contain papers relating to the *Suprema*, Regency and the administration of King Joseph. These are listed in *Indice de los Papeles de la Junta Central Suprema Gubernativa, del Reino y del Consejo de Regencia* (Madrid, 1904).

Reference and introductory works

Many relevant texts treat the French Revolutionary and Napoleonic periods as a single entity stretching from 1789 to 1815. There are, however, two substantial bibliographies which focus primarily on the Napoleonic era: *Napoleonic Military History: A Bibliography* (edited by D.D. Horward, New York, 1986); and *An Annotated Bibliography of the Napoleonic Era* (edited by J.A. Meyer, Westport, CT, 1987). Dictionaries include D.G. Chandler, *Dictionary of the Napoleonic Wars* (London, 1979) and *Historical Dictionary of Napoleonic France, 1799–1815* (edited by O. Connelly, Westport, CT, 1985). The best collection of maps relating to the Napoleonic campaigns is unquestionably to be found in V.J. Esposito and R. Elting, *A Military History and Atlas of the Napoleonic Wars* (New York, 1964).

So far as introductory and background texts on Napoleonic Europe are concerned, *New Cambridge Modern History: War and Peace in an Age of Upheaval, 1793–1815* (edited by C.W. Crawley, vol. IX, Cambridge, 1965); F.L. Ford, *Europe, 1780–1830* (London, 1989); G. Rudé, *Revolutionary Europe, 1783–1815* (London, 1964 and 1985); and D.M.G. Sutherland, *France 1789–1815: Revolution and Counter-Revolution* (London, 1985) contain much to recommend them. C. Emsley, *The Longman Companion to Napoleonic Europe* (London, 1993) provides a solid grounding in the subject, as does O. Connelly, *French Revolution and Napoleonic Era* (Fort Worth, TX, 1991), and M. Broers, *Europe under Napoleon, 1799–1815* (London, 1996). A pivotal work on Europe's economic development during this period is A. Milward and N. Saul, *The Economic Development of Continental Europe, 1780–1870* (London, 1979), as is C. Trebilcock, *The Industrialization of the Continental Powers, 1780–1914* (London, 1981).

Napoleon, France and the Empire

To begin with Napoleon himself, the reader has numerous sources to choose from, among them several biographies such as I. Collins, *Napoleon: First Consul and Emperor of the French* (London, 1986); V. Cronin, *Napoleon* (London, 1971), which is rather simplistic; P. Geyl, *Napoleon: For and Against* (London, 1964); R.B. Jones, *Napoleon: Man and Myth* (London, 1977); G. Lefebvre, *Napoleon* (English edition, London, 1969); F. Markham, *Napoleon* (New York, 1963); J.M. Thompson, *Napoleon Bonaparte* (Oxford, 1952); J. Tulard, *Napoleon: The Myth of the Saviour* (English edition, London, 1984), though this has lost something in translation from the original work, *Mythe de Napoleon* (Paris, 1971); F.A. Kafker and J.M. Laux, *Napoleon and his Times: Selected Interpretations* (Malabar, FL, 1989), which contains material on both the emperor and major issues he was concerned with; and M. Lyons, *Napoleon Bonaparte and the Legacy of the French Revolution* (London, 1994). Alongside the (often contrasting) impressions gained from such works as these, one might also gain an insight into Napoleon's personality from J.C. Herold (ed.), *The Mind of Napoleon: A Selection from his Written and Spoken Words* (New York, 1955), or from D.G. Chandler, 'Napoleon as Man and Leader', CREP, I (1989). 'Napoleon: Civil Executive and Revolutionary', CREP (1972) also contains much interesting material in this connection. For a straightforward study of the emperor as a military commander, D.G. Chandler, *The Campaigns of Napoleon* (London, 1966) is hard to beat.

Turning now to France and the Napoleonic Empire, L. Bergeron, *France under Napoleon* (English edition, Princeton, 1981) is of great help in exploring political and socio-economic trends and questions of the time, while D.M.G. Sutherland's *France, 1789–1815* (see above) also provides a good overview in this regard. R. Holtman, *The Napoleonic Revolution* (Philadelphia, 1967) remains a seminal text so far as social, political and economic matters are concerned, while Holtman's *Napoleonic Propaganda* (Baton Rouge, 1950) is one of numerous works which explore particular aspects of Napoleonic history. Others include: J. Godechot, 'The Sense and Importance of the Transformation of the Institutions of the Revolution in the Napoleonic Epoch', in *Napoleon and his Times* (edited by F.A. Kafker and J.M. Laux, Malabar, FL, 1989); E.A. Arnold, *Fouché, Napoleon and the General Police* (Washington, 1979); A. Boime, *A Social History of Modern Art: Art in an Age of Bonapartism, 1800–15* (Chicago, 1993); J.K. Burton, *Napoleon and Clio: Historical Writing, Teaching and Thinking during the First Empire* (Durham, NC, 1979); D.G. Chandler, ' "To Lie Like a Bulletin": An Examination of Napoleon's Re-Writing of the History of the Battle of Marengo', in *Proceedings of the Annual Meeting of the Western Society for French History*, XVIII (1991); C. Church, *Revolution and Red Tape: The French Ministerial Bureaucracy, 1770–1850* (Oxford, 1981); two works by I. Collins, *Napoleon and his Parliaments* (London, 1979) and 'Napoleon's Wars: The Parliamentary Dimension', in *Men, Women and War* (edited by T. Fraser and K. Jeffery, Dublin, 1993); G. Ellis, *Napoleon's Continental Blockade: The Case of Alsace* (Oxford, 1981), which furnishes a splendid case-study of Napoleon's economic policies at both the macro and micro levels; and R. Hodges, *The Eagle and the Spade: The Archaeology of Rome during the Napoleonic Era, 1809–14* (Cambridge, 1992). E.E.Y. Hales, *Napoleon and the Pope: The Story of Napoleon and Pius VII* (London, 1962) and H.H. Walsh, *The Concordat of 1801: A Study of the Problem of Nationalism in the Relations of Church and State* (London, 1933) tackle contrasting aspects of the thorny but important question of Church–State relations. Similarly, F. Kobler, *Napoleon and the Jews* (New York, 1976), F. Malino, *The Sephardic Jews of Bordeaux: Assimilation and Emancipation in Revolutionary and Napoleonic France* (Birmingham, AL, 1978), S. Schwarzfuchs, *Napoleon, the Jews and the Sanhedrin* (London, 1979) and Z. Szajkowski, *Agricultural Credit and Napoleon's Anti-Jewish Decrees* (New York, 1953) shed much light on relations between the French state and its Jewish subjects. Broader examinations of Judaism during our period can be found in R. Mahler, *A History of Modern Jewry* (London, 1971).

With regard to popular resistance to the Napoleonic regime, G. Artom, *Napoleon is Dead in Russia* (New York, 1970), which covers the Malet conspiracy, G. Lewis, *The Second Vendée: The Continuity of Counter-Revolution in the Department of the Gard, 1789–1815* (Oxford, 1978), L. de Villefosse and J. Bouissounouse, *The Scourge of the Eagle: Napoleon and the Liberal Opposition*

(London, 1972) and D. Hamilton-Williams, *The Fall of Napoleon: The Final Betrayal* (London, 1994), which is somewhat simplistic, deal with various strands of this phenomenon. R. Cobb, *The Police and the People: French Popular Protest, 1789–1820* (Oxford, 1970) and C. Emsley, 'Policing the Streets of Early Nineteenth-Century Paris', *French History*, 1/2 (1987) can also be of use in this connection, while resistance to the draft is explored in E.A. Arnold, 'Some Observations on the French Opposition to Napoleonic Conscription, 1804–6', *French Historical Studies*, 4/4 (1966). A. Forrest, 'Conscription and Crime in Rural France during the Directory and Consulate', in *Beyond the Terror: Essays in French Regional and Social History, 1794–1815* (edited by G. Lewis and C. Lucas, Cambridge, 1983) and A. Forrest, *Conscripts and Deserters: The Army and French Society during the Revolution and Empire* (Oxford, 1989). For a wider view of the impact of war, G. Best, *War and Society in Revolutionary Europe, 1770–1870* (London, 1982) furnishes an insight into the relationships between society, politics, armed forces and warfare, while C. Esdaile, *The Wars of Napoleon* (London, 1995) is also less concerned with military operations *per se* than with the impact of the Napoleonic conflict on Europe's social, political and economic structures. Parts of general works such as M.E. Howard, *War in European History* (London, 1976), J. Gooch, *Armies in Europe* (London, 1980) and A. Vagts, *A History of Militarism, Civilian and Military* (London, 1959) also delve into such matters.

With regard to the upper echelons of French society and the decision-making apparatus, two works by E.A. Whitcomb, 'Napoleon's Prefects', *American Historical Review*, 79 (1974) and *Napoleon's Diplomatic Service* (Durham, NC, 1979), are important. R. Horricks, *Napoleon's Elite* (New Brunswick, NJ, 1995) is somewhat superficial but does provide thumbnail sketches of key figures in Napoleonic society. P. Mansel, *The Eagle in Splendour: Napoleon I and his Court* (London, 1987) is narrower but good. D. Seward, *Napoleon's Family* (London, 1986) is the most recent in a long list of works covering some or all of the emperor's relations. Among these are: A.H. Atteridge, *Joachim Murat, Marshal of France and King of Naples* (London, 1911); J. Bear, *Caroline Murat: A Biography* (London, 1972); H. Cole, *The Betrayers: Joachim and Caroline Murat* (London, 1972); O. Connelly, *The Gentle Bonaparte: A Biography of Joseph, Napoleon's Elder Brother* (New York, 1968); C. Oman, *Napoleon's Viceroy: Eugène de Beauharnais* (London, 1966); M. Ross, *The Reluctant King: Joseph Bonaparte, King of the Two Sicilies and Spain* (London, 1976); and M. Weiner, *The Parvenu Princesses: Elisa, Pauline and Caroline Bonaparte* (London, 1964). The best studies of Talleyrand in English are those by E. Dard, *Napoleon and Talleyrand* (London, 1937) and by J.F. Bernard, *Talleyrand: A Biography* (London, 1973).

Of the many books that have appeared on the marshalate, *Napoleon's Marshals* (edited by D.G. Chandler, New York, 1987) and P. Young, *Napoleon's Marshals* (Reading, 1973) are among the most recent which cover all of the 26 marshals created under the First French Empire, while studies of individual marshals include Sir Peter Hayman, *Soult: Napoleon's Maligned Marshal* (London,

1990) and A. Palmer, *Bernadotte: Napoleon's Marshal, Sweden's King* (London, 1990). The fashion in which the forces of the Revolutionary *leveé en masse* gradually developed into the essentially professional *Grande Armeé* is explored in J. Lynn, 'Toward an Army of Honour: The Moral Evolution of the French Army, 1789–1815', *French Historical Studies*, 16/1 (1989) and in J. Bertaud, *The Army of the French Revolution: From Citizen Soldiers to Instrument of Power* (Princeton, 1988). The French Army's officer corps as a whole is discussed in J. Bertaud, 'Napoleon's Officers', *Past and Present*, 112 (1986). So far as the humbler ranks are concerned, the wide-ranging and excellent work by A. Forrest, *Conscripts and Deserters* (see above) is invaluable, while I. Woloch, 'Napoleonic Conscription: State Power and Civil Society', *Past and Present*, 111 (1986) also provides a glimpse of, among other things, the darker side of '*la gloire*'.

Works which relate to Greater France and the empire include S. Woolf, *Napoleon's Integration of Europe* (London, 1991) and G. Ellis, *The Napoleonic Empire* (London, 1991), which both examine inter- and intranational relationships. O. Connelly, *Napoleon's Satellite Kingdoms* (New York, 1965) looks at the establishment and administration of the Napoleonic vassal states in Spain, Italy, Naples, Westphalia and Holland. The last of these is also dealt with in G. Bond, 'Louis Bonaparte and the Collapse of the Kingdom of Holland', CREP (1974). S. Schama, *Patriots and Liberators: Revolution in the Netherlands, 1780–1813* (London, 1977) and E.H. Kossmann, *The Low Countries, 1780–1940* (Oxford, 1978). Also of help are S. Schama, 'The Exigencies of War and the Policies of Taxation in the Netherlands, 1795–1810,' in *War and Economic Development: Essays in Memory of David Joslin* (edited by J. Winter, Cambridge, 1975) and G.J. Renier, *Great Britain and the Establishment of the Kingdom of the Netherlands, 1813–15* (London, 1930).

Turning to other works which focus on distinct regions of the empire, a general introduction to affairs relating to Italy is provided by P. Villani, *Italia Napoleonica* (Naples, 1978). S. Woolf, *A History of Italy, 1700–1860* (London, 1979), H. Hearder, *Italy in the Age of the Risorgimento, 1790–1870* (London, 1983) and R. Johnston, *The Napoleonic Empire in Southern Italy and the Rise of the Secret Societies* (2 volumes, London, 1904). The French kingdom of Naples is examined in J.A. Davis, 'The Impact of French Rule on the Kingdom of Naples, 1806–15', *Ricerche Storiche*, 20/2–3 (1990) and in E. Noether, 'Change and Continuity in the Kingdom of Naples, 1806–15', CREP (1988). Two important articles on Piedmont are M. Broers, 'Revolution as Vendetta: Napoleonic Piedmont, 1800–14', *Historical Journal*, 33 (1990) and D. Outram, 'Education and Politics in Piedmont, 1796–1814', *Historical Journal*, 19 (1976). Sicily, of course, evaded occupation by Napoleon. However, much material concerning Sicilian–Neapolitan affairs can be extracted from J. Rosselli, *Lord William Bentinck and the British Occupation of Sicily, 1811–14* (Cambridge, 1956) and from D. Gregory, *Sicily: The Insecure Base: A History of the British Occupation of Sicily, 1806–15* (Rutherford, NJ, 1988). Two works which deal with Sicily and Bourbon Naples are H. Acton, *The Bourbons of Naples* (London, 1956) and

D. Mack Smith, *Modern Sicily after 1713* (London, 1968). M. Finley has produced several works on relevant military matters, notably *The Most Monstrous of Wars: The Napoleonic Guerilla War in Southern Italy, 1806–11* (Columbia, SC, 1994), while two pieces by W.H. Flayhart, *Counterpoint to Trafalgar: The Anglo-Russian Invasion of Naples, 1805–6* (Columbia, SC, 1992) and 'The Neapolitan Reaction to the Allied Invasions of 1805–6', CREP, II (1989), explore novel topics, as does F. della Peruta, 'War and Society in Napoleonic Italy: The Armies of the Kingdom of Italy at Home and Abroad', in *Society and Politics in Italy in the Age of the Risorgimento* (edited by J. Davis and P. Ginsborg, Cambridge, 1991). Lastly, events beyond the Adriatic, in the Illyrian provinces, are discussed in H. Bjelovic, *The Ragusan Republic: Victim of Napoleon and its own Conservatism* (Leiden, 1970) and F.W. Carter, *Dubrovnik (Ragusa): A Classic City-State* (London, 1972).

A superb background text on Germany (and Austria) is J.J. Sheehan, *German History, 1770–1866* (Oxford, 1989), while J. Gagliardo, *Reich and Nation: The Holy Roman Empire as Idea and Reality, 1763–1806* (Bloomington, IN, 1980) deals with the German political scene inherited by Napoleon. Though a little dated, H.A.L. Fisher, *Studies in Napoleonic Statesmanship: Germany* (Oxford, 1903) is still worth reading. Specialist explorations written in English of the impact of French influence include: T.C.W. Blanning, 'The French Revolution and the Modernisation of Germany', *Central European History*, 2 (1989); G.P. Gooch, 'Germany's Debt to the French Revolution', in *Studies in German History* (edited by G.P. Gooch, London, 1948); H. Kohn, *Prelude to Nation States: The French and German Experience, 1789–1815* (Princeton, 1967); and H. Segeberg, 'Germany', in *Nationalism in the Age of the French Revolution* (edited by O. Dann and J. Dinwiddy, London, 1988). Prominent among the many German studies of aspects of individual *Rheinbund* states are: H. Berding, *Napoleonische Herrschafts- und Gesellschaftspolitik im Königreich Westfalen, 1807–13* (Göttingen, 1973); W. Demel, *Der bayerische Staatsabsolutismus, 1806/8–1817* (Munich, 1983); and K. Möckl, 'Die bayerische Konstitution von 1808', in *Reformen im rheinbündischen Deutschland* (edited by E. Weis, Munich, 1984). Among the handful of works in English are: C. Anderson, 'State-Building and Bureaucracy in Early Nineteenth-Century Nassau', *Central European History*, 24/3 (1991); A. Cronenberg, 'Montgelas and the Reorganisation of Napoleonic Bavaria', CREP (Bicentennial Consortium, 1989); J.M. Diefendorff, *Businessmen and Politics in the Rhineland, 1789–1834* (Princeton, 1980); L.E. Lee, 'Baden between Revolutions: State-Building and Citizenship', *Central European History*, 24/3 (1991); and H.C. Vedeler, 'The Genesis of the Toleration Reforms in Bavaria under Montgelas', *Journal of Modern History*, 10/4, (1938).

Finally, we should mention Denmark and the Grand Duchy of Warsaw. Not a popular topic with researchers writing in English, the latter is covered primarily in general histories of Poland, two of which are pre-eminent: *The Cambridge History of Poland: From Augustus II to Pilsudski (1697–1935)* (edited by W.F. Reddaway *et al.*, Cambridge, 1951) and P. Wandycz, *The Lands of Partitioned Poland, 1795–1918* (Seattle, 1974). Similarly, Denmark's part in the Napoleonic War has attracted little attention from scholars writing in English. Other than S. Oakley, *The Story of Denmark* (London, 1972) and T. Derry, *A Short History of Norway* (London, 1957), both of which are rather cursory, general histories, there is little literature available. The Copenhagen Expedition features in some British texts, but one invariably receives a very one-sided view. Indeed, in seeking to give a Danish perspective on an aspect of the Napoleonic War, R. Ruppenthal, 'Denmark and the Continental System', *Journal of Modern History*, 15/1 (1943), is as novel as it is old.

Diplomacy and interstate relations

H. Butterfield, *The Peace Tactics of Napoleon* (Cambridge, 1929), H.C. Deutsch, *The Genesis of Napoleonic Imperialism* (Cambridge, MA, 1938) and and R.B. Mowat, *The Diplomacy of Napoleon* (London, 1924) are all a little dated but still of value, while P. Schroeder, 'Napoleon's Foreign Policy: A Criminal Enterprise', CREP (1989 Bicentennial Consortium) is both more recent and provocative. P.W. Schroeder, *The Transformation of European Politics, 1763–1848* (Oxford, 1994) contains a thoughtful and challenging thesis concerning war's impact on international relations and diplomacy during our period. Other substantial pieces on interstate relations in general can be found in D. McKay and H. Scott, *The Rise of the Great Powers, 1648–1815* (London, 1983), *The Great Powers and the European States System, 1815–1914* (edited by F.R. Bridge and R. Bullen, London, 1980) and *Europe's Balance of Power, 1815–48* (edited by A. Sked, London, 1979). Works which concentrate more on bilateral relations include: H. Barnes, 'Canning and the Danes, 1807', *History Today*, 15/8 (1965); E.E. Kraehe, *Metternich's German Policy: Volume I: The Contest With Napoleon, 1799–1814* (Princeton, 1963); R. Muir, *Britain and the Defeat of Napoleon, 1807–15* (New Haven and London, 1996); A.C. Niven, *Napoleon and Alexander I: A Study in Anglo-Russian Relations, 1807–12* (Washington, 1978); V. Puryear, *Napoleon and the Dardanelles* (Cambridge, 1951); H. Ragsdale, *Détente in the Napoleonic Era: Bonaparte and the Russians* (Lawrence, KA, 1980); E. Roach, 'Anglo-Russian Relations from Austerlitz to Tilsit', *International History Review*, 5/2 (1983); J.H. Rose, 'Canning and the Spanish Patriots in 1808', *American Historical Review*, 12/1 (1906); and A. Ryan, 'An Ambassador Afloat: Vice-Admiral Saumarez and the Swedish Court, 1808–12', in *The British Navy and the Use of Naval Power in the Eighteenth Century* (edited by J. Black and P. Woodfine, Leicester, 1988).

Napoleon's adversaries

Britain

Britain consistently opposed Napoleon from the outbreak of the war until its end. Good background texts on her participation in the war include: A. Briggs, *The Age of Improvement* (London, 1959); I. Christie, *Wars and Revolutions: Britain, 1760–1815* (London, 1982); N. Crafts, *British Economic Growth during the Industrial Revolution* (Oxford, 1985); C. Emsley, *British Society and the French Wars, 1793–1815* (London, 1979); A. Gayer, W. Rostow and A. Schwartz, *The Growth and Fluctuation of the British Economy, 1790–1815* (Oxford, 1953); A.D. Harvey, *Britain in the Nineteenth Century* (London, 1978); *Britain and the French Revolution* (edited by H.T. Dickinson, Basingstoke, 1989), which contains some superb insights into various issues; C. More, *The Industrial Age: Economy and Society in Britain, 1750–1855* (London, 1989); J.S. Watson, *The Reign of George III, 1760–1815* (Oxford, 1960); and S. Wood, *Britain and the French Wars* (London, 1973). Britain's part in the French emperor's downfall is carefully chronicled in R. Muir, *Britain and the Defeat of Napoleon* (see above), while her strategic approach to the challenge is covered by C.D. Hall, *British Strategy in the Napoleonic War* (Manchester, 1992), which is good, if a touch uneven. P. Mackesy, 'Strategic Problems of the British War Effort', in *Britain and the French Revolution, 1789–1815* (edited by H.T. Dickinson, London, 1989) and C. Fedorak, 'Maritime vs. Continental Strategy: Britain and the Defeat of Napoleon', CREP (Bicentennial Consortium, 1989) also shed some light on the formulation of strategy.

So far as foreign policy is concerned, C.K. Webster, *The Foreign Policy of Castlereagh, 1812–15* (London, 1931) is pre-eminent, together with J.M. Sherwig, *Guineas and Gunpowder: British Foreign Aid in the Wars with France, 1793–1815* (Cambridge, MA, 1969) and P. Schroeder, *The Transformation of European Politics* (see above). C.S.B. Buckland, *Metternich and the British Government* (London, 1932), G.J. Renier, *Great Britain and the Establishment of the Kingdom of the Netherlands* (see above), and J. Rosselli, *Lord William Bentinck and the British Occupation of Sicily* (see above) are all important if more sharply focused, as is H. Butterfield, *Charles James Fox and Napoleon* (London, 1962). The *Cambridge History of British Foreign Policy, 1783–1919* (edited by A. Ward and G. Gooch, Cambridge, 1919) is old but still meritorious, while two more recent studies are M. Chamberlain, *Pax Britannica? British Foreign Policy, 1789–1914* (London, 1988) and J. Clarke, *British Diplomacy and Foreign Policy, 1782–1865: The National Interest* (London, 1989). Lastly, to get the flavour of how at this time the British regarded other nations, and vice versa, see A. Harvey, 'European Attitudes to Britain during the French Revolutionary and Napoleonic Wars', *History*, 63/209 (1978) and C.J. Bartlett, 'Gentlemen versus Democrats: Cultural Prejudice and Military Strategy in Britain in the War of 1812', *War in History*, 1/2 (1994). Parts of F.G. Stephens and M.D. George, *Catalogue of Political and*

Personal Satires, Preserved in Department of Prints and Drawings in the British Museum (11 volumes, British Museum, London, 1870–1954 and 1978) can also be useful in this regard, as can M.D. George, *English Political Caricature* (2 volumes, Oxford, 1959).

Many details concerning the formulation of British policy can be gleaned from the numerous biographies of prominent British statesmen. Among these are: C.J. Bartlett, *Castlereagh* (London, 1966); N. Gash, *Lord Liverpool: The Life and Political Career of Robert Banks Jenkinson, Second Earl of Liverpool, 1770–1828* (London, 1984); J. Derry, *Charles James Fox* (London, 1972); P. Dixon, *Canning, Politician and Statesman* (London, 1976); J. Derry, *Castlereagh* (London, 1976); D. Gray, *Spencer Perceval, 1762–1812: The Evangelical Prime Minister* (Manchester, 1963), which is still the finest work available on Perceval; B. Hilton, 'The Political Arts of Lord Liverpool', *Transactions of the Royal Historical Society*, 5th Series, 38 (1988); W. Hinde, *George Canning* (London, 1973), which is both highly informative and enjoyable); P. Jupp, *Lord Grenville, 1759–1834* (Oxford, 1985), which is outstanding; P. Rolo, *George Canning: Three Biographical Studies* (London, 1965); E.A. Smith, *Lord Grey, 1764–1845* (Oxford, 1990), which is excellent; and P. Ziegler, *Addington: A Life of Henry Addington, First Viscount Sidmouth* (London, 1965). Also of value in this connection are B. Hill, *British Parliamentary Parties, 1742–1832* (London, 1985), F. O'Gorman, *The Emergence of the British Two-Party System, 1760–1832* (London, 1982) and J. Sack, *The Grenvillites* (Chicago, 1979), as is M. Roberts, *The Whig Party, 1807–12* (London, 1939 and 1965), despite its advancing years. Helpful if more circumscribed pieces include: G. Davies, 'The Whigs and the Peninsular War', *Transactions of the Royal Historical Society*, 4th Series, 4 (1919); J. Dinwiddy, 'Charles James Fox and the People', *History*, 55/185 (1970); A. Harvey, 'The "Ministry of All the Talents": The Whigs in Office, February 1806–March 1807', *Historical Journal*, 15/4 (1972); J. McQuiston, 'Rose and Canning in Opposition, 1806-7', *Historical Journal*, 14/3 (1971); J. Severn, 'The Peninsular War and the Ministerial Crisis of 1812', CREP (1992); and R. Willis, 'Fox, Grenville and the Recovery of the Opposition', *Journal of British Studies*, 11/2 (1972).

Peaceful, extra-parliamentary opposition is adequately dealt with in J. Cookson, *The Friends of Peace: Anti-War Liberalism in England, 1793–1815* (Cambridge, 1982). However, it is often difficult to disentangle pacifist resistance to the war from brands of political radicalism. See, for example: H.T. Dickinson, *British Radicalism in the French Revolution, 1789–1815* (Oxford, 1985); J.R. Dinwiddy, 'Sir Francis Burdett and Burdettite Radicalism', *History*, 65/213 (1980); J.A. Hone, *For the Cause of Truth: Radicalism in London, 1796–1821* (Oxford, 1982); and N.C. Miller, 'John Cartwright and Radical Parliamentary Reform, 1808–19', *English Historical Review*, 83/329 (1968). Similarly, popular unrest can be attributed in many instances to economic hardship for which the war and related policies were, rightly or wrongly, often blamed. Works worthy of consultation in this regard include: J. Bohstedt, *Riots and Community Politics in England and Wales, 1790–1810* (Cambridge, MA,

1983); F. Darvall, *Popular Disturbances and Public Order in Regency England* (Oxford, 1934); J. Dinwiddy, 'Luddism and Politics in the Northern Counties', *Social History*, 4/1 (1979); F.K. Donnelly, 'Ideology and Early English Working-Class History: Edward Thompson and his Critics', *Social History*, 1/2 (1976); P. Holt, *Threats of Revolution in Britain, 1789–1848* (London, 1977); D. Moss, 'Birmingham and the Campaign against the Orders-in-Council and the East-India-Company Charter, 1812–13', *Canadian Journal of History*, 11/2 (1976); A.J. Randall, 'The Shearmen and the Wiltshire Outrages of 1802: Trade Unionism and Industrial Violence', *Social History*, 7/3 (1982); J. Stevenson, 'Food Riots in England, 1792–1818', in *Popular Protest and Public Order: Six Studies in British History, 1790–1820* (edited by J. Stevenson and R. Quinault, London, 1974); and E.P. Thompson, *The Making of the English Working Class* (London, 1963).

As a counterpart to all this, among the leading works on internal stability and national cohesion are L. Boyd, *The Role of the Military in Civil Disorders in England* and Wales, 1780–1811 (Knoxville, Tennessee, 1977) and K. Fox, *Making Life Possible: A Study of Military Aid to the Civilian Power in Regency England* (Kineton, 1982). A thorough examination of how the Napoleonic War helped give the English, Scots, Welsh and Irish a sense of common national identity can be found in L. Colley, *Britons: Forging the Nation, 1707–1837* (London, 1994), while two other works by the same author are central to the study of the monarchy and social hierarchy at this time: 'The Apotheosis of George III: Loyalty, Royalty and the British Nation, 1760–1820', *Past and Present*, 102 (1984) and 'Whose Nation? Class and National Consciousness in Britain, 1750–1830', *Past and Present*, 113 (1986). Also of use in this regard is W. Stafford, 'Religion and the Doctrine of Nationalism at the Time of the French Revolution and the Napoleonic Wars', in *Religion and National Identity* (edited by S. Mews, Oxford, 1982).

The British economy was, at the time of the Napoleonic War, the most developed in the world. Indeed, Britain's economic prowess, and the creditworthiness which this brought her, were major factors in bringing about her victory in the conflict. So far as fiscal matters are concerned, significant works include: S. Cope, *The Goldsmids and the Development of the London Money Market during the Napoleonic Wars* (London, 1942); A. Cunningham and J. Lasalle, *British Credit in the Last Napoleonic War* (Cambridge, 1910); A. Hope Jones, *Income Tax and the Napoleonic Wars* (Cambridge, 1939); and L. Neal, *The Rise of Financial Capitalism: International Capital Markets in the Age of Reason* (Cambridge, 1990). Highly recommended works among studies of other aspects of the economy include three pieces by G. Hueckel: 'War and the British Economy, 1793–1815: A General Equilibrium Analysis', *Explorations in Economic History*, 10/4 (1973); 'Relative Prices and Supply Response in English Agriculture during the Napoleonic Wars', *Economic History Review*, 39/3 (1976); and 'English Farming Profits during the Napoleonic Wars, 1793–1815', *Explorations in Economic History*, 13/3 (1976). W. Galpin, *The Grain Supply of England during the Napoleonic Period* (New York, 1925) contains much useful material, as do M. Olson, *The Economics of Wartime Shortage: A History of British Food Supplies in the Napoleonic Wars and World Wars One and Two* (Durham, NC, 1963), A. John, 'Farming in Wartime, 1793–1815', in *Land, Labour and Population in the Industrial Revolution* (edited by E. Jones and G. Mingay, London, 1967) and D. Thomas, *Agriculture in Wales during the Napoleonic Wars* (Cardiff, 1963). Aspects of the development of British trade are covered in: M. Edwards, The *Growth of the British Cotton Trade, 1780–1815* (Manchester, 19167); J. Frankel, 'The 1807–9 Embargo against Great Britain', *Journal of Economic History*, 43/2 (1982); D. Goebel, 'British Trade to the Spanish Colonies, 1796–1823', *American Historical Review*, 43/2 (1938); C. N. Parkinson, *The Trade Winds: A Study of British Overseas Trade during the French Wars, 1793–1815* (London, 1948); J.H. Rose, 'British West-India Commerce as a Factor in the Napoleonic Wars', *Cambridge Historical Journal*, 2/1 (1929); and A. Ryan, 'Trade with the Enemy in the Scandinavian and Baltic Ports during the Napoleonic War: For and Against', *Transactions of the Royal Historical Society*, 5th Series, 12(1962).

Austria

Though not quite as consistent in her resistance to Napoleon as Britain, Austria constituted his other principal opponent. There are, however, few texts in English which are specifically concerned with this dimension of the conflict. As a general introduction, the following might be consulted: C.W. Ingrao, *The Habsburg Monarchy, 1618–1815* (Cambridge, 1994); R.A. Kann, *A History of the Habsburg Empire, 1526–1918* (Los Angeles, 1974); E. Kraehe, *Napoleon's German Policy: The Contest with Napoleon* (see above); K. Roider, *Baron Thugut and Austria's Response to the French Revolution* (Princeton, 1987); parts of J.J. Sheehan's outstanding *German History, 1770–1866* (see above); and S. Musulin, *Vienna in the Age of Metternich: From Napoleon to Revolution, 1805–48* (London, 1975).

Sections of two works in German by R. Sandgruber give a valuable insight into Austrian economic issues: *Österreichische Agrarstatistik 1750–1918* (Munich, 1978) and *Die Anfänge der Konsumgesellschaft: Konsumgüterverbrauch, Lebensstandard und Alltagskultur in Österreich im 18. und 19. Jahrhundert* (Munich, 1982). So far as nationalism and patriotism are concerned, W.C. Langsam, *The Napoleonic Wars and German Nationalism in Austria* (New York, 1930) is of interest despite being somewhat obsolete in places, while, again for readers of German, C. Prignitz, *Vaterlandsliebe und Freiheit: Deutscher Patriotismus von 1750–1850* (Wiesbaden, 1981) can be of help. Napoleon's impact on the Hungarians and Czechs is explored in B. Kiraly, 'Napoleon's Proclamation of 1809 and its Hungarian Echo', in *Intellectual and Social Developments in the Habsburg Empire from Maria Theresa to World War I* (edited by S. Winters and J. Held, New York, 1975), and in two works by J. Zacek: 'Contemporary Czech Popular Sentiment towards the French Revolution and Napoleon', CREP (Bicentennial Consortium, 1989) and 'The French Revolution, Napoleon and the Czechs', CREP, I (1980).

Prussia

Predictably, most of the major studies of Prussia during our period are composed in German. However, there are several important texts in English covering Prussian social and economic issues, notably those relating to Stein's reforms. These include: R. Berdahl, *The Politics of the Prussian Nobility: The Development of a Conservative Ideology, 1770–1848* (Princeton, 1988); F.L. Carsten, *A History of the Prussian Junkers* (Aldershot, 1989); G.A. Craig, 'The Failure of Reform: Stein and Marwitz', in *The End of Prussia* (edited by G.A. Craig, Madison, WI, 1984); G.S. Ford, *Stein and the Era of Reform in Prussia, 1807–15* (Princeton, 1922); M. Gray, *Prussia in Transition: Society and Politics under the Stein Reform Ministry of 1808* (Philadelphia, 1986); R.C. Raack, *The Fall of Stein* (Cambridge, MA, 1965); J.R. Seeley, *Life and Times of Stein* (Cambridge, 1878); sections of J.J. Sheehan, *German History, 1770–1866* (see above); and W.M. Simon, *The Failure of the Prussian Reform Movement, 1807–19* (New York, 1971). So far as the interwoven issues of German patriotism, Romanticism and nationalism are concerned, works in German are legion, as a glance at, say, Chapter XIII of *Napoleonic Military History* (see above) reveals. However, there is a significant amount of literature composed in English: G.A. Craig, 'German Intellectuals and Politics, 1789–1815: The Case of Heinrich von Kleist', *Central European History*, 2/1 (1969); S. Heit: 'German Romanticism: An Ideological Response to Napoleon', CREP, I (1980); O. Johnston, 'The Spanish Guerrilla in German Literature during the Peninsular War', in *New Lights on the Peninsular War* (edited by A.D. Berkeley, Lisbon, 1991), and 'British Pounds and Prussian Patriots', CREP (1986); H. Kohn, 'Father Jahn's Nationalism', *Review of Politics*, 11/4 (1949); G. Mann, *Secretary of Europe: The Life of Friedrich von Gentz, Enemy of Napoleon* (New Haven, Connecticut, 1946); A.G. Pundt, *Arndt and the Nationalist Awakening in Germany* (New York, 1935); and H. Schulze, *The Course of German Nationalism: From Fichte to Bismarck, 1763–1867* (Cambridge, 1991). A view of the contribution of the *Rheinbund* to German national sentiment is expounded in W.O. Shanahan, 'A Neglected Source of German Nationalism: The Confederation of the Rhine, 1806–13,' in *Nationalism: Essays in Honour of Louis L. Snyder* (Westport, CT, 1981), while H. Schmitt, 'Germany Without Prussia: A Closer Look at the Confederation of the Rhine', *German Studies Review*, 6/1 (1983) also treats the *Rheinbund* in this fashion.

Russia

Russia and her part in the war are not particularly well covered, with much of the material that is available being printed in Cyrillic. Moreover, there is a large quantity of literature dealing with the French invasion of 1812, whereas other campaigns and operations are largely neglected. A. Palmer, *Russia in War and Peace* (London, 1972) is not particularly detailed but does concentrate on the Napoleonic period, while there are relevant sections to be found in English-language texts such as D. Saunders, *Russia in the Age of Reaction and Reform, 1801–1881* (London, 1992), H. Seton Watson, *The Russian Empire, 1801–1917* (Oxford, 1967) and E. Thaden, *Russia since 1801: The Making of a New Society* (New York, 1971). Biographies of the Tsar Alexander include M. Dziewanowski, *Alexander I: Russia's Mysterious Tsar* (New York, 1990), J. Hartley, *Alexander I* (London, 1994) and A. McConnel, *Alexander I: Paternalistic Reformer* (Arlington Heights, IL, 1970), while his predecessor is dealt with in R. McGrew, *Paul I of Russia, 1754–1810* (Oxford, 1992) and *Paul I: A Reassessment of his Life and Reign* (edited by H. Ragsdale, Pittsburgh, 1979). Among items on Speransky are: D. Christian, 'The Political Deals of Michael Speransky', *Slavonic and East European Review*, 54/2 (1976); J. Gooding, 'The Liberalism of Michael Speransky', *Slavonic and East European Review*, 54/3 (1986); and M. Raeff, *Michael Speransky, Statesman of Imperial Russia, 1772–1839* (The Hague, 1957). Selected aspects of the reform era are covered in O. Narkiewicz, 'Alexander I and Senate Reform', *Slavonic and East European Review*, 47/1 (1969) and E.E. Roach, 'The Origins of Alexander I's Unofficial Committee', *Russian Review*, 28/3 (1969). With regard to Russian foreign policy, P.K. Grimsted, *The Foreign Ministers of Alexander I: Political Attitudes and the Conduct of Russian Foreign Policy, 1801–25* (Los Angeles, 1969) is a good starting point, while the key studies of Czartorysky and his policies are: M. Kukiel, *Czartorysky and European Unity, 1770–1861* (Ithaca, New York, 1955); C. Morley, 'Alexander I and Czartorysky: The Polish Question from 1801 to 1813', *Slavonic and East European Review*, 25/65 (1947); and three pieces by W.H. Zawadzki, *A Man of Honour: Adam Czartorysky as a Statesman of Russia and Poland, 1795–1831* (Oxford, 1993), 'Prince Adam Czartorysky and Napoleonic France, 1801–1805: A Study in Political Attitudes', *The Historical Journal*, 18/2 (1975) and 'Russia and the Reopening of the Polish Question, 1801–14', *International History Review*, 7/1 (1985). The very beginning of our period is discussed by H. Ragsdale, 'A Continental System in 1801: Paul I and Bonaparte', *Journal of Modern History*, 42/1 (1970), which can be supplemented by some of P. Schroeder's observations in *The Transformation of European Politics* (see above), while Russia's Mediterranean policy up to the time of Tilsit and Cintra is explored in N. Saul, *Russia and the Mediterranean, 1797–1807* (Chicago, 1970).

Portugal and Spain

Portugal and Spain have received considerable attention from scholars writing in English, if only because they formed the venue for the bulk of Wellington's campaigns. That said, there are more works concerning Spain than Portugal. The beginnings of the wartime alliance between Portugal and Britain are explored in M. Fryman, 'Charles Stuart and the "Common Cause": Anglo-Portuguese

Diplomatic Relations, 1810–14', CREP (1977) and in M. Goldstein, 'The Stuart–Vaughan Mission of 1808: The Genesis of the Peninsular Alliance', CREP (1977). C. MacKay, 'Conflicting Goals: Napoleon, Junot and the Occupation of Portugal', CREP (1992) deals with the first French invasion, while F. de la Fuente, 'Portuguese Resistance to Napoleon: Don Miguel Forjaz and the Mobilisation of Portugal', CREP (1983) and F.O. Cetre, 'Beresford and the Portuguese Army, 1809–14', in *New Lights on the Peninsular War* (see above) both deal with dimensions of the attempts to repel the French. Similarly, there is a succinct study of Wellington's endeavours in this regard by D. Horward, 'Wellington and the Defence of Portugal', *International History Review*, 11/1 (1989).

Turning to Spain, G. Lovett, *Napoleon and the Birth of Modern Spain* (2 volumes, New York, 1965) remains *the* core text. The background to the revolution of 1808 is explored in two works by R. Herr, *The Eighteenth Century Revolution in Spain* (Princeton, 1958) and 'Good, Evil and Spain's Uprising against Napoleon', in *Ideas in History* (edited by R. Herr and H. Parker, Durham, NC, 1965). J. Lynch, *Bourbon Spain, 1700–1808* (Oxford, 1989) is also valuable as an introductory piece. Recent works on Godoy and his relationship with the royal family include J. Chastenet, *Godoy: Master of Spain, 1792–1808* (London, 1953) and D. Hilt, *The Troubled Trinity: Godoy and the Spanish Monarchs* (Tuscaloosa, AL, 1987), while Jovellanos is examined in J. Polt, *Gaspar Melchor de Jovellanos* (New York, 1971). More generally, politics within Spain during the *Guerra de la Independencia* are covered by such works as: C.W. Crawley, 'English and French Influences in the Cortes of Cadiz', *Cambridge Historical Journal*, 6/2 (1939); B. Hamnett, 'Spanish Constitutionalism and the Impact of the French Revolution, 1808–14', in *The Impact of the French Revolution on European Consciousness* (edited by T. Mason and W. Doyle, Gloucester, 1989); and G. Lovett, 'The Fall of the First Spanish Liberal Regime, 1813–14', CREP (1974). The last of these items revolves around the topic of civil–military relations on which C. Esdaile has produced an impressive amount of scholarship. Besides sections of his *The Spanish Army in the Peninsular War* (Manchester, 1988) are other more specialist items: 'Wellington and the Spanish Army, 1812: The Revolt of General Ballesteros', CREP (1987); 'War and Politics in Spain, 1808–14', *Historical Journal*, 31/2 (1988); and 'The Marqués de la Romana and the Peninsular War: A Case Study in Civil–Military Relations', CREP (1993).

An overview of Spanish social, political and economic trends during our period can be obtained from two works by W. Callahan, *Church, Politics and Society in Spain, 1750–1854* (London, 1985) and 'The Origins of the Conservative Church in Spain, 1789–1823', *European Studies Review*, 10/2 (1980), together with two by E.J. Hamilton, *War and Prices in Spain, 1651–1800* (Cambridge, MA, 1947) and 'War and Inflation in Spain, 1780–1800', *Quarterly Journal of Economics*, 59/1 (1944). Two pieces on the state finances are also important in this regard: J. Barbier and H. Klein, 'Revolutionary Wars and Public Finances: The Madrid Treasury, 1784–1807', *Journal of Economic History*, 41/2

(1981), and R. Herr, *Rural Change and Royal Finances in Spain at the End of the Eighteenth Century* (Los Angeles, 1989), as is B. Hamnett, 'The Appropriation of Mexican Church Wealth by the Spanish Bourbon Government: The Consolidation of the *vales reales*, 1805–9', *Journal of Latin American Studies*, 1/2 (1969). The last of these brings us to relations between the Latin American colonies and their motherlands. Here, T. Anna, *Spain and the Loss of America* (Lincoln, NB., 1983), two works by M.P. Costeloe, *Response to Revolution: Imperial Spain and the Latin-American Revolutions* (Cambridge, 1986) and 'Spain and the Spanish-American Wars of Independence: The Comisión de Reemplazos, 1811–1820', *Journal of Latin American Studies*, 13/2 (1981), are, together with J. Lynch, *The Spanish-American Revolutions, 1808–26* (London, 1973), recommended reading. For British and French attitudes towards the Latin American colonies, see W. Kaufmann, *British Policy and the Independence of Latin America, 1804–28* (London, 1967) and W. Robertson, *France and Latin-American Independence* (Baltimore, 1939) respectively.

Sweden

While there are no major works in English which concentrate on Sweden in the Napoleonic era exclusively, there is a profile of Bernadotte in A. Palmer, *Bernadotte: Napoleon's Marshal, Sweden's King* (London, 1990). H. Barton, 'Late Gustavian Autocracy in Sweden: Gustav IV Adolf and his Opponents, 1792–1809', *Scandinavian Studies*, 46/3 (1974) serves as an introduction to Swedish politics during the period prior to the revolution of 1809, while relations between the ill-fated king and the British cabinet are traced in R. Carr, 'Gustavus IV and the British Government, 1804–9', *English Historical Review*, 60/1 (1945). In other respects, one is obliged to rely on general histories, notably those by I. Anderson, *A History of Sweden* (London, 1955) and F. Scott, *Sweden: The Nation's History* (Minneapolis, 1977). T. Derry, *A History of Scandinavia* (London, 1979) is also worthy of mention in this connection.

Military thought, armies, navies and individual campaigns

Relevant sections of two excellent pieces of scholarship by A. Gat, *The Origins of Military Thought* (Oxford, 1989) and *The Development of Military Thought* (Oxford, 1992), are to be recommended as invaluable aids for comprehending the era's military doctrines and the fashion in which broader social, cultural and political factors shaped their evolution. So far as the Napoleonic military reform movements are concerned, Prussia is particularly well covered. Among works on this theme are: G.A. Craig, *The Politics of the Prussian Army, 1640–1945* (Oxford, 1955); J. Ellis, *Armies in Revolution* (London, 1973); M.E. Howard, *Clausewitz* (Oxford, 1983); P. Paret, *Clausewitz and the State* (Oxford, 1976),

'Education, Politics and War in the Life of Clausewitz', *Journal of the History of Ideas*, 29/3 (1968), and *Yorck and the Era of Prussian Reform, 1807–15* (Princeton, 1966); G. Ritter, *The Sword and the Sceptre: The Problem of Militarism in Germany* (London, 1972); W. Shanahan, *Prussian Military Reforms, 1786–1813* (New York, 1945); and C.E. White, *The Enlightened Soldier: Scharnhorst and the Militärische Gesellschaft in Berlin, 1801–5* (New York, 1989).

Material on Russia is rare, but C. Duffy, *Russia's Military Way to the West: Origins and Nature of Russian Military Power, 1700–1800* (London, 1981) can serve as an introductory text, while J. Keep, 'The Russian Army's Response to the French Revolution', CREP (1980) is also of value. Even biographies of Russian generals are unusual, but there are two relevant ones: M. Jenkins, *Arakcheev: Grand Vizier of the Russian Empire* (London, 1969) and M. Josselson, *The Commander: A Life of Barclay de Tolly* (Oxford, 1980). Similarly, the principal specialist sources in English on the Austrian Army's thinking and leaders during this period remain three works by G.E. Rothenberg: *Napoleon's Great Adversaries: The Archduke Charles and the Austrian Army, 1792–1814* (London, 1982); 'The Archduke Charles and the Question of Popular Participation in War', CREP (1982); and *The Military Border in Croatia: A Study of an Imperial Institution* (Chicago, 1966). Military thought, reform and training in the British Army is covered in D. Gates, *The British Light Infantry Arm c. 1790–1815: Its Creation, Training and Operational Role* (London, 1987) and in R. Glover, *Peninsular Preparation: The Reform of the British Army, 1795–1802* (Cambridge, 1963). Further material can also be gleaned from the monumental work of Sir J. Fortescue, *A History of the British Army* (13 volumes, London, 1899–1930). Biographies of prominent commanders are legion, among them being L. James, *The Iron Duke: A Military Biography of Wellington* (London, 1992), C. Oman, *Sir John Moore* (London, 1953) and G.F. Teffeteller, *The Surpriser: The Life of Rowland, Lord Hill* (East Brunswick, NJ, 1983).

This brings us to the study of the campaigns waged by the period's armies and navies. Works on this field abound, but there is a tremendous amount of repetition. G. Rothenberg, *The Art of Warfare in the Age of Napoleon* (London, 1977) and R. Quimby, *The Background to Napoleonic Warfare* (New York, 1957) are essential introductory reading. The relevant sections of M. van Creveld, *Supplying War: Logistics from Wallenstein to Patton* (Cambridge, 1977), H. Strachan, *European Armies and the Conduct of War* (London, 1983) and A. Jones, *The Art of War in the Western World* (Urbana, IL, 1987) can be helpful, and there is a selection of interesting essays on topical issues in D.G. Chandler, *On The Napoleonic Wars* (London, 1994). R.M. Epstein, *Napoleon's Last Victory and the Emergence of Modern War* (Lawrence, KA, 1994) is a good case-study of the growth of mass armies and the interlinked changes in strategic thinking and the organization of forces which it engendered, while battlefield tactics and manœuvres are covered in some detail in G. Jeffrey, *Tactics and Grand Tactics of the Napoleonic Wars* (New York, 1982), P. Griffith, *Forward into Battle: Tactics from Waterloo to Vietnam* (Chapter III), (Chichester, 1981) and

B. Nosworthy, *Battle Tactics of Napoleon and His Enemies* (London, 1995). Griffith's work should be read alongside two other interpretations: C. Oman, 'Column and Line in the Peninsula', in *Studies in the Napoleonic Wars* (edited by C. Oman, London, 1929) and J.R. Arnold, 'A Reappraisal of Column versus Line in the Napoleonic Wars', *Journal of the Society for Army Historical Research*, 60/4 (1982). Two core studies of tactical thought, particularly so far as it concerned the creation and preparation of sophisticated infantry forces, are D. Gates, *The British Light Infantry Arm* (see above) and P. Paret, *Yorck and the Era of Prussian Reform* (see above). Much briefer and more limited but also of interest here are two items by D. Showalter, 'Manifestation of Reform: The Rearmament of the Prussian Infantry.1806–13', *Journal of Modern History*, 44/4 (1972) and 'The Prussian *Landwehr* and its Critics. 1813–19', *Central European History*, 4/1 (1971).

Expositions of the recruitment, composition, organization, equipment and tactics of the armies of particular countries include: J.R. Elting, *Swords around a Throne: Napoleon's Grande Armée* (London, 1989); *The Road to Waterloo: The British Army and the Struggle against Revolutionary and Napoleonic France, 1793–1815* (edited by A. Guy, London, 1990); G.E. Rothenberg, *Napoleon's Great Adversaries: The Archduke Charles and the Austrian Army, 1792–1814* (see above); J.H. Gill, *With Eagles to Glory: Napoleon and his German Allies in the 1809 Campaign* (London, 1992); C. Esdaile, *The Spanish Army in the Peninsular War* (see above); C. Oman, *Wellington's Army, 1809–14* (London, 1913); H.C.B. Rogers, *Wellington's Army* (Shepperton, Surrey, 1979); D. Nash, *The Prussian Army, 1808–15* (New Malden, Surrey, 1972); and M. Yaple, 'The Auxiliaries: Foreign and Miscellaneous Regiments in the British Army, 1802–17', *Journal of the Society for Army Historical Research*, 50/201 (1972). Studies of particular arms and regiments, especially French and British ones, abound. Typical of these is E. Bukhari, *French Napoleonic Line Infantry* (New Malden, 1973) and three short works by M.G. Head: *French Napoleonic Artillery* (New Malden, 1970), *French Napoleonic Lancer Regiments* (New Malden, 1971) and *Foot Regiments of the Imperial* Guard (New Malden, 1973). Last but by no means least, the role of females in the French military is explored in S. Conner, 'Les Femmes Militaires: Women in the French Army, 1792–1815', CREP (1982), just as F. Page, *Following the Drum: Women in Wellington's Wars* (London, 1986) chronicles the life of women alongside the British forces in the Peninsula.

Predictably, accounts of battles and individual campaigns have been and remain a firm favourite with authors, but coverage is somewhat patchy. Waterloo in particular has been written on *ad nauseam*, whereas in-depth studies of the 1807 campaign in Poland, for instance, are extremely novel. Although those who can should read the great accounts composed by Count Toreño, *Historia del Levantamiento, Guerra y Revolucion de Espana* (3 volumes, Paris, 1838) and José Goméz de Arteche y Moro, *Guerra de la Independencia: Historia militar de España de 1808 a 1814* (14 volumes, Madrid, 1868–1903), the finest chronicle of the entire Peninsular War in English remains C. Oman, *A History of the*

Peninsular War (7 volumes, Oxford, 1902–30; second edition London, 1996–7). However, there are recent, interesting accounts of some corners of it which are especially worth reading: R. Rudorff, *The War to the Death: The Sieges of Saragossa, 1808–9* (London, 1974) and D. Horward, *Napoleon and Iberia: The Twin Sieges of Ciudad Rodrigo and Almeida* (Tallahassee, 1984). Similarly, D.W. Alexander, *Rod of Iron: French Counterinsurgency Policy in Aragon during the Peninsular War* (Wilmington, DE, 1985) tackles a complex and neglected issue with commendable success.

David Chandler's *Campaigns of Napoleon* is a very readable yet elegant and authoritative guide to the operations conducted by the emperor himself and has become the work most readers instinctively turn to today. However, this is a book based essentially on secondary sources written in French and English, notably the works of F.L. Petre, which cover all of Napoleon's great campaigns except those of 1805 and 1812: *Napoleon's Campaign in Poland, 1806–7* (London, 1907); *Napoleon's Conquest of Prussia, 1806* (London, 1907); *Napoleon and the Archduke Charles: A History of the Franco-Austrian Campaign . . . in 1809* (London, 1909); *Napoleon's Last Campaign in Germany, 1813* (London, 1912); and *Napoleon at Bay, 1814* (London, 1914). These, in turn, were based on some of the colossal studies of the Napoleonic campaigns which were produced during the course of the nineteenth century, notably by the personnel of the historical sections of the various general staffs of the European states. These examinations include, for example, the work of the staff of the *Kriegsarchiv*, Vienna, *Österreich in den Befreiungskriegen* (10 volumes, Vienna, 1911–14). Though mostly soldiers rather than scholars – and their analytical style tends to reflect their background – these men laboured for years over original manuscript collections to produce the backbone of what we take to be the history of the land campaigns of the Napoleonic Wars. Their endeavours had a tremendous impact on writers such as Oman and Petre; and students today should, if possible, grasp any opportunity to read these early studies alongside more recent works.

Turning to maritime matters, the 'standard' text on this period remains A.T. Mahan's *The Influence of Seapower upon the French Revolution and Empire, 1793–1812* (2 volumes, London, 1892), while P. Kennedy, *The Rise and Fall of British Naval Mastery* (London, 1976) includes an excellent overview chapter on the significance of Britain's naval strength. Though worth reading, D.D. Horward, 'The Influence of British Seapower upon the Peninsular War, 1808–14', *Naval War College Review*, 31 (1978) has a narrower focus and is less erudite, as is R. Glover, 'The French Fleet, 1807–14: Britain's Problem and Madison's Opportunity', *Journal of Modern History*, 39/3 (1967). J. Harbron, *Trafalgar and the Spanish Navy* (London, 1988), C.N. Parkinson, *The War in the Eastern Seas, 1793–1815* (London, 1954), J.H. Rose, 'Napoleon and Seapower', *Cambridge Historical Journal*, 1/2 (1924), P. Crowhurst, *The French War on Trade: Privateering, 1793–1815* (London, 1989), A.N. Ryan, 'The Defence of British Trade with the Baltic, 1808–13', *English Historical Review*, 74 (1959), L. Sondhaus, *The Habsburg Empire and the Sea: Austrian Naval Policy, 1797–1866* (West Lafayette, IN, 1989) and O. von Pivka, *Navies of the*

Napoleonic Era (Newton Abbot, 1980) are also worth consulting. R. Morriss, *The Royal Dockyards during the Revolutionary and Napoleonic Wars* (Leicester, 1983), P.L.C. Webb, 'Construction, Repair and Maintenance in the Battlefleet of the Royal Navy, 1793–1815', in *The British Navy and the Use of Naval Power in the Eighteenth Century* (see above), D. Pope, *Life in Nelson's Navy* (Annapolis, 1991) and M. Lewis, *A Social History of the Navy, 1793–1815* (London, 1960) provide a glimpse of, among other things, the unglamorous side of naval power. We should also mention here the principal maritime operation of the Napoleonic Wars, the economic blockade of continental Europe, and its effects. Besides the strategic analysis of F.E. Melvin, *Napoleon's Navigation System: A Study of Trade Control during the Continental Blockade* (London, 1919), two core texts on this theme are: E.F. Hecksher, *The Continental System: An Economic Interpretation* (Oxford, 1922) and F. Crouzet, 'Wars, Blockade and Economic Change in Europe, 1792–1815', *Journal of Economic History*, 24/4 (1964). A. Grab, 'The Kingdom of Italy and Napoleon's Continental Blockade', CREP (1988) deals with a neglected dimension of the economic war, while, for those who read French, Crouzet's *L'Économie Britannique et le Blocus Continental, 1806–13* (2 volumes, Paris, 1958 and 1987) is of immense assistance. Indeed, the second edition contains a new, large introduction which discusses other pieces of relevant literature, many of them in English.

Index